Developments in Petroleum Science, 5

OIL SHALE

Developments in Petroleum Science, 5

OIL SHALE

Edited by

TEH FU YEN

Associate Professor,
Department of Chemical Engineering,
University of Southern California, Los Angeles,
Calif., U.S.A.

and

GEORGE V. CHILINGARIAN

Professor,
His Imperial Majesty Shahanshah Arya Mehr Chair of
Petroleum Engineering, University of Southern California,
Los Angeles, Calif., U.S.A., and Abadan Institute of Technology,
Abadan, Iran

ELSEVIER SCIENTIFIC PUBLISHING COMPANY
Amsterdam — Oxford — New York   1976

ELSEVIER SCIENTIFIC PUBLISHING COMPANY
335 Jan van Galenstraat
P.O. Box 211, Amsterdam, The Netherlands

AMERICAN ELSEVIER PUBLISHING COMPANY, INC.
52 Vanderbilt Avenue
New York, New York 10017

ISBN 0-444-41408-8

Printed in The Netherlands

Dedicated to

His Imperial Majesty Shahanshah Arya Mehr Mohammad Reza Pahlavi of Iran for his very important contributions to higher education.

"The importance of oil is so great that the industrial countries have based the foundations of their economies on this vital commodity, which some day, willing or not, will come to an end. I had stated that oil is a valuable product and too precious to be used as a fuel or for power."

"Therefore, the other energy-giving sources such as oil shales, coals, etc. have to be used. In the future, raw materials, such as oil and gas, must be utilized for better and more essential purposes. In this manner, we can hope to have oil not only for 20 or 30 years more but maybe for another 100 or 200 years."

HIS IMPERIAL MAJESTY
SHAHANSHAH ARYA MEHR **MOHAMMAD** REZA PAHLAVI

FOREWORD

In 1694 the British Crown issued Patent Number 330 to Martin Eele and his colleagues who reported to have found a way to extract and make great quantities of pitch, tar and oil out of a "sort of stone". This is the first verified report of oil products derived from oil shale. In the March 1874 issue of *Scientific American*, there was a news item that during the construction of a railroad in the Green River region, workmen piled together a few pieces of excavated rock as protection from a dinner fire and soon observed the stone itself ignited. This marked the first discovery of oil shale in North America, the tri-state area of Colorado, Utah and Wyoming, which has one of the most abundant single deposits of organic-rich shale. By the 1920's, the development of oil shale was considerable, especially in the United States. Actually, a journal was published entitled *The Shale Review* to establish communication between different areas of oil-shale technology. In the interim years, there were ups and downs for the actual development of oil shale for practical uses. Although a progress was made in several locations of the world in commercial utilization of oil shales, a full development of this industry was not achieved.

Up to this time, thousands of patents have been issued on the theme of retorting of oil shale. There is, however, very little basic knowledge of oil-shale science and technology available, especially in a complete text and monograph form. Therefore, we undertook the responsibility of inviting a group of internationally known oil-shale experts to furnish background information on different aspects of oil-shale science and technology. The coverage ranges from origin, distribution, mineralogy, and chemistry to the exploration, engineering and environmental considerations of this important energy source, oil shale. The purpose of the present endeavor is to stimulate further growth of the maturing oil-shale industry. It can be stated that without the fundamental knowledge of oil-shale science and technology, the technological growth will be retarded.

We take this opportunity to thank the contributors for their patience in developing this book. We also express our thanks to the publishers for their farsight and cooperation.

TEH FU YEN
GEORGE V. CHILINGARIAN

CONTRIBUTORS

R.F. CANE — The Queensland Institute of Technology, Brisbane, Qld., Australia

G.V. CHILINGARIAN — Department of Petroleum Engineering, University of Southern California, Los Angeles, Calif., U.S.A.

G.U. DINNEEN — Laramie Energy Research Center, Laramie, Wyo., U.S.A.

D.C. DUNCAN — U.S. Department of the Interior, Geological Survey, Washington, D.C., U.S.A.

W.H. FERTL — Research and Development Department, Continental Oil Co., Ponca City, Okla., U.S.A.

E.J. GALLEGOS — Chevron Research Co., Richmond, Calif., U.S.A.

D.W. HENDRICKS — Civil Engineering Department, Colorado State University, Fort Collins, Colo., U.S.A.

W.C. MEYER — Department of Geological Sciences, University of Southern California, Los Angeles, Calif., U.S.A.

TH.J. O'NEIL — Department of Geological Sciences, University of Southern California, Los Angeles, Calif., U.S.A.

C.H. PRIEN — Chemical Division, Denver Research Institute, University of Denver, Denver, Colo., U.S.A.

W.E. ROBINSON — Laramie Energy Research Center, Bureau of Mines, U.S. Department of the Interior, Laramie, Wyo., U.S.A.

J.D. SAXBY — Mineral Research Laboratories, C.S.I.R.O., North Ryde, N.S.W., Australia

W.E. SEYFRIED — Department of Geological Sciences, University of Southern California, Los Angeles, Calif., U.S.A.

W.C. SHANKS — Department of Geological Sciences, University of Southern California, Los Angeles, Calif., U.S.A.

J.C. WARD — Civil Engineering Department, Colorado State University, Fort Collins, Colo., U.S.A.

T.F. YEN — Department of Chemical Engineering, University of Southern California, Los Angeles, Calif., U.S.A.

CONTENTS

Chapter 1. INTRODUCTION TO OIL SHALES
    T.F. Yen and G.V. Chilingar

Chapter 2. GEOLOGICAL SETTING OF OIL-SHALE DEPOSITS AND WORLD
    PROSPECTS
    D.C. Duncan

Chapter 3. THE ORIGIN AND FORMATION OF OIL SHALE
    R.F. Cane

Chapter 4. ORIGIN AND CHARACTERISTICS OF GREEN RIVER OIL SHALE
    W.E. Robinson

Chapter 5. MINERALOGY OF OIL SHALE
W.C. Shanks, W.E. Seyfried, W.C. Meyer and Th.J. O'Neil

Chapter 6. CHEMICAL SEPARATION AND CHARACTERIZATION OF KERO-
GEN FROM OIL SHALE
J.D. Saxby

Chapter 7. STRUCTURAL ASPECTS OF ORGANIC COMPONENTS IN OIL
SHALES
T.F. Yen

Chapter 8. BIOLOGICAL FOSSIL HYDROCARBONS IN SHALES
E.J. Gallegos

Chapter 9. RETORTING TECHNOLOGY OF OIL SHALE
G.U. Dinneen

Chapter 10. EVALUATION OF OIL SHALES USING GEOPHYSICAL WELL-
LOGGING TECHNIQUES
W.H. Fertl

Chapter 11. ENVIRONMENTAL ANALYSIS OF AN OIL-SHALE INDUSTRY IN
THE UPPER COLORADO REGION
D.W. Hendricks and J.C. Ward

Chapter 12. SURVEY OF OIL-SHALE RESEARCH IN THE LAST THREE DE-
CADES
C.H. Prien

Chapter 1

INTRODUCTION TO OIL SHALES

T.F. YEN and GEORGE V. CHILINGAR

As petroleum is a natural resource that is being rapidly consumed, there are widespread efforts to seek possible substitutes for it. The reserves of oil shale stand out as a very important source of substitutes for petroleum. In Australia, France, and Scotland, oil shales have been the source of products similar to those obtained from petroleum for a long time. In the United States, the Interior Department studies indicate that there are over 700 billion barrels of economically recoverable synthetic crude spread over 11 million acres (17,000 sq miles) of Colorado, Utah, and Wyoming in the Green River Formation. Non-commercial deposits occur beneath additional 5 million acres (8,000 sq miles) in these states (Fig. 1-1). The total deposits in this tri-state area constitute 1.8 trillion barrels of crude shale oil. The thickness of the Green River Formation ranges from 10 to 2,000 ft, with an overburden ranging from 0 to 1,600 ft. The most economical deposits are those which are at least 30 ft in thickness and average about 30 gallons of oil per ton of oil shale. Poorly defined deposits having a yield of approximately 15 gal/ton are not considered economical at the present time. Of the total world potential of 30 trillion (1 trillion = 10^{12}) bbl of shale oil, only about 2% is available for present-day commercial exploitation. This percentage will probably change in the near future as a result of extensive research which is being conducted at the present time, and there will be a rapid development of oil-shale resources over the next few years. In terms of energy resource banks, oil shale has a huge potential of 160 million Q*, of which about 300 Q are available under present-day technology and economics.

Definition

Oil shales are diverse fine-grained rocks, which contain refractory organic material that can be refined into fuels. Soluble bitumen fraction constitutes about 20% of this organic material, whereas the remainder exists as an insoluble kerogen. All oil shales appear to have been deposited in shallow lakes, marshes, or seas, which supported a dense algal biota. The latter was a probable source for the shale-bound organic fuel precursors.

---

* Q = one quadrillion, i.e., 10^{15}, Btu. One Btu is the amount of heat necessary to raise the temperature of 1 lb of water by 1°F.

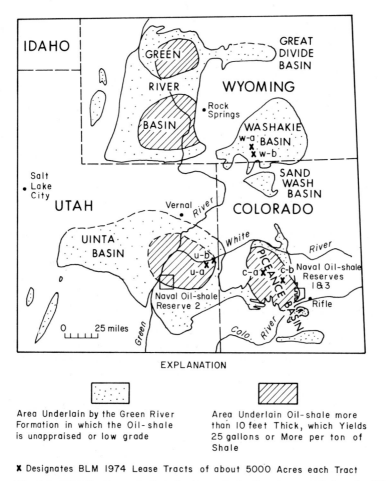

EXPLANATION

Area Underlain by the Green River Formation in which the Oil-shale is unappraised or low grade

Area Underlain Oil-shale more than 10 feet Thick, which Yields 25 gallons or More per ton of Shale

X Designates BLM 1974 Lease Tracts of about 5000 Acres each Tract

Fig. 1-1. Distribution of oil-shale deposits in the states of Colorado, Wyoming, and Utah, U.S.A. (After U.S. Department of the Interior, 1973.)

Gavin [1]* defined the oil shale as follows: "Oil shale is a compact, laminated rock of sedimentary origin, yielding over 33% of ash and containing organic matter that yields oil when distilled, but not appreciably when extracted with the ordinary solvents for petroleum." In distinguishing between the coal and oil shale, it seems that the material which yields less than 33% ash should be considered as coal.

Oil shale can be classified as "composites" of tightly-bound organics and inorganics as shown in Fig. 1-2. The ratio of organics to inorganics rarely exceeds 1/4. The weight percentage of organics in a typical oil shale, yielding

---

* Numbers in brackets refer to items in the references at the end of each chapter.

Oil shale
- Inorganic matrix
  - Quartz
  - Feldspars
  - Clays (mainly illite and chlorite)
  - Carbonates (calcite and dolomite)
  - Pyrite and other minerals
- Bitumens (soluble in CS_2)
- Kerogens (insoluble in CS_2)
  (containing U, Fe, V, Ni, Mo)

Fig. 1-2. General scheme of the oil-shale components.

FeS_2 0.86%			
$NaAlSi_2O_6 \cdot H_2O$ (analcite) 4.3%			
SiO_2 (quartz) 8.6%			
$KAl_4Si_7AlO_{20}(OH)_4$ (illite) montmorillonite muscovite 12.9%			
$KAlSi_3O_8$ (K-feldspar) $NaAlSi_3O_8$-$CaAl_2Si_2O_8$ (plagioclase) 16.4%			
O 22.2%	$CaMg(CO_3)_2$ (dolomite) and calcite 43.1%	Mineral matter 86.2%	Oil shale
Ca 9.5%			
Mg 5.8%			
C 5.6%			
S, N, O 1.28%	bitumen 2.76 %	Organic matter 13.8%	
H 1.42%	kerogen 11.04%		
C 11.1%			

Fig. 1-3. Average chemical composition of Green River oil shale, as determined by the writers for several samples from Rifle, Colorado.

25 gal of oil per ton, is only about 14%. As an example, the composition of the Green River oil shale is presented in Fig. 1-3. The mineralogy of oil shales is discussed in Chapter 5.

Inasmuch as kerogen constitutes the bulk of available organic material in an oil shale, the liberation of hydrocarbons will depend upon the degree to which kerogen can be degraded to liquid fuel precursors. Green River oil shale kerogen consists of polycyclic subunits interconnected by long-chain alkanes and isoprenoids. The matrix also contains substantial amounts of entrapped, uncondensed alkanes and fatty acids. The extensive cross-linking of these subunits gives rise to the insoluble character of kerogen [2]. A hypothetical structural model of Green River oil shale kerogen is discussed in Chapter 7.

Origin of oil shale

It is possible to present only a very generalized concept of the genesis of oil shales, because of the wide range of their properties observed in different areas. Certain factors, however, appear to be necessary for deposition and accumulation of the inorganic and organic material, which become oil shale upon burial and diagenesis. Oil shales result from the contemporaneous deposition of fine-grained mineral debris and organic degradation products derived from the breakdown of biota. Conditions required for the formation of oil shales, therefore, include abundant organic productivity, early development of anaerobic conditions, and a lack of destructive organisms.

Oil shales were probably deposited in bodies of tranquil, either marine or fresh-water, depositional environment, such as isolated marine basins, lakes, or deltaic swamps. The prevailing climate during deposition was similar to that favorable for coal formation.

Continued sedimentation, perhaps coupled with subsidence, provided overburden pressure necessary for the compaction and diagenesis of organically-rich strata. Chemical activity at low temperature ($\approx 150°C$) results in the loss of volatile fractions, which ultimately produces a sedimentary rock having a high content of refractory organic residues.

Most investigators agree that kerogen and bitumen are of biological origin and are largely derived from the lipid fraction of algae. During taphonomy and biostratinomy further conversion is possible for the fossilized material.

The origin of oil shales is discussed in Chapters 3 and 4.

Types of oil shales

Torbanites constitute the richest type of oil shales, characterized by the low ratio of mineral to organic material content. Major deposits of this type occur in Australia, Pennsylvania (U.S.A.), and Illinois (U.S.A.). It appears that they all formed primarily as a result of accumulation of debris from a single species of algae. Torbanites generally occur as lenticular bodies, often associated with coal deposits. This suggests deposition in a shallow, partially emergent, fresh-water environment.

The majority of torbanite deposits occur close to, and often are bounded by, coal horizons. Although the lateral facies changes from torbanite to coal are not uncommon, they do not occur as a mixed seam. This suggests that the general environments for the formation of the two deposits were similar, but perhaps chemicals, which inhibited algal growth, were produced during the formation of coal deposits.

Tasmanites which are marine deposits, are atypical oil shales. They formed in very shallow seas adjacent to the coastline and are often laterally related to the terrestrial spore-containing coals. Their organic matter is composed of spherical disseminules believed to be algal spores. These deposits are not broadly distributed, occurring in major concentrations only in Tasmania and Alaska.

The Alaskan tasmanite outcrops along the northern slopes of the Brooks Mountain range. Although rich in organic material, it has received little attention due to the remote location.

A third type of oil shale, the Green River oil shale, may be the most important oil-shale deposit. These oil shales, which are of lacustrine origin, are intermixed with varying amounts of tuff, siltstone, halite, trona, and nahcolite. The sediments of the Green River Formation were deposited principally from the large Eocene lakes — Lake Uinta in Colorado and Utah, and Lake Gosiute in Wyoming. Oil shale is present in the following basins: Uinta, Piceance Creek, Sandwash, Green River, Great Divide, Washakie, and Fossil (see Fig. 1-1).

Potential resources

The oil-shale deposits in the United States occur through the span of a geological time from the Late Tertiary to the Ordovician or, even, to the Precambrian period. The major resources in the United States of America could be roughly grouped as follows:

(1) Tertiary deposits of the Green River Formation of the Eocene age and the Monterey Formation of the Miocene age.

(2) Jurassic and Triassic marine shales in Alaska.

(3) Permian deposits of the Phosphoria Formation in Montana.

(4) Pennsylvanian cannel-shale in coal fields.

(5) Devonian and Mississippian shales of central and eastern U.S.A. (Chattanooga Shale).

(6) Ordovician black shales in the Appalachian Basin (Maquoketa Shale and Utica Shale).

(7) Nonesuch Shale of Precambrian age in Michigan and Wisconsin.

The United States of America resources in terms of billion barrels of oil

TABLE 1-I

Oil shale resources of U.S.A. (in billion bbl)

Deposits	Oil equivalent (in billion bbl)		
	25—100*	10—25	5—10
Green River Formation	1,200	2,800	4,000
Devonian and Mississippian oil shales	—	1,000	2,000
Alaskan marine oil shales	250	200	large
Shales associated with coal	60	250	210
Other shales:	500	22,000	134,000
Appalachian black shales			
Permian Phosphoria Formation			
Monterey Formation			
Cretaceous shales			

* Oil yield in gal/ton.

are summarized in Table 1-I. It should be pointed out that all oil shales other than those of the Green River Formation have not been thoroughly studied, and no accurate figures of the proven resources are available. For example, the estimates of oil and gas potential of the Devonian and Mississippian oil shales of central and eastern U.S.A. vary widely. Winchester [5] estimated that 18.6 billion bbl were available in strippable deposits in Indiana and Kentucky. Rubel [6], on the other hand, estimated a total of 1,500 billion bbl of shale oil for the same region. The low estimate of 18.6 billion bbl corresponds to 130 trillion cu ft of methane upon gasification. It has been estimated that the methane yield of the Devonian and the Mississippian oil shales amounts to about 8—16 quadrillion cu ft. The geological setting of oil-shale deposits and world prospects are discussed in Chapter 2.

Recovery methods

Extraction of oil from oil shales

The organic matter in oil shale contains both bitumen and kerogen. Inasmuch as the bitumen fraction is soluble in most organic solvents, it is not difficult to extract it from oil shale. Unfortunately, bitumen content in oil shale constitutes only a minor portion. The bulk of the organic matter is composed of kerogen, which is insoluble and inert.

Several approaches are used for the separation of oil (organics) from the mineral matrix (inorganics): (1) to drastically break the bonds of the organics, (2) to mildly degrade the organics, and (3) to erode the inorganics and keep the organics intact. The first approach is used widely in the industry at the present time. It involves a "retorting" process, which had been developed as early as 1850 by James Young of Ireland (see Chapter 9). The latter two approaches are being investigated at the University of Southern California since 1972, using a biochemical technique.

Surface retorting

In the case of surface retorting processes, oil shale is mined (surface or underground), crushed, and then conveyed to a retorter, where it is subjected to temperatures ranging from 500 to 550°C. As a result, the chemical bonds linking the organic compounds to the remainder of the rock matrix are broken. The liberated compounds, in the gaseous state, are collected, condensed, and upgraded into a liquid product that is the rough equivalent of a crude oil. This oil is shipped by pipeline to a refinery, where it is refined into the final product.

The first major experimental retort, which was built and operated by the Bureau of Mines in Rifle, Colorado, 25 years ago, was capable of processing 6 tons of oil shale daily. Since that time, many private firms have become interested in the oil-shale extraction and have developed alternate retorting methods. Among these are the Union Oil, Cameron and Jones, Tosco, NTU and Lurgi-Ruhrgas processes. These systems have several limiting factors in common:

(1) Each system requires the use of energy to produce energy.

(2) Current retorting methods are very inefficient with respect to liberating the organic material found in oil shale and, at best, can remove only 70% of the organic material contained in oil shale. The remaining 30% is closely tied to the inorganic matrix and, therefore, cannot be extracted.

(3) The retorting processes give rise to a large volume of expended shale that must be disposed. A 100,000-bbl/day plant would require the daily disposal of 4,000 tons of spent shale. Not only must this amount of material be moved and stored, but means must be found to insure that the minerals contained in the spent shale are not introduced into the ground water and/or the local streams flowing in the area. Thus, ecologists fear a "nightmare".

In the opinion of the writers, although these factors represent drawbacks in the current processes, the enormous gain resulting from the energy made available by their use more than outweighs the disadvantages. Retorting processes have been discussed in detail in Chapter 9.

In-situ processing

In-situ processes do not require removal of shale from underground. The three steps inherent in this process, i.e., fracturing, injection to achieve communication, and fluid migration, take place at the underground location of the shale bed. Several processes, which have been developed to accomplish each step, are discussed here. In-situ processing does not require removal of shale, which is, perhaps, the single most important factor from both the environmental and economical standpoint. Consequently, there is a sharp rise in interest in developing the in-situ processes.

Fracturing. Fracturing can be achieved through the use of explosives, both conventional and nuclear.

In conventional fracturing, a series of wells are drilled and explosives are placed at the bottom of each well. The degree of fracturing resulting from detonation of these explosives is a function of the explosive power, rock strength, and depth of the well.

It has been suggested that nuclear explosives can be used in a similar manner. The resulting explosion will form a "nuclear chimney" which is a mass of fractured rock [7]. The extensive fracturing and the great amount of shale oil available for extraction would seem to make this an ideal method. The associated environmental hazards, however, are great. There is a possibility of (1) radioactive gases being released to the atmosphere and (2) incorporation of radioactive materials into the ground water. In addition, the radioactive materials would have to be removed from the shale oil. The Test Ban Treaty has presently eliminated any possibility of carrying out experiments in this area.

A second method to achieve fracturing is to drill a series of wells and use electrical arcing to fracture the rock. A limited amount of success on using this method has been reported in the literature.

Injection of fluids to achieve intercommunication. Hot gases, water, and other fluids can be injected into the wells and forced through the fractures. These fluids are able to expand the width of the fractures and push the fractures deeper into the shale bed, i.e., extend the fractures. The possible use of direct electric current to achieve flow should be investigated [16]. If the wells are very close to each other, then it is feasible to have continuous fractures to extend from one well to another; this has been reported in the literature.

Fluid migration. If hot gases are passed through the rock bed, liberation of organic compounds may occur. The latter may, then, flow along with the gases to a producing well where they can be brought to the surface.

As a result of the sharp increases in oil prices, the commercial exploitation of oil shale by in-situ methods may become a reality. Occidental Petroleum Company has announced recently the formation of a chimney with the use of conventional explosives. A detailed description of an in-situ recovery method is presented in Chapter 12.

Disadvantages of retorting processes

The limitations and disadvantages of retorting processes can be summarized as follows:

(1) Shale for surface retorting must be mined and transported to the processing plant, which may cause environmental damage in addition to transport expense.

(2) Present retorting methods all require an expenditure of thermal energy, which may be supplied by electrical arc, gas combustion, or other energy sources. Even in-place retorting methods still require expenditure of a considerable fraction of the energy contained in the fuels released from oil shales. This diminishes the net energy production.

(3) Retorting is not an efficient method for the liberation of organic material locked in oil shales. For example, shales that produce 25 gallons of oil per ton of rock by retorting, may produce 40 gal/ton if all available kerogen is removed.

(4) Present retorting techniques require high temperatures (about 550°C), which, in the presence of minerals in the rock, cause the formation of organic chemicals that are difficult to refine into fuel. In addition, these high temperatures burn off a great deal of otherwise useful organic material.

(5) Retorting produces large volumes of waste rock, which undergoes a volume increase (about 10%) during processing. These large volumes of spent shale present an important disposal problem.

(6) Preliminary findings by the Denver Research Institute have shown that retorting results in the formation of large amounts of the carcinogenic compounds found in the smoked meat by the Food and Drug Administration, i.e., 3,4-benzopyrene.

(7) At high temperatures, dehydrogenation of hydrocarbons precedes aromatization. As a consequence, large amounts of hydrogen have to be used during subsequent refining processes.

In conclusion, one can state that retorting is not an efficient recovery method. Consequently, there is a need for research and development of economically and environmentally more favorable alternative methods to recover oil from oil shales.

Biochemical recovery method

Principles of bioleaching

Broadly speaking, any interaction of biological agents with the oil-shale matrix, regardless of whether the reaction is biochemical, chemical, or physical, is termed bioleaching. The term bioleaching has been adopted in hydrometallurgy for the erosion of low-grade ores by microorganisms. The special concern here is the biodegradation and biodisintegration of the inorganic components in the oil-shale matrix. The organic—inorganic linkages can be disrupted by microorganisms to cause the organic components to separate. The main drawback of bioleaching is the large amount of water required by this process.

Inorganic components of oil shales (see Fig. 1-2) are known to vary considerably. Different bioleaching techniques may be advisable with varying mineralogical composition of oil shales. In the case of the Green River Formation, for example, the concentration of carbonates is unusually high and these are easily accessible to the attack of acid-producing bacteria [8]. On the other hand, the Swedish oil shale ("kolm"), which is also a low-grade uranium ore (uranium content ≈0.01%), can be easily disintegrated with microbial oxidants, such as hydrogen peroxide or ferric ion [9].

Actually the stabilities of sediments are governed by pH and Eh; the deposition and dissolution of many minerals are controlled by both pH and Eh. For example, pyrites and chalcocite are unstable at high Eh values. Calcites are unstable at low pH values. A proper combination of both pH and Eh may render silicates or clay minerals soluble. Silica is stable over a wide range of pH and Eh values. Some bacteria seem to decompose silicates. The biochemical fuel cell is an excellent example of redox-potential changes caused by microbial methods.

Biochemical methods

Extensive research on biochemical recovery methods [10—14] is being conducted at the University of Southern California under the direction of Dr. T.F. Yen.

The oil shales of the Green River Formation, for example, contain large amounts (≈50%) of acid-soluble carbonates, which are susceptible to degradation by acid-producing bacteria. The erosion of oil-shale minerals by bacteria may lead to the partial release of bound kerogens and facilitate their subsequent production from either mined or weathered oil shales.

Ample evidence is available to indicate that biochemical methods may be used for mineralogic degradation of oil shale:

(1) Coal mines in Pennsylvania are plagued with acidic drainage supporting a thriving population of *Thiobacillus thiooxidans*.

(2) *Ferrobacillus ferrooxidans* has been successfully utilized to remove pyrite from coal.

(3) Pot holes in asphalt roads have been caused by the degradative activities of *Desulfovibrio desulfuricans*.

(4) Sulfate-reducing bacteria are commonly used in industry to convert gypsum and anhydrite to sulfur.

(5) Concrete sewer pipes and cooling towers deteriorate and disintegrate in the presence of *Thiobacillus concretivorous*.

(6) Dental caries form as a result of the action of lactic acid bacteria.

Research workers at the University of Southern California have used certain species of bacteria to break down the mineral matrix of Green River oil shale. The following methodology was used:

The aerobic bacteria *Thiobacillus thiooxidans* and other *Thiobacillus* sp. depend mainly on the oxidation of sulfur (S^0) to sulfate for energy. They also need carbon dioxide for propagation. These bacteria function best in the acidic environment (pH range of 2—4) and can survive at pH of 0.5. Their metabolic waste — sulfuric acid — dissolves acid-soluble carbonates, while the bacteria feed on sulfur. The CO_2, released as a result of dissolution of carbonates could be utilized by the sulfur-oxidizing bacteria for cell building material.

The sulfur in the sulfate form can be recovered as a sulfide using a culture of sulfate-reducing bacteria *Desulfovibrio vulgaris* and *D. gigas*. Nutrients for these anaerobic bacteria are the remains of the sulfur-oxidizing bacteria. Additional ammonia sources can be derived from a nitrifier *Nitrosomonas europeae* in oil-shale culture. The CO_2 produced from dissolution of carbonates in the oil shale will serve as an inert environment for anaerobic growth. This reversible, redox cycle will require little additional water or sulfur once started and will result in partially disintegrated oil shale.

Acknowledgment

Partial support of NSF Grant No. G1-35683 AER-74-23797, A.G.A. BR-48-12 and PRF 6272-AC2 is acknowledged.

References

1. J.M. Gavin, *Oil Shale*, Washington Government Printing Office, 201 pp. (1924).
2. T.F. Yen, "A New Structural Model of Oil Shale Kerogen", *ACS Div. Fuel Chem. Preprints*, *19*, 109—114 (1974).
3. T.F. Yen, *Application of Microbiology to Energy and Environment*, Ann Arbor Science Publishers, 400 pp. (1975).
4. D.C. Duncan and V.E. Swanson, "Organic-rich Shale of the United States and World Land Areas", *Geol. Surv. Circ. 523*, 30 pp. (1965).
5. E.E. Winchester, "The Oil Possibilities of the Oil Shales of the United States", Federal Oil Conservation Board of the President of the United States, Sept. 2, app. 1, 13—14 (1928).
6. A.C. Rubel, "Shale Oil as a Future Energy Resource", *Mines Mag.*, Oct., 72—76 (1955).
7. D.B. Lombard, "Recovering Oil from Shale with Nuclear Explosives", *J. Pet. Technol.*, *17* (8), 877—882 (1965).
8. J.E. Findley, M.D. Appleman and T.F. Yen, "Degradation of Oil Shale by Sulfur-Oxidizing Bacteria", *Appl. Microbiol.*, *28* (3), 460—464 (1974).
9. J.E. Zajic, *Microbial Biochemistry*, Academic Press, 186—191 (1969).
10. W.C. Meyer and T.F. Yen, "Solubility of Silica in Basic Organic Matter", *ACS Div. Fuel Chem. Preprints*, *19* (2), 242—245 (1974).

11. W.C. Meyer and T.F. Yen, "The Effect of Bioleaching on Green River Oil Shale", *ACS Div. Fuel Chem. Preprints, 19* (2), 94—99 (1974).
12. A.J. Davis and T.F. Yen, "Development of a Biochemical Desulfurization Procedure for Fuels", *ACS Div. Fuel Chem. Preprints, 19*, 218—223 (1974).
13. D.K. Young, S. Shih and T.F. Yen, "Stepwise Oxidation of Bioleached Oil Shale", *ACS Div. Fuel Chem. Preprints, 19* (2), 169—174 (1974).
14. M. Moussavi, D.K. Young and T.F. Yen, "Correlation of Oil Shale Particle Size to Rate of Dissolution of Mineral Matrix", *ACS Div. Fuel Chem. Preprints, 19* (2), 300—305 (1974).
15. R.H. McKee, *Shale Oil*, The Chemical Catalog Co., New York, 326 pp. (1925).
16. G.V. Chilingar, A. El-Nassir and R.G. Stevens, "Effect of Direct Electrical Current on Permeability of Sandstone Cores", *J. Pet. Technol.*, July, 830—836 (1970).

Chapter 2

GEOLOGIC SETTING OF OIL-SHALE DEPOSITS AND WORLD PROSPECTS

D.C. DUNCAN

Introduction

Numerous occurrences of oil shale are known, but, with a few exceptions, interest in their development has not been sufficient either to support thorough exploration and appraisal of known deposits or to stimulate search for additional deposits. If, as appears likely, technologic advances make oil shale a competitive source of energy in the near future, the tasks of prospecting, exploration, and appraisal may soon become far more important than they have been in the past.

Oil shales are diverse in composition, lithologic association, and genesis; however, some meaningful generalizations can be made about them that may aid in identifying favorable terranes and in exploring and appraising individual deposits. In this chapter, the lithology of oil shales, their depositional environments, and their world distribution are summarized. Some of the guides that may be useful in prospecting and in identifying terranes favorable for the occurrence of new deposits are also presented.

The reported occurrences of oil shale number several hundred. Recent summary descriptions and references to most deposits are included in reports and bibliographies by Jaffe [1], Duncan and Swanson [2], and Ozerov [3].

Lithology

In this chapter "oil shale" is defined as a fine-textured sedimentary rock that contains indigenous organic matter, mostly insoluble in ordinary petroleum solvents, from which substantial amounts of oil can be extracted by heating. The amount of oil that can be retorted from oil-shale deposits ranges from about 4% to more than 50% of the weight of the rock, or about 10—150 gal of oil per ton of rock.

Many oil shales so defined are not shales in the restrictive sense of fine-grained, fissile, clastic rocks. The mineral or textural features of many oil shales would allow them to be classed as other types of rock, such as siltstone, impure limestone, black shale, or impure coal. They range in color from light shades of brown, green, or even red, to dark brown, gray, or black, and in thin sections their organic matter may be translucent red, yellow, orange, or opaque black.

Although most oil shales do not contain much oil as such, nearly all have at least small amounts of soluble organic matter (bitumen), and most contain veinlets, veins, or blebs of solid or viscous hydrocarbons, which probably have migrated from the shale into the fractures. These secondary deposits are usually small, but minable veins of asphalt, gilsonite and other asphaltites, and similar materials are associated with some oil-shale formations.

The organic matter in most oil shales is so altered and finely divided that the organisms from which it was derived are not identifiable. Algal remains, spores, and pollen are common in some deposits. Well-preserved megafossils (such as larger plants, molluscs, arthropods, and fish) are present in many deposits, but generally are not the predominant organic material of the rock. Some of the identifiable organic remains are of organisms that contain extraordinary amounts of oils, fats, or waxes, and it is often presumed that it is such organisms (some blue-green algae and, to a lesser degree, other single-celled plants and animals such as diatoms and radiolaria) that are the chief sources of the unidentifiable organic matter in oil shales.

The inorganic constituents of oil shales differ substantially from one deposit to another. They may be predominantly composed of (1) quartz plus feldspar, clay, opal, or chert, or (2) carbonates, such as calcite or dolomite. Saline minerals — trona, dawsonite, halite, and many others — are sometimes present in oil shale or in closely associated sediments. Volcanic ash is frequently a constituent of the shale itself or is prominent in accompanying sediments. The less abundant minerals commonly include pyrite or other metallic sulfides, and phosphatic minerals.

Three general categories of oil shale deserve special mention: (1) carbonate-rich shale, (2) siliceous shale, and (3) a kind of coaly shale, designated here as cannel shale. These oil-shale types are not uncommonly found in the same formation and, in some places, intergrade.

Carbonate-rich shale

Oil-shale deposits containing substantial amounts of carbonate minerals are of particular interest because they include some of the higher-grade oil-shale accumulations. The carbonate minerals, commonly calcite or dolomite, are fine-grained and may be the dominant mineral constituent of the shale. Most of the carbonates probably were precipitated at the time of deposition of the shale, but some of them may have formed as a result of the alteration of organic debris. The process of oxidation of part of the organic matter to CO_2 and its combination with calcium, magnesium, and other elements may have begun with the decay of organic matter during deposition and continued during the early stages of compaction of the shale. Milton [4] has described more than 20 such carbonate minerals in the oil shale and marlstone of the Green River Formation of Eocene age in Wyoming and Utah.

Carbonate-rich oil shale, particularly that of lacustrine deposition, is commonly varved; a cyclic layer rich in organic matter alternates with a cyclic layer composed mostly of carbonate. These shales are generally hard, tough rocks that are resistant to weathering. The process of compaction and cementation evidently sealed the volatile and mobile constituents in the rock at a very early stage.

Siliceous shale

Oil shales devoid of significant amounts of carbonate minerals may have detrital minerals (quartz, feldspar, or clay) as their main constituents, but chert or opal, some in the form of diatoms and other fossil remains, is not uncommon. The siliceous shales are generally dark brown or black and are less resistant to weathering than the carbonate-rich shales. Some of the Mesozoic and Tertiary deposits of siliceous shale have rich oil yields, but the yield of older deposits is generally poor. The effects of compaction, deformation, and metamorphism apparently have led to the progressive release and migration of their mobile and volatile constituents.

Cannel shale

Cannel shale is an oil shale that burns with a bright flame and consists predominantly of organic matter that completely encloses other mineral grains. Such rocks are sometimes classed as impure cannel coal, torbanite, or some varieties of marine coals. Cannel shale is composed largely of algal remains, and generally contains so much mineral impurity that it is excluded from commercial categories of coal. Cannel shale is usually dark brown or black. A large proportion of its organic matter is convertible to oil with normal distillation methods. The oil yield of cannel shales does not seem to be appreciably affected by compaction and does not diminish with age. Deposits are not known, however, in areas of intense deformation and low-grade metamorphism.

Environment of deposition

The principal environments in which oil shale is deposited are (1) large lakes; (2) shallow seas on continental platforms and continental shelves, generally in areas where circulation of water near the sea floor was restricted; and (3) small lakes, bogs, and lagoons associated with coal-producing swamps.

Large lake basins

Some of the richest and most extensive oil shales have been deposited in large lake basins, particularly tectonic basins that formed as a result of block faulting or crustal warping during mountain building. The oil shales of the Green River Formation of Eocene age in western United States, the Albert Shale of Early Carboniferous (Mississippian) age in New Brunswick, Canada, and deposits of Triassic age in the Stanleyville Basin of the Congo are of this type. Tuffaceous sediments are commonly interspersed with the oil shales, and volcanic debris may have been the source of the nutrients required for the large amounts of aquatic life that must have been a prerequisite to the formation of the oil shale. The presence of saline minerals in the Green River Formation and some of the other lacustrine deposits implies aridity during at least part of the history of the lakes, but evidence also indicates that a tropical or subtropical climate prevailed during the deposition of some lacustrine oil shales.

Generally, the oil shales deposited in the large lacustrine basins are of the calcareous type. The associated sediments are volcanic tuffs, clastics, and carbonate rocks.

The oil shale deposited in the large lake basins include the thickest deposits known. The Green River deposits thicken substantially toward the center of the basins, where they are as much as 2,000 ft thick. They may extend over thousands of square miles and yield 40 gal of oil or more per ton.

Shallow seas on continental platforms and shelves

The marine oil shales deposited in shallow seas on continental platforms include the widespread black shales of (1) Cambrian age in northern Siberia and northern Europe; (2) Devonian age in eastern and central North America; (3) Permian age in southern Brazil, Uruguay, and Argentina; and (4) Jurassic age in Europe, eastern Asia, and Alaska. Characteristically, the platform shales are thin — a few feet to a few tens of feet thick. Most yield less than 30 gal of oil per ton, but they may extend over hundreds or thousands of square miles. They are mostly of the siliceous type, but there are carbonate-rich shales of the latter environmental origin also, and most of the higher-grade shales are of this type. The platform shales are generally associated with limestone, quartz sandstone, and chert or cherty limestone; phosphate nodules are also a common associate.

Oil shales deposited on continental shelves include those formed in subsiding geosynclinal basins. They are generally dark brown or black shales associated with limestone, phosphate rock, sandstone, and chert, in assemblages much thicker than the platform types. These deposits appear to have formed in part as a result of upwelling of nutrient-rich waters (as observed in modern seas along the western coasts of the continents and certain other environments) onto a shoaling bottom [5,6]. Most of the oil shales in this assemblage are of the siliceous type, but some are calcareous. Only the younger ones, such as the Miocene shales of California and similar deposits in Sicily, yield large amounts of oil. Tuffaceous sediments associated with some of them may also have supplied nutrients for luxuriant marine life. Lower-grade oil shales of Permian age in the Phosphoria Formation in the north-western United States, of Mississippian age in the Brooks Range in northern Alaska, and of Late Cretaceous and Early Eocene age in north Africa and the Middle East are other examples.

Small lakes, bogs, and lagoons associated with coal-forming swamps

Oil-shale deposits associated with coal-bearing rocks are relatively small, although many are high grade, yielding a barrel (=42 gal) or more of oil per ton of rock. A few are both thick and of wide extent. At Fushun, Manchuria, for example, a thick deposit intertongues with and overlies a thick coal sequence of Tertiary age; the Kenderlick deposits, mostly of Late Carboniferous age in Kazakhstan, USSR, are also large. In some areas of the interior provinces of the United States, extensive, thin, low-grade oil-shale deposits of marine origin overlie some coal beds in a cyclic sequence of alternating marine and fluviatile sediments.

Many of the oil shales associated with coal measures are of the higher-grade cannel type, but lower-grade siliceous and calcareous shales are also found.

Age and world distribution

As mentioned previously, few of the known occurrences of oil shale have been completely explored. Undoubtedly, many deposits are still to be discovered on all the continents, but the reported occurrences constitute favorable prospects in many areas. The distribution of known oil shales is in itself, therefore, a guide to prospecting; it is illustrative of the geologic settings favorable for the occurrence of new deposits. In this chapter, known occurrences are grouped by age, and their approximate locations are shown on Figs. 2-1—2-5.

The reported deposits of Early Paleozoic (Cambrian and Ordovician) age (Fig. 2-1) are all marine-platform types and are in northern Europe, northern Asia, and east-central North America. Most are siliceous black shale yielding relatively small amounts of oil. Generally, only a small proportion of their contained organic matter converts to oil with demonstrated methods. The Kukersite deposits of Ordovician age in Estonia and the adjacent Leningrad region in the USSR are exceptional. These deposits are represented by relatively thin but high-grade calcareous oil shales, rich in organic material of

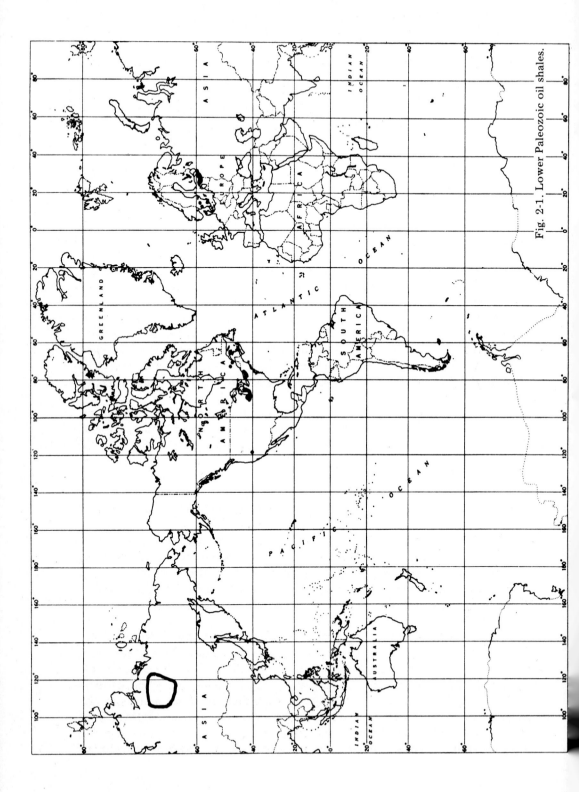

Fig. 2-1. Lower Paleozoic oil shales.

algal origin, interbedded with limestones. They have been used for several decades as a source of shale oil and, more recently, also of gas.

The Middle Paleozoic (Silurian—Devonian) oil-shale deposits (Fig. 2-2) are marine-platform deposits in the eastern and central United States, where they are mostly black shale yielding relatively small amounts of oil (10—20 gal/ton). In central European USSR, thin marine oil shales are marginal to a deeper salt basin and are presumed to thicken toward the central part of the basin.

Oil shales are reported in rocks of Late Paleozoic age (Fig. 2-3) on all the continents. Most are associated with coal-bearing rocks and are represented by small cannel shale or related deposits. Such deposits have been mined in a small way at times in Scotland, France, Spain, South Africa, Australia, USSR, and in other countries.

The oldest reported large tectonic lake-basin deposit is the Albert Shale of Early Carboniferous age in eastern Canada. One of the world's largest oil-shale deposits is a marine black shale, the Irati Shale of Late Permian age in southern Brazil. Shale of approximately correlative age is also present in Uruguay and southern Argentina. Less extensive, low-grade marine deposits in the black shale—phosphorite—chert assemblage are reported in southern Montana in the Phosphoria Formation of Permian age of northwestern United States. Similar low-grade deposits of Mississippian age are known in the Brooks Range of northern Alaska.

Oil shales of Mesozoic age are reported in all continents except Australia (Fig. 2-4). In the Stanleyville Basin of the Congo in central Africa, extensive, high-grade, lacustrine oil shale of Triassic age is interbedded with limestone and volcanic materials. The thickest oil-shale sequence is in the deeper part of the sedimentary basin. Deposits in northern and eastern Asia are mostly associated with coal-bearing rocks of Jurassic (and Cretaceous) age. Extensive marine-platform deposits of the black shale—phosphorite—chert assemblage of Cretaceous age are reported in Israel, Jordan, Syria, and the southern part of the Arabian Peninsula. In Europe, extensive marine-platform deposits, mostly black shales, of Jurassic age are widely distributed. They include many thin but high-grade deposits, as well as extensive thicker lower-grade accumulations. Some oil shale associated with Jurassic and Cretaceous coal is reported in eastern and southern Europe. Minor deposits of Triassic age are reported in south-central Europe.

In North America, large marine-platform deposits are reported in Alaska and central Canada. Triassic deposits in eastern Alaska and Jurassic and Cretaceous deposits in northern Alaska both contain thin high-grade oil shale in thicker lower-grade sequences. In Saskatchewan and Manitoba, Canada, platform deposits of low-grade oil shale of Cretaceous age are extensive. Numerous other low-grade marine oil-shale deposits of Cretaceous age are known in western United States, but few have been explored for their oil potential. Small oil-shale deposits associated with coal-bearing rocks

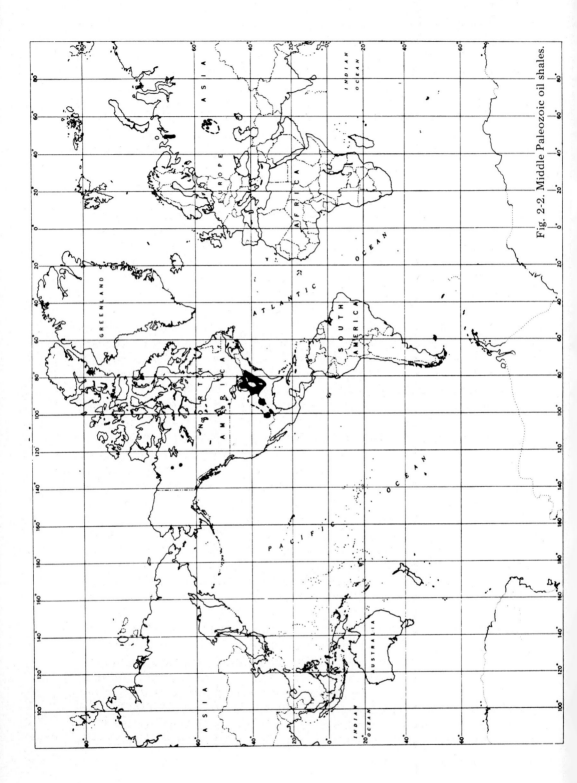

Fig. 2-2. Middle Paleozoic oil shales.

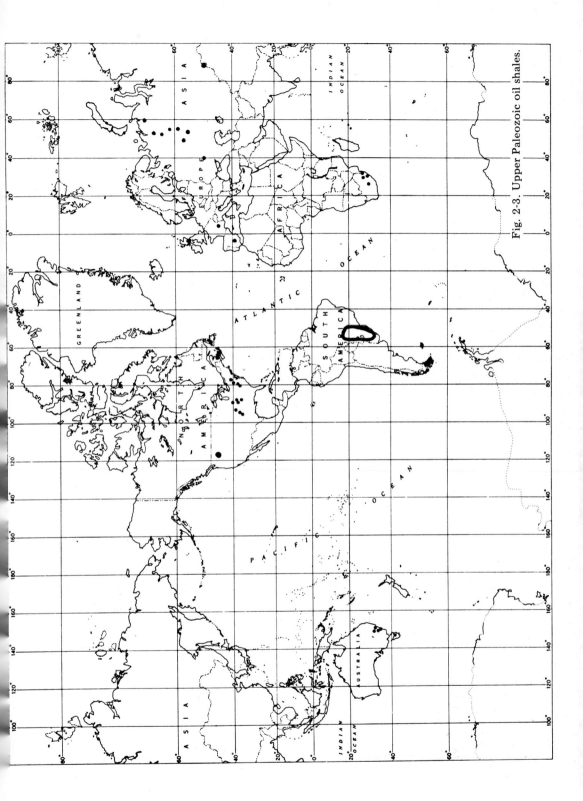

Fig. 2-3. Upper Paleozoic oil shales.

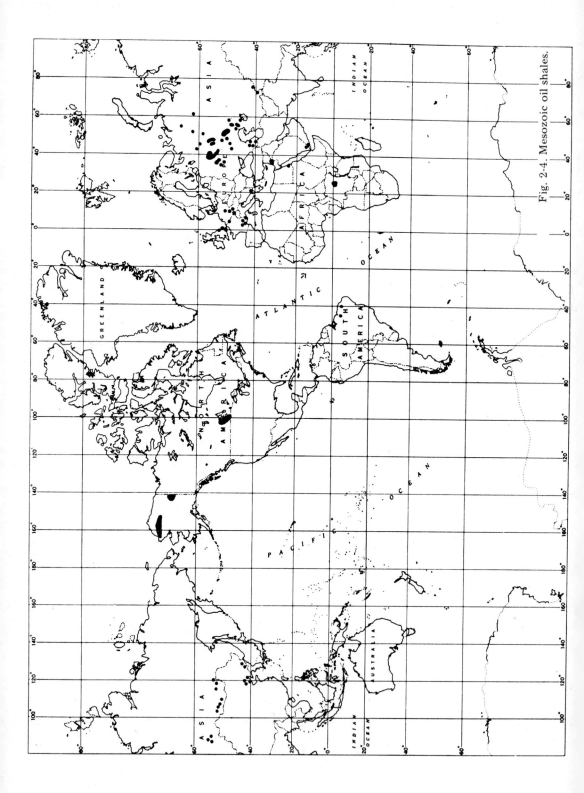

Fig. 2-4. Mesozoic oil shales.

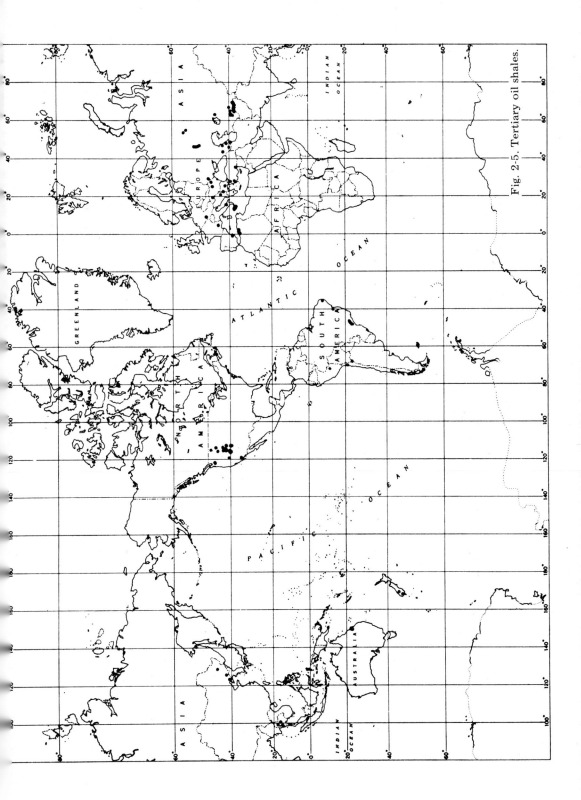

Fig. 2-5. Tertiary oil shales.

are reported in the Triassic sedimentary rocks of eastern United States and in rocks of Cretaceous age in a few localities in western United States and Canada.

Many of the reported oil-shale deposits of Tertiary age (Fig. 2-5) are of nonmarine origin. They accumulated in large lake basins or as smaller deposits associated with coal-bearing strata. Several marine deposits are reportedly large, but generally lower in grade. Small deposits are reported in New Zealand, in several areas of Europe, in the Andean Mountains of South America, and in the Cordilleran and Coast ranges of western North America.

The larger lake-basin deposits, mostly of Early and Middle Tertiary age, include oil shale in the Green River Formation and other basin deposits in western United States, in the Paraiba Valley of southern Brazil, the Aleksinac and other deposits in Yugoslavia, in the intermountain basins of the southern USSR, and in eastern China. Most are in regions that were marginal to the major orogenic movements that produced the modern folded and faulted mountains.

Marine deposits of the black shale—phosphorite—chert assemblage, mostly of Late Tertiary age, are reported in southern California, Algeria, Sicily, and the Caucasus region of southern USSR. They are mainly diatomaceous shale with substantial bitumen content in addition to kerogen.

Quaternary deposits not shown on maps include a number of modern lake, bog, lagoon, and marine-basin deposits containing organic debris that can yield oil. Most contain so much water, however, that they have not been considered economic sources of shale oil. Some have been studied for clues as to origin and preservation of the organic matter in oil shale, but not as potential resources of oil.

Geologic settings favorable for prospecting

As indicated at the outset, oil shales are so diverse in character and origin, and so poorly understood, that it is not possible at this stage to give definitive guides to the search for all types of deposits or to define all the terranes favorable for their occurrence. Some guides, however, can be set up, which will be useful in the search for some deposits.

Oil shales range in age from Cambrian to Recent. The better-grade oil shales of marine origin are mainly black shales, many of which extend over areas of hundreds or thousands of square miles, but most of which are only a few feet to a few tens of feet in thickness. Those with a siliceous matrix tend to decrease in yield with age, and Paleozoic black shales generally yield less than 20 gal of oil per ton of rock. Shales with a carbonate matrix are likely to be richer and even those of Paleozoic age may yield 20—50 gal/ton. From the standpoint of prospecting, many thin marine black shale sections are worth testing. Black shales associated with limestone, chert, and phosphate rocks are particularly favorable. The platform sections of the world and the younger geosynclinal sections are, in general, favorable provinces.

The large lake basins contain the thickest and some of the richest oil shales. Such shales may extend over areas of hundreds or thousands of square miles, be measurable in hundreds of feet, and yield 20—50 gal of oil or more per ton of rock. Many are associated with pyroclastics. Not enough is known about the origin of the lacustrine shales to make it possible to identify the most favorable basins. In general, however, the tectonic lake basins formed during mountain building in the younger orogenic belts around the world deserve examination. In the western United States alone, for example, more than 165 extensive lake-basin deposits contain rocks of Cenozoic age [7]. Several contain oil shale that has not been explored and further prospecting is likely to disclose oil shale in many others. The Tertiary orogenic belts in Europe and Asia are known to contain large lake-basin deposits, most of which have not been fully explored. Some probably contain large, but unrecognized, oil-shale deposits.

The oil-shale deposits associated with coal measures are mostly of small extent and thickness, but may have a rich oil yield. They are likely to range from a fraction of a square mile to hundreds of square miles in extent, from a few feet to a few tens of feet in thickness, and to contain zones that yield 50 gal of oil or more per ton. Their yield is less likely to be diminished by compaction and deformation, but the metamorphism associated with intense deformation may substantially reduce the oil yield. Coal measures in many parts of the world have not been adequately prospected for such deposits, and coal-bearing sections of some regions may in general be considered favorable for exploration.

Conclusions

The known resources of oil shale are tremendous [2], but they are made up of a few large deposits — the Green River Formation of western United States, the Devonian shales of eastern and central United States, the Permian Irati Shale of Brazil, the Cambrian deposits of northern Asia, and a few others. If technologic advances would make shale oil competitive, it will be competitive at first only in areas close to the source. Rich, cheaply minable, small deposits may, therefore, have great significance in the local scene. In conclusion, one can state with confidence that further prospecting and exploration will identify valuable deposits in many parts of the world where they are now unknown.

References

1. F.C. Jaffe, "Oil Shale. I Nomenclature, Uses, Reserves, and Products", *Colo. Sch. Mines, Miner. Ind. Bull.*, 5 (2), 11 pp. (1962).
2. D.C. Duncan and V.E. Swanson, "Organic-rich Shale of the United States and World Land Areas", *U.S. Geol Surv., Circ. 523*, 30 pp. (1965).

3. G. Ozerov, *Progress and Prospects in the Utilization of Oil Shale*, U.N. Dep. Econ. Soc. Aff., Resour. Transp. Div., New York, Pap. *1*, 102 pp. (1965).
4. C. Milton, "Green River Mineralogy", in: *Encyclopedia of Geology*, New York (1967).
5. V.E. McKelvey, "Changes in Patterns of Energy Consumption and Their Bearing on Exploration", *Indian Miner.*, *19* (2), 134—138 (1965).
6. R.P. Sheldon, "Paleolatitudinal and Paleogeographic Distribution of Phosphorite", *U.S. Geol. Surv., Prof. Pap. 502-C*, C106—C111 (1964).
7. J.H. Feth, "Review and Annotated Bibliography of Ancient Lake Deposits (Precambrian to Pleistocene) in the Western States", *Bull. U.S. Geol. Surv.*, *1080*, 119 pp. (1964).

Chapter 3

THE ORIGIN AND FORMATION OF OIL SHALE

R.F. CANE

Introduction

Any consideration of the origin and mode of formation of oil shale must be, with little exception, highly speculative. As oil shales from different parts of the earth vary widely in composition, it is obviously impossible, in this short survey, to provide adequate treatment of many of the world's deposits, indeed, even of the main representatives. A satisfactory hypothesis of the origin of one type of rock may not be applicable to another and there is no doubt that a wide variety of source materials must be considered. Nevertheless, there are several features appertaining to all oil shales which enable limiting criteria to be applied; these features will be discussed herein.

During the last century, there has been much research into the composition of oil-shale kerogen and many theories have been put forward regarding the nature of this organic material. These theories have resulted mainly from microscopical and geological observations and often led to greater confusion than existed before. Although much has been done by the microscopist in explaining a probable origin of selected types of oil shale, the results provide practically no evidence at all of its present chemical structure. The recent availability of highly selective physical methods of analysis is, however, rapidly changing the situation.

Ab initio, it is believed desirable to define the proper meaning of the word "kerogen". The name "kerogen" was first coined by Professor Crum Brown [1] in 1912 to denote specifically the insoluble organic matter in oil shale. He used the word "kerogen" to cover the material which, on heating and decomposition, gives rise to shale oil. This precise meaning remained unaltered for nearly half a century but, unfortunately, since the rise of a new generation of organic geochemists, its specificity has now been lost [2]. The original significance of the word shall be used in this contribution.

Many substances have been suggested as the source material of oil-shale kerogen, including resins, spores, lignin, inspissated petroleum, algae, bitumen and animal remains. It is now generally agreed, however, that some, if not many, oil shales owe their origin to algal growth. Although algae may have been the main contributor, it is undeniable that a variety of miscellaneous detrital material has been associated with all depositions. Wind-borne plant debris is important in some deposits and, in all cases, the effects of microbial action can never be ignored. Thorne et al. [3] have adequately expressed the present concensus in the following terms: "Oil shale was formed by the deposition and lithification of finely divided mineral matter and organic debris in the bottom of shallow lakes and seas. The organic debris resulted from the mechanical and chemical degradation of small aquatic algal organisms."

Because of its exceptional inertness, a satisfactory solution to the problem of kerogen constitution is a difficult one. Degradative chemical methods such as oxidation or pyrolysis, although providing some clues, have many inadequacies and it seems likely that they only provide information on specific reactive entities within the polymer matrix. Other chemical methods, such as hydrogenolysis or chlorination have been even less rewarding. One must also remember that the properties of a single kerogen sample always represent an average of the properties of the constituent maceral species. Natural kerogen, which behaves macroscopically and chemically as a single entity, is revealed under the microscope as grossly heterogeneous. In most cases, the nature of the causative organism has been so changed by diagenetic processes as to render it structureless and unrecognizable.

Although much useful detail is now known about many aspects of kerogen, it would seem unlikely that a complete picture of the origin and nature of this complex organic matter will ever be obtained. No doubt, there is a general pattern of constitution in kerogen, and maybe fragments of this pattern can be translated into some sort of chemical picture; however, at best, one cannot regard the result as other than a rough sketch. One faces here a problem very similar to that of the constitution of coal. For over a century, even with considerable economic incentive, the structural chemistry of coal has baffled some of the best scientific brains and, although some parts of the picture are known in considerable detail, the entire canvas is still ill-defined.

General considerations

As it is impracticable to discuss the nature of all varieties of oil shale, it has been decided to present a broad consideration of the origin and deposition of oil shales in general. This is followed by a detailed treatment of three specific, but widely different, types. Two examples are included in the present chapter, whereas the third is given separate treatment in Chapter 4. The three examples are:

(1) *Torbanite*, which originated from a morphologically recognizable colonial alga of terrestrial and fresh-water origin. The deposits are lenticular and associated with Permian coals. An hypothesis of the mode of formation and the chemical constitution of this kerogen now seems well established.

(2) *Tasmanite*, which is constituted from spherical disseminules of organized structure, believed to be algae of unknown affinity. The deposits are

stratified and of marine origin. The chemical nature of the kerogen is only partly explored.

(3) The *Green River Formation* oil shale is composed of disorganized and unrecognizable organic matter. Although thought to be of algal genesis, it would appear that several biological types have contributed. It is of lacustrine origin associated with saline waters. Because of its potential economic importance, a separate chapter (Chapter 4) has been devoted to this deposit.

The salient features of each type are given in Table 3-I.

Information on the genesis of petroleum has been helpful in suggesting likely processes in the early stages of deposition and formation of oil shale. As a result of various studies, it is believed that the conditions of sedimentation and compaction were not too dissimilar from those existing at present and that similar processes may be still occurring. If this be so, it is surprising that one does not recognize such conversions today and make direct observation. This lack of record is primarily caused by human inability to appreciate the magnitude of geological time. Even though the thickness of some oil-shale deposits may be measured in thousands of feet, Bradley [4] has shown that the rate of deposition, on a dry basis, of kerogenous ooze is less than 1 mm per century, a circumstance hardly likely to arouse one's interest during a lifetime.

TABLE 3-I

Main features of selected oil shales

	Torbanite (N.S.W.)	Tasmanite (Tasmania)	Oil shale (Colorado)
Geological era	Permian	Permian	Eocene
Depositional conditions	fresh water	marine	saline
Source	Algae	Algae?	?
Inorganic matter	silica, clays	mudstones	silicates and carbonates
Analysis (% w/w) — (d.a.f. basis):			
Carbon	83.6	78.1	79.2
Hydrogen	11.3	10.2	10.5
Oxygen	3.5	6.0	6.5
Nitrogen	0.6	0.6	2.6
Sulphur	1.0	5.1	1.2
C/H wt. ratio	7.4	7.7	7.5
S.G. of pure organic matter	0.96	0.99	1.04

Likely source materials in kerogen formation

Organic components

Many substances have been suggested as giving rise to oil-shale kerogen, but most chemical types must be rejected for the same reasons that they have been rejected by petroleum geochemists. Thus one must disregard carbohydrates, lignins, proteins and waxes. Assuming that today's biochemical degradative processes are the same as those existing in past geological ages, the fate of these groups may be summarized as follows:

Carbohydrates can be broken down by either chemical processes or biological agencies. Under the gentle environmental conditions present during deposition, purely chemical decomposition may be discounted. Any preferential removal of hydroxyl groups or scission of the strong ether linkages cannot be entertained. One can, however, envisage bacterial or enzymatic attack to produce saccharides and their subsequent hydrolysis to carbon dioxide and water. This mode of complete degradation is so prevalent that the chance of cellulose, or carbohydrates generally, making any appreciable contribution to kerogen in oil shales may be neglected. Likewise, *proteins* are not stable enough to be considered. Enzymatic attack on the peptide linkages would be followed by further breakdown, with the ultimate production of ammonia and amines.

Of course, the simple molecules arising from the decomposition of complex proteins or carbohydrates probably had some role in kerogen formation. Hydrogen sulphide is a typical reactive decomposition intermediate which is associated with sapropelic formations. It seems likely that some of the hetero-atoms, originating from proteins, were present in the intermediate breakdown products and, eventually, were "built into" the kerogen matrix. It has been shown (Cane, unpublished work) that added nitrogenous compounds such as gluten are "molecularly enmeshed" during the polymerization of polyene fatty acids. If such a polymer containing "occluded" aliphatic nitrogen compounds is pyrolysed under conditions similar to oil-shale retorting, the product oil contains alkyl pyridines. In a similar manner, dihydric phenols are produced during the pyrolysis of polymerized polyene acids which have been oxidized by exposure to the atmosphere.

Lignins are essentially aromatic derivatives of phenyl propane and can be envisaged as giving rise to kerogenous material [5] by demethylation, ring rupture and polymerization. The pyrolysis liquids of polymers from such sources, however, would certainly exhibit a much more aromatic character than does shale oil. Thus it seems unlikely that lignins played a significant role in kerogen formation, although some contribution by lignin-type material cannot be ignored, particularly in the coaly oil shales.

Waxes consist of straight chain or cyclic hydrocarbons of moderate to high molecular weight. Waxes are chemically and thermodynamically stable enough to remain unchanged over geological periods. They are reasonably soluble and, by the definition of kerogen, are excluded as a source material other than being considered as part of the lipid component or the extractibles of biological substances.

One is, therefore, left with the inescapable conclusion that lipid matter is the only likely major contributor which should be given serious consideration. Lipids have the desired stability, the required chemical configuration and the availability. It is less certain, but not unlikely, that lipids (perhaps of marine origin) constitute the main source of petroleum. The important distinguishing feature of kerogen diagenesis was that the source material on ageing increased in molecular weight and became solid, tough and insoluble, whereas in petroleum it decreased in molecular size and became more volatile and less complex. Both kerogen and petroleum could owe their origin to mixed lipid matter, characterized, in the case of petroleum, by a relatively low degree of chemical reactivity, whereas in kerogen, similar but more reactive molecules were capable of extensive inter- and intra-molecular bonding. Because of the relative stability of the petroleum precursors, thermodynamic factors governed a slow breakdown into liquids and gases. On the contrary with proto-kerogen, the chemical reactivity of a similar "monomer" quickly built up an energetically well-protected more stable polymer. Hence the precursor to both is probably a chemical type in which a minor difference in structure leads to a vastly different behavior during diagenesis and resulting end-product, over geological time. If one accepts that polymerization and condensation are the major reactions during kerogen formation, it seems inevitable that molecular unsaturation is the variable that decides the diagenetic route. It is conceivable that, after a suitable burial period, intermediates derived from the less reactive lipids would be extensively decomposed into petroleum-like molecules, whereas polymeric matter originating in more reactive members of the same class of compound could be still at the inert kerogen stage.

One of the stumbling blocks to the ready acceptance of the lipid theory of naphthogenesis has been the actual chemical composition of crude oil, its lack of unsaturation, the peculiarly high content of C_7, C_8, C_9 and C_{10} hydrocarbons, the low "carbon preference index",[1] and the occurrence of unique cyclic structures in petroleum. There are no such problems in the case of oil shale kerogen. The composition of the polymer, such as is known, can be explained in terms of a variety of lipid monomers. Compared with petroleum, no one has ever isolated a range of homologous hydrocarbons from kerogen and the extractives have the required high C.P.I. Another difficulty in the lipid theory of petroleum origin is that it has proved impossible,

---

[1] Carbon preference index (C.P.I.) — Ratio of the amount of odd-carbon-numbered n-alkanes to the amount of even-carbon-numbered ones [23].

so far, to provide a satisfactory simulated diagenetic process. On the contrary, it has been possible to synthesize kerogens from certain plant fats. Thus it seems reasonable to accept the hypothesis that the algal lipids were the major contributors to most kerogens, either as hydrocarbons or as fatty acids which became partially decarboxylated to hydrocarbon residues. Bacteria and other predators also had an important role in kerogen formation by acting as "chemical factories" ingesting a variety of primitive foods in the deposited matter and excreting other compounds to further modify the sediment.

Type of lipids. Because the concensus is that algal residues played a major role in kerogen formation it is useful to examine the lipid types likely to have been involved. The main chemical compounds justifying consideration are esters of fatty acids and hydrocarbons. It seems that both had important roles, either conjointly or separately. It is believed that some kerogens were formed nearly exclusively from hydrocarbon lipids, whereas others owe their origin mainly to fatty acids; by far the larger contributor would be of the latter type. The ubiquity and chemistry of fatty acids provide all the desiderata for kerogen formation. Fatty acids are present in nearly all life forms and occur in ample quantity. Suitable members of the group possess sufficient chemical reactivity to polymerize to hard, insoluble and inert material similar to kerogen. Stadnikoff [6] has laid great stress on the oxidation and polymerization of such fatty oils in the formation of petroleum and kerogenous material. Polyene acids, so characteristic of algal fats, are highly reactive and Cane [7] has suggested several mechanisms for the formation of kerogen-like polymers. Many workers have reported the 'disappearance' of polyene acids in algal fats. Abelson [8] studied *Chlorella* in relation to the C18:3 acid and states "on heating at 190°C for 3 days, this compound largely disappears" ... whereas the saturated and mono-unsaturated acids ... "could last for millions of years". The simple explanation is, of course, that the polyenes had completely polymerized and were no longer observable as a chemical entity.

After a few years under burial conditions, fats are hydrolyzed to the free acid and the carboxyl group can be eliminated in a number of ways. Once the fatty acid has been liberated, biological and microbial attack can convert it into a variety of other chemical types subsequent to the attack on the reactive $\alpha\beta$-carbon link. Bacterial attack can lead to the formation of $\alpha\beta$-unsaturated acids followed by further reactions of the Diels-Alder type.

Algal fatty acids. The algal families most likely to contribute to kerogen formation are members of the Chlorophyceae or Cyanophyceae. These algae contain large amounts of saturated and unsaturated fatty acids in a variety of molecular weights and degrees of unsaturation. The actual composition of the lipid acid is not important to this discussion, but, in general, the chain length ranges from C_{14} to C_{22} with a maximum at C_{16} for the saturated acids. Large amounts of C_{16} and C_{18} unsaturated acids are also usually present. These acids are represented by several contributors including trienoic and higher members although the dominant ones are usually oleic and the 18:2 acid [9]. In a few algal species the 18:3 acid is the main component, but acids containing up to six double bonds have been reported. As distinct from fatty acids, specific algae are capable of secreting hydrocarbons, sometimes in phenomenally large amounts. The hydrocarbons are generally maximized at C_{17} for both the green and the blue-green genera. A second peaked concentration is found in some species in which the distribution is bimodal with one maximum at C_{17} and another in the $C_{27}-C_{31}$ range, the latter often being represented by dienes. One particular species produces C_{34} hydrocarbons almost exclusively.

Alkane acids, other than the normal fatty series, have been found in some algal communities, but these are probably secondary products. Leo and Parker [10] have shown that bacteria are active in transforming n-fatty acids to iso- and anteiso-acids and in assisting other conversions. Bacteria have additional effects on acids' composition, being capable of hydrogenating oleic and linoleic acids [11], of decarboxylating and polymerizing alkanoic acids [12] and hydrolyzing lipids [13].

It is a well-known phenomenon that algae, under adverse conditions, may show greatly increased lipid formation concomitant with decreased amounts of protein and carbohydrate. With plentiful food under natural conditions, the total fat content of most algae is only a few percent. By reducing the oxygen and lowering the temperature, *Chlorella* can be caused to secrete lipids up to 86% of its dry weight [14], a large proportion of which is unsaturated. In the case of *Chlorella pyrenoidosa* the figures in Table 3-II are pertinent [15].

TABLE 3-II

Lipid secretion by *Chlorella*, in controlled atmospheres

Experiment number	1	2	3	4
Total lipids (%, dry wt.)	23.4	33.2	63.0	75.5
Fatty acids (F.A.) (% of lipids)	6.6	16.4	52.3	65.6
$C_{16} + C_{18}$ unsat. F.A. (% of total F.A.)	83	85	88	85

Conditions:
1   5% CO_2 in air   — 80 days, natural light
2   5% CO_2 in air   — 17 days, natural light
3   5% CO_2 in air   — 83 days, natural light
4   5% CO_2 in nitrogen — 75 days, artificial light

In exceptional cases, the organism may even change its physiological processes to cope with adverse circumstances. The hydrocarbon-producing alga believed responsible for the formation of some oil shales, not only changes the structure of its hydrocarbons but changes color as well. In the rapid growth form it is green from chlorophyll, whereas, in the resting stage, it is rusty-orange in color from carotenes.

Inorganic components

Oil shale contains two distinct and dissimilar types of matter, the ratio of which may vary greatly from one sample to another: the organic portion, consisting of small particles of biological origin, and the inorganic part composed of clays, sand, dolomite or other adventitious mineral matter. All physical and chemical properties, therefore, are a function of the amount of each component present, and will vary between limits determined by the maximum amount of either. Although the composition of the inorganic portion of oil shale is outside the province of this chapter, the effect of such material on kerogen formation should be considered. The inorganic components also provide much useful information on the manner of deposition.

Considerable research has gone into the study of possible catalytic effects of clays on petroleum formation. Although evidence is not strong, it is believed by some researchers that surface catalysis directs reactions in naphthogenesis [16]; no such "magic powder" is needed to explain the formation of kerogen. Extensive non-catalytic polymerization of many polyene structures will take place readily at ambient temperature by free radical mechanisms yielding solid tough polymers. Cane [7] suggested that trienoic aliphatic acids were suitable sources of some kerogens and showed that satisfactory synthetic kerogens could be obtained from them with gentle incubation for some years. The addition of clays to the monomer did not appear to affect the chemistry or the reaction kinetics, but, by acting as a reinforcing filler, certainly produced a much stronger product.

The extremely fine particle size of much inorganic matter in oil shale demonstrates unequivocally that these deposits were formed under very still conditions. This does not always follow, however, as the ultrafine silica of some torbanites is not allochthonous but was precipitated in the form of chalcedony from siliceous waters during the early stages of maturation. There are other instances where sulphides have been formed within the tissues after deposition and some calcareous oil shales have an autochthonous mineral matrix. With these exceptions, it appears that the mineral matter was added to the organic ooze as a finely suspended argillaceous or arenaceous silt containing small amounts of metallic salts, often iron. Calcined oil shales show heterogeneous patterns indicating changes in the composition of the mineral matter during deposition. Marine oil shales often contain shells and pebbles. The inorganic matter of torbanites is discussed later.

Some metals occur in oil shales as organic complexes. Erdman et al. [17] have shown that one such complex contains vanadyl compounds. As the presence of vanadium is limited to very few life forms, it has been suggested that the vanadium was removed from igneous rocks by weathering and then chelated during deposition and maturation. Other metals such as nickel, uranium and molybdenum occur as organic complexes in kerogen and also may arise from weathering processes.

The discussion so far has been of a general nature to serve as a background to an explanation of the formation of kerogen. Before proceeding to such a description, three additional topics will be presented, as they provide useful evidence on specific features of kerogen genesis. The topics to be discussed are: (1) Biological markers, (2) Chemical analyses, and (3) Nature of shale oil.

(1) *Biological markers.* The early biological history of petroleum precursors is of great importance because the identity of the primary source material is far from being established. The problem of naphthogenesis is made particularly difficult because the organic matter has been transformed and then transported away from the site of deposition; the diagenesis has left no morphological clues to the progenitors. The position with oil shale is much simpler because transportation after deposition did not occur and, in many cases, petrographic examination shows the occurrence of morphologically recognizable remains. Only in a few deposits has the decomposition and rock distortion been so extensive that the material is now structureless. In all cases, useful information may be obtained from certain biological evidence which is to be found in kerogen itself.

Since the discovery of gas—liquid chromatography and the consequent development of extremely sensitive analytical methods for organic compounds, a great deal of research has been expended searching for traces of biogenetic compounds in rocks. Particular emphasis has been placed on the detection of isoprenoid compounds as it seems impossible that this type of hydrocarbon configuration could be produced other than by life processes. Cummins and Robinson [18] have found phytane, pristane and associated trimethylalkanes in Green River oil shale in high amounts. Other isoprenoids have been found by other workers [19,20,21]. There seems to be a general decrease in isoprenoid concentration with geological age and, in this respect, kerogen resembles petroleum.

A second biological marker in oil shale is the presence of organo-metallic compounds, the importance of which does not rest on the composition of the complex, but on the thermal sensitivity of such compounds. For example, it is known that porphyrins are not stable over about $180°C$ and, therefore, their occurrence in oil shale sets an upper temperature limit to the whole diagenetic process. Treibs' [22] monumental work on the occurrence of chlorophyll, mesoporphyrins and hemin derivatives in European oil shales, petroleum and bitumens, has shown that kerogens have not been exposed to temperatures exceeding 150°C. Like petroleum, kerogen has been formed by a low-temperature process.

A third important parameter in the study of rock biogenesis is termed the "Carbon Preference Index". The C.P.I. may be defined [23] as the ratio of the amount of odd-carbon-numbered n-alkanes to the content (count) of even-carbon ones; however, there are other definitions. It can readily be seen that if bio-lipids are largely glyceride esters of even-carbon-numbered fatty acids, then odd-carbon-numbered n-alkanes derived from such bio-acids, are likely to predominate in any extractive. Some oil shale n-alkanes have a high C.P.I. and are comparable to extracts from recent soils and muds [24]; no such relationship has been found in petroleum which has a peculiarly high content of C_7, C_8, C_9 and C_{10} hydrocarbons. Typical C.P.I. values are:

n-Alkane Source	C.P.I.
Crude oil	1
Ancient sediments	1.1—2.4
Recent sediments	2.3—5.5
Oil shales	1.0—4.8

With regard to actual hydrocarbon distribution in many kerogens, particularly those in the geologically younger deposits, there is the expected large contribution from hydrocarbons in the C_{13}—C_{19} range together with peaking of the associated acids [25]. The large C_{17} alkane concentration is consistent with the ubiquitous C_{18} acids, but many kerogens show a second "hump" in C_{27}—C_{31} range [18,27]. It is suggested by the writer that the C_{27}—C_{31} alkanes arise not from fatty acids, but from unchanged algal hydrocarbons, such as those which give rise to torbanite [28], and less likely from triterpanes as has been suggested. In all cases, the significance and specificity of the C.P.I. decreases with the age of the deposit and tends to approach unity at depth, as in the case of petroleum and coal [29].

(2) *Chemical analyses.* Because of its inertness and insolubility, classical chemical analysis has not provided much useful data on the constitution of kerogen. Chemical attack by conventional reagents has been unrewarding and the published material is largely conjectural. Kerogens are known to contain varying amounts of carboxyl, hydroxyl and ester functions based on their infra-red spectra, and some quantitative chemical information is available [30]. Carbon unsaturation is always present.

An elemental analysis gives an average figure for all constituents in the sample and includes contributions from non-kerogen components, as well as mineral matter. Nevertheless, elemental analyses are reasonably accurate when done on purified kerogen and enable some differentiation to be made between various types. Himus [31] and Robinson [30] have presented surveys of elemental analyses and showed that they range between the following limits (% w/w): carbon — 64—89, hydrogen — 7.1—12.8, nitrogen — 0.1—3.1, sulphur — 0.1—8.7, oxygen — 0.8—24.8.

These rather scattered data may be narrowed by excluding a few exceptional deposits of doubtful character. A further restriction may be applied by the calculated exclusion of nitrogen and sulphur. The latter artifice introduces errors, but they are probably no worse than the overall accuracy of the analyses. When these modifications are made, representative kerogen analyses are presented in Table 3-III.

With advantage, the analyses may be presented as areas on the modified Ralston diagram shown in Fig. 3-1. The figure shows that kerogens occupy an area between those of fatty acids and hydrocarbon mixtures such as petroleum.

The C/H ratio of kerogen varies from about 7½ to 10, and lies between ca. 15 for coal and 6—7 for petroleum. In general, the ratio indicates open unsaturated or saturated cyclic hydrocarbon structures. In view of the likely source materials discussed earlier, the biological markers, and the elemental analyses, one can postulate with some assurance that most kerogens are derived from lipids (1) by a process of decarboxylation and polymerization of fatty acids or (2) by a process of oxidation and polymerization of hydrocarbons.

Although, as mentioned earlier, the intractability of kerogen to chemical examination has proved one of the main stumbling blocks to constitutional

TABLE 3-III

Elemental analyses of kerogen

	Carbon (%)	Hydrogen (%)	Oxygen (%)
Oil shale			
Colorado (U.S.A.)	82.3—87.5	8.7—10.9	3.8— 6.7
France	84.3—87.7	8.1— 8.4	4.1— 7.3
Scotland	81.4—83.0	7.9— 8.8	8.8—10.6
South Africa	81.0—82.2	8.4— 9.3	7.6— 8.9
Torbanite			
Australia	81.2—87.2	10.1—11.9	2.3— 6.4
Scotland	86.4—87.7	9.9—10.9	3.8— 5.1
South Africa	80.2—82.4	7.3—10.5	8.3—10.4
Kukersite	76.5—78.4	9.2— 9.4	11.8—14.6
Tasmanite	82.4—84.8	10.5—10.9	5.2— 7.1

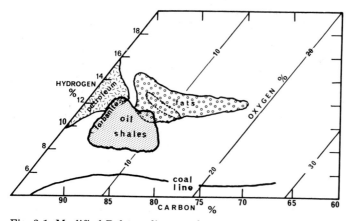

Fig. 3-1. Modified Ralston diagram showing oil shales and possible precursors.

studies, some success has been achieved using aqueous oxidation. Arising from early work on the chemistry of coal, Down and Himus [32] studied the action of alkaline potassium permanganate on a variety of oil shales. This research had the very important result that it clearly differentiated oil-shale kerogens into two types depending upon whether benzenoid acids were formed or not. A second major differentiation could be made based on extent of attack. Thus, torbanites yielded virtually no benzenoid acids[1] and were very resistant to oxidation, leaving large amounts of unoxidized carbon. Green River oil shale, on the other hand, also yielded no aromatic acids, but was nearly completely solubilized. Kimmeridge oil shale was also completely attacked, but yielded much aromatic acid material.

Further research has led to the belief that at least two types of kerogen are likely to be present in oil shale: (1) an algal portion which may or may not be oxidation resistant and (2) a quasi-aromatic portion, the nature of which is more humic or coaly. Dancy and Giedroyc [33] stated "the residue from the oxidation of the Ermelo (oil shale) showed that a large part of the algal matter had been concentrated" in the non-oxidized portion, which was "very similar to that of the N.S.W. torbanite, which is almost of pure algal origin", the black humic portion of the oil shale having been oxidized away "almost entirely", yielding benzenoid acids. By gentle oxidation of Green River oil shale, further reaction of the initial products was minimized and Robinson [34] has been successful in obtaining principally carbon dioxide and alkane dicarboxylic acids ranging from oxalic to adipic. The residue was characterized in a later paper [35] and was shown to consist of highly complex aromatic, napthenic and heterocyclic acids. The oxidation results of several workers and portion of Robinson's [36] table is reproduced in Table 3-IV in a modified form.

Permanganate oxidation techniques have been carried to a further stage

[1] See note added in proof, p. 60.

TABLE 3-IV

Permanganate oxidation of kerogens

Oil shale	Benzenoid acids	Non-volatile non-oxalic acids (%)	Carbon dioxide (%)	Volatile and oxalic acids (%)	Unoxidized residue (%)
Green River (U.S.A.)	—	1	63	35	1
Kukersite (Estonia)	—	4	51	37	8
Torbanite (N.S.W.)	—	3	13	10	74
Ermelo (South Africa)	+	17	31	18	34
Pumperston (Scotland)	+	13	21	15	51
St Hilaire (France)	+	10	35	7	48

by Stefanovic and Vitorovic [37]. These workers showed that, under very gentle conditions in acetone solution, aliphatic polycarboxylic acids could be obtained. They concluded that this (Yugoslav) kerogen "consists of comparatively long aliphatic chains which are partially unsaturated and are probably interconnected by cross linkages . . . the unsaturated bonds are mainly present as isolated double bonds".

In the opinion of the writer, the resistance to oxidation is directly related to the kerogen structure and hence to the source material, rather than to any diagenetic process. All true torbanites and certain oil shales, such as "Green River" and kukersite, yield no benzenoid acids on oxidation. Torbanite, however, consists largely of hydrocarbon polymers [28] lacking oxygen, whereas the latter two contain much oxygen function as carboxyl and ester. The opinion is here put forward that the absence of benzenoid acids indicates a substantial algal contribution with little humic content, whereas the resistance to oxidation within this group depends primarily on the ratio of the two types of algal lipid, i.e., hydrocarbons to fatty acids.

A second major kerogen class may be defined as that possessing a humic or coaly character yielding benzenoic acids on permanganate oxidation. Two limiting subtypes are shown in Table 3-V.

TABLE 3-V

Kerogen classification based on oxidation behavior

KEROGEN A yielding no benzenoid acids. Algal origin.
    Subtype A(i) — derived largely from algal fatty acids.
    Subtype A(ii) — derived largely from algal hydrocarbons.

KEROGEN B yielding benzenoid acids. The kerogen contains humic contributors.
    Subtype B(i) — admixed with kerogen A(i).
    Subtype B(ii) — admixed with kerogen A(ii).

Although some gradation may be expected, most of the worlds' oil shales can be neatly fitted into one of the above classes.

(3) Nature of shale oil. Although much technological work has been done on shale oil, there is little that helps to explain the origin and composition of kerogen. It has been amply demonstrated [26] that the primary discernible decomposition product of kerogen is a rubbery "depolymerized" intermediate which, on further heating, yields a semi-solid bitumen. This, on further reaction, breaks down to a viscous secondary tar. Given sufficient thermal energy, the tar, in turn, decomposes into a mixture of fluid hydrocarbons called shale oil as well as gas and coke. During the early changes, a substantial portion of the hydrogen sulphide and carbon dioxide is evolved, although the pyrolysis gases are relatively free from hydrocarbons. Only in the tertiary-tar/oil transformation is there active decomposition of the organic mass and copious hydrocarbon evolution.

Although the decomposition is progressive and no stage occurs to the exclusion of another, one may illustrate the decomposition as shown in Fig. 3-2. It is thus a matter of definition at what stage of pyrolysis can shale oil be considered to exist as such. It is also obvious that the oil composition is not constant but varies with decomposition conditions.

Shale oil formed by this cracking reaction looks like petroleum. Unlike petroleum, however, shale oil is a man-made product formed under conditions in which energetics demand certain structures to be stable and others to be destroyed; for this reason its chemistry is significantly different. "Normal" shale oil is about 40% unsaturated, contains a relatively high proportion of nitrogen and sulphur bodies, and, disregarding these heteromolecules, has a composition more like that produced by destructively decomposing high-molecular-weight fatty acids or ketones.

The variation in oil composition with pyrolysis conditions is not great provided the reaction temperature does not exceed $600°C$. At higher temperatures, as might be expected, there is a spectacular increase in aromatics at the expense of other hydrocarbon groups. On the contrary, by performing the pyrolysis over very long periods at low temperatures ($180-220°C$) negligible amounts of oil but heavy soluble intermediates are generated from which "bitumen" may be recovered by extraction. If one regards "proto-petroleum" as a high-molecular weight naphthenic "honey", then proto-shale oil is undoubtedly represented by this thermally produced extractable bitumen.

In an effort to gain some insight into kerogen and its decomposition, the mechanism of the thermal transformation to oil was extensively studied in

Fig. 3-2. Scheme of the reaction stages of the pyrolysis of algal kerogen [79].

the 1920's [38,39,40]. Studies of the kinetics of the solubilizing process showed that the reaction was pseudo-first order with an activation energy of 160—250 kJ/mol, which is similar to that encountered in petroleum cracking. The pyrolysis mechanism would thus seem to be the fracture of long-chain carbon—carbon bonds. Additionally, the presence of paraffin wax in many shale oils shows that, at least, corresponding lengths of carbon chains occur in the particular kerogen. It is thermodynamically impossible to synthesize, by purely thermal means, long-chain alkanes from other hydrocarbon configurations.

Before the advent of G.L.C.[1], much work had been expended on the isolation and identification of a few tar acids and tar bases in shale oil. In 1961, using G.L.C., Brown and Buck [41] identified twenty-nine alkyl pyridines and quinolines in a single shale-oil sample. All possible mono-substituted alkyl thiophenes up to butylthiophene have been identified in Colorado shale oil, the inference being that the early work detected only major components. Cane (unpublished work) has shown that alkyl pyridines occur in the pyrolysate from a polyene polymer to which 2% gluten had been added at the monomer stage. Phenols have been identified in the pyrolysate of a polymer of pure linolenic acid. These results again emphasize the fact that compounds found in the oil may have little relation to the structure of the parent kerogen. They are there simply because they are the ones which are thermodynamically favored during pyrolysis.

The limited amount of biogenetic information to be gleaned from the oil composition and formation may be summarized as follows:

(1) Long-chain hydrocarbon structures are important in some kerogens.

(2) Kerogen pyrolysis is, fairly generally, the scission of carbon—carbon bonds.

(3) Hetero-atoms, such as sulphur, nitrogen and oxygen, occur in kerogen. They may be part of the kerogen "molecule" or represent exogenous entities within the polymer matrix.

(4) Sulphur appears to be in two combinations, one loosely held, which gives rise to hydrogen sulphide in the early stages of decomposition, and the other, which is released later as organo-sulphur compounds, is much more firmly held. The type of nitrogen combination appears to be different as ammonia occurs only as a tertiary product at the end of the decomposition.

The formation of oil shale

Past research on oil-shale formation has been based largely on one of two approaches to the problem: (a) the analytic or (b) the synthetic.

(a) The analytic approach is that characterized by degradation of the "kerogen molecule" into identifiable fragments. Later, the information from

---

[1] Gas—liquid chromatography.

a multiplicity of fragments is correlated to ascertain whether a comprehensive picture can be obtained.

(b) The synthetic approach is that based on deduction from known facts plus conjecture of unknown ones, followed by the synthesis of a variety of "kerogens" from likely source materials. The data from synthetic models are then compared with those of the natural substance and the process repeated with a "better fit".

In the preceding pages, selected aspects of the genesis of kerogen have been presented as a background to the consideration of an overall picture of the formation of oil shale. At the present state of knowledge, only a general qualitative hypothesis can be drawn from the available information; one must never lose sight of the fact that kerogen is only a type of lithified organic mud. Any hypothesis must provide an explanation for the origin of both the organic and inorganic constituents and make allowances for the wide range of properties found in oil shale.

Deposition stage

It is self evident that the material of oil shale is the result of the codeposition of inorganic silt and clay and the organic matter of ancient biological organisms. Suitable environmental conditions for such deposition to lead to the production of petroleum have been set down by Hedberg [42] as: (1) abundant production of organic matter, (2) early development of an anaerobic environment, and (3) absence of total destructive organisms. These would apply equally well to the formation of oil shale.

Microscopic examination reveals that oil shales were laid down in quiet ecosystems containing lakes, lagoons or coastal strips of shallow seas. It appears that the major deposits were formed from the remains of algae which flourished in still waters, either marine or terrestrial, and that algal lipids were the main source of kerogen itself. Minor contributors were spores, pollen and remains of higher plants. Adventitious foreign matter is always present, which may be made up of insects, parts of small animals, fishes, minute crustacea, or other miscellania. In certain torbanites, complete leaf fossils are to be found in the form of films of coal embedded, without distortion, in the seam.

Conditions of deposition

It has been stated above that the aqueous environment, into which kerogen precursors were introduced, was characterized by very tranquil conditions. One can envisage small or large lakes, a series of interconnected lagoons or even inland seas being the sites of fresh-water deposits. Other oil shales appear to have been formed in river deltas or shallow estuaries, whereas further types were formed under marine conditions in shallow coastal ecosystems of quiet bays and lagoons or temporary inshore basins. These near-shore deposits received a substantial contribution from terrestrial matter brought down by river systems [43] and, in specific cases, this allochthonous matter makes up a major portion of the kerogen. Most inland deposits were of fresh- or, sometimes, brackish-water origin, an important exception being the Green River Formation which was formed under saline conditions. The inland water areas were usually surrounded by a thick margin of swamp vegetation which acted as an effective filter for all but the finest silt and clay brought in by rivers. The fine-grained material consisted mostly of clays, plus finely comminutated plant debris. Coarser matter and much mud were introduced during flood periods.

One can thus imagine a system of waterways of one kind or another in which a flourishing algal vegetation provided an enormous organic contribution to the ecosystem. Inflowing rivers brought further organic matter which, together with clay and silt, was mixed in various proportions with the autochthonous matter of the lakes. Regular changes in growth pattern tended to produce stratification within the existing algal mass. Some added matter sank to the bottom because of occluded mineral grains, whereas nearly pure organic matter might have floated. Both aerobic and anaerobic conditions might have coexisted.

All deposits are microstratified and contain banded structures showing that the environmental conditions were not steady but varied on an annual, seasonal or irregular basis. Even algae themselves tended to produce a stratified pattern. Parker [44] has described the formation of extensive algal mats in lagoons and mudflats as follows: "The living mat covers the mud bottom like a sheet of leather. Directly under the living mat is a layer of black mud, at times, a few centimeters thick. The remains of a former mat are under the first mud layer and they too have a mud layer under them. This pattern of mat and mud repeats itself."

Generally, the climate appears to have been fairly dry and conditions were not unlike that believed suitable for the formation of coal. Indeed, in some cases, coal-forming vegetation surrounded the lakes and lagoons. In many deposits there is unquestionable evidence that these lakes occasionally dried up and were covered by chemical precipitates and/or mud cracks so that the rock now shows a broken banded structure. Certain oil shales show distinct zones of spores, pollen, "resin grains", or even animal remains, indicating that the basin was subjected to periodic departures from normal conditions. At other times, coarse material or nearly pure inorganic matter was introduced into the basin. Other circumstances produced circumscribed areas within lakes where conditions were suitable for pure organic matter to be deposited. During normal deposition there was virtually no lateral movement of the sediment and convection disturbances of any kind were negligible. Some oil shales even show the prints of plants in a vertical growing position undisturbed since Permian times.

In the lagoons, the mixture of algal debris and other organic matter would be subject to attack by bacteria, the metabolites of which would add further to the sapropel. Although microbial depletion of the biodegradable components of such ooze would occur, Bradley [4] has demonstrated that the modern equivalent of such ancient oozes has remarkable preservative properties, so the expected balance may not, in fact, have been obtained. Modern subtropical lakes are capable of accumulating vast quantities of organic matter suitable to behave as a source material for kerogen. Bradley [4] stated that "the algal ooze does not pack down; it stays loose and essentially fluid for one foot or so below the mud—water interface", while the "dense mat of vegetation along the shores" effectively removes all but the finest silt. These sub-tropical oozes show little tendency to decay, even under anaerobic conditions, and it is probable that such algal sapropel and copropel constitute the real primary source of many kerogens.

With the gradual subsidence of the basin, a series of layers was built up in which the organic matter was protected by the continuous addition of clay and silt and, occasionally, sealed by a cover of pure inorganic matter. Storms could upset the balance of the ecosystem or water levels might be established which would be unsuitable for algal growth. In a few instances, it seems that subsidence caused a lagoonal area to be estuarine, or, in the extreme, marine. Thus, one occasionally finds a change from an argillaceous to arenaceous horizon.

After the depositional stage, the composite decaying debris—mineral matter stratum was covered by successive layers of sediments. With subsidence over geological time, the pressure of the overlying strata resulted in the compaction of the mixture and the final chemical changes took place. Once again it is necessary to remind oneself of the extent of geological time. The depositional events outlined above could take place slowly over centuries or millennia, or some layers might be quickly built up over years.

Diagenetic processes

Based on experimental evidence, the complete formation process probably did not occur at temperatures in excess of 150°C and changes in chemical composition commenced from the moment of deposition. With ageing of the algal mats, polymerization and biochemical decay would cause a decrease in chemical unsaturation, whereas proteins and carbohydrates would be preferentially removed under aerobic and anaerobic conditions. Later under anaerobic conditions, polyene fatty acids would lose carboxylic and other groups by condensation or bacterial attack. Bacteria can also modify structures, increase the chain length of organic molecules [45], and destroy or hydrogenate double bonds. The main composition change in the juvenile stage of diagenesis was polymerization and loss of oxygen. Some oxygen was lost as water because of condensation reactions and a further quantity was converted by anaerobes. The fresh debris might have contained 15—25% oxygen and this was slowly reduced to 3—8% over long periods. Until the diagenetic processes can, at least in part, be simulated by experiments, this aspect of the chemistry must remain largely speculative.

Throughout all these changes, more stable forms of matter were created at the expense of the less stable ones. The effect of the maturation was a uniform decrease in oxygen of the protokerogen and the generation of an essentially hydrocarbon structure. The actual mechanism of the conversion of fatty matter to the quasi-hydrocarbon is difficult to explain and still needs further experimental evidence. In the case of torbanites, and perhaps with some other oil shales, an explanation of the conversion of fatty acid to "hydrocarbon" is not necessary because the alga itself provides the requisite hydrocarbons. Experiments with model substances provide evidence that, in their transformation to kerogen, most of the chemical reaction takes place relatively early during the diagenesis. An intermediate phase allows increase in molecular cross-linking and development of structure, whereas the geological burial period serves only to "mature the chemistry with increase in rank and strength". The final product is a tough inert organic polymer which binds together a reinforcing inorganic "filler". The product is called oil shale.

It appears that pressure alone had little effect on the diagenesis of organic matter. Cane [46] subjected suitable synthetic lipids to pressures as great as 22,000 atm but found no appreciable change in the hardening process. The complete absence of any flow patterns in most torbanites provides additional evidence.

Once again it is necessary to emphasise that an idealized situation has been presented. Vascular plant matter made some contribution to most oil shales, with some being quite "coaly". When examined by ultra-violet radiation, no deposit, even the richest, is entirely free from coal macerals. In addition, many oil shales contain appreciable amounts of non-kerogen extractables and this clearly differentiates them from others such as torbanites, which contain very little soluble matter.

In the portion of the text dealing with the chemical behavior of kerogen (p. 39), it was pointed out that kerogen can be divided into two main classes depending on whether benzenoid acids are produced by permanganate oxidation or not, and that this difference is related to possible humic structures. A consideration of the properties of "coaly" kerogen, or rather of the coaly components of algal kerogen, leads to the suggestion of the differentiation of three main types of organic matter in oil shale. These are defined herein as follows:

(1) Kerogen (a) — that giving rise to the "coaly maceral" of oil shale and which yields benzenoid acids during permanganate oxidation.
(2) Kerogen (b) — that originating from algal fatty acids.
(3) Kerogen (c) — that arising from algal hydrocarbons.

Kerogen (a), which has a large contribution from vascular plant tissue, provides the opaque dark ground-mass of oil shale, including even the high-grade torbanites. The aromaticity of kerogen (a) is high, but its oil yield is small. It is the "matrosite" of Dulhunty [47].

Kerogen (b) is the important constituent of nearly all oil shales and appears as the yellow-orange matter in rock sections. It is derived from algal fatty acids and, except in torbanites, is the main oil-yielding component.

Kerogen (c) is similar to kerogen (b), but it is derived from algal hydrocarbons and not from fats. From present knowledge only one alga, or its ancestral equivalent, provides kerogen (c). Torbanite is derived largely from this type of kerogen, which provides the "yellow bodies" of boghead coal and alginites. The yield of oil from kerogen (c) is particularly high, being about 96% on an organic mass basis.

Within limits, it is suggested that all oil shales are mainly made up of various tertiary mixtures of kerogens (a), (b) and (c). As it has been established that the oil yield, based on organic carbon, varies widely from deposit to deposit, it seems probable that this variation in yield is caused by differences in the proportions of the three types of organic matter. Bradley [74] has reported that the kerogen of the Green River Formation is bipartite, i.e., one part yields oil whereas the other yields very little oil. Kurth [48] has found this to be true for tasmanite. It is interesting to speculate whether this hypothesis will stand up to experimental verification or not.

Torbanites: their nature and origin

The richest kind of oil shale is represented by a class of organic rocks variously called torbanite, cannel coal, boghead coal, kerosene shale, or alginite. Torbanite presents a specially interesting study to the organic geo-chemist, because its kerogen was formed largely from a single recognizable organism with a verifiable biological history. Torbanite occurs in the Ermelo district in the Transvaal (South Africa), in the Midlothian and West Lothian counties in Scotland, and in the Sydney Basin of New South Wales in Australia. Other minor deposits occur in France, U.S.S.R., Kentucky and elsewhere.

Torbanites are characterized by a minor contribution from mineral matter and, hence, are very rich in organic material and have a low specific gravity (less than unity for particularly rich samples [49]). The color of torbanite is shiny black, although exceptionally rich samples are deep green by reflected light and orange-red by transmitted light. Torbanite has a bright golden-yellow fluorescence, whereas materials allied to kerogen (a) and coal show no such phenomenon. Examination of rich specimens under ultraviolet light enables one to observe non-fluorescent veins running at random throughout the material, even though a close examination under visible light fails to resolve them. It is believed that these coaly veins arise from vascular plant material, which has been added to the algal ooze at an early stage. They should be differentiated from the large sheets of "jet", sometimes containing fossils of *Glossopteris* or *Gangamopteris* parallel to, or of *Vertebraria* at right angles to the bedding plane. These carbonized fossils demonstrate the "coal-ification" conditions and tranquil environment during the deposition period.

When viewed in thin sections, torbanite is resolved into an opaque brown structureless groundmass in which are embedded innumerable translucent yellow ellipsoidal bodies of vague fibrous internal structure and specific char-acteristics. These entities are scattered throughout the matrix in no fixed manner except that their long axis is generally oriented towards the bedding plane. It would seem that they represent flattened spheroids or compressed rounded particles. Thin sections also show occasional spores, fragments of quartz, and small particles of calcite. As microscopical examination of tor-banites from various places shows similar structures and, as it appears that their kerogens had much the same biological history, it is believed that a detailed discussion of the formation of the Australian deposit would be applicable, with some modification, to most torbanites found elsewhere.

The New South Wales torbanites

The great accumulation of torbanite in Australia is situated in the Sydney Basin of New South Wales and covers an area of approximately 2,000 sq miles. This field is made up of a number of deposits, which vary in size from about 7 sq mi to isolated small patches. At least 38 deposits have been de-scribed in the literature and it seems probable that many more exist under the 1,500-ft thick Triassic sandstone plateau which overlies the Permian strata.

The torbanites appear close to the western margin of the Upper Coal Measures and extend for nearly 250 miles north and south in the central coastal region of New South Wales. Roughly speaking, they can be said to occupy an inverted acute triangle with the deposits of Ulan and Baerami as the base line and Joadja as the vertex. A map of the area is given in Fig. 3-3, in which the extent of both the coal and torbanite deposits is indicated. The coal seams reach to the western margin of the torbanite deposits, but are not shown as overlying or underlying the torbanite because of consequent dia-grammatic complexity.

The Permian rocks, which can be up to 600 ft thick, include both the Coal Measures and the Torbanites. The deposits are widely dispersed over four separate horizons with nearly 300 ft between the Ilford deposit, which is less than 30 ft below the Triassic sandstone, and the Mount Marsden deposit in the lowest coal horizon immediately above the Marangaroo Conglomerate, overlying the Devonian basal rock.

The majority of known torbanite deposits occurs fairly close to the coal horizons and, in some places, are both overlaid and underlaid by coal.

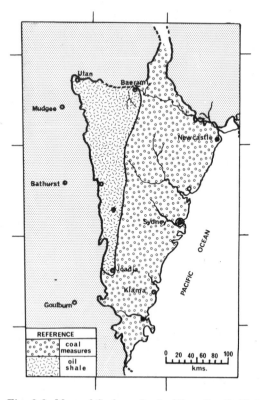

Fig. 3-3. Map of Sydney Basin (New South Wales, Australia) showing Permian coal measures and area of oil shale formation.

Although torbanite may thin out at the edges and be replaced by coal, the two do not occur as a mixed seam. This would suggest that the ecosystems for coal and for torbanite formation were similar and, within limitations, this is true. As they are not found together, it seems probable that conditions for the growth of one were exclusive for the other. Perhaps some of the polyhydric phenols which exist in peat bogs may have prevented algal growth. Alternatively, the changes in water level, with periods of near dryness, associated with origin of oil shale were not suitable for permanent growth of swamp vegetation. Compared with the extensive coal measures throughout the world, the restricted deposits of torbanite indicate that rather special environmental conditions were necessary for their formation.

Torbanite deposits are lenticular in shape, having flat upper surfaces and a dished-convex contour on the lower horizon. Many lenses are overlaid with a flat cover of clay or mediocre coal. The thickness of torbanite may be up to 5 ft at the center, contracting to a few inches at the edges, usually into carbonaceous shales or poor coal. The whole structure is patently characteristic of a lacustrine formation. A torbanite deposit may be joined irregularly at an edge to another deposit or they may be quite separate. The whole system clearly originated in a string of lakes and lagoons surrounded by large swamp lands and higher areas. The following description from "The Origin of the New South Wales Torbanites" by Dulhunty [50] is reproduced with permission:

"The presence of lenticular deposits of torbanite, cannel coal, clay shales and other accessory materials on the main coal-bearing horizons in the Upper Coal Measures indicates shallow-water conditions, with the surface of sedimentation only partially covered by water, rather than the deposition of the coal-forming debris in large completely submerged areas. Large rivers, bringing water and sediments to the regions of sedimentation, must have passed across the marginal areas in wide, meandering watercourses of ever changing form with banks of peat and sub-aerial swamp-vegetation. Towards the central portions of the basin, these watercourses dispersed by means of distributaries, and eventually became lost in swampy areas and peat bogs. Isolated lakes would be formed in marginal areas by the washing out of peat bogs, and meanders being cut off during periods of flood. Similar lakes were formed, less frequently, in the central areas by unequal deposition of sediments from floods, and lowering of the general water-level during normal periods. Such lakes, both marginal and central, received supplies of water by percolation through peat beds and marshes from the main channels of moving water. In marginal areas, the water, penetrating to the isolated lakes, would be comparatively fresh from the mountain streams, and would carry dissolved gases and mineral matter, but would not have been in contact with the decaying vegetation of peat bogs long enough to become heavily charged with humic product. This provided the necessary physical as well as chemical environment for the formation of algal sapropel."

"The isolated lakes in the central areas would receive supplies of stagnant water, poorly aerated and containing a high concentration of humic product, gathered during its passage through, perhaps, fifty miles of decaying vegetation. These conditions, accompanying sluggish deposition, are most unlikely to have supported an abundant growth of the alga, for reasons already given; and it is considered that, in Upper Coal Measures time, they were the principal factors determining the absence of torbanite deposits in the whole of the North-Western Region."

Origin of torbanite

The problem of the origin of torbanite has been the subject of research for over 120 years. Even in the 1850's, investigators were suggesting many different sources for the "yellow bodies" seen by microscopic examination. In 1889, David [51] put forward the suggestion that "it may be found that these spherical bodies are to be referred to some variety of fresh-water alga". During the next thirty years, over a dozen papers dealing with the possible algal origin of torbanite were published. Although Bertrand [52] and Renault [53] produced further evidence supporting David's beliefs, some authorities were not in accord with an algal origin, pointing out that such algae were unlikely to resist decay sufficiently to give rise to torbanite.

The similarity between the presumed algal fossils in torbanite and the extant alga *Botryococcus braunii* (Kutzing) was first recognized by Zalessky

[54] while working on Russian deposits. Zalessky's findings were supported by later work of Thiessen [55], Kogerman [56], and Bertrand [57], so that by the early 1930's, there was general agreement that torbanite originated from algal growth. Zalessky's deductions were based, in part, on his investigation of a peculiar rubbery deposit found at Lake Balkhash, Siberia, and its comparison with kukersite, the oil shale of Estonia. Stadnikov [58] also suggested a relationship between the deposits at Lake Balkash and oil shales. He stated: "The chemical entities contributing to the kerogen were fatty acids, aliphatic alcohols, esters and alkane hydrocarbons originating in some form of algal growth". A material similar to balkashite is found near the 90-mile Coorong waterway in South Australia.

In all the extant deposits (coorongite, balkashite, n'hangellite) the mode of occurrence is much the same. The gummy residue is found in the hollows of undulating ground where either brackish or saline waters could collect and then disperse by evaporation or slow drainage. The substance originates, particularly after flood rains, as a prolific greenish scum floating on ponds and lagoons. The local algal mat is fed by further growth until an enormous quantity of the alga has collected. The decaying alga usually builds up in certain parts of the waterway because of transport and accumulation as a result of prevailing winds. On the partial drying of the lagoonal system, the green algal mass gradually coalesces into a gummy yellowish skin lying on the sand, or on the ground which has been exposed by the receding waters. The material at Lake Balkhash is also found at the margins of shallow inlets at the southern extreme of the lake. The residue may be up to two inches thick covering strips 15 ft wide; areal extent has been reported in terms of acres. Broughton [59] described the early stages of formation of coorongite in the following terms:

"... like green paint ¼ inch thick, it covers hundreds of square yards of water and, as it dries, it forms a skin like linseed oil drying on an overturned mass of paint ... Every stage from the green liquid paint-like substance to the tough elastic sand-containing coorongite may be observed."

Fresh coorongite is a soft, greenish-yellow gelatinous mass, which, in sections, clearly shows its algal origin. On exposure, the material gradually hardens, particularly the upper surface which tends to become scaly. Old samples, found at shallow depths, are black and leathery, but still sectile. Specimens lying in the open in semi-desert country are little affected by microbial attack or exposure. The only outward effect of weathering from decades of exposure to sunlight and water is a slow hardening of the original deposit, concomitant with a color darkening to nearly black. The resistance to decay is quite extraordinary, the reason for which is discussed later. From both the biological and chemical viewpoints, coorongite must be regarded as the "peat stage" in the formation of one type of algal kerogen, i.e., kerogen (c) of this text.

Botany and phytochemistry of Botryococcus. The alga giving rise to coorongite — *Botryococcus braunii* (Kutzing) — is a polymorphic colonial alga belonging to the Chlorophyceae [60]. *Botryococcus* is found throughout the
world in fresh or saline waters in ponds, lakes and lagoons. It has been found
in glacial muds, peats, clays, and a variety of other deposits, both ancient
and recent. The alga is a small organism which, under as yet undefined conditions, propagates prodigiously to form enormous water blooms. These
exceptional growths have been particularly noted in arid regions after floods,
when conditions are becoming adverse again. The species exhibits two principal modes of growth, one of which is colored green by chlorophyll and the
other (the resting stage) is colored rusty orange by carotenes.

The microscopic features of the alga have been the subject of considerable
research and details should be sought in the original literature [55,61,62].
The main morphological feature of the alga is a thick fleshy skeletal matrix
which is largely made up of oily "cups" surrounding each cell. The material
of the cups is very high in lipids and, until recently, these were believed to
consist of fatty esters. Stadnikov [58] and others had already suggested that
it was the polymerization and oxidation, followed by decarboxylation, of
such fatty acids or acid anhydrides that gave rise to kerogen. Cane [7] put
forward cogent argument and presented convincing experimental data to
show that torbanite kerogen was constituted from polymers of fatty polyene
acids, and that alkatrienoic acids fitted both the required behavioral pattern
and the elemental analyses.

Studies of the polymerization of polyene fats show that the primary stage
involves dimerization and ring closure to form a hydroaromatic dibasic molecule with side chains. Both free radical and step growth polymerization
would be possible and ring closure would be, normally, by a Diels-Alder
mechanism. Examples of such dimers are shown in Fig. 3-4; the carbon
atoms marked by ψ are part of a carboxylic group and thus capable of other
reactions by condensation.

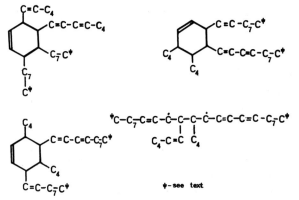

Fig. 3-4. Structural model dimers of C_{18} trienoic fatty acids.

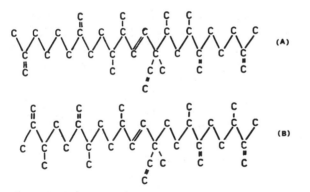

Fig. 3-5. Suggested carbon skeletons of Botryococcene.

The decarboxylated dimer would fit the kerogen building block suggested by Aarna and Lippmaa [63].

The fatty acid theory of torbanite genesis was invalidated in 1968 by Maxwell et al. [64] who showed that the lipids of one physiological form of the alga consist not of fatty acids as previously believed, but of two novel isomeric hydrocarbons to which the names botryococcene and isobotryococcene have been given. The botryococcenes are highly reactive polyenes of which a suggested structure [46], based on the findings of Maxwell et al., is given in Fig. 3-5(A). Recently, Cox et al. [78], using ^{13}C n.m.r. spectra obtained by pulsed Fourier Transform Operation, have suggested a modification to that given by Cane [46] and the carbon skeleton of this alternative structure is shown in Fig. 3-5(B). Under suitable conditions, these branched-chain hydrocarbons can amount to ca. 80% of the dry weight of the alga, whereas the remaining lipids consist of small amounts of monocarboxylic fatty acids, both saturated and unsaturated. Smaller amounts of C_{18} and C_{28} dienoid and dicarboxylic acids are also present, whereas there are only traces of straight-chain hydrocarbons [65]. The discovery that this alga directly synthesizes hydrocarbons in large quantities completely altered the theories on torbanite origin and diagenesis. The need to explain a decarboxylation reaction was eliminated and the assumed proto-kerogen equivalent was available for chemical investigation.

The existence of the botryococcenes appeared to provide the obvious answer that the $C_{34}H_{58}$ model compound postulated by Cane [7] was not a dimeric alkyl residue from fatty acids, but biogenetic hydrocarbons with the same elemental composition and degree of unsaturation. In contradiction to this, in an extensive study of coorongite, Cane and Albion [28] could find little evidence of the expected botryococcene polymers. This led them to reassess the problem and look for other contributors. Brown et al. [66] and Knights et al. [67] showed that B. braunii exists in two physiological states, an orange resting stage and a green exponential-growth form. It is the former state which is characterized by the production of botryococcenes. The green form of the alga produces straight-chain alkadienes of the general formula:

$$CH_2{=}CH(CH_2)_x{-}CH{=}CH{-}(CH_2)_7{-}CH_3, \text{ where } x = 15, 17, 19.$$

The latter form of the alga gives rise to coorongite. Further research has made it fairly certain that the alkadienes produced by the green form of alga are the true building blocks of torbanite kerogen. It seems logical to postulate that these or similar alkadienes provide the foundation for the kerogen (c) of oil shale, which has been discussed earlier in this chapter.

Once again an idealized situation has been depicted. No doubt, other contributors should be considered, e.g., fatty acids always have some role. In addition, the ubiquitous microbial transformations have been neglected and the effect of higher plant debris has been disregarded. The richest torbanite so far reported [49], however, approaches the ideal case and appears to be nearly pure alkadiene polymer; it has an ash of ca. 2% as mined. It is hoped that the constitution of all torbanites may be satisfactorily explained in terms of such polymers plus minor extraneous components. The mixed polymer needs little modification to make the hypothesis entirely acceptable in terms of the composition of the present-day rock.

Tasmanite

Tasmanite is an atypical oil shale, often erroneously called a spore coal or a torbanite. Because of its anomalous character, Down and Himus [68] in their classification of oil shales set it apart from all others under the name of "spore shale". The kerogen of tasmanite occurs as particulate amber-colored discs (in reality, flattened sacs), having a distinct structure and clearly defined cell walls. These disseminules were believed to be spores and their progenitor was given the generic name *Tasmanites*. Although the genus is scattered geographically and over a wide range of sediments from the Ordovician to Recent, tasmanite deposits of any reasonable size are limited to Alaska and Tasmania. Both deposits are marine and are associated with shallow seas near ancient coastlines. Minor deposits are found in Brazil, Sahara, U.S.A., and Thailand.

Alaskan tasmanite occurs as contorted outcrops along the northern slopes of the Brooks Range in Northern Alaska. The rock, in general appearance, is more like a low-grade torbanite, nearly black in color, more compact than that from Tasmania, and considerably richer in organic matter. There is some doubt whether the species of *Tasmanites* is identical with that in the Tasmanian deposits. As yet its kerogen has received little scientific examination.

Tasmanian tasmanite occurs in the northwest of the island over a relatively restricted area fairly close to the existing coast. Insignificant patches of tasmanite have been reported at other isolated places in northern Tasmania, as well as on the mainland of Australia. The Tasmanian oil-shale beds occur in numerous isolated areas separated by later faulting and diabase intrusions. The tasmanite seam is interbedded with other rocks of the Permian system and occurs as two main bands separated by a layer of mudstone up to 2 ft in thickness. The nature of this mudstone is similar to the inorganic matrix of tasmanite, but contains insignificant organic matter. The composite seam has a fairly uniform thickness of ca. 5 ft and shows no thinning out at the edges. It appears that the sea floor did not shelve up at the coast, but the contour changed abruptly at the land margin. In places, tasmanite is replaced by coal as if a low-lying, coal-forming swamp ran right down to the shore line. Unlike the deposits of torbanite elsewhere in Australia, coal does not occur above or below the tasmanite, but is found laterally adjacent to it. It seems that tasmanite was formed in very shallow seas at, or near to, the Permian coastline and that a spore-containing coal was contemporaneously formed in low swampy lands in the same basin surrounded by hills composed of schist, slate, and conglomerate.

Embedded in the tasmanite seam are marine fossils, shells and other littoral debris, as well as pebbles, pieces of pyritic schist, quartzite and, even, large rock fragments. Occasional erratics show that isolated icebergs must have been in the area at the period of deposition. Pyrite replacement is not uncommon, so that some fossils are now pyritic rather than calcitic; pyrite is also found as veins in some pebbles. Three hundred feet of fossiliferous mudstone overlie the tasmanite, whereas other mudstones associated with pebbly conglomerates underlie this deposit.

There has been little study of the mode of deposition of tasmanite from the organic geochemical viewpoint. It may be inferred that the source material was laid down in a quiet ecosystem of shallow bays, inlets and river estuaries in which the alga was free to multiply. The kerogen resulted from prodigious algae blooms when conditions were propitious for completion of the life cycle and "spore" build-up in the marginal waters. Although the tasmanite kerogen is individualistic and of marine origin, one cannot ignore the enormous amounts of organic terrestrial debris contributed to near-shore deposits by river drainage [43]. Tasmanite is no exception and higher plant contribution cannot be disregarded.

Kerogen of tasmanite

Tasmanian tasmanite is a fine-grained arenaceous mudstone containing innumerable discrete yellowish discs of biological origin, the exact nature of which was a matter of debate for over one hundred years [69]. For a long time, these disc-like microfossils were regarded, not without suspicion, as belonging to a plant possibly allied to the *Lepidodendrales* or *Equisetales*. In 1941, Krausel [70] showed, however, that the tasmanite discs were fossil leiospheres and this has remained the concensus, with the genus retaining the name *"Tasmanites"*. If this fossil genus be regarded as equivalent to the present-day *Pachysphaera* [71], one can regard the tasmanite disseminules as cysts of a planktonic alga belonging to the class Prasinophyceae, although the taxonomy is still equivocal.

As mentioned above, tasmanite kerogen occurs as discs with creased and sculptured surfaces, or rather as just visible, amber-colored, discrete, flattened sacs. The best description of their appearance was given by Johnson [72] nearly a century ago, when he wrote: "the discs are welded together like grains of meal in an oat cake. The discs resemble diminutive flattened flabby gooseberry skins rent or fractured on one side as by sporadic emission of contents". It is obvious that the undistorted disseminules were spheroids, which have been flattened and broken by overburden pressure, although there is evidence that many may have burst just prior to deposition. Simoneit and Burlingame [75] reported that the flattened "spore cases" contain an interior dark oil which can be removed by extraction. Tasmanite kerogen also contains very small spherical bodies, which appear to have a bacterial origin [76].

The fundamental mode of origin of tasmanite appears to have been much the same as that of other oil shales, i.e., an environment in which tranquil waters supported algal and other lowly forms of plant life, which were free to form enormous water blooms. The residues from these growths were later codeposited with fine inorganic silt. Because of the physical characteristics of the "spores", one might erroneously surmise that the chemistry of tasmanite might differ from the complex lipid-derived polymer of other kerogens. Elemental analyses, infrared examination, and microspectroscopy [77] provide data not much at variance from those of other kerogens. Figure 3-6

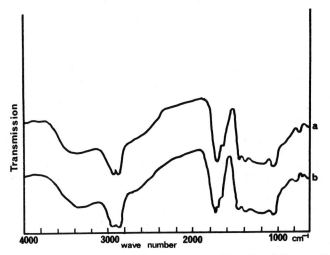

Fig. 3-6. Infrared microspectra of the cell walls of *Tasmanites punctatus* and *Tasmanites erraticus*. (After Kjellstrom [77], with permission.)

shows infrared micro-spectra of the cell walls of the "spores" of two species of *Tasmanites* and substantiates a structure composed of complex lipid substances containing hydroxy, alkyl and carboxylic groups. No tentative composition can be put forward with confidence, however, and the exact structural nature must still be considered as uncertain.

Tasmanite kerogen also shows the dichotomy discussed earlier and behaves as if it contained both kerogen (a) and kerogen (b). Kurth [48] has demonstrated that the "non-spore", non-marine organic material occurs to an extent of about 20%, but has an oil yield of only 6.2%. This residual organic matter is made up of spore fragments, cuticles, vegetal dust and other extraneous matter, most probably contributed by fresh-water, allochthonous detritus.

Envoi

It has been stated that the organic matter in oil shale represents the greatest global accumulation of energy defined by the two simple equations:

$$C + O_2 \rightarrow CO_2$$

and:

$$H_2 + \tfrac{1}{2}O_2 \rightarrow H_2O.$$

The energy potential of the oil shale of the Green River Formation alone is equivalent to many times that of the cumulative production of all American petroleum from the time of discovery of the Drake well. The "energy crisis" of 1973 and the dramatic increase in selling price of the world's crude oil has only emphasized a situation well recognized by fuel technologists. This situation is that the competitive position and the choice of a particular fossil fuel is nearly entirely predicated upon the cost of the carbon therein, just before transforming it to carbon dioxide in the energy converter.

While international politics are presently "juggling" with the cost of carbon, groups of research workers at various places in the world continue to explore the molecular architecture of the world's oil shales and their kerogen. These men are motivated partly by curiosity, partly by dedication, and partly by cussedness, because the problem is one of the most difficult of constitution studies, usually left well alone by other scientists exploring natural products. Within this context the attitude of the latter type of worker has been aptly expressed by Breger [80]: "Blame them not, for they know what they do not do."

In 1694, the British Crown issued Patent No. 330 to Martin Eele, Hancock and Portlock, who "after much paines and expences hath certainly found out '*A way to extract and make great quantityes of pitch, tarr and oyle out of a sort of stone*' of which there is sufficient plenty within our Dominions ... and wee, being willing to cherish and encourage all laudable endeavours and designes of all such persons as have by theire industry found out useful and profitable arts, misteryes and invencons." Before this text appears in print the situation could well be that "oyle from a sort of stone" could be a permanent and fruitful additional source of energy for mankind.

References

1. A. Crum-Brown, "The Oil Shales of the Lothians", (3rd ed.), *Geol. Surv. Mem. (Scotl.)*, 274 pp., ref. p. 160, H.M. Stationery Office, London (1927).
2. R.F. Cane, "Geological Semantics", *Nature, 228*, 1009 (1970).
3. H.M. Thorne, K.E. Stanfield, G.U. Dinneen and W.I. Murphy, "Oil Shale Technology, A Review", *U.S. Bur. Mines, Inf. Circ.* 8216, 1—24. U.S. Dep. of the Interior, Washington (1964).
4. W.H. Bradley, "Tropical Lakes, Copropel and Oil Shale", *Geol. Soc. Am. Bull., 77*, 1333—1337 (1966).
5. I.A. Breger, "Diagenesis of Metabolites and a Discussion on the Origin of Petroleum", *Geochim. Cosmochim. Acta, 19*, 297—308 (1960).
6. G.L. Stadnikov, "Die Entstehung von Kohle und Erdöl — Die Umwandlung der organischen Substanz im Laufe der geologischen Zeitperioden", in: *Schriften auf Gebiet der Brennstoffe Geologie*, Enke, Stuttgart (1930).
7. R.F. Cane, "The Constitution and Synthesis of Oil Shale", *Proc. 7th World Pet. Congr., III*, 681—689, Elsevier (1967).
8. P.H. Abelson, T.C. Hoering and P.L. Parker, "Fatty Acids in Sedimentary Rocks", in: U. Colombo and G.D. Hobson (Editors), *Advances in Organic Geochemistry*, Pergamon, London, pp. 169—174 (1964).
9. P.L. Parker, C.V. Baalen and L. Maurer, "Fatty Acids in Eleven Species of Blue Green Algae", *Science, 155*, 707—708 (1967).
10. R.F. Leo and P.L. Parker, "Branched Chain Fatty Acids in Sediments", *Science, 152*, 649—650 (1966).
11. J. Schonbrunner, "Über die bakterielle Hydrierung von Ölsäure und Sorbinsäure und über ihre Beeinflüssung durch Gallensäure", *Biochem. Z., 304*, 26—36 (1940).
12. C.E. ZoBell, *"Annual Report for 1944"*, American Petroleum Institute, Research Project 34A, Washington (1944).
13. W.D. Rosenfeld, "Fatty Acid Transformations by Anaerobic Bacteria", *Archiv. Biochem., 16*, 263—273 (1948).
14. H.A. Spoehr and H.W. Milner, "The Chemical Composition of Chlorella — Effect of Environment Conditions", *Plant Physiol., 24*, 120—149 (1949).
15. H.W. Milner, "The Fatty Acids of Chlorella", *J. Biol. Chem., 176*, 813—818 (1948).
16. A.K. Galwey, "Heterogeneous Reactions in Petroleum Genesis and Maturation", *Nature, 223*, 1257—1260 (1969).
17. J.G. Erdman, V.G. Ramsey, N.W. Kalenda and W.E. Hansen, "Synthesis and Properties of Porphyrin Vanadium Complexes", *J. Am. Chem. Soc., 78*, 5844—5847 (1956).
18. J.J. Cummins and W.E. Robinson, Normal and Isoprenoid Hydrocarbons isolated from Oil Shale Bitumen", *J. Chem. Eng. Data, 9*, 304—307 (1964).
19. S. Sever and P.L. Parker, "Fatty Alcohols (Normal and Isoprenoid) in Sediments", *Science, 164*, 1052—1054 (1969).
20. J.W. Moore and H.N. Dunning, "Interfacial Activities and Porphyrin Contents of Oil Shale Extracts", *Ind. Eng. Chem., 47*, 1440—1444 (1955).
21. G. Eglinton, A.G. Douglas, J.R. Maxwell and S. Ställberg-Stenhagen, "The Occurrence of Isoprenoid Fatty Acids in Green River Oil Shales", *Science, 153*, 1133—1135 (1966).

22. A. Treibs, "On the Occurrence of Chlorophyll Derivatives in an Oil Shale of the Upper Triassic Period", *Ann. Chim.*, *509*, 103—114 (1934).
A. Treibs, "Chlorophyll and Hemin Derivatives in Bitumenous Rocks", *Ann. Chim.*, *517*, 172—183 (1935).
. . . and other papers.

23. E.E. Bray and E.D. Evans, "Distribution of n-Paraffins as a Clue to Recognition of Source Beds", *Geochim. Cosmochim. Acta*, *22*, 2—15 (1961).

24. E.E. Bray and G.S. Kenny, Personal communication cited by N.P. Stevens, "Origin of Petroleum — A Review", *Bull. Am. Assoc. Pet. Geol.*, *40*, 51—61 (1956).

25. D.L. Lawlor and W.E. Robinson, "Fatty Acids in Green River Formation Oil Shale", *ACS Div. Pet. Chem. (Detroit Meet., Mich.), Preprint 1*, 5—9 (1965).

26. R.F. Cane, "The Chemistry of the Pyrolysis of Torbanite", *Aust. Chem. Inst. J. and Proc.*, *15*, 62—68 (1948).

27. G. Eglinton, P.M. Scott, T. Belsky, A.L. Burlingame, W. Richler and M. Calvin, "Occurrence of Isoprenoid Alkanes in a Precambrian Sediment", in: G.D. Hobson and M. Louis (Editors), *Advances in Organic Geochemistry*, Pergamon, Oxford, pp. 41—74 (1964).

28. R.F. Cane and P.R. Albion, "The Organic Geochemistry of Torbanite Precursors", *Geochim. Cosmochim. Acta*, *37*, 1543—1549 (1973).

29. J.D. Brooks and J.W. Smith, "The Diagenesis of Plant Lipids During the Formation of Coal, Petroleum and Natural Gas", *Geochim. Cosmochim. Acta*, *31*, 2389—2397 (1967).

30. W.E. Robinson and G.U. Dinneen, "Constitutional Aspects of Oil Shale Kerogen", *Proc. 7th World Pet. Congr. (Mexico)*, pp. 669—680 (1967).

31. G.W. Himus, "Observations on the Composition of Kerogen Rocks and the Chemical Constitution of Kerogen", in: *Oil Shale and Cannel Coal*, 2, Institute of Petroleum, London, pp. 112—133 (1951).

32. A.L. Down and G.W. Himus, "A Preliminary Study of the Chemical Constitution of Kerogen", *J. Inst. Pet.*, *27*, 426—445 (1941).

33. T.E. Dancy and V.L. Giedroyc, "Further Investigations of the Chemical Constitution of the Kerogen of Oil Shales", *J. Inst. Pet.*, *36*, 607—623 (1950).

34. W.E. Robinson, J.J. Cummins and K.E. Stanfield, "Constitution of Organic Acids Prepared from Colorado Oil Shale", *Ind. Eng. Chem.*, *48*, 1134—1138 (1956).

35. W.E. Robinson and D.L. Lawlor, "Constitution of Hydrocarbon-like Materials Derived from Kerogen Oxidation Products", *Fuel*, *40*, 375—388 (1961).

36. W.E. Robinson, H.H. Heady and A.B. Hubbard, "Alkaline Permanganate Oxidation of Oil Shale Kerogen", *Ind. Eng. Chem.*, *45*, 788—791 (1953).

37. G. Stefanovic and D. Vitorovic, "Nature of Oil Shale Kerogen Oxidations with Potassium Permanganate in Acetone Solution", *J. Chem. Eng. Data*, *4*, 162—167 (1959).

38. R.A. McKee and E.E. Lyder, "The Thermal Decomposition of Shales", *Ind. Eng. Chem.*, *13*, 613—618 (1921), *13*, 678—684 (1921).

39. A.J. Franks and B.D. Goodier, "Preliminary Study of the Organic Matter of Colorado Oil Shale", *Q. Colo. Sch. Mines*, *17*, 1—16 (1922).

40. C.G. Maier and S.R. Zimmerley, "Chemical Dynamics of the Transformation of the Organic Matter to Bitumen in Oil Shale", *Bull. Univ. Utah*, *14*, 62—81 (1924).

41. A.R. Brown and K.R. Buck, "Pentamethylpyridine in Shale Oil Bases", *Chem. Ind. (Lond.)*, p. 1347 (1961).
A.R. Brown and K.R. Buck, "Gas Chromatography of Quinoline Bases", *Chem. Ind. (Lond.)*, p. 714 (1961).

42. H.D. Hedberg, "Geological Aspects of the Origin of Petroleum", *Bull. Am. Assoc. Pet. Geol.*, *48*, 1758—1803 (1964).

43. I.A. Breger and A. Brown, "Distribution and Types of Organic Matter in a Barred Marine Basin", *N.Y. Acad. Sci. Trans.*, *Ser. II*, *25*, 741—755 (1963).

44. P.L. Parker and R.F. Leo, "Fatty Acids in Blue Green Algal Mat Communities", *Science, 148*, 373—374 (1965).
45. W.D. Rosenfeld, "Lipolytic Activities of Anaerobic Bacteria", *Arch. Biochem., 11*, 145—154 (1946).
46. R.F. Cane and P.R. Albion, "The Phytochemical History of Torbanites", *J. Proc. R. Soc. N.S.W., 104*, 31—37 (1971).
47. J.A. Dulhunty, "The Torbanites of New South Wales", *J. Proc. R. Soc. N.S.W., 72*, 179—198 (1939).
48. E.E. Kurth, *The Oil Shales of Tasmania and New South Wales*, Unpubl. D.Sc. thesis, University of Tasmania, Hobart, 389 pp. (1934).
49. R.F. Cane, "A rich Torbanite from Marangaroo", *Aust. J. Sci., 5*, 156—157 (1943).
50. J.A. Dulhunty, "The Origin of the New South Wales Torbanites", *Proc. Linn. Soc. N.S.W., 69*, 26—48 (1944).
51. T.W.E. David, "Note on the Origin of Kerosene Shale", *Proc. Linn. Soc. N.S.W., 4* (2), 483—500 (1889).
52. C.E. Bertrand, "Conférences sur les Charbons de Terre; Les Bogheads à Algues", *Soc. Belge Géol. Pal. Hydrol. Bull., 1*, 45—81 (1893).
53. M.B. Renault, "Sur Quelques Microorganismes des Combustibles Fossiles", *Soc. Ind. Min. St. Étienne, Bull., 13* (3), 865—1169 (1899).
54. M.D. Zalessky, "On the Nature of the Yellow Bodies of Boghead and on Sapropel of the Ala-Kool Gulf of Lake Balkash", *Bull. Com. Géol. Petersbourg, 33*, 495—507 (1914).
   M.D. Zalessky, "Sur les Nouvelles Algues Découvertes dans le Sapropelogène du Lac Beloe et sur une Algue Sapropelogène *Botryococcus Braunii* Kutzing", *Bull. Gen. Bot., 38*, 30—42 (1926).
   . . . and other papers.
55. R. Thiessen, "Origin of Boghead Coals", *U.S. Geol. Surv. Prof. Pap.* 132-I (1925).
56. P.N. Kogerman, "On the Chemistry of the Estonian Oil Shale 'Kukersite' ", *Arch. Naturk. Estlands, 1*, Ser. X, Tartu (1931).
57. P. Bertrand, "Les Botryococcacées Actuelles et Fossiles et les Consequences de Leur Activité Biologique", *Soc. Biol. (Paris) C.R. et Mém., 96*, 695—696 (1927).
58. G.L. Stadnikov and A. Weizmann, "Ein Beitrag zur Kenntnis der Umwandlung der Fettsäuren in Laufe der geologischen Zeitperioden", *Brenn. Chem., 10*, 401—408 (1929).
59. A.C. Broughton, "Coorongite", *Trans. Proc. R. Soc. S. Aust., 44*, 386 (1920).
60. J.H. Belcher and G.E. Fogg, "Biochemical Evidence of the Affinities of Botryococcus", *New Phytol., 54*, 81—83 (1955).
61. K.B. Blackburn, "A Reinvestigation of the Alga *Botryococcus Braunii* Kutzing", *Trans. R. Soc. Edinb., 58* (3), 841—854 (1936).
62. B.N. Temperley, "The Boghead Controversy and the Morphology of the Boghead Algae", *Trans. R. Soc. Edinb., 58* (3), 855—868 (1936).
63. A.Y. Aarna and E.T. Lippmaa, "Structure of the Carbon Skeleton of the Kerogen of Estonian Oil Shale", *Zh. Prikl. Khim. (J. Appl. Chem.), 30*, 419—426 (1957).
64. J.R. Maxwell, A.G. Douglas, G. Eglinton and A. McCormick, "The Botryococcenes — Hydrocarbons of Novel Structure from the Alga *Botryococcus Braunii* Kutzing", *Phytochem., 7*, 2157—2171 (1968).
65. A.G. Douglas, K. Douraghi-Zadek and G. Eglinton, "Fatty Acids of the Alga *Botryococcus Braunii*", *Phytochem., 8*, 285—293 (1969).
66. A.C. Brown, B.A. Knights and E. Conway, "Hydrocarbon Content and Its Relationship to Physiological State in the Green Alga, *B. Braunii*", *Phytochem., 8*, 543—547 (1969).
67. B.A. Knights, A.C. Brown, E. Conway and B.S. Middleditch, "Hydrocarbons from the Green Forms of the Freshwater Alga, *Botryococcus Braunii*", *Phytochem., 9*, 1317—1324 (1970).

68. A.L. Down and G.W. Himus, "The Classification of Oil Shales and Cannel Coals", *J. Inst. Pet.*, *26*, 329—333 (1940).
69. A.H. Church, "On Tasmanite: A New Mineral of Organic Origin", *Phil. Mag.*, *28*, 465—470 (1854).
70. R. Krausel, "Die Sporokarpien Dawsons, eine neue Thallophyten Klasse des Devons", *Palaeontographia*, *86*, 113—135 (1941).
71. D. Wall, "Evidence from Recent Plankton Regarding the Biological Affinities of *Tasmanites* (Newton 1875) and *Leiosphaeridia* (Eisenack 1958)", *Geol. Mag.*, *99*, 353—362 (1962).
72. R.M. Johnson, "Tasmanite or Mersey "Yellow Coal"", private printing, Hobart, 8 pp. (1877).
73. D.M. Collyer and G.E. Fogg, "Studies on Fat Accumulation by Algae", *Exp. Bot. J.*, *6*, 256—275 (1955).
74. W.H. Bradley, "Green River Oil Shale — Concept of Origin Extended", *Geol. Soc. Am. Bull.*, *81*, 985—1000 (1970).
75. B.R. Simoneit and A.L. Burlingame, "Carboxylic Acids Derived from Tasmanian Tasmanite by Extractions and Kerogen Oxidations", *Geochim. Cosmochim. Acta*, *37*, 595—610 (1973).
76. A. Combez, "Microsphérules Muriformes dans les Roches-mères du Pétrole", *C.R. Acad. Sci. Paris*, *270*, 2240—2243 (1970).
77. G. Kjellstrom, "Remarks on the Chemistry and Ultrastructure of the Cell Wall of Some Palaeozoic Leiospheres", *Geol. Foren. Stockholm Forh.*, *90*, 221—228 (1968).
78. R.E. Cox, A.L. Burlingame, D.M. Wilson, G. Eglinton and J.R. Maxwell, "Botryococcene — a Tetramethylated Acyclic Triterpenoid of Algal Origin", *J. Chem. Soc., Chem. Comm.*, pp. 284—285 (1973).
79. R.F. Cane, "The Mechanism of the Pyrolysis of Torbanite", in: *Oil Shale and Cannel Coal, 2*, Institute of Petroleum, London (1951).
80. I.A. Breger, "Organic Colloids and Natural Waters", in: D.W. Hood (Editor), *Organic Matter in Natural Waters*, Univ. Alaska, Institute of Marine Science Publ. 1, pp. 563—574 (June 1970).

Note added in proof (see p. 38)
Editorial comment: According to M.V. Djuricic et al. (*Adv. Org. Geochem., 1971, Proc. Int. Congr., 5th*, Pergamon, pp. 305—321), however, the major degradation products from Australian torbanites were found to be various isomers of benzene di-, tri-, and tetra-carboxylic acids.

Chapter 4

ORIGIN AND CHARACTERISTICS OF GREEN RIVER OIL SHALE

WILBUR E. ROBINSON

Introduction

The Green River Formation of Colorado, Wyoming, and Utah consists of an organic-rich shale or marlstone. This deposit consists of varying amounts of soluble organic material, insoluble organic material, and minerals. The mineral composition depended upon the amounts of soluble and insoluble minerals washed into the basin lakes and upon conditions which caused precipitation of minerals from the aqueous phase. Precursors for organic material consisted of algae which grew profusely in the saline lakes, and plant spores and pollen grains which were wind borne into the lakes. The amount of organic material remaining in the sedimentary shale depended upon the amount of accumulation, preservation, and alteration of the original precursor organic material.

The Green River Formation located in the tri-state area of northwestern Colorado, southwestern Wyoming, and northeastern Utah (see Fig. 1-1) contains organic-rich shale which represents an enormous energy resource. The extent of the resource has been evaluated periodically with a tendency for the estimated amount of shale oil equivalent in the formation to increase with each evaluation. Duncan and Swanson [1] concluded that the Green River Formation has a known shale-oil resource, recoverable under present technology, of 80 billion barrels with marginal and submarginal oil equivalent in the formation for a total resource of 8,000 billion barrels. The 80 billion barrels of shale oil represent about a 15-year reserve of crude oil for the United States at the 1973 consumption rate.

The organic-rich material of the Green River Formation, which has been described as mainly marlstone, consists of varying amounts of a wide variety of mineral matter, varying amounts of soluble organic material, and varying amounts of insoluble organic material commonly called "kerogen". The latter insoluble organic material is converted to a volatile and condensible crude-oil-like material, referred to as shale oil, upon the application of heat. A common temperature used to convert kerogen to shale oil in a reasonable period of time is 500°C (932°F).

From the mid 1800's, when the first written description of the formation was made, to the present time, much time and effort have been devoted to the determination of the composition and origin of this sediment. During this same period of time, industry, governmental agencies, colleges and universities, and private individuals have devoted vast amounts of time and money to the development of economically and environmentally sound methods of utilizing this valuable resource.

The published literature abounds with descriptions of studies related to the characteristics and origin of Green River oil shale. Much useful information is available on the geology of the formation, the mineral composition of the formation, and the characteristics of the organic material of the formation. The complex and insoluble nature of the kerogen, however, complicates structural determinations of this material. General information about the nature of this material is available, but detailed information about structure is not available and probably will not be obtained with present techniques. The reactions and conditions involved in the formation of this sedimentary material are equally as speculative; however, plausible postulates have been made, which add much to the understanding of this material.

In preparing this chapter, no attempt was made to include a review of the published literature. Only those references were included which contributed to the overall viewpoint relative to the origin and characteristics of Green River Formation oil shale.

Characteristics of Green River oil shale

Green River Formation oil shale has been defined as a compact, laminated, sedimentary rock containing organic material from which appreciable amounts of oil can be obtained by the application of heat but not by extraction with solvents. Bradley [2] referred to the rock as marlstone.

The sedimentary material of the Green River Formation contains organic material, mineral matter, and small amounts of moisture. The organic content varies from less than 1% to as much as 40% with an average for the Mahogany zone (a rich mineable bed of about 75 ft in the Piceance Creek Basin of Colorado) of about 16%. The remaining portion of the sediment consists of mineral constituents and moisture. A description of the mineral constituents and the organic constituents is presented here.

Mineral constituents

The geology of the Green River Formation has been studied extensively by Bradley [2], Duncan and Belser [3], Donnell et al. [4], and others. According to published information based upon field surveys, core drilling operations, and rotary drill cuttings, the Green River Formation occurs in four main basins: (1) the Uinta Basin of Utah, (2) the Green River Basin and (3) the Washakie Basin of Wyoming, and (4) the Piceance Creek Basin of Colorado. Bradley [5,6] believed that the Green River Formation was deposited in two large fresh-water lakes and one somewhat smaller lake. Lake Uinta (Utah and Colorado), the largest lake, was in existence for 5—8 million years during the Eocene Epoch ($50 \cdot 10^6$ years). Lake Gosiute (Wyoming) was in existence for about 4 million years during the Eocene Epoch. Bradley postulated further that at the end of the Upper Cretaceous, when the Rocky Mountain ranges were upfolded, the intermountain basins were formed. The streams flowing into the basins eroded these new mountains with a tendency to fill the basins. For these lakes to have lasted for 8 million years, a progressive downwarp that exceeded the rate of deposition had to have taken place.

The deposition of minerals in the lake basins, both stream carried and precipitated in place, was subject to many variations so that the Green River Formation is not homogeneous. This non-uniformity of the Piceance Creek Basin is described by Donnell et al. [4], who divided the formation into four definable members from lithologic observations. The Douglas Creek Member lies immediately above the Wasatch Formation and consists of about 800 ft of buff-colored sandstone and gray-colored shale with a few algal limestone beds. Immediately above the Douglas Creek Member is the Garden Gulch Member which consists of about 200 ft of gray marlstone, some gray and brown shale, and a few thin beds of oil shale. Above this member lies the Parachute Creek Member which consists of 400—750 ft of gray-black, gray, and brown marlstones which comprise the principal oil-shale units. This member includes the Mahogany marker, an analcitized tuff bed used for identification purposes, and the Mahogany zone [7]. Above the Parachute Creek Member to the surface lies the Evacuation Creek Member of about 600 ft of gray or brown fine- to medium-grained sandstone with interbedded gray marlstone and a few thin oil-shale beds.

The mineral composition of Green River oil shale is variable; however, most samples contain dolomite, calcite, quartz, illite clay, soda feldspar, potash feldspar, pyrite, and analcite [8]. Minor constituents as determined by X-ray fluorescence spectroscopy contain the following elements: titanium, strontium, manganese, barium, chromium, boron, lead, vanadium, nickel, rubidium, zinc, and zirconium. Minerals of commercial potential are present in some samples in rather large quantities. Smith and Milton [9] found dawsonite [$NaAl(OH)_2CO_3$], a potential source of aluminum, and nahcolite ($NaHCO_3$) in oil shale below the Mahogany zone in the Piceance Creek Basin of Colorado. Presently, trona ($NaHCO_3 \cdot Na_2CO_3 \cdot 2H_2O$), which occurs in the Green River Formation, is being mined in southwestern Wyoming. Milton [10] lists over 70 authigenic mineral species that have been found in the Green River Formation of Utah, Wyoming, and Colorado.

Most of the Green River oil-shale deposit consists of minute, seasonal pairs of laminae called varves. As described by Bradley [11], the oil-shale varves are thin laminations of light and dark colored material, the latter being the result of inclusion of organic material into the inorganic matrix. Dolomite and calcite are major minerals in Green River oil shale and constitute a significant portion of the light colored portion of the varves. Smith and Robb [12] effectively described the coexistence of aragonite, calcite, and dolomite and postulated geochemical conditions necessary for this coexistence. They believed that the genesis and preservation of these carbonates in varved oil shale involved formation of the minerals in a permanently stratified lake. The noncirculating part of the lake water was a strongly basic sodium carbonate solution. Calcite, formed from calcium and carbonate ions, was precipitated upon solution of fine silicate particles that fell into the lake's lower alkaline layer. Aragonite formed each summer, in the surface layer of the lake, preceded the settlement of annual crop of organic matter to the lake bottom. Dolomite formed from aragonite in the sediment at the lake bottom, after the pH of the sediment's interstitial water had been lowered sharply by the evolution of CO_2 from organic matter. Smith and Robb indicated further that the limiting conditions for deposition of Mahogany zone oil shale are pH ranging from 8.0 to 10.0 and oxidation-reduction potential (Eh) of 0.3—0.45 V at pH 8.0 and 0.4—0.58 V at pH 10.0.

Tisot [13,14,15] found that about 75% of the mineral matter consisted of particle sizes between 2 and 20 μ, the size of silt; 17% were less than 2 μ, the size of clay; and 8% ranged between 20 and 200 μ, the size of fine sand. This nonspherical mineral matter along with the organic matter forms a highly consolidated system with no significant micropore structure, pore volume, or internal surface. Tisot estimated that only a small part of the organic matter is bonded either physically or chemically to the mineral constituents, and that less than 4% of the organic material can be located within micropore volume of the inorganic constituents.

Organic constituents

Vast quantities of debris from organisms that grew in the upper portion of the chemically stratified lakes were deposited into this inorganic mixture. The organic material, after being subjected to extensive physical, biological, and chemical alteration exists in the form of soluble organic material sometimes referred to as bitumen and the insoluble organic material referred to as kerogen. The hydrocarbon portion of the soluble material has been amenable to modern analytical techniques and most of the compounds present in this portion of the bitumen have been identified. Some of the low-molecular-weight polar constituents have been identified, but most of the complex high-molecular-weight polar constituents have eluded characterization. Similarly, only general structural information is known about the complex and insoluble kerogen which constitutes most of the total organic material.

Soluble organic material. The major portion of the soluble extract from Mahogany zone oil-shale samples can be fractionated into about 1% n-alkanes, 3% branched alkanes, 21% cyclic alkanes, 2% aromatic oil, 63% resins, and 10% pentane-insoluble material. Average values for the same components

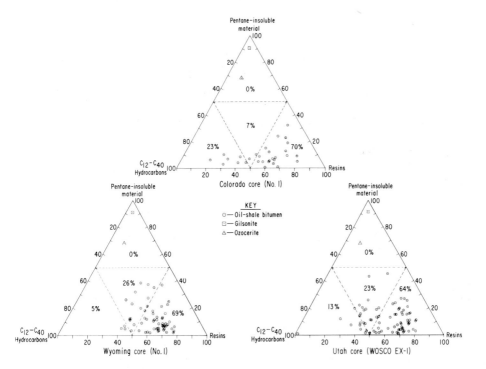

Fig. 4-1. Correlation of components of Green River Formation bitumen.

from a 2,300-ft core from Piceance Creek Basin in Colorado [16,17], a 745-ft core from the Green River Basin in Wyoming [18], and a 1,200-ft core from the Uinta Basin in Utah were as follows: n-alkanes, 3.4—3.9 wt.%; branched plus cyclic alkanes, 23.6—30.3 wt.%; aromatic oil, 2.7—3.3 wt.%; resins, 54.4—57.4 wt.%; and pentane-insoluble material, 9.0—12.5 wt.%. Overall averages for the three cores suggest that the soluble organic material was very uniform; however, analysis of individual samples from the cores show major compositional differences as illustrated in Fig. 4-1. The results of the analyses are shown in the triaxial diagram along with the percentages of the samples analyzed that are represented in each quarter section of the diagram. The soluble extracts showing the most evidence of maturation were from the Colorado core, as 23% of its extracts contained more than 50% hydrocarbons compared to 5 and 13% for the other two cores. None of the core samples had compositions comparable to that of gilsonite or ozocerite, two soluble organic materials that occur in or near the Green River Formation of the Uinta Basin. One sample from the Utah core contained about 97% hydrocarbons. There were significant differences in the extraction ratios (grams of extract per gram of organic carbon) for the three cores. The Green River Basin (Wyoming) core had an average extraction ratio of 0.07, the Piceance Creek Basin (Colorado) core had an average extraction ratio of

0.11, and the Uinta Basin (Utah) core had an average extraction ratio of 0.22 with a maximum value of 1.19. The extraction ratios for the three cores did not increase with increase in depth of burial, suggesting that the soluble material was not degraded from kerogen by depth-related factors such as increased temperature and pressure. The extremely high content of soluble material in the Uinta Basin, relative to the other basins, may be due to source material differences, environmental differences, significant difference of loss of soluble material from the sediment, or other factors.

The n-alkanes present in the bitumen range from about C_{13} to C_{35} compounds [19,16,18]. Samples taken from the Mahogany zone of the formation have bimodal carbon-number distribution with maxima at about C_{17} and C_{29} with an odd—even predominance of 3 or 4 to 1. At the greatest depth of burial, the odd—even predominance is reduced to nearly unity and the carbon-number distribution assumes the characteristic envelope of thermally or biologically altered n-alkanes. The largest amount of n-alkanes found for any of the three core samples was from a Uinta Basin sample and represented 17.1 wt.% of the soluble organic material. In Mahogany zone samples, the quantity of the C_{22} n-alkane exceeds adjacent carbon numbers, but in samples below the Mahogany zone this predominance is much less and disappears at the greatest depths of burial. This difference in C_{22} n-alkane content is probably explained by source material differences.

The branched plus cyclic alkane fraction of the soluble extract from Mahogany zone oil shale of the Piceance Creek Basin (Colorado) has probably received more attention than any portion of the organic material in the Green River oil shale. Identification of five chain isoprenoid compounds (C_{15} farnesane; C_{16}, C_{18}, C_{19} pristane; and C_{20} phytane) in this alkane fraction by Cummins and Robinson [19] initiated considerable research on the extracts from Green River oil shale. Part, if not most of the interest, was from researchers studying extraterrestrial sediments and the relationship of these sediments to living organisms. Because these and other isoprenoid compounds can be interpreted in terms of previous biological existence and were undoubtedly derived from living organisms that grew in the lakes, it appeared that these compounds could serve as so-called "biological markers". Unfortunately the chain isoprenoid compounds are of a ubiquitous nature and their usefulness as indicators has lessened, but the interest in compound identification from this alkane fraction has continued. Table 4-I shows the empirical formulas, number of saturated rings, and the molecular weight of the compounds identified mass spectrally in the branched plus cyclic alkane fraction from a Mahogany zone oil-shale sample. Positive identification of many of the compounds has been made by mass spectral and adjunct analyses, and at present approximately 75% of the compounds in this fraction are known. The type of compound present includes C_{15}, C_{16}, C_{18}, C_{19}, and C_{20} chain isoprenoid compounds [19]; C_{27}, C_{28}, and C_{29} steranes [20,21] and sterane degradation products [22,23]; C_{30} and C_{31} pentacyclic triter-

TABLE 4-I

Branched and cyclic alkanes in Green River Formation oil-shale bitumen

Molecular formula	Mole weight	No. of rings	Reference	Molecular formula	Mole weight	No. of rings	Reference
$C_{13}H_{26}$	182	1	[22]	$C_{25}H_{50}$	350	1	[22]
$C_{14}H_{26}$	194	2	[22]	$C_{25}H_{52}$	352	0	[23]
$C_{14}H_{28}$	196	1	[22]	$C_{26}H_{44}$	356	5	[22]
$C_{15}H_{30}$	210	1	[22]	$C_{26}H_{46}$	358	4	[22]
$C_{15}H_{32}$	212	0	[19]	$C_{26}H_{48}$ I	360	3	[23]
$C_{16}H_{32}$	224	1	[22]	$C_{26}H_{48}$ II	360	3	[23]
$C_{16}H_{34}$	226	0	[19]	$C_{26}H_{52}$	364	1	[22]
$C_{18}H_{38}$	254	0	[19]	$C_{27}H_{46}$	370	5	[22]
$C_{19}H_{38}$	266	1	[22]	$C_{27}H_{48}$ 5α	372	4	[20]
$C_{19}H_{40}$	268	0	[19]	$C_{27}H_{48}$ 5β	372	4	[25]
$C_{20}H_{36}$ I	276	3	[22]	$C_{27}H_{54}$	378	1	[22]
$C_{20}H_{36}$ II	276	3	[23]	$C_{27}H_{56}$	380	0	[23]
$C_{20}H_{38}$	278	2	[22]	$C_{28}H_{48}$	384	5	[22]
$C_{20}H_{40}$	280	1	[22]	$C_{28}H_{50}$ 5α	386	4	[20]
$C_{20}H_{42}$	282	0	[19]	$C_{28}H_{50}$ 5β	386	4	[25]
$C_{21}H_{36}$ 5α	288	4	[23]	$C_{28}H_{56}$	392	1	[22]
$C_{21}H_{38}$ I	290	3	[22]	$C_{29}H_{50}$	398	5	[25]
$C_{21}H_{38}$ II	290	3	[23]	$C_{29}H_{52}$ 5α	400	4	[20]
$C_{21}H_{40}$	292	2	[22]	$C_{29}H_{52}$ 5β	400	4	[25]
$C_{21}H_{42}$	294	1	[22]	$C_{29}H_{58}$	406	1	[22]
$C_{21}H_{44}$	296	0	[23]	$C_{29}H_{60}$	408	0	[23]
$C_{22}H_{40}$	304	3	[22]	$C_{30}H_{52}$ I	412	5	[24]
$C_{22}H_{42}$	306	2	[22]	$C_{30}H_{52}$ II	412	5	[20]
$C_{22}H_{44}$	308	1	[22]	$C_{30}H_{52}$ III	412	5	[25]
$C_{22}H_{46}$	310	0	[23]	$C_{30}H_{52}$ IV	412	5	[25]
$C_{23}H_{40}$ I	316	4	[22]	$C_{30}H_{54}$	414	4	[22]
$C_{23}H_{40}$ II	316	4	[23]	$C_{30}H_{56}$	416	3	[25]
$C_{23}H_{42}$ I	318	3	[22]	$C_{30}H_{60}$	420	1	[22]
$C_{23}H_{42}$ II	318	3	[23]	$C_{31}H_{54}$ I	426	5	[25]
$C_{23}H_{44}$	320	2	[22]	$C_{31}H_{54}$ II	426	5	[25]
$C_{23}H_{46}$	322	1	[22]	$C_{31}H_{62}$	434	1	[22]
$C_{24}H_{40}$	328	5	[22]	$C_{32}H_{56}$	440	5	[22]
$C_{24}H_{42}$	330	4	[22]	$C_{32}H_{64}$	448	1	[22]
$C_{24}H_{44}$	332	3	[22]	$C_{33}H_{64}$	460	2	[25]
$C_{24}H_{46}$	334	2	[22]	$C_{34}H_{68}$ I	476	1	[25]
$C_{24}H_{48}$	336	1	[22]	$C_{34}H_{68}$ II	476	1	[25]
$C_{25}H_{42}$	342	5	[22]	$C_{40}H_{78}$ I	558	2	[26]
$C_{25}H_{44}$	344	4	[22]	$C_{40}H_{78}$ II	558	2	[23]
$C_{25}H_{46}$ I	346	3	[22]	$C_{40}H_{80}$	560	1	[22]
$C_{25}H_{46}$ II	346	3	[23]				

panes [20,24,25]; C_{40} carotanes [26]; and other branched and cyclic alkanes [22,23].

Recent papers by Anders et al. [27] and Gallegos [28] describe studies of the aromatic fraction of Green River bitumen by mass spectrometry, infrared, gas chromatography, and dehydrogenation techniques. According to Anders et al. [27], the C_nH_{2n-6} compounds represented 10% of the total fraction and ranged from $C_{12}H_{18}$ to $C_{32}H_{58}$. These compounds were alkylbenzenes. The C_nH_{2n-8} compounds represented 31% of the total fraction and ranged from $C_{12}H_{16}$ to $C_{30}H_{52}$. These compounds were alkyltetralins. The C_nH_{2n-10} compounds represented 18% of the fraction and ranged from $C_{15}H_{20}$ to $C_{33}H_{56}$. These compounds contained one aromatic ring and two saturated rings. The C_nH_{2n-12} compounds represented 12% of the fraction and ranged from $C_{17}H_{22}$ to $C_{33}H_{54}$. These compounds contained one aromatic ring and three saturated rings. The C_nH_{2n-14} compounds represented 8% of the fraction and ranged from $C_{18}H_{22}$ to $C_{33}H_{52}$. These compounds contained two aromatic rings and one saturated ring. Twenty percent of the fraction was represented by a series of monoaromatic alkanes ranging in molecular weight from 536 to 550 and differing from the next homolog by two mass units. This suggested that the differences in structure may be related to differences in double bond content similar to that resulting from varying degrees of saturation of carotenoid compounds with hydrogen during geologic time.

The nonhydrocarbon constituents of the soluble extract from Green River oil shale have not been extensively investigated. According to Robinson and Cummins [29] the material insoluble in pentane at $0°C$ has an average molecular weight of 1,320 and contains about 0.2% nitrogen, 1.0% sulfur, and 7.4% oxygen. The polar portion of the pentane-soluble material, eluted from alumina by benzene and benzene—methanol mixtures, had an average molecular weight of 625 and contained 0.9% nitrogen, 1.4% sulfur, and 7.8% oxygen. Recently Doolittle et al. [30] obtained the exact mass and other spectral data for six oxygen and oxygen—nitrogen-containing compounds which were removed from the Resin I fraction (eluted from alumina with benzene) by molecular distillation. Four of the compounds were of a homologous series with empirical formulas of $C_{11}H_{12}O$ to $C_{14}H_{18}O$. Spectral data suggest that these compounds may be either indanones, tetralones, or acetyl indans. A compound, having an empirical formula of $C_6H_{11}NO$, may be a hydroxypyrrole. Another compound, having an empirical formula of $C_7H_9NO_2$, may be a diketo pyrrole.

Moore and Dunning [31] extracted organic matter from Green River oil shale successively with solvents of increasing polarity and determined the interfacial activities and the porphyrin, nitrogen, and metal contents of the extracts. Porphyrins of the phyllo type were identified in Green River oil shale by Morandi and Jensen [32]. Other nitrogen-containing compounds have been reported by Simoneit et al. [33]. The fatty acids present in this sediment were reported by Abelson and Parker [34] and Lawlor and Robinson [35], who found a predominance of C_{14}, C_{16}, and C_{18} fatty acids and a homologous series of fatty acids from C_{10} to C_{34}, respectively. Eglinton et al. [36] have shown the presence of isoprenoid fatty acids ranging from C_{14} to C_{21} with the exception of the C_{18} acid. Haug et al. [37] identified C_7 to C_{12} normal acids, C_9 and C_{10} isoprenoid acids, C_{12} to C_{18} dicarboxylic acids, C_{13} and C_{15} mono-α-methyl dicarboxylic acids, and C_{11} and C_{14} methyl ketoacids. Sever and Parker [38] identified C_{14} to C_{22} normal alcohols (except C_{19} and C_{21}) and the isoprenoid alcohol, dihydrophytol, in extracts of Green River oil shale. Identification of precursors for the cycloalkane constituents of the soluble extracts from Green River oil shale was recently accomplished by Steel and Henderson [39]. Tetrahymanol, other triterpenoid alcohols, and C_{27} to C_{29} sterols probably represent reduction intermediates during geologic time to gammacerane, other triterpenoid hydrocarbons, the C_{27} to C_{29} steranes, and other cyclo-alkane constituents of Green River oil shale. All of these compounds were isolated. Palacas [40], as well as Kvenvolden and Peterson [41], obtained evidence of amino acids. Palacas also found evidence of the presence of small amounts of carbohydrates in the Green River sediments.

Insoluble organic material. The major portion of the organic material in Green River oil shale consists of the insoluble kerogen. Considerable research has been conducted on kerogen during the past few decades, most of which up to 1960 was abstracted by Robinson and Stanfield [42]. Kerogen of the Green River Formation and other oil shales is described in articles by Robinson and Dinneen [43] and Robinson [44].

Green River kerogen of the Mahogany zone as seen under the microscope consists of organic material of two types: the major portion has a yellowish-amber color and the minor portion is brown or brownish-black in color. The yellow-amber structureless organic material occurs in long, thin bands or stringers laid parallel to the bedding laminae and is intimately mixed with inorganic material; whereas the brown organic material occurs in thin stringers and as irregular masses. Occasionally, lenses of nearly pure organic material occur in the formation, some of which are soluble and some are insoluble. Some sections of cores from the Uinta Basin are impregnated with such high contents of soluble materials that they ooze out as soon as the core is withdrawn. Some samples, especially those taken from the bottom of the formation, show some alteration as evidenced by darkening of the kerogen when viewed with a microscope; however, there does not appear to be a direct relationship between depth of burial and aromatization of the kerogen [27,29].

Based on elemental analysis by Smith [45], the empirical formula for Green River Formation kerogen at the Mahogany zone level may be represented by $C_{215}H_{330}O_{12}N_5S$ with a minimum formula weight of about 3,200. The atomic H/C ratio of 1.53 shows this kerogen to be of a highly aliphatic nature. The atomic C/O ratio of 18, the atomic C/N ratio of 43, and the atomic C/S ratio of 215 illustrate the average amount of carbon atoms associated with each heteroatom. Upon thermal conversion at 500°C, the kerogen from the Mahogany zone level produced an average of 0.68 g of oil per g of organic carbon. This represents a significantly high conversion of the carbonaceous material to an oily product and further illustrates the predominance of aliphatic structures (straight chain and cyclic) in this kerogen.

One method of studying the structures present in kerogen is to degrade the complex and insoluble material to lower-molecular-weight materials by complete oxidation or by controlled step oxidation [46,47,48,49,50]. The studies by Robinson et al. [46] revealed that Green River kerogen is nearly completely oxidized to oxalic acids, volatile acids, and CO_2 in 100 hours using a boiling alkaline potassium permanganate solution. The oxidation behavior distinguishes this kerogen from most other kerogens of the world as many of the latter contain varying amounts of aromatic structures that are not oxidized beyond the benzenoid acid stage [43]. Coal and coal-like materials contain large amounts of aromatic structures that are not oxidized with permanganate beyond the benzenoid acid stage; whereas other kerogens — for, for example, Australian torbanite and Alaskan algal shale — are not oxidized significantly with permanganate because of their high fatty or paraffinic content. The complete or carbon balance oxidation tests showed conclusively that Green River kerogen from the Mahogany zone contains very little aromatic structure and few long-chain structures.

Controlled or step oxidation techniques, using an alkaline potassium permanganate solution, converts about 77% of the kerogen carbon to intermediate-molecular-weight products and 23% to final oxidation products. By a series of reactions, Robinson et al. [51,52] converted the intermediate-molecular-weight products to esters, alcohols, iodides, and finally hydrocarbon-like materials. Based on X-ray diffraction, mass spectra, and infrared spectra, the reduced product contained 2% normal alkanes, 2% branched alkanes, 34% cycloalkanes (1—6 rings), 15% aromatic compounds (1—2 rings), and 47% heterocyclic compounds. Average molecular weight of the various fractions ranged from 270 to 1,220.

More recent studies by Burlingame et al. [49] showed the presence of normal, branched, isoprenoid, cyclic, pentacyclic, and aromatic acids of carbon-number range from C_3 to C_{32} in Green River kerogen oxidation products. Djuricic et al. [50] found evidence of normal, isoprenoid, keto, and aromatic acids ranging from C_4 to C_{29} compounds in oxidation products. Based on the general type analyses for the oxidation products found by Robinson and Lawlor [52], Green River kerogen from the Mahogany zone appears to be predominantly a saturated cyclic material containing numerous heteroatoms. It is visualized that this kerogen consists of linear networks of cyclic rings of methylene groups with or without hetero groups. Associated with the saturated rings are some long chains and aromatic structures with the entire system being held together by short methylene interconnections and crosslinks of oxygen bridges. These oxygen bridges and oxygen on ring structures would serve as points for ready oxidative cleavage. The imaginary structure for this kerogen accounts for many of the determined properties of the kerogen, but it differs significantly from the polymethylene bridge-type structure proposed by Djuricic et al. [50]. The structure envisioned by Djuricic should give strong infrared absorption in the 720 cm^{-1} region; however, Green River kerogen from the Mahogany zone gives weak absorption in this region [44], showing the presence of small amounts of methylene chains greater than C$_4$. Also, the polymethylene bridge-type structure would probably be more resistant to complete oxidation than is found for this kerogen.

Low-temperature thermal degradation of Green River kerogen from the Mahogany zone by Robinson and Cummins [29] and Hubbard and Fester [53] confirm the cyclic structural interpretations derived from oxidation studies. In the first study, Green River kerogen was degraded at temperatures from 25 to 350°C in the presence of tetralin, a hydrogen-donor solvent. Increasing amounts of kerogen were made soluble as the temperature increased and at 350°C about 95% of the kerogen was converted to a soluble extract after 144 hours of heating. At 350°C the kerogen was degraded to 10—15% normal and branched alkanes, 20—25% cycloalkanes, 10—15% aromatic structures, and 45—60% heterocyclic material. In the second study, Hubbard and Fester degraded kerogen at 355°C in the presence of hydrogen (4,200 psig pressure) and stannous chloride catalyst. The hydrogenolysis product contained n-alkanes, branched alkanes, cycloalkanes, and a polar oil fraction that contained O, N, and S and was essentially nonaromatic in character. Both the oxidative and thermal degradations gave similar type products, which would not be expected if the degradation products were rearrangement products. These degradation products undoubtedly portray some of the structural features of the original kerogen.

Fester and Robinson [54] determined the oxygen functional groups present in the Green River kerogen from the Mahogany zone. Carboxyl and ester groups represented 15 and 25% of the kerogen oxygen, respectively. An additional 7% of the kerogen oxygen was accounted for as hydroxyl, carbonyl, and amide oxygen, leaving 53% of the kerogen oxygen accounted for as unreactive oxygen. They suggested that the unreactive oxygen is probably ether oxygen.

The infrared spectrum [44] of a Green River kerogen concentrate shows strong absorption in the region of 2,900 and 1,460 cm^{-1} assigned to methylmethylene groups, strong absorption in the 1,680 to 1,720 cm^{-1} region assigned to carbonyl groups, medium absorption in the 1,580 to 1,610 cm^{-1} region assigned to aromatic structures or carboxyl salts, medium absorption in the 1,380 cm^{-1} region assigned to methyl or cyclic methylene groups, and weak absorption in the 720 cm^{-1} region assigned to chain methylene groups greater than C$_4$. Absorption of radiation in the ultraviolet region was investigated by McDonald and Cook [55] who showed that Green River kerogen of the Mahogany zone contains about 5—10% aromatic structures. The X-ray diffraction pattern of Green River kerogen relative to other carbonaceous materials shows the predominantly saturated character of this kerogen. These and other physical properties of Green River kerogen are given in a report by Robinson [44].

Recent studies by Robinson and Cook [16,18] of cores taken from the Piceance Creek Basin (Colorado), the Green River Basin (Wyoming), and the Uinta Basin (Utah) show that there are significant differences in the properties of kerogen taken from different stratigraphic and geographic locations within the Green River Formation. To illustrate this point, variations in the determined values for one property — namely, the atomic hydrogen to carbon ratio — will be given. The H/C ratios for 60 selected samples from the 2,300-ft Colorado No. 1 core ranged from 0.92 to 1.77 with an average of 1.48. The 61 selected samples from the 750-ft Wyoming No. 1 core had H/C ratios that ranged from 1.12 to 1.67 and averaged 1.49. The H/C ratios for 75 selected samples from the 1,200-ft WOSCO EX-1 core (Utah) ranged from 0.70 to 1.61 and averaged 1.44. The lowest values for H/C ratios are about in the range of sub-bituminous coals; however, only 6% of the selected samples from the three cores had H/C ratios less than 1.3 and only 9% of the samples had H/C ratios of 1.6 or greater. The H/C ratios and other determined physical properties of the kerogen did not appear to be related to depth of burial.

Average amounts of the total organic carbon not volatilized at 500°C from samples of the three cores ranged from 29 to 32%. This carbon residue test illustrates the cyclic nature of the portion of the organic material not volatilized at 500°C, because noncyclic materials produce little carbon residue when heated at 500°C. Because other tests have shown that aromatic structures represent a small part of Green River kerogen, it is deduced that most of the carbon residue was derived from the dehydrogenation of complex and nonvolatile saturated cyclic structures during the thermal decomposition reaction. Also, as discussed earlier, the volatile and soluble organic material produced thermally at rather slow reaction rates at 350°C were predominantly saturated cyclic materials.

Origin of Green River oil shale

For several decades arguments have been waged as to whether the carbonaceous deposits of the world are of biological or of abiological origin. Except in very limited and isolated cases, it is generally believed that most of the carbonaceous materials are derived from biological organisms that grew in aquatic environments. Bradley [2] was one of the early investigators to propose that the organic material in Green River oil shale was of biological origin. This conclusion was based upon the masterful work he did in identifying fossils and microfossils in Green River oil shale. Bradley stated that two kinds of organic material can be clearly distinguished in thin sections of Green River oil shale. One is entirely structureless, translucent, and lemon-yellow to reddish brown in color. The other kind of organic matter consists of remains of complete or fragmentary organisms such as bacteria, algae, fungi, protozoa, insects, and parts of higher plants (spores, pollen grains, or minute pieces of tissue). The structureless material makes up the major portion of the total organic material and was derived from the partial putrefaction of aquatic organisms. Bradley concluded that the lakes were rather shallow at times in order for fungi to grow in such abundance on the surface of the organic ooze. Also, algae apparently dominated the flora of the ancient lakes; however, zooplankton production was probably large. Bradley concluded that the preservation of such vast quantities of organic matter must have been determined by a copious supply of the organisms, an effective check upon the microbian activity, and the absence of strong oxidizing conditions.

Equally convincing of the biological origin of the organic material in Green River oil shale is the large number of "biological marker" compounds that have been positively identified in the soluble organic material in Green River oil shale. With but few exceptions, the hydrocarbon portion of this material can be directly related to a biological precursor. Undoubtedly, as more of the complex components of the soluble organic material are characterized, they will also be found to be directly related to a biological entity.

Contribution of organic matter to the formation of Green River Formation came from three different sources: (1) bodies of fresh water (nonmarine), which contained adequate nutrients for abundant aquatic plant growth, (2) streams flowing into the basin and carrying soluble organic material from terrestrial plants that grew in the subtropical environment, and (3) wind-borne material derived from the terrestrial plants. Most of the organic debris came from organisms that grew in the lakes. Bradley [6] estimated that the annual deposition of organic debris from organisms that grew in the lakes was between 0.5 and 1.1 kg m^{-2}.

According to Bradley [56], only three classes of non-marine algae need to be considered as precursors for the organic matter of Green River oil shale — yellow-green algae (Xanthophyceae), green algae (Chlorophyceae), and blue-green algae (Cyanophyceae). Evidence of diatoms has not been found in Green River oil shale. He excluded *Botryococcus* because no recognizable fossil or a trace of a fossil of this algae has ever been found in Green River oil shale. In Bradley's opinion blue-green algae were the predominant organisms that served as precursors for the organic material of Green River oil shale. Also, he was equally sure that the only significant contribution of plant material other than the algal material was a considerable amount of pollen, which was wind-blown or floated into the lake from the land plants that grew on the banks surrounding the lake. What part animal remains may have contributed to the organic matter content is unknown. Likewise, it is not known what portion of the total organic material was carried into lakes by streams. The most abundant deposition of carbonaceous residue is located in the central portions of the basin, suggesting that the most abundant biological growth was in the mid sections of the lakes.

Although identification of a large variety of specific compounds in the soluble extract from Green River oil shale has shown the biological nature of this carbonaceous material, it has not shown the exact precursors. Future studies similar to those of Eglinton [57] and Balogh et al. [58], e.g., correlation of absolute stereochemistry of naturally-occurring compounds with those found in the sediment, carbon isotope ratio studies, carbon-number dominance, or other techniques, may be helpful in showing the exact precursors for the organic material in Green River oil shale.

Conditions of deposition

Several deductive conclusions have been made about the conditions that existed during the deposition of the Green River Formation, and they are as follows: (1) fresh-water lakes (non-marine) containing adequate nutrients for an abundant growth of organisms; (2) stratification of the lakes (probably chemical) which prevented complete thermal overturns; (3) a reducing environment in the bottom sections of the stratified lakes; (4) a natural preservation of the organic debris; and (5) compaction and desiccation of the sediment.

At the time of the deposition of the Green River Formation, the Cretaceous seas had withdrawn and the region was under the influence of the Laramide orogeny. For this reason the basin lakes that were the progenitors of the Green River Formation are classified as fresh-water lakes even though they were highly saline. The lake environment was ideally suited for abundant plant growth as evidenced by the amount of carbonaceous material that remains in the sediment. The streams feeding the lake basins were fairly well regulated mountain streams carrying an adequate amount of phosphates and other nutrients into the lake beds. Bradley [6] suggested that the climate was semitropical with flora on the watershed being similar to that of the present coastal area of the Gulf of Mexico. The annual average temperature was about 66—67° F and the average yearly rainfall was about 35—40 inches. At various times the lakes overflowed their outlets and at other times the water level was extremely low with the marginal areas being very shallow and on occasions drying to the point where mud cracks developed. Probably at the greatest depth the lakes did not exceed 100 ft and in most cases the average depth of the lakes was much less. Because the existing sediment is highly calcareous and dolomitic, it is assumed that the streams feeding the lakes carried high concentrations of calcium, magnesium, and sodium ions. Bradley estimated that the stream waters may have contained about 55 ppm of calcium, 18 ppm of magnesium, 40 ppm of sodium, 204 ppm of bicarbonate, 14 ppm of silicone dioxide, 108 ppm of sulfate, and 22 ppm of other salts for a total of 461 ppm of dissolved salts.

The preservation of enormous quantities of organic material in the Green River Basins necessitated a rapid exclusion of oxygen and aerobic bacteria from the deeper sections of the lake. A permanent stratification of the lake waters has been envisioned by various researchers, whereby the annual or semiannual thermal overturns did not occur and thus prevented oxygen from entering the bottom waters known as the hypolimnion. Because other evidence suggests that the lakes were not deep enough to cause permanent stratification, it has been proposed that the hypolimnion was saline enough to cause differences in density sufficient to prevent overturns. The upper layer of water, or the epilimnion, maintained the abundant growth of organisms which upon dying were subjected to oxidative conditions and aerobic bacteria until the biomass settled into the hypolimnion. Because of exclusion of oxygen, decay and rotting conditions in the hypolimnia soon produced a highly reducing environment. Evidence for a highly reducing environment is the presence of significant amounts of iron pyrite in the sediments and essentially complete absence of sulfate ion. Also, the soluble hydrocarbons identified in the sediment are mostly in a highly reduced form.

The organic debris falling into the reducing environment of the hypolimnion was degraded to a gelatinous material similar to the deposits in present-day lakes described as algal ooze. In this state, the components of the original biological precursors were subjected to polymerization, chemical reduction, anaerobic alteration, and other chemical and physical changes. The stable portion of the precursor components, for example, the hydrocarbons, retained their structural identity and appear in the soluble portion of the organic material. Other components of the precursor organisms, for example, the sterols, terpenes, diterpenes, triterpenes, carotenoid compounds, chlorophyll and so forth, were altered slightly by oxidative, reductive, or biological reactions; however, some semblance of their original structure was retained. This type of structure constitutes a significant portion of the soluble organic material and some evidence suggests that these components may have contributed significantly to the kerogen material. The labile portion of the precursor components, for example, unsaturated hydrocarbons, unsaturated alcohols, unsaturated fatty acids and so forth, entered into polymerization reactions forming more stable materials of varying molecular weight. These constituents served as precursor material for the insoluble kerogen and for the high-molecular-weight components of the soluble material. Differences in solubility of the resulting organic materials may be due mainly to differences in molecular size of the polymers. Another possible contributor to the total organic material is the unknown amount of organic debris deposited in the form of bacterial metabolite. Because of the complex nature of the organic material in Green River oil shale, it seems likely that most of the above proposed reactions may have contributed to the origin of organic material and that it was not derived from a single organism. Differences in the ecology of the biologically active lakes produced different source material at different times and, perhaps, even different chemical compositions of the same organism. Also, a multitude of different chemical and biological reactions were involved in the production of the resulting complex organic material.

After deposition of the organic—inorganic debris, water was expelled from the bottom portions of the inorganic—organic mass. With additional weight from more debris, the sediment was finally compacted and desiccated to form the highly impermeable Green River sediment. How much biological alteration occurred after compaction is unknown, but at the present time the sediment is essentially sterile. Some maturation, especially with respect to the normal alkanes, occurred after deposition, but generally evidence of maturation of the kerogen was not related to depth of burial. The absence of appreciable maturation seems reasonable in view of the estimated static pressure of 210 kg cm^{-2} and an ambient temperature of between 90° and 125°C [6] for the bottom of the formation.

Conclusions

The existing evidence suggests that the organic material present in the Green River Formation is of biological origin. The exact precursors are not known; however, it is believed that a variety of organisms contributed to the organic debris and a wide variety of reactions produced the resulting carbonaceous material. Environmental conditions changed during the deposition of the Green River Formation sediment as evidenced by significant differences in both the mineral and organic compositions. For example, the composition of the soluble extracts from samples taken from the top of the formation differs from that from the bottom of the formation. Some of these differences are related to source material variations and some are related to burial depth. Also, significant differences in the amounts of soluble organic material per unit of organic carbon were found for samples taken from different geographical locations within the formation. All of these variations probably reflect differences in the source material, conditions of the aquatic environment, alteration of the organic material, and so forth. Further research will undoubtedly clarify some of these questions and will contribute to a better understanding of the nature of Green River oil shale and how it can be utilized best.

References

1. D.C. Duncan and V.E. Swanson, "Organic-rich Shale of the United States and World Land Areas", *U.S. Geol. Surv. Circ.*, *523*, 30 pp. (1965).

2. W.H. Bradley, "Origin and Microfossils of the Oil Shale of the Green River Formation of Colorado and Utah". *U.S. Geol. Surv. Profess. Pap.*, *168*, 58 pp. (1931).
3. D.C. Duncan and C. Belser, "Geology and Oil Shale Resources of the Eastern Side of the Piceance Creek Basin, Rio Blanco and Garfield Counties, Colorado", *U.S. Geol. Surv. Map*, OM 119, *Oil Gas Inv. Ser.* (1950).
4. J.R. Donnell, W.B. Cashion and J.H. Brown Jr., "Geology of the Cathedral Bluffs Area, Rio Blanco and Garfield Counties, Colorado", *U.S. Geol. Surv. Map*, OM 134, *Oil Gas Inv. Ser.* (1953).
5. W.H. Bradley, "Limnology and the Eocene Lakes of the Rocky Mountain Region", *Bull. Geol. Soc. Am.*, *59*, 635—648 (1948).
6. W.H. Bradley, "Paleolimnology", in: D.G. Frey (Editor), *Limnology in North America*, University of Wisconsin Press, Madison, Wisc., pp. 621—652 (1963).
7. K.E. Stanfield, I.C. Frost, W.S. McAuley and H.N. Smith, "Properties of Colorado Oil Shale", *U.S. Bur. Mines Rep. Invest.* 4825, 27 pp. (1951).
8. J.W. Smith and K.E. Stanfield, "Oil Yield and Properties of Green River Oil Shale in the Uinta Basin, Utah", in: *Guidebook to the Geology and Mineral Resources of the Uinta Basin*, Intermountain Assoc. Petrol. Geologists, pp. 213—221 (1964).
9. J.W. Smith and C. Milton, "Dawsonite in the Green River Formation of Colorado", *Econ. Geol.*, *61*, 1029—1042 (1966).
10. C. Milton, "Authigenic Minerals of the Green River Formation", *Contrib. Geol.*, *10*, 57—63 (1971).
11. W.H. Bradley, "The Varves and Climate of the Green River Epoch", *U.S. Geol. Surv. Profess. Pap.*, *158-E*, 87—110 (1929).
12. J.W. Smith and W.A. Robb, "Aragonite and the Genesis of Carbonates in Mahogany Zone Oil Shales of Colorado's Green River Formation", *U.S. Bur. Mines Rep. Invest.*, 7727, 21 pp. (1973).
13. P.R. Tisot, "Alterations in Structure and Physical Properties of Green River Oil Shale by Thermal Treatment", *J. Chem. Eng. Data*, *12*, 405—411 (1967).
14. P.R. Tisot, "Properties of Green River Oil Shale Determined from Nitrogen Adsorption and Desorption Isotherms", *J. Chem. Eng. Data*, *7*, 405—410 (1962).
15. P.R. Tisot and W.I.R. Murphy, "Physicochemical Properties of Green River Oil Shale — Particle Size and Particle-Size Distribution of Inorganic Constituents", *J. Chem. Eng. Data*, *5*, 558—562 (1960).
16. W.E. Robinson and G.L. Cook, "Compositional Variations of the Organic Material of Green River Oil Shale — Colorado No. 1 Core", *U.S. Bur. Mines Rep. Invest.*, 7492, 32 pp. (1971).
17. D.E. Anders and W.E. Robinson, "Geochemical Aspects of the Saturated Hydrocarbon Constituents of Green River Oil Shale — Colorado No. 1 Core", *U.S. Bur. Mines Rep. Invest.*, 7737, 23 pp. (1973).
18. W.E. Robinson and G.L. Cook, "Compositional Variations of the Organic Material of Green River Oil Shale — Wyoming No. 1 Core", *U.S. Bur. Mines Rep. Invest.*, 7820, 32 pp. (1973).
19. J.J. Cummins and W.E. Robinson, "Normal and Isoprenoid Hydrocarbons Isolated from Oil-Shale Bitumen", *J. Chem. Eng. Data*, *9*, 304—307 (1964).
20. A.L. Burlingame, P. Haug, T. Belsky and M. Calvin, "Occurrence of Biogenic Steranes and Pentacyclic Triterpanes in an Eocene Shale (52 Million Years) and in an Early Precambrian Shale (2.7 Billion Years), A Preliminary Report", *Proc. Nat. Acad. Sci.*, *54*, 1406—1412 (1965).
21. P.C. Anderson, P.M. Gardner, E.V. Whitehead, D.E. Anders and W.E. Robinson, "The Isolation of Steranes from Green River Oil Shale", *Geochim. Cosmochim. Acta*, *33*, 1304—1307 (1969).
22. D.E. Anders and W.E. Robinson, "Cycloalkane Constituents of the Bitumen from Green River Shale", *Geochim. Cosmochim. Acta*, *35*, 661—678 (1971).

23. E.J. Gallegos, "Identification of New Steranes, Terpanes, and Branched Paraffins in Green River Shale by Combined Capillary Gas Chromatography and Mass Spectrometry", *Anal. Chem., 43*, 1151–1160 (1971).

24. I.R. Hills, E.V. Whitehead, D.E. Anders, J.J. Cummins and W.E. Robinson, "An optically Active Triterpane, Gammacerane, in Green River Oil-Shale Bitumen", *Chem. Commun., 20*, 752–754 (1966).

25. W. Henderson, V. Wollrab and G. Eglinton, "Identification of Steroids and Triterpenes from a Geological Source by Capillary Gas-Liquid Chromatography and Mass Spectrometry, in: P.A. Schenck and I. Havenaar (Editors), *Advances in Organic Geochemistry*, Pergamon Press, Oxford, pp. 181–207 (1969).

26. M.T.J. Murphy, A. McCormick and G. Eglinton, "Perhydro-β-carotene in the Green River Oil Shale", *Science, 157*, 1040–1042 (1967).

27. D.E. Anders, F.G. Doolittle and W.E. Robinson, "Analysis of Some Aromatic Hydrocarbons in a Benzene-soluble Bitumen from Green River Shale", *Geochim. Cosmochim. Acta, 37*, 1213–1228 (1973).

28. E.J. Gallegos, "Identification of Phenylcycloparaffin Alkanes and Other Monoaromatics in Green River Shale by Gas Chromatography—Mass Spectrometry", *Anal. Chem., 45*, 1399–1403 (1973).

29. W.E. Robinson and J.J. Cummins, "Composition of Low-Temperature Thermal Extracts from Colorado Oil Shale", *J. Chem. Eng. Data, 5*, 74–80 (1960).

30. F.G. Doolittle, D.E. Anders and W.E. Robinson, *Spectral Characteristics of Heteroatom Compounds in Oil Shale*, presented at the Pittsburgh Conference on Analytical Chemistry and Applied Spectroscopy, Cleveland, Ohio, Paper 167 (1973).

31. J.W. Moore and H.N. Dunning, "Interfacial Activities and Porphyrin Content of Oil-Shale Extracts", *Ind. Eng. Chem., 47*, 1440–1444 (1955).

32. J.R. Morandi and H.B. Jensen, "Comparison of Porphyrins from Shale Oil, Oil Shale and Petroleum by Absorption and Mass Spectroscopy", *Chem. Eng. Data, 11*, 81–88 (1966).

33. B.R. Simoneit, H.K. Schnoes, P. Haug and A.L. Burlingame, "High Resolution Mass Spectrometry of Nitrogenous Compounds of the Colorado Green River Formation Oil Shale", *Chem. Geol., 7*, 123–141 (1971).

34. P.H. Abelson and P.L. Parker, "Fatty Acids in Sedimentary Rocks", *Carnegie Inst. Year Book, Washington, 61*, 181–184 (1962).

35. D.L. Lawlor and W.E. Robinson, "Fatty Acids in Green River Formation Oil Shale", *Preprints, Div. Petrol. Chem., ACS, 10* (1): 5–9 (1965).

36. G. Eglinton, A.G. Douglas, J.R. Maxwell, J.N. Ramsey and S. Stallberg-Stenhagen, "Occurrence of Isoprenoid Fatty Acids in Green River Shale", *Science, 153*, 1133 (1966).

37. P. Haug, H.K. Schnoes and A.L. Burlingame, "Studies of the Acid Components of the Colorado Green River Formation Oil Shale: Mass Spectrometric Identification of the Methyl Esters of Extractable Acids", *Chem. Geol., 7*, 213–236 (1971).

38. J. Sever and P.L. Parker, "Fatty Alcohols (Normal and Isoprenoid) in Sediments", *Science, 164*, 1052–1054 (1969).

39. G. Steel and W. Henderson, "Isolation and Characterization of Stanols from the Green River Shale", *Nature, 238*, 148–149 (1972).

40. J.G. Palacas, *Geochemistry of Carbohydrates*, thesis, Univ. Minnesota (1959).

41. K.A. Kvenvolden and E. Peterson, "Amino Acid Enantiomers in Green River Formation Oil Shale", *Abs. Ann. Meet. Geol. Soc. Am.*, Atlantic City, N.J., pp. 132–133 (1969).

42. W.E. Robinson and K.E. Stanfield, "Constitution of Oil-Shale Kerogen", *U.S. Bur. Mines Rep. Invest.*, 7968, 79 pp. (1960).

43. W.E. Robinson and G.U. Dinneen, "Constitutional Aspects of Oil-Shale Kerogen", *Proc. 7th World Pet. Congr., 3*, 669–680 (1967).

44. W.E. Robinson, "Kerogen of the Green River Formation", in: G. Eglinton and M.T.J. Murphy (Editors), *Organic Geochemistry — Methods and Results*, Springer, Berlin, pp. 619—637 (1969).
45. J.W. Smith, "Ultimate Composition of Organic Material in Green River Oil Shale", *U.S. Bur. Mines Rep. Invest.*, 5725, 16 pp. (1961).
46. W.E. Robinson, H.H. Heady and A.B. Hubbard, "Alkaline Permanganate Oxidation of Oil-Shale Kerogen", *Ind. Eng. Chem.*, 45, 788—791 (1953).
47. W.E. Robinson, D.L. Lawlor, J.J. Cummins and J.I. Fester, "Oxidation of Colorado Oil Shale", *U.S. Bur. Mines Rep. Invest.*, 6166, 33 pp. (1963).
48. T.C. Hoering and P.N. Abelson, "Fatty Acids from the Oxidation of Kerogen", *Carnegie Inst. Year Book, Wash.*, 64, 218—223 (1965).
49. A.L. Burlingame, P.A. Haug, H.K. Schnoes and B.R. Simoneit, "Fatty Acids Derived from Green River Formation Oil Shale by Extraction and Oxidation — A Review", in: P.A. Schenck and I. Havenaar (Editors), *Advances in Organic Geochemistry*, Pergamon, Oxford, pp. 85—129 (1969).
50. M. Djuricic, R.C. Murphy, D. Vitorovic and K. Biemann, "Organic Acids Obtained by Alkaline Permanganate Oxidation of Kerogen from Green River (Colorado) Shale", *Geochim. Cosmochim. Acta*, 35, 1201—1207 (1971).
51. W.E. Robinson, J.J. Cummins and K.E. Stanfield, "Constitution of Organic Acids Prepared from Colorado Oil Shale Based Upon Their n-Butyl Esters", *Ind. Eng. Chem.*, 48, 1134—1138 (1956).
52. W.E. Robinson and D.L. Lawlor, "Constitution of Hydrocarbon-like Materials Derived from Kerogen Oxidation Products", *Fuel*, 40, 375—388 (1961).
53. A.B. Hubbard and J.I. Fester, "Hydrogenolysis of Colorado Oil-Shale Kerogen, *Chem. Eng. Data Ser.*, 3, 147—152 (1958).
54. J.I. Fester and W.E. Robinson, "Oxygen Functional Groups in Green River Oil-Shale Kerogen and Trona Acids", in: R.F. Gould (Editor), *Coal Science*, Am. Chem. Soc., Washington, D.C., pp. 22—31 (1966).
55. F.R. McDonald and G.L. Cook, "A Method of Obtaining the Ultraviolet and Visible Spectra of Insoluble Material — Use of Low-Molecular-Weight Polyethylene as a Matrix Material", *U.S. Bur. Mines Rep. Invest.*, 6439, 10 pp. (1964).
56. W.H. Bradley, "Green River Oil Shale — Concept of Origin Extended", *Geol. Soc. Am. Bull.*, 81, 985—1000 (1970).
57. G. Eglinton, "Hydrocarbons and Fatty Acids in Living Organisms and Recent and Ancient Sediments", in: P.A. Schenck and I. Havenaar (Editors), *Advances in Organic Geochemistry*, Pergamon, Oxford, 1—24 (1969).
58. B. Balough, D.M. Wilson and A.L. Burlingame, "Carbon-13 NMR Study of the Stereochemistry of Steranes from Oil Shale of the Green River Formation (Eocene)", *Nature*, 233, 261—263 (1971).

Chapter 5

MINERALOGY OF OIL SHALE

WAYNE C. SHANKS, WILLIAM E. SEYFRIED, W. CRAIG MEYER and
THOMAS J. O'NEIL[1]

Introduction

Oil shales from different localities show large compositional variation, but are generally fine-grained, indurated sedimentary rocks containing a high-molecular-weight mineraloid of indefinite composition, predominantly derived from algae, spores, or pollen [1]. Classifications of oil shales and canneloid deposits have been based on a number of criteria, including organic composition, mineralogy, specific gravity, and age [1,4,5]. None of the proposed schemes has been totally accepted, however, perhaps because they are too complex, or lack indication of definitive genetic relationships. A convenient and meaningful geologic classification could be based on the environments of deposition (i.e., deltaic, swamp, estuarine, or coastal marine basin), but as yet there is insufficient data on field relationships, mineralogy, and sedimentary petrology for most oil-shale deposits. Detailed environmental interpretation of facies relationships within oil-shale deposits would contribute greatly to the knowledge of oil-shale genesis, as well as serve as a base for the much needed genetic classification.

A reasonable descriptive criterion which can be used to differentiate oil shales from coals is their abundant ($> 33\%$) mineral content [2,3]. There are, however, a number of sedimentary deposits of oil-producing potential which have an inorganic content between coal and oil shale. The nomenclature pertaining to these deposits (e.g., tasmanites, torbanites, boghead coals) has been best described as chaotic [4]. In order to avoid semantic problems arising from such historical and parochial terminology, the term oil shale will be used in this chapter in a generalized sense, referring to all sedimentary rocks capable of yielding economic quantities of oil by retorting.

General characteristics of oil shales

It appears that there are three general depositional frameworks in which oil shales form: shallow seas on continental platforms and shelves (Miocene shales of California), small lakes, bogs, and lagoons associated with coal-

[1] University of Southern California, Department of Geological Sciences, Contribution No. 350.

TABLE 5-I

Mineralogy of some oil shales (After Himus, 1951 [6])

Shale	Ash (%)	Mineral matter (%)	Amorphous silica and quartz (%)	Feld-spar (%)	Clay minerals (%)	Gypsum (CaSO$_4$·2H$_2$O) (%)	Pyrite (FeS$_2$) (%)	Calcite (CaCO$_3$) (%)	Magnesite[1] (MgCO$_3$) (%)	Siderite (FeCO$_3$) (%)
Kukersite, Estonia	36.3	47.87	9.0	6.75	13.9	1.1	4.25	56.1	—	—
Kohat, N.W.F.P. India	68.7	88.83	12.40	2.47	40.68	0.49	trace	22.68	8.34	3.76
Broxburn, Main	67.4	76.15	16.55	11.30	45.85	0.43	1.76	2.91	2.63	11.24
Kimmeridge, Dorset	37.8	40.89	38.97	5.74	20.68	8.56	4.64	3.51	—	—
Ermelo, Transvaal	44.9	47.85	50.13	5.14	29.45	0.24	2.03	1.73	0.24	—
Tasmanite, Tasmania	79.2	82.05	56.3	6.0	23.75	1.45	1.64	—	—	—
Amherst, Burma	43.9	46.78	34.33	5.63	27.45	5.49	0.19	trace	—	—
Boghead, Autun	65.0	79.2	32.4	n.d.	17.4	1.1	0.7	37.3	—	—
Pumpherston I	75.0	83.45	24.6	n.d.	22.9	trace	2.35	5.8	4.15	2.15
Pumpherston II	66.3	86.77	19.3	n.d.	22.9	0.3	1.35	26.7	12.1	5.1
Middle Dunnet	77.6	84.76	26.5	n.d.	54.65	0.3	0.55	4.25	3.65	—
Newnes, N.S.W.	20.1	20.79	74.0	n.d.	17.9	0.3	0.4	—	3.3	—
Cypris shale, Brazil	65.9	69.50	66.33	n.d.	17.13	0.78	1.24	5.25	0.62	—
Massive shale, Brazil	72.8	48.5	n.d.	37.2	37.2	0.4	1.4	2.6	1.1	—

forming swamps (Kinderlick, Kazakhstan, USSR), and large terrestrial lake basins (Green River Formation, USA). The inorganic constituents of each of these deposits may be divided into detrital, biogenic, and authigenic minerals, but, with the exception of the Green River deposits, no extensive studies have been made of the mineral content of oil shales. The best available information on bulk-oil-shale mineralogy is provided by Himus [6], who used the metal-oxide analysis of oil-shale ash to calculate proximate mineral content (Table 5-I). From the available information, it is possible to draw only the most general conclusions about the mineralogy of most oil-shale deposits.

The detrital material in oil shales is composed principally of quartz, feldspars, certain clay minerals, and volcanic debris (the percentage of each constituent in the oil shale being a function of the source area, mode of transport, and distance transported). Biogenic minerals are primarily amorphous silica and calcium carbonate, but are not generally abundant. Authigenic minerals are pyrite and other metal sulfides, carbonates (calcite, dolomite, siderite), chert, phosphates, and saline minerals such as trona, dawsonite, and halite. Authigenic minerals are of importance because they may provide information concerning redox conditions during or soon after sedimentation, nature of the original solution, and climatic conditions. Organic matter and authigenic metal sulfides ubiquitously present in oil shales suggest formation in a reducing (low Eh) environment, which, considering the oxidizing nature of the oceans and atmosphere, indicates deposition in areas of limited water circulation. The fine grain size (argillaceous to sandy argillaceous) of detrital sediments included in oil shale is indicative of low-energy environments and supports this interpretation.

Sulfide for pyrite and metal sulfide precipitation is produced by oxidation of organic matter causing concomitant reduction of sulfate in the aqueous solution:

$$2CH_2O + SO_4^{2-} = H_2S + 2HCO_3^- \tag{5-1}$$

$$Fe^{2+} + H_2S + S^0 = FeS_2 + 2H^+ \tag{5-2}$$

Authigenic carbonates and saline minerals are formed by evaporative concentration of the original solution and, when present, indicate an arid climate. Limestones may also form in response to an increase in dissolved carbonate concentration brought about by bacterial degradation of organic matter:

$$2CH_2O + SO_4^{2-} = H_2S + 2HCO_3^- \tag{5-3}$$

or:

$$2CH_2O + H_2O = CH_4 + HCO_3^- + H^+ \tag{5-4}$$

$$2HCO_3^- + Ca^{2+} = CaCO_3 + H_2CO_3 \tag{5-5}$$

The association of phosphate nodules with lower-grade oil shales (e.g., Phosphoria Formation) implies that these deposits were formed in part as a result of upwelling of nutrient-rich waters onto a shoaling ocean bottom [7,8].

Non-authigenic minerals in oil shales are generally detrital and indicative of source area. Comprehensive mineralogic and petrologic analysis of the detrital fraction necessary for environmental interpretation have not been performed for most oil shales. An important exception is the Green River oil shale, which, due to its importance as a domestic U.S. energy source, has been extensively examined and will be discussed in detail here.

Green River Formation

The Green River Formation of Wyoming, Utah, and Colorado contains one of the world's largest known reserves of oil shale. These kerogen-containing marlstones were deposited in several different sedimentary basins (Fig. 5-1) occupied by the quiet waters of the Lower and Middle Eocene lakes Gosiute and Uinta. At their maximum extent these lakes occupied 16,000 and 20,000 sq miles, respectively. Oil-shale-bearing rocks of the Green River Formation presently cover an area of about 16,500 sq miles [11] (Fig. 5-1).

The Green River Formation was primarily deposited as two lenticular

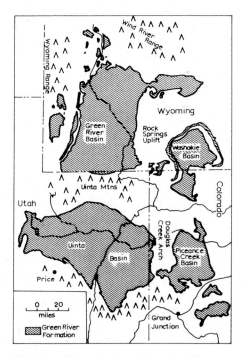

Fig. 5-1. Map of the Colorado—Wyoming—Utah area. Shows present outcrop extent (shaded) and depositional basins of the Green River Formation.

bodies separated by the Uinta uplift, consisting of fine-grained, generally finely laminated, lacustrine sediments. Sediments were deposited during an extended period of progressive downwarping, allowing these areas to remain as negative features for approximately four million years (Early to Middle Eocene). The lakes passed through several episodes of varying water depth and chemistry, but their history can be generalized into three major changes in size.

Stage one marks an initial period during which the large fresh-water lakes were depositing varved, organic-rich sediments. After approximately 1 million years this first stage was terminated by the onset of arid climatic conditions which resulted in a significant volume decrease. The Rock Springs Uplift and Douglas Creek Arch (Fig. 5-1) existed as positive structural features throughout much of Green River time. During the second stage, these features became emergent, causing the ancestral lakes to be dissected into a number of small desiccating basins (Washakie, Green River, Uinta, and Piceance Creek) in which strikingly different saline mineralogies are developed. Trona deposits are of primary importance in the Green River Basin, nahcolite is predominant in the Piceance Creek and Uinta Basins, whereas dawsonite is known exclusively from the Piceance Creek Basin (Fig. 5-1). A return to more humid conditions characterized the third stage during which the lake system reached its maximum extent and deposited typical organic-rich, deep-water shales and marlstones. Eventually, ash beds from the Yellowstone—Absaroka volcanic province to the north and detrital material supplied by continuous stream deposition, led to the infilling of these basins.

Lithology

In order to describe the principal lithologies and the occurrence of important oil shale and saline rocks, it is necessary to briefly consider stratigraphic relationships of the Green River Formation in its various basins (Fig. 5-2). Much of the following discussion is from McDonald [12] who provided a more detailed and comprehensive treatment.

During the Lower Eocene, deposition of fluvial sandstones, siltstones, and shales in the southwestern Uinta Basin formed the Colton Formation, a lateral extension of the more centrally located Wasatch Formation. In the Western Uinta Basin, the Colton grades transitionally into the Flagstaff Limestone. Throughout the Green River, Uinta, Piceance Creek, and Washakie Basins, the upper Colton—Wasatch deposits are complexly intertongued with the Green River Formation. In all basins, the Wasatch is essentially a redbed unit deposited in alluvial environments.

The end of the Lower Eocene marked the onset of Green River deposition initiated by restriction of outlets to the sea [13]. This resulted in deposition of a series of lacustrine, shoreline, and evaporative rocks in response to fluctuating lake levels. Green River Formation lithology is complex and variable

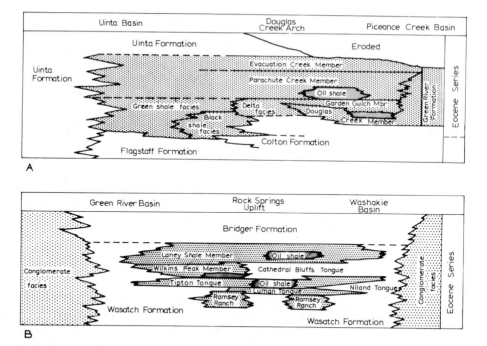

Fig. 5-2. Schematic west—east stratigraphic section through deposits of the Green River Formation (shaded). (After Van West, 1972, [10].)

(Fig. 5-3), but generally consists of lacustrine shales and varved dolomitic marlstones (especially in rich oil shale zones).

The major stratigraphic units deposited in Lake Uinta (Fig. 5-2A) are as follows:

Black shale facies. Black shale facies occurs only in the Uinta Basin where it conformably overlies the Flagstaff Limestone. It consists of locally carbonaceous, dolomitic or calcareous, pyritic shales, which may be interbedded with thin sandstones or carbonaceous limestones.

Douglas Creek Member and Delta facies. The Douglas Creek Member occurs throughout the Uinta Basin, crossing the Douglas Creek Arch into the Piceance Creek Basin. The predominant lithology is nearshore or shallow-water lacustrine sandstones, siltstones and shales, and oolitic, algal and ostracodal limestones [12]. The Delta facies occurs in the southern and southwestern Uinta Basin, correlating with the Douglas Creek Member and indicating a prominent southern source of detrital sediments.

Garden Gulch Member. Garden Gulch Member occurs mainly in the Piceance Creek Basin, pinching out to the west in the Uinta Basin. It consists primarily of shales, thinly interbedded with marlstones, and shallow lacustrine beds of similar lithology to those in the Douglas Creek Member.

Parachute Creek and Evacuation Creek Members. Parachute Creek and

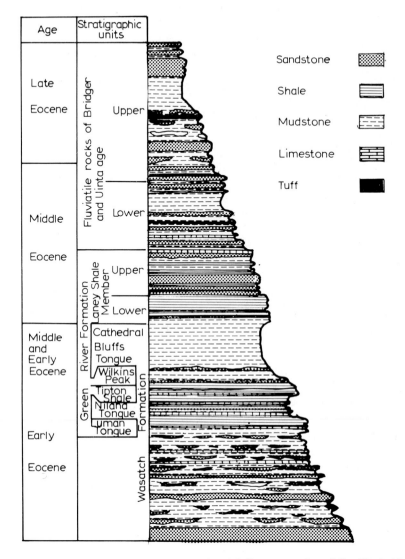

Fig. 5-3. Composite columnar section of Eocene rocks of the Washakie Basin, showing lithologic variations in the Green River Formation. (After Roehler, 1970, [14].)

Evacuation Creek Members are persistent throughout both the Uinta and Piceance Creek Basins, and clearly represent the maximum extent of Lake Uinta. The lower part of the Parachute Creek Member, however, contains extensive deposits of bedded evaporites containing nahcolite, dawsonite, and halite. The Upper Parachute Creek and much of the Evacuation Creek members reflect a return to deep-water, low-energy, lacustrine environments. The Parachute Creek Member is mainly a dolomitic marlstone containing some of the largest oil shale concentrations (Fig. 5-2A). The Evacuation Creek Member, however, is composed of sandstone, siltstone, shale, and marlstone beds of variable thickness, reflecting an environment transitional from lacustrine to fluvial.

The major stratigraphic units deposited in Lake Gosuite are as follows:

Ramsey Ranch Member. Deposition of the sediments of Ramsey Ranch Member, the oldest member of the Green River Formation in Wyoming, was restricted to topographic lows in the Washakie Basin, Great Divide Basin, and Rock Springs Uplift (Fig. 5-1). It is composed of shales deposited in shallow to moderate depths, sandstones, and coquinal limestones.

Luman Tongue and Tipton Tongue. The Luman Tongue was deposited predominantly in the Washakie Basin as shallow-water, low-energy, lacustrine mudstones, siltstones, sandstones, and low-grade oil shales. The lithology of Tipton Tongue varies from shale and marlstone in the Washakie Basin to algal, oolitic, and ostracodal marls interbedded with sandstone and shale beds in the Green River Basin. These deposits also contain numerous thin tuff beds and some economically significant oil shales (Fig. 5-2).

Wilkins Peak Member. Dolomitic mudstones and marls of this member, deposited in small, closed, evaporite basins, are restricted to the southern portions of the Green River Basin. Thick-bedded evaporites consisting principally of trona, halite, shortite, and some rich oil shales are also included in these deposits.

Laney Shale Member. This uppermost unit of the Green River Formation represents the maximum extent of Lake Gosiute. The Laney Shale contains a variety of normal lacustrine deep-water sediments including marlstones, shales, muddy sandstones, some low-grade oil shales, and numerous tuff beds.

The upper portions of the Green River Formation show a marked increase in the amount of tuffaceous material and contain heavy mineral suites indicative of volcanic activity [14]. It has been proposed [13] that the increased volcanic influx contributed greatly to the demise of lakes Gosiute and Uinta. The end of the period represented by the Green River Formation is marked by the onset of fluviatile sedimentation, which formed the overlying Middle and Upper Eocene Bridger and Uinta formations.

Authigenic minerals

The early work of Bradley [9,15] established that the bulk of the minerals in the Green River Formation are non-detrital in origin.[1] To date, over 70 authigenic minerals, including 12 previously undescribed (Table 5-II), have been identified within these rocks [16].

Unfortunately, most discussions concerning authigenic minerals have been

---

[1] The role of compaction fluids in the formation of authigenic minerals should be thoroughly investigated (editorial comment).

TABLE 5-II

New minerals discovered in Green River Formation

Name of mineral	Reference
Neighborite	Chao et al., 1961, [17]
Shortite	Fahey, 1939, [18]
Loughlinite	Fahey, 1947, [19]
	Fahey et al., 1960, [20]
Bradleyite	Fahey, 1941, [21]
Wegscheiderite	Fahey and Yorks, 1963, [22]
Reedmergnerite	Milton et al., 1954, [23]
Eitelite	Milton et al., 1954, [23]
Garrelsite	Milton et al., 1955, [24]
McKelveyite	Milton et al., 1965, [25]
Norsethite	Mrose et al., 1961, [26]
Ewaldite	Donnay and Preston, 1968—1969, [27]
Ferroan northupite	Milton and Meyrowitz, 1964, [28]

largely descriptive or have been concerned with the genesis of specific mineral assemblages [29,30]. It has, therefore, been somewhat difficult for the
casual reader to glean much information concerning the occurrence of authigenic minerals in a regional framework.

Saline minerals

The minerals listed in Table 5-III are those which probably formed without direct interaction with, or alteration of, pre-existing silicates. Most of
these minerals formed by precipitation from brine pools or interstitial brines
[31] and are, therefore, primarily associated with the Wilkins Peak Member
in Wyoming and the Parachute Creek Member of Utah and Colorado. The
common carbonate minerals of this group are predominant throughout the
Green River Formation. Dolomite and calcite are the most abundant, although
calcite is reported to be less important than dolomite in the Piceance Creek
Basin [32]. Microprobe analyses of samples from the Mahogany Ledge of
the Parachute Creek Member, however, produced anomalously high weight
percent ratio of calcium to magnesium (Ca/Mg = 4.0), indicating that calcite
may be locally more abundant with respect to dolomite than previously
reported.

The saline minerals of the Green River Formation have been extensively
studied, not only because of scientific interest in the rare mineral assemblages,
but also because of the economic potential of the evaporites. Dawsonite, a
potential aluminum ore, and the primary ores of soda ash (Na_2CO_3), especially nahcolite and trona, are of principal economic interest.

The only major accumulations of trona in the Green River Formation

TABLE 5-III

Saline minerals in Green River Formation (modified after Milton, 1971, [16])

Name of mineral	Formula	Abundance
Halides		
Halite	$NaCl$	locally abundant
Fluorite	CaF_2	rare
Cryolite	Na_3AlF_6	rare
Neighborite	$NaMgF_3$	rare
Carbonates		
Calcite	$CaCO_3$	ubiquitous
Dolomite	$CaMg(CO_3)_2$	ubiquitous
Shortite	$Na_2Ca_2(CO_3)_3$	widespread
Barytocalcite	$BaCa(CO_3)_2$	widespread
Nahcolite	$NaHCO_3$	locally abundant
Trona	$Na_2CO_3 \cdot NaHCO_3 \cdot 2H_2O$	locally abundant
Dawsonite	$NaAl(CO_3)(OH)_2$	locally abundant
Pirssonite	$Na_2Ca(CO_3)_2 \cdot 2H_2O$	locally abundant
Gaylussite	$Na_2Ca(CO_3)_2 \cdot H_2O$	locally abundant
Ankerite	$(Mg_{0.85}Fe_{0.15}Ca)(CO_3)_2$	locally abundant
Wegscheiderite	$Na_2CO_3 \cdot 3NaHCO_3$	rare
Thermonatrite	$Na_2CO_3 \cdot H_2O$	rare
Natron	$Na_2CO_3 \cdot 10H_2O$	rare
Magnesite	$MgCO_3$	rare
Strontianite	$SrCO_3$	rare
Witherite	$BaCO_3$	rare
Siderite	$FeCO_3$	rare
Aragonite	$CaCO_3$	rare
Norsethite	$MgBa(CO_3)_2$	rare
Burbankite	$Na_2(Ca, Sr, Ba, Ce)_4(CO_3)_5$	rare
Eitelite	$Na_2Mg(CO_3)_2$	very rare
McKelveyite	$(Na_2Ca_1)(Ba_4REE_{1.7}U_{0.3})(CO_3)_9$	very rare
Ewaldite	$(Na_2Ca_1)(Ba_4REE_{1.7}U_{0.3})(CO_3)_9$	very rare
Compound carbonates		
Northupite	$Na_2Mg(CO_3)_2 \cdot NaCl$	locally abundant
Bradleyite	$MgNa_3CO_3PO_4$	rare
Ferroan northupite	$Na_2(Mg_1Fe)(CO_3)_2 \cdot NaCl$	rare
Tychite	$Na_2Mg(CO_3)_2 \cdot Na_2SO_4$	very rare
Burkeite	$Na_2CO_3 \cdot 2Na_2SO_4$	very rare
Sulfates		
Barite	$BaSO_4$	rare
Celestite	$SrSO_4$	rare
Gypsum	$CaSO_4 \cdot 2H_2O$	rare
Siderotil	$FeSO_4 \cdot 4H_2O$	rare
Phosphates		
Collophanite	$Ca_{10}(PO_4)_6CO_3 \cdot H_2O$	widespread
Fluorapatite	$Ca_{10}(PO_4)_6F_2$	rare

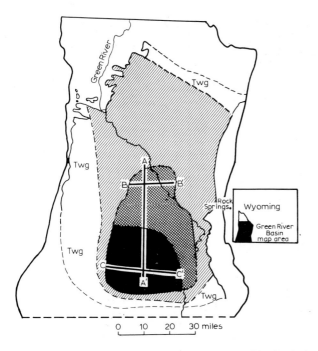

Fig. 5-4. Map of the Wilkins Peak Member (*Twg*) of the Green River Formation in the Green River Basin. Shows saline zone (hachured), bedded trona zona (cross-hachured), bedded halite (shaded), and cross-section lines for Fig. 5-5. (Modified after Culbertson, 1971, [33].)

occur in the Green River Basin where trona and trona—halite beds up to 37 ft in thickness can be traced throughout much of the saline facies in the lowermost Wilkins Peak Member [30,33]. In this basin, at least 42 trona beds underly an area of about 13,000 sq miles (Fig. 5-4) at depths ranging from 400 to 3,500 ft. The 25 most important beds (Fig. 5-5) may contain as much as 100 billion tons of trona and trona—halite [33].

Bedded trona occurs primarily in the south—central portion of the Green River Basin (Fig. 5-4). The occurrence of halite in the trona beds is restricted, being limited to the lower 17 beds. Shortite occurs as disseminated crystals throughout most of the basin, whereas other saline minerals (northupite, gaylusite, pirssonite, nahcolite, and wegscheiderite) are important locally and are generally, but not exclusively, in association with trona beds [30,34,33].

Materials interbedded with saline beds include oil shale, marlstone, detrital sandstones, and numerous thin tuff beds. Culbertson [33] noted that most trona beds are directly underlain by oil shales. Eugster and Surdam [35] proposed that such units form during flooding in a playa lake environment. Carbon dioxide formed by decay of organic matter in underlying muds could, upon evaporation of the playa lake, account for precipitation of car-

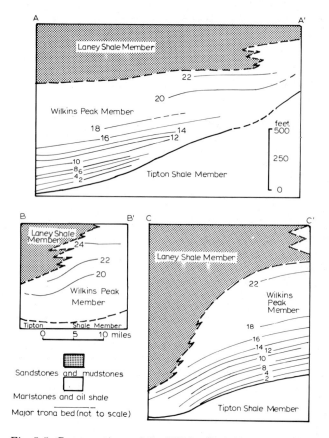

Fig. 5-5. Cross sections of the Wilkins Peak Member in the Green River Basin showing vertical extent of the major trona beds. Location of cross sections in Fig. 5-4. (Modified after Culbertson, 1971, [33].) Numbers in diagrams denote some major trona beds.

bonate minerals such as trona, nahcolite, and dawsonite:

$$2CH_2O + Na^+ + H_2O = NaHCO_3 + CH_4(g) + H^+ \qquad (5\text{-}6)$$
$$\text{nahcolite}$$

Important dawsonite and nahcolite deposits are concentrated in the saline zones of the lower Parachute Creek Member of the Piceance Creek Basin of Colorado (Fig. 5-6). Nahcolite deposits of unknown areal extent are also known to occur in the Uinta Basin of Utah [37].

Three bedded nahcolite units from 1 to 9 ft in thickness occur in the lowermost Parachute Creek Member and can be traced over an area of 180 sq miles. Nahcolite also occurs in two lensoid halite-bearing zones (Fig. 5-6) where these two minerals are cyclically interbedded and associated with wegscheiderite, shortite, northupite, searlesite, and trona [38]. Additional

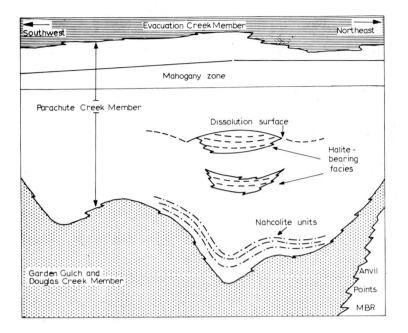

Fig. 5-6. Cross section through the depositional center of the evaporite deposits of the Green River Formation in the Piceance Creek Basin. (After Dyni et al., 1970, [36].)

nahcolite occurs as vug-fillings, disseminated crystals and thin layers in inter-bedded marlstones and oil shales.

The saline zone of the Parachute Creek Member contains some of the world's richest oil shales intercalated with the evaporites. The X-ray analysis of oil shales from the Mahogany Zone (Fig. 5-6) within this member indicates that dolomite, calcite, and quartz are predominant minerals, whereas con-stituents of minor importance are pyrite, feldspar, analcite, smectite[1], and illite [39]. Dawsonite is significantly concentrated in these oil shales and occurs primarily in a fine-grained disseminated form. The thickness of dawsonite-bearing beds increases toward the basin depocenter (Fig. 5-7), as do the nahcolite-rich beds described previously [11,36]. Dawsonite-rich oil shales may contain 25% of this mineral and reach a thickness of over 800 ft.

Silicates

The Green River Formation contains abundant and widely distributed thin (0.5—3 cm) beds of originally rhyolitic to rhyodacitic volcanic ash [40], especially in the upper portions of the section. The tuff beds are generally

---

[1] Smectite is used throughout this paper for any sheet-silicate which expands to 17 Å in glycol, and when heat treated at 550°C for 1 hour will contract to 9—10 Å.

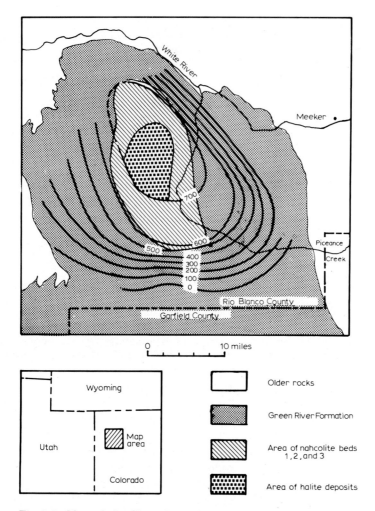

Fig. 5-7. Map of the Green River Formation in the northern part of the Piceance Creek Basin showing the distribution of dawsonite, nahcolite, and halite. Isopachs, in feet, of dawsonite-bearing oil shale. (After Dyni et al., 1970, [36].)

highly reactive, and it is believed that many of the authigenic silicates (Table 5-IV) were formed as a direct or indirect result of tuff alteration. For example, alteration of glass shards within the tuffs would have provided an abundant supply of dissolved silica which, combined with sodium bicarbonate enriched brines, could readily produce minerals such as reedmergnerite or searlesite [29]. Alternatively, tuffaceous glass may have undergone in situ devitrification to form the common authigenic silicates, i.e., quartz, albite, and orthoclase [16].

Recently, several studies have been made of authigenic minerals within

TABLE 5-IV

Authigenic silicates in Green River Formation (modified after Milton, 1971, [16])

Name of mineral	Formula	Abundance
Clay minerals		
Kaolinite	$H_4 Al_2 Si_2 O_9$	locally abundant
Stevensite	$(Al_{0.06} Fe_{0.04} Mg_{2.81} Li_{0.04})$ $(Si_{3.98} Al_{0.02})O_{10}(OH)_2 Na_{0.04}$	locally abundant
Loughlinite	$H_{16} Na_2 Mg_3 Si_6 O_{24}$	locally abundant
Sepiolite	$H_4 Mg_2 Si_3 O_{10}$	rare
Talc	$Mg_3(OH)_2 Si_4 O_{10}$	rare
Zeolites		
Analcite	$NaAlSi_2 O_6 \cdot H_2 O$	widespread
Natrolite	$Na_2 Al_2 Si_3 O_{10} \cdot 2 H_2 O$	rare
Harmotome-wellsite	$(Ba, Ca, K_2)Al_2 Si_6 O_{10} \cdot 6 H_2 O$	rare
Clinoptilolite- Mordenite	$(Ca, Na_2, K_2)(AlSi_5 O_{12}) \cdot 6 H_2 O$	rare
Borosilicates		
Searlesite	$NaBSi_2 O_6 \cdot H_2 O$	locally abundant
Garrelsite	$(Ba, Ca, Mg)B_2 SiO_6(OH)_3$	rare
Leucosphenite	$CaBaNa_3 BTi_3 Si_9 O_{29}$	rare
Reedmergnerite	$NaBSi_3 O_8$	rare
Other silicates		
Quartz	SiO_2	ubiquitous
Orthoclase	$KAlSi_3 O_8$	widespread
Albite	$NaAlSi_3 O_8$	widespread
Acmite	$NaFeSi_2 O_6$	rare
Riebeckite	$Na(FeMg)_3 Fe_2(OH, F)(Si_4 O_{11})_2$	rare
Labuntsovite	$(K, Ba, Na, Ca, Mn, Ti, Nb)$ $(Si, Al)_2(O, OH)_7 H_2 O$	rare
Vinogradovite	$Na_5 Ti_4 AlSi_6 O_{24} \cdot 3 H_2 O$	very rare
Elpidite	$H_6 Na_2 ZrSi_6 O_{18}$	very rare
Natron-catapleiite	$H_4(Na_2 Ca)ZrSi_3 O_{11}$	very rare
Biotite	$K(Fe, Mg)_3 AlSi_3 O_{10}(OH)_2$	very rare
Hydrobiotite	$(K, H_2 O)(Mg, Fe, Mn)_3 AlSi_3 O_{10}$ $(OH, H_2 O)_2$	very rare

tuff beds [41,42,43,44]. Parker and Surdam [42] summarized the distribution of authigenic silicates in tuffs of the Washakie Basin (Fig. 5-8). The time-stratigraphic zonation of alteration types provides a good indication of the response of alteration mineralogy to environmental conditions. Additional work on this aspect will help realize the economic potential of zeolites in these deposits as well as contribute greatly to the knowledge of the geochemistry of volcanic rock alteration.

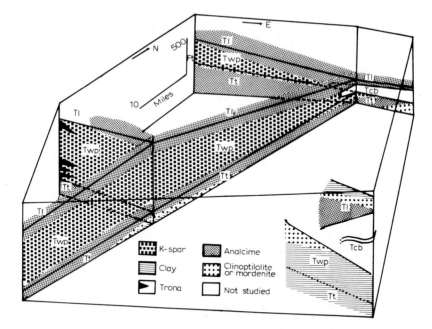

Fig. 5-8. Three-dimensional composite section showing distribution of authigenic alumino-silicate minerals in the tuffaceous rocks of the Green River Formation in Green River and Washakie basins. *Tl* = Laney Shale Member; *Twp* = Wilkins Peak Member; *Tt* = Tipton Shale Member; *Tcb* = Cathedral Bluffs Member of the Wasatch Formation. (After Parker and Surdam, 1971, [42].)

Clay mineralogy

Few studies have been published on the clay mineralogy of oil shales; those that exist deal exclusively with the Green River Formation [45,46]. Clay minerals contained in this formation were deposited in water ranging from fresh to saline. These varied environments may have affected the clays through diagenetic adjustments, but many appear to be clearly detrital and largely unaltered.

Interpretation of the clay mineralogy of the Green River Formation will be based on those sediments located in the Green River Basin, because the published analyses of these sediments provide the only sufficient data. A comprehensive paper by Tank [46] provides the bulk of the data utilized here and should be consulted for more detailed information.

During the first stage in the evolution of Lake Gosiute, the Tipton Shale Member was deposited under fresh-water conditions. In the area of the Green River Basin it is composed of approximately 175 ft of carbonaceous and tuffaceous oil shales which are commonly varved. Illite, smectite, and chlorite, as well as a small amount of loughlinite, are found throughout this

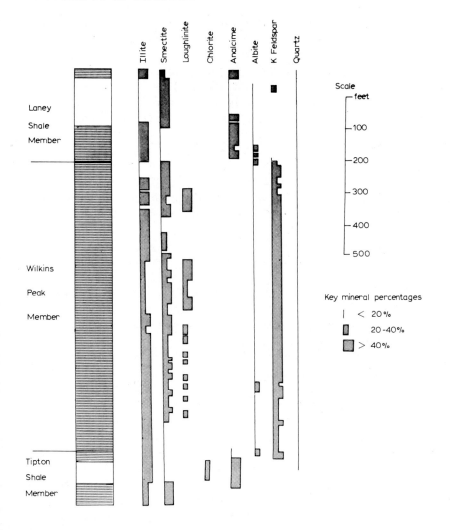

Fig. 5-9. Relative abundances of clay minerals and silicates from the Green River Formation in the Green River Basin. (After Tank, 1972, [46].)

member (Fig. 5-9). Illite and smectite are generally concentrated in the basal oil shales, whereas an illite—chlorite suite characterizes the sands in the middle of the member. Illite is the dominant clay mineral and is found throughout the entire member, whereas mixed-layered clays and amorphous material are present in subordinate amounts.

The Wilkins Peak Member contains abundant saline minerals, marking the evaporative stage in the history of Gosuite Lake. The clay minerals composing this unit are loughlinite, sepiolite, illite, smectite, and mixed-layered clays in conjunction with small amounts of chlorite and talc [13]. The X-ray analysis indicates that the smectite minerals vary considerably; however, a consistent and fairly thick bed of stevensite (Table 5-IV) has been reported within this member [47].

The Laney Shale Member represents the uppermost and final fresh-water phase, containing brown to buff, calcareous to dolomitic mudstones and shales. The clay mineralogy consists mainly of illite and smectite. Illite is the dominant clay mineral, as it is in the entire basin, and occurs alone as well as randomly interstratified with smectite.

Quantitative analysis of these clay minerals, which requires tedious pre-treatment for removal of organic matter [48], is limited by problems arising from varying orientation, crystallinity, size, and shape of mineral grains [49]. Tank [46], however, has derived the relative composition of Green River clays by standardizing techniques and has advanced several arguments in favor of their in situ origin:

(1) There is unequivocal evidence that over 50 authigenic non-clay miner-als occur in the Green River Formation, suggesting the possibility of similar modes of development for clay minerals.

(2) The physical nature of the strata, particularly in the central basin area, suggests a low-energy environment which would preclude large-scale influx of detrital material, thereby providing a favorable physical environment for the formation of non-detrital minerals.

(3) The alkaline milieu of Gosiute Lake would have been suitable for the authigenic evolution of clay minerals.

Although these arguments can be used in support of the authigenic forma-tion of some of the clays, especially in the Wilkins Peak Member, it is too simple a generalization for the Green River Formation as a whole. Clay min-erals, because of their fine grain size, are highly mobile, passing from one geological environment to another with a minimum of transport energy. Biscaye [50] and Hathaway [51] have clearly demonstrated detrital origin of many recent clays found in low-energy environments such as deep-sea sediments and estuaries. Contrary to the conclusions of previous investiga-tors [45,46], it is likely that many of the Green River clays are detrital and, thus, may contribute information concerning clay provenance rather than the diagenetic environment.

During the Early Eocene, Gosiute Lake was adjacent to three eroding high-lands (Rock Springs Uplift, Wyoming Range, Uinta Uplift), which contained micaceous material [13] that upon transport could have been transformed into the 1 md polytype illite. In fact, Roehler [14] has established that the major detrital heavy mineral in the Wilkins Peak Member is biotite. Also, the presence of illite throughout the multiple environments of the Green River Formation suggests that its precursor was originally detrital, but underwent diagenetic modification subsequent to deposition.

Illite and mica (muscovite) are structurally very similar; both are 10 Å phases, but illite is slightly more hydrous with a layer charge less than unity and interlayer positions not being completely occupied by potassium ions. Hence, the illite has a d_{001} slightly greater than 10 Å, whereas that for muscovite is slightly less.

The neoformation of illite [52] has been shown to take place at higher pressure and temperature conditions, such as those brought about through burial diagenesis [53,54,55,56]. It has been conclusively shown by these investigators that the formation of illite passes through an illite—smectite mixed-layer phase by gradual isomorphic substitutions into the tetrahedral and octahedral layers. The increased layer charge is satisfied by the uptake of K^+ and the formation of additional illite layers. The process is very slow and depends greatly on the geothermal gradient.

Clearly, loughlinite, sepiolite, and stevensite [15,20,47] are authigenic throughout the evaporite-rich Wilkins Peak Member. Silica needed for the formation of these clays probably came from the alteration of volcanic ash beds [57,58]. Subsequent evaporation could have affected concentration of dissolved constituents (such as Na^+, Mg^{2+}, H^+, and H_4SiO_4) until the resultant solution entered the stability fields of sepiolite and loughlinite [59].

Much additional work remains to be done including detailed sampling of the Green River Formation as well as other oil shales in order to establish clay mineral trends within various lithofacies. The nature of the clay mineral-organic complex also merits further study to ascertain if the organics bond with clays and, if so, where and how. It would also be important to determine the composition of organic materials and establish relationships with the clay minerals.

Conclusions

Mineralogical investigations of oil shales are few and, as yet, do not permit detailed geologic interpretation of the environment of formation. In general, however, oil shales are low-energy sediments, usually deposited under reducing conditions in large lake basins, on continental platforms and shelves in quiet seas, and in small lakes, bogs, and lagoons associated with coal-forming swamps.

There is abundant geologic data on the Green River oil shale (marl), but these deposits are not necessarily representative of oil shales in general. Deposition of the Green River Formation occurred in the Eocene Gosiute—Uinta lake system during one of three climatic episodes. It is composed of detrital and authigenic clays, carbonates, and silicates. The second (arid) climatic episode resulted in deposition of oil-rich marls, associated with numerous exotic evaporite minerals. In addition to the obvious economic value of oil produced from these deposits, a number of the associated authigenic minerals show economic potential as sources of aluminum, soda ash, zeolites, and other industrially important materials.

Much future geological and geochemical investigation of oil shales is warranted in order to establish the details of oil-shale genesis and provide a meaningful genetic classification of oil-shale deposits. Particularly fruitful research topics appear to be: (1) detailed sedimentological (depositional environments) study; (2) descriptive petrographical and mineralogical investigations of oil shales from various parts of the world; (3) geochemistry of evaporite minerals and altered volcanic rocks; and (4) clay mineral analysis of various oil shales.

References

1. F.C. Jaffe, "Oil Shale — Pt. 2, Geology and Mineralogy of the Oil Shales of the Green River Formation, Colorado, Utah, Wyoming", *Colo. Sch. Mines, Min. Ind. Bull.*, 5 (3), 15 pp. (1962).
2. F.C. Jaffe, "Oil Shale — Pt. 1, Nomenclature, Uses, Reserves and Production", *Colo. Sch. Mines, Min. Ind. Bull.*, 5 (2), 11 pp. (1962).
3. R.E. Gustafson, "Shale Oil", in: E. Kirk and D.R. Othmer (Editors), *Encyclopedia of Chemical Technology*, *18*, 1—20 (1969).
4. R.A. Mott, "The Nomenclature of the Canneloid Materials", *Oil Shale and Cannel Coal, Inst. Pet., Lond.*, *2*, 134—149 (1951).
5. A.L. Down and G.W. Himus, "The Classification of Oil Shales and Cannel Coals", *J. Inst. Petrol.*, *26*, 329—332 (1940).
6. G.W. Himus, "Observations on the Composition of Kerogen Rocks and the Chemical Constitution of Kerogen", *Oil Shale and Cannel Coal, Inst. Pet., Lond.*, *2*, 112—135 (1951).
7. R.P. Sheldon, "Paleolatitudinal and Paleogeographic Distribution of Phosphorite", *U.S. Geol. Surv. Prof. Pap.*, *501-C*, C106—C111 (1964).
8. V.E. McKelvey, "Changes in Patterns of Energy Consumption and Their Bearing on Exploration", *Indian Miner.*, *19* (2), 134—138 (1965).
9. W.H. Bradley, "Origin and Microfossils of the Oil Shale of the Green River Formation of Colorado and Utah", *U.S. Geol. Surv. Prof. Pap.*, *168*, 58 pp. (1931).
10. F.P. Van West, "Green River Oil Shale", in: *Geologic Atlas of the Rocky Mountain Region*, Denver, Colo., Rocky Mtn. Assoc. Geol., pp. 287—289 (1972).
11. J.W. Smith and C. Milton, "Dawsonite in the Green River Formation of Colorado", *Econ. Geol.*, *61* (6), 1029—1042 (1966).
12. R.E. McDonald, "Eocene and Paleocene Rocks of the Southern and Central Basins", in: *Geologic Atlas of the Rocky Mountain Region*, Denver, Colo., Rocky Mtn. Assoc. Geol., pp. 243—256 (1972).
13. W.H. Bradley, "Geology of Green River Formation and Associated Eocene Rocks in Southwestern Wyoming and Adjacent Parts of Colorado and Utah", *U.S. Geol. Surv. Prof. Pap.*, *496-A*, 86 pp. (1964).
14. H.W. Roehler, "Nonopaque Heavy Minerals from Sandstone of Eocene Age in the Washakie Basin, Wyoming", in: *Geological Survey Research 1970, U.S. Geol. Surv. Prof. Pap.*, *700-D*, D181—D187 (1970).
15. W.H. Bradley, "The Varves and Climate of the Green River Epoch", *U.S. Geol. Surv. Prof. Pap.*, *158-E*, 87 pp. (1929).
16. C. Milton, "Authigenic Minerals of the Green River Formation", *Wyo. Univ. Contrib. Geol.*, *10* (1), 57—63 (1971).
17. E.C.T. Chao, H.T. Evans Jr., B.J. Skinner and C. Milton, "Neighborite, $NaMgF_3$, A New Mineral from the Green River Formation, South Ouray, Utah", *Am. Mineral.*, *46* (3—4), 379—393 (1961).

18. J.J. Fahey, "Shortite, A New Carbonate of Sodium and Calcium", *Am. Mineral., 24* (8), 514—518 (1939).
19. J.J. Fahey, "Loughlinite, A New Hydrous Magnesium Silicate", *Bull. Geol. Soc. Am., 58* (12), 1178—1179 (1947).
20. J.J. Fahey, M. Ross and J.M. Axelrod, "Loughlinite, A New Hydrous Sodium Magnesium Silicate", *Am. Mineral., 45* (3—4), 270—291 (1960).
21. J.J. Fahey, "Bradleyite, A New Mineral, Sodium Phosphate-Magnesium Carbonate (with X-ray Analysis by George Tunnell)", *Am. Mineral., 26* (11), 646—650 (1941).
22. J.J. Fahey and K.P. Yorks, "Wegscheiderite ($Na_2CO_3 \cdot 3NaHCO_3$), A New Saline Mineral from the Green River Formation, Wyoming", *Am. Mineral., 48* (3—4), 400—403 (1963).
23. C. Milton, J.M. Axelrod and F.S. Grimaldi, "New Minerals Reedmergnerite ($NaO \cdot B_2O_3 \cdot 6SiO_2$) and Eitelite ($Na_2O \cdot MgO . 2CO_2$) Associated with Leucosphenite, Shortite, Searlesite, and Crocidolite in the Green River Formation, Utah", *Bull. Geol. Soc. Am., 65* (2), 1286 (1954).
24. C. Milton, J.M. Axelrod and F.S. Grimaldi, "New Mineral Garrelsite ($Ba_{0.65}Ca_{0.29}$-$Mg_{0.06})_4H_6Si_2B_6O_{20}$ from the Green River Formation, Utah", *Bull. Geol. Soc. Am., 66* (12), 1597 (1955).
25. C. Milton, B. Ingram, J.R. Clarke and E.J. Dwornik, "McKelveyite, A New Hydrous Sodium Barium Rare-Earth Uranium Carbonate Mineral from the Green River Formation, Wyoming", *Am. Mineral., 50* (5—6), 573—612 (1965).
26. M.E. Mrose, E.C.T. Chao, J.J. Fahey and C. Milton, "Norsethite, $BaMg(CO_3)_2$, A New Mineral from the Green River Formation, Wyoming", *Am. Mineral., 46* (3—4), 420—429 (1961).
27. G. Donnay and H. Preston, "Progress Report on Ewaldite", *Annual Report of the Director, Geophysical Laboratory — Carnegie Institution Year Book, 68*, 288—290 (1968—1969).
28. C. Milton and R. Meyrowitz, "Ferroan Northupite in the Green River Formation of Wyoming", in: *Geological Survey Research 1964 — U.S. Geol. Surv. Prof. Pap., 501-B*, B66—B68 (1964).
29. C. Milton and H.P. Eugster, "Mineral Assemblages of the Green River Formation, in: P.H. Abelson (Editor), *Researches in Geochemistry*, I, Wiley, New York, N.Y., pp. 118—150 (1959).
30. W.H. Bradley and H.P. Eugster, "Geochemistry and Paleolimnology of the Trona Deposits and Associated Authigenic Minerals of the Green River Formation", *U.S. Geol. Surv. Prof. Pap., 496-B*, 71 pp. (1969).
31. C.A. Wolfbauer, "Criteria for Recognizing Paleoenvironments in a Playa-Lake Complex: The Green River Formation of Wyoming", *Wyo. Geol. Assoc. Guideb., 25*, 87—91 (1973).
32. J.W. Smith, L.G. Trudell and K.E. Stanfield, "Characteristics of Green River Formation Oil Shales at Bureau of Mines Wyoming Corehole No. 1", *U.S. Bur. Mines Rep. Invest., 7172*, 92 pp. (1968).
33. W.C. Culbertson, "Stratigraphy of the Trona Deposits in the Green River Formation, Southwest Wyoming", *Wyo. Univ. Contrib. Geol., 10* (1), 15—23 (1971).
34. J.J. Fahey, "Saline Minerals of the Green River Formation, with a Section on X-ray Powder Data for Saline Minerals of the Green River Formation, by M.R. Mrose", *U.S. Geol. Surv. Prof. Pap., 405*, 50 pp. (1962).
35. H.P. Eugster and R.C. Surdam, "Depositional Environment of the Green River Formation of Wyoming: A Preliminary Report", *Geol. Soc. Am. Bull., 84*, 1115—1120 (1973).
36. J.R. Dyni, R.J. Hite and O.B. Raup, "Lacustrine Deposits of Bromine-Bearing Halite, Green River Formation, Northwestern Colorado, in: *Symposium on Salt, 3rd, Northern Ohio Geol. Soc.*, Cleveland, Ohio, pp. 166—180 (1970).

37. R.J. Hite, "Salines", in: *Mineral and Water Resources of Utah, Utah Geol. Mineral. Surv. Bull.*, *73*, 206—215 (1964).

38. R.J. Hite and J.R. Dyni, in: *Symposium on Oil Shale, 4th, Q. Colo. Sch. Mines.*, *62* (3), 25—38 (1967).

39. W.C. Meyer and T.F. Yen, "Effects of Bioleaching on Oil Shale", *Am. Chem. Soc. Div. Fuel Chem., Preprint*, *19* (2), 242—248 (1974).

40. A. Iijjima and R.L. Hay, "Analcime Composition of Tuffs of the Green River of Wyoming", *Am. Mineral.*, *53* (1—2), 184—200 (1968).

41. J.H. Goodwin and R.C. Surdam, "Zeolitization of Tuffaceous Rocks of the Green River Formation, Wyoming", *Science*, *157*, 307—308 (1967).

42. R.B. Parker and R.C. Surdam, "A Summary of Authigenic Silicates in the Tuffaceous Rocks of the Green River Formation", *Wyo. Univ. Contrib. Geol.*, *10* (1), 69—72 (1971).

43. R.A. Sheppard, "Zeolites in Sedimentary Deposits of the United States — A Review", *Am. Chem. Soc., Adv. Chem. Ser.*, *101*, 279—310 (1971).

44. D.A. Brobst and J.D. Tucker, "Analcime, Its Composition and Relation to Dawsonite in Tuff and Shale in the Green River Formation, Piceance Creek Basin, Colorado", *Geol. Soc. Am., Abstr. Progr.*, *4* (6), 369—370 (1972).

45. J.W. Hosterman and J.R. Dyni, "Clay Mineralogy of the Green River Formation, Piceance Creek Basin, Colorado", in: *Geological Survey Research 1972, U.S. Geol. Surv. Prof. Pap., 800-D*, D159—D163 (1972).

46. R.W. Tank, "Clay Minerals of the Green River Formation (Eocene) of Wyoming", *Clay Miner.*, *9*, 297—307 (1972).

47. W.R. Bradley and J.J. Fahey, "Occurrence of Stevensite in the Green River Formation of Wyoming", *Am. Mineral.*, *47* (7—8), 996—998 (1962).

48. M.L. Jackson, *Soil Chemical Analysis*, Prentice-Hall, Englewood Cliffs, N.J., 498 pp. (1958).

49. J.M. Pierce and W. Siegal, "Quantification in Clay Mineral Studies of Sediments and Sedimentary Rocks", *J. Sediment. Petrol.*, *39* (1), 187—193 (1969).

50. P.E. Biscaye, "Mineralogy and Sedimentation of Recent Deep-Sea Clay in the Atlantic Ocean and Adjacent Seas and Oceans", *Geol. Soc. Am. Bull.*, *76*, 803—832 (1965).

51. J.C. Hathaway, "Regional Clay Mineral Facies in Estuaries and Continental Margins of the United States East Coast", in: *Environmental Framework of Coastal Plain Estuaries, Geol. Soc. Am. Mem.*, *133*, 293—316 (1972).

52. G. Millot, *Geology of Clays*, Springer, New York, N.Y., 600 pp. (1970).

53. J.F. Burst, "Diagenesis of Gulf Coast Clay Sediments and Its Possible Relation to Petroleum Migration", *Bull. Am. Assoc. Petr. Geol.*, *53* (1), 73—93 (1969).

54. E.A. Perry and J. Hower, "Burial Diagenesis in Gulf Coast Pelitic Sediments", *Clays Clay Miner.*, *18* (1), 165—177 (1970).

55. R.M. Garrels and F.T. MacKenzie, "Chemical History of the Oceans Deduced from Post-Depositional Changes in Sedimentary Rocks", in: *Studies in Paleo-Oceanography*, 1973, in press.

56. E.A. Perry, "Diagenesis and the K—Ar Dating of Shales and Clay Minerals", *Geol. Soc. Am. Bull.*, *85* (5), 827—830 (1974).

57. R.C. Surdam and R.B. Parker, "Authigenic Aluminosilicates in the Tuffaceous Rocks of the Green River Formation", *Geol. Soc. Am. Bull.*, *83* (3), 689—700 (1972).

58. H.W. Roehler, "Zonal Distribution of Montmorillonite and Zeolites in the Laney Shale Member of the Green River Formation in the Washakie Basin, Wyoming", *U.S. Geol. Surv. Prof. Pap., 800-B*, B121—B124 (1973).

59. R. Wollast, F.T. MacKenzie and O.P. Bricker, "Experimental Precipitation and Genesis of Sepiolite at Earth-Surface Conditions", *Am. Mineral.*, *35*, 1645—1662 (1968).

Chapter 6

CHEMICAL SEPARATION AND CHARACTERIZATION OF KEROGEN FROM OIL SHALE

J.D. SAXBY

Introduction

From the viewpoint of energy potential, the crucial component of oil shales is kerogen. An understanding on a molecular level of the source of the energy available from oil shales requires data on the chemical structure of kerogen. Definitions of the terms oil shale and kerogen vary and some confusion exists, but in this chapter definitions used by many recent workers have been adopted. Hence in its broadest sense kerogen (or kerabitumen) is the insoluble organic matter present in any rock. In the narrow field of oil-shale studies, from which the term is derived historically, kerogen is the indigenous insoluble organic matter in fine-textured sedimentary rocks, from which "substantial" amounts of oil can be generated by heating [1].

"Oil shale" is largely an economic term and it is difficult to define the extreme points at which oil shales merge into "carbonaceous" shales and coals. Some early workers required that for a genuine oil shale more than 50% of the organic material should be converted to oil on heating to 500°C. From the point of view of chemical separation and characterization of the insoluble organic matter, however, the same basic principles apply regardless of whether the organic material is present in traces or in amounts approaching 100%.

Organic matter in sedimentary rocks may originate from terrestrial, aquatic or mixed sources. The three main geochemical properties characterizing a kerogen are its quantity, origin, and degree of diagenesis as revealed by its chemical and physical structure. It is instructive to compare oil-shale kerogens not only with each other, but also with coals and, especially, with kerogen sparsely distributed in shales, siltstones, sandstones and carbonate rocks. The ultimate aim of kerogen research is to relate, both theoretically and practically, oil shale kerogen and the organic matter in petroleum source rocks to the carbon cycle of nature and the estimated $2.5 \cdot 10^{16}$ metric tons of carbon on earth [2,3]. This chapter examines recent progress on the separation and characterization of kerogen and briefly presents some new data on a number of Australian sediments.

Isolation of kerogen

Separation of kerogen from inorganic minerals is necessary because the latter tend to interfere with the determination of most chemical and physical properties of kerogen. Minerals commonly encountered in oil shales include quartz, feldspars (e.g., albite), clays (e.g., illite), carbonates (e.g., dolomite, calcite), pyrite and saline minerals (e.g., trona, dawsonite, halite) [1,4]. Numerous methods of isolation have been discussed and reviewed [5—8], but it remains true that there is no universal ideal procedure for the separation and characterization of kerogen. Furthermore, as in most geochemical studies, it is important to choose samples which are uncontaminated and preferably unweathered [9]. A quantitative recovery of unchanged material is desirable followed by the application of techniques leading to "average" macroscopic and molecular structures.

Solvent extraction

The amount and properties of kerogen isolated from a sample may vary considerably with the solvent used initially to remove soluble matter, because all undissolved organic material remains as part of the kerogen. Clearly, for an accurate definition of the term "insoluble", the solvent and conditions of extraction need to be specified. In most cases "complete" extraction of the ground rock is approached by ultrasonic agitation at room temperature or Soxhlet extraction at the boiling point of the organic solvent [10]. The following solvents are typical of those used: benzene [11]; benzene/methanol (1:1) [12,13]; benzene/methanol (2:1) [14]; benzene/methanol (3:1) [15—17]; benzene/methanol (4:1) [18]; benzene/methanol (70:30) [19]; benzene/methanol/acetone (70:15:15) [20,21]; benzene/methanol/acetone (70:15:15) [22]; chloroform [23,24]; ether [25]; and cyclohexane [26,27].

The amount of extractable material increases with extraction temperature and with polarity and chemical reactivity of the solvent. Vitorovic and Pfendt [28] have investigated the solubility of Aleksinac oil shale in a wide range of solvents and have found solubilities ranging from 0.53% in petroleum ether to 11.44% in dioxane and 52.63% in aniline. In the latter case, oxidation and chemical alteration occurred and similar effects have been observed during extractions with tetralin at temperatures up to 400°C [29]. The achievement of complete extraction with non-reactive solvents may not always be straight-forward. Preheating of Aleksinac oil shale has been shown to increase the amount of extractable matter [30]. Arpino and Ourisson [31] have suggested that when methanol or ethanol is used as a solvent, esterification of acidic groups may occur, particularly when clay minerals are present to act as catalysts. Standardization of extraction procedures may never be achieved, but in all kerogen studies it is desirable that the initial extraction be carried out using a non-reactive solvent at low temperatures in an inert atmosphere.

Physical methods

A variety of procedures aimed at physically separating organic matter from inorganic minerals have been described [6,7,32]. Such methods depend mainly upon flotation and centrifugation in pure or mixed heavy liquids or on the different "wettability" properties of organic and inorganic matter in water and liquid hydrocarbons. Combinations of physical methods involving ultrasonic, electrostatic and magnetic techniques have also been employed.

Two methods which have been used successfully on Green River oil shale have been described in detail by Robinson [7]. The modified Quass method depends on preferential wetting of kerogen by n-hexadecane during prolonged grinding and in favorable cases this results in the ash yield being reduced by over 90%. The second method involves centrifuging powdered rock in $CaCl_2$ solution (specific gravity = 1.06 to 1.15 g/cm^3) or in carbon tetrachloride—benzene mixtures (specific gravity = 1.15 to 1.40 g/cm^3). In the case of Green River Formation kerogen, the latter procedure leads to a final float concentrate yielding 9% ash, but representing only 1% of the original kerogen. The problems of physical separation are three-fold: (1) If the initial concentration of kerogen is low, even repeated separations may not prove successful. (2) The loss of material often results in only a small yield of low-ash kerogen. (3) Fractionation of kerogen on the basis of particle size or mineral association is likely. In certain instances, the main advantage of physical methods, namely the absence of chemically altered kerogen, may be successfully achieved in a combined physical-chemical procedure.

Chemical methods

The most common and, usually, the most satisfactory method for isolating kerogen and removing inorganic minerals is successive chemical treatment of the ground, extracted rock. For many oil-shale samples containing > 10% kerogen, treatments with hydrochloric acid (to remove carbonates) and with hydrofluoric acid (to remove silica and silicates) are sufficient to give a more or less mineral-free kerogen. On the other hand, when the organic content is low and the pyrite (FeS_2) content is high, subsequent removal of FeS_2 is necessary. The interaction of demineralizing reagents with organic functional groups in kerogen may not be negligible and a general summary of reactions which may occur is given in Table 6-I.

Of the reagents for the removal of pyrite, lithium aluminium hydride ($LiAlH_4$) and dilute nitric acid (HNO_3) will be considered later, while sodium borohydride ($NaBH_4$) does not appear to react readily enough to be entirely satisfactory [8,22]. Powdered zinc in concentrated HCl has been widely used [6,18,33,34] to reduce and hence solubilize FeS_2, but as with $NaBH_4$ repeated treatments are necessary. Both of these reagents probably have a similar reducing effect on carbonaceous material. Chemical methods using 10% aqueous sodium hydroxide [35] or aqueous ferric salts [36] have been suggested for removing pyrite from coals, but it is doubtful if these will be applicable to kerogens. Pyrite (and other resistant minerals such as rutile

TABLE 6-I

Effect of reagents on possible organic functional groups in kerogens

Reagent	Type of reaction	Functional groups or molecules affected
Hydrochloric acid	hydrolysis	R—COOR (ester), R—CONH$_2$ (amide), poly-saccharides, (—NHCHR—CO—)$_n$ (proteins, etc.), (R—COO)$_2$ M(II) (metal salts)
	addition	R$_2$C=CR$_2$ (olefin), quinones
	quaternization	R$_3$N (amine)
	alkyl halide formation	R—OH (alcohol)
Hydrofluoric acid	hydrolysis	as for HCl
	addition	as for HCl
	condensation[1]	R$_2$C=CR$_2$ + R—H, R—X + R(arom.)H, R—OH + R(arom.)OH
Lithium aluminium hydride	reduction	R—CHO (aldehyde), R$_2$CO (ketone), R—COOH (acid), (R—CO)$_2$O (acid anhydride), R—COCl (acid chloride), R—COOR (ester), R—CONH$_2$ (amide), R—CN (nitrile), R—NO$_2$ (nitro compound), RX (alkyl halide), R—SSR (disulphide), R$_2$SO (sulphoxide), R$_2$SO$_2$ (sulphone), R—OSO$_2$R (sulphonic ester), some olefins, certain heterocycles
Nitric acid	oxidation	R—OH (alcohol), R—CHO (aldehyde), R$_2$CO (ketone), R$_2$C=CR$_2$ (olefin), R$_2$S (sulphide), certain hydrocarbons, aliphatic side chains, heterocycles, etc.
	nitration	R—H (hydrocarbon), R$_2$O (ether), R$_3$N (amine), R(arom.)OH (phenol), various aliphatic side chains, aromatic and heterocyclic nuclei, etc.
Sodium boro-hydride	reduction	R—CHO (aldehyde), R$_2$CO (ketone), R—COCl (acid chloride), R—SSR (disulphide), R$_2$SO (sulphoxide), R$_2$SO$_2$ (sulphone), R—OSO$_2$R (sulphonic ester), some heterocycles

[1] Usually under anhydrous conditions.

and zircon) can also be decomposed with 40% hydrofluoric acid, but only at unacceptably high temperatures (>112°C) [37].

Palynologists and petrologists often use chemical methods to concentrate and, if necessary, separate kerogen for microscopic analysis. In some cases, such as fluorescence microscopy and where surface properties are measured, it may be desirable to observe both kerogen and soluble organic matter together in the natural state, and so removal of the latter with an organic solvent is not carried out. Particularly when many samples are being examined, care is required to prevent unnecessary alteration or loss during treatment and recovery of kerogen. For the examination of spores, rocks may be crushed before treatment, whereas in the examination of plant fragments slow disintegration of uncrushed rock is preferable. Ultrasonic vibration may sometimes break up geomicrobiological remains [38].

Comparison of selected Australian kerogens

Quantitative data on the effect of chemical demineralization on kerogen are largely lacking in the literature. Hence, five widely varying samples have been chosen and treated in the same way to give information on the loss of kerogen and on chemical alteration of kerogen during successive treatments. The results on these samples are discussed here and compared with existing data on chemical separation of kerogen.

Samples and method

The following samples were ground to ~ 70% —200 mesh, washed with water at room temperature and dried:
  (1) Carbonaceous sediment from the Coorong area, South Australia.
  (2) Oil shale from Julia Creek, Queensland.
  (3) Oil shale from Sydney Basin, NSW.
  (4) Carbonaceous shale from Sydney Basin, NSW.
  (5) Bituminous coal from Sydney Basin, NSW.
The Sydney Basin oil shale was from Glen Davis, while the Sydney Basin carbonaceous shale and bituminous coal were drill-core samples from a depth of 3,922 ft in Terrigal No. 1 well. The Coorong sample is an unconsolidated sediment and, having a high mineral content, is not a genuine "coorongite" as described by Cane [39].

Each sample was extracted ultrasonically with benzene/methanol (3:1) before treatment with $3N$ HCl at $70°C$ for 1 h and then similarly with a 1:1 mixture of 50% HF and $3N$ HCl. Half of the product at this stage was treated twice with $LiAlH_4$ in tetrahydrofuran [34,40], while the other half was twice subjected to reaction with $2N$ HNO_3 at $70°C$ for 1 h. At each stage, products were dried under vacuum at $40°C$ and samples kept for subsequent analysis. Results are summarized in Tables 6-II—6-IV. All oxygen values were obtained by difference and, hence, are subject in many cases to considerable error.

Table 6-II shows the extent to which carbon present in kerogen is lost during HCl, HF, $LiAlH_4$ or HNO_3 treatments. The percentage losses are "total" values, including mechanical losses during filtering or centrifuging as well as solubilized material due to reaction of the kerogen. The effect of chemical treatment on hydrogen/carbon and oxygen/carbon atomic ratios

TABLE 6-II

Effect of chemical demineralization on recovery of kerogen[1]

	Coorong sediment	Julia Creek oil shale	Sydney Basin oil shale	Sydney Basin carbonaceous shale	Sydney Basin bituminous coal
Organic carbon in untreated sample	19.0	14.4	56.5	9.2	79.0
Carbonate carbon in untreated sample	0.0	7.1	0.0	0.0	0.0
Extractable organic matter	3.0	4.0	0.9	0.6	0.7
Kerogen carbon removed with HCl and HF	(75)	(3)	1.8	13.2	6.7
Kerogen carbon removed with LiAlH$_4$	(4)	(0)	0.0	0.2	5.6
Kerogen carbon removed with HNO$_3$	(12)	(8)	2.7	6.2	5.6

[1] All values given as percentages; uncertain values in parentheses.

is shown in Table 6-III (H/C atomic ratio = 12 × %H/%C; O/C atomic ratio = 0.75 × %O/%C). Before HF treatment and particularly where the ash yield is high, both ratios may be considerably affected by water associated with clay and other minerals. Full analyses at each stage of treatment are given for the Sydney Basin oil shale in Table 6-IV.

Effect of hydrochloric acid

As shown in Table 6-I, HCl can react with certain groupings particularly by hydrolysis, but for most consolidated sediments such as those presented in Table 6-II, the fraction of organic matter solubilized is relatively small. During treatment with 5N HCl, Dancy and Giedroyc [41] observed a 0.45% loss of oil-shale kerogen, while Smith [42] attributed a drop of 2.5% in kerogen content mainly to "mechanical losses". When the nitrogen content of kerogen decreases during HCl treatment, the appearance of porphyrins,

TABLE 6-III

Effect of chemical demineralization on atomic ratios of kerogen[1]

	Coorong sediment		Julia Creek oil shale		Sydney Basin oil shale		Sydney Basin carbonaceous shale		Sydney Basin bituminous coal	
Ratios:	H/C	O/C	H/C	O/C	H/C	O/C	H/C	O/C	H/C	O/C
Original sample[2]	(1.8)	(0.6)	(1.4)	(0.8)	1.52	0.04	(1.3)	(0.2)	0.69	0.03
After HCl treatment	(1.8)	(0.3)	1.35	0.11	1.56	0.03	(1.3)	(0.1)	0.68	0.07
After HF treatment	1.48	0.20	1.27	0.03	1.53	0.01	0.66	0.01	0.64	0.06
After LiAlH₄ treatment	1.46	0.20	1.29	0.10	1.57	0.02	0.66	0.05	0.69	0.05
After HNO₃ treatment	1.28	0.28	1.16	0.26	1.47	0.07	0.54	0.19	0.56	0.22

[1] Uncertain values given in parentheses.
[2] After removal of soluble matter.

amino acids, amino sugars, etc. in the extract confirms the reaction of proteinaceous and porphyrinic material [43]. An increase in the amount of extractable fatty acids in shales after HCl treatment is often a sign of the decomposition of metal salts of these acids within the kerogen [44,45]. This effect, together with increased accessibility of solvent molecules to soluble

TABLE 6-IV

Analytical data on Sydney Basin oil shale

	C	H	N	O[1]	S	Ash	Cl	F
	(%, dry, ash-free basis)					(%)	(%)	(%)
Untreated sample	83.8	10.5	1.1	3.8	0.9	32.6	<0.5	<0.3
After solvent extraction	82.8	10.5	0.8	5.0	0.9	30.7	<0.5	<0.3
After HCl treatment	84.3	10.9	0.9	2.9	0.9	32.6	<0.5	<0.3
After HF treatment	86.0	11.0	1.0	0.9	1.0	1.7	<0.5	0.9
After LiAlH₄ treatment	85.1	11.1	0.6	2.5	0.7	3.9	<0.5	<0.3
After HNO₃ treatment	79.9	9.8	2.0	7.6	0.7	0.6	<0.5	0.4

[1] By difference.

material, probably accounts at least in part for the increase of 50% in the solubility of Aleksinac oil shale after HCl treatment [46].

In certain cases, acetic and carbonic acids have been used in place of HCl. Results on Colorado oil shale have shown that kerogens obtained after HCl or H_2CO_3 treatment are analytically almost indentical [47].

Effect of hydrofluoric acid

As HF acid will react with organic functional groups in a similar way to HCl, a significant additional loss or change in composition of the kerogen is not to be expected. This is supported by the data of Tables 6-II—6-IV. The low Cl and F contents as shown in Table 6-IV confirm that at least for this oil shale, additional reactions and adsorption of HCl and HF are negligible. Oxidation of organic matter may occur if the sample is evaporated to dryness during HCl—HF treatment and, therefore, high temperatures and complete evaporation should be avoided.

The principal problem encountered in HF treatment is the formation of insoluble fluorides such as CaF_2, $MgAlF_5 \cdot xH_2O$, $NaAlF_4 \cdot xH_2O$, and $Fe(II)[Al,Fe(III)]F_5 \cdot xH_2O$ [37]. Dilute HF solutions and the presence of excess HCl tend to prevent the formation of such fluorides. Methods for dissolving complex fluorides have been suggested, using ammonium carbonate [6] or saturated boric acid [7].

As carbonaceous matter may be altered during HCl and HF treatments, kerogen has sometimes been defined as organic material which cannot be further extracted with organic solvents and which will not react further with acids such as HCl and HF [48]. The data in Table 6-II suggest that for oil shales and "high-rank" kerogens any loss of organic material is relatively small. Tables 6-III and 6-IV show that the elemental composition of the kerogen is also not greatly changed as a result of these treatments. For more immature kerogens, the content of hydrolyzable organic groupings could be much larger, resulting in significant losses of material and consequent changes in average composition. A very large loss of organic carbon occurs during HCl and HF treatments of the very immature Coorong sediment.

Effect of lithium aluminium hydride

Pyrite reacts with $LiAlH_4$ through the formation of a complex which decomposes in water:

$$FeS_2 \xrightarrow[\text{(ii) } H_2O]{\text{(i) } LiAlH_4} FeS + S^{2-} \xrightarrow{H^+} Fe^{2+} + 2H_2S \qquad (6\text{-}1)$$

Functional groups which are reduced by $LiAlH_4$ are given in Table 6-I and of these, particularly important are carboxyl and ester groupings, which will be reduced to alcohols. Infrared spectra of Colorado oil-shale kerogen after

$LiAlH_4$ treatment exhibit decreased carbonyl absorptions (5.9 μ) and increased alcohol absorptions (9—10 μ) [34]. From the data in Table 6-II, however, it is clear that for these sediments reaction with $LiAlH_4$ usually results in only small losses of organic carbon. This is consistent with the hypothesis that the products of any organic reduction by $LiAlH_4$ are virtually insoluble in water or HCl. Jones and Dickert [49] have similarly found that $LiAlH_4$ (or even lithium in ethylenediamine) does not increase the solubility of Green River kerogen, whereas Fedina and Danyushevskaya [40] report insignificant chemical changes in kerogens during pyrite removal with $LiAlH_4$.

The atomic ratios in Table 6-III and the ash-free analyses in Table 6-IV are consistent with a lack of any substantial change in chemical structure of the kerogen during treatment under reducing conditions. A slight increase in H/C ratio is just discernible, whereas variations in O/C ratio are considered to be within experimental error. As noted for HCl and HF, less mature kerogens would probably in general show greater losses of organic carbon and more extensive reaction with $LiAlH_4$.

Effect of nitric acid

Dilute HNO_3 is the simplest reagent for dissolving pyrite, but oxidation and nitration of the accompanying kerogen limit its usefulness. Furthermore, oxidation of pyrite with dilute HNO_3 may result in the formation of a significant amount of elemental sulphur, which must subsequently be removed (e.g., by washing with benzene). St. Hilaire oil-shale kerogen had its nitrogen content increased from 1.33% to 2.31% by nitric acid treatment [41] and bands at $\sim$ 1330 and $\sim$1540 cm^{-1} in the infrared spectra of HNO_3-treated kerogens have been attributed to $R—NO_2$ groups [50]. Tables 6-II—6-IV clearly show that organic matter is lost during HNO_3 treatment, particularly from the very immature Coorong sediment, and that in all cases the H/C ratio is lowered and the O/C ratio is increased due to chemical alteration. Significantly, the nitrogen content of Sydney Basin oil shale increases due presumably to nitration, whereas the large increase in oxygen content is due both to nitration and to the introduction of carboxyl groups.

The conditions used in the present studies are relatively mild and much more severe alteration of kerogen would be expected to occur at higher temperatures with more concentrated acid. A fact not often acknowledged is that severe oxidation may result in a kerogen relatively poor in oxygen. Low-hydrogen humic material may be oxidized and solubilized, whereas lipids from algal material, having a low oxygen content, may be resistant and hence concentrated [51]. The present results are consistent with mild oxidation mainly on the surfaces of organic particles. Moreover, it is clear that if a single method of FeS_2 removal is desired, $LiAlH_4$ is much more preferable to HNO_3, even under the mildest of conditions.

Chemically resistant minerals

For each of the five samples tested (p. 109), the products after $LiAlH_4$ or HNO_3 treatment were virtually free of resistant minerals. For shales containing less kerogen, however, X-ray diffraction of the final product may reveal variable quantities of rutile, anatase, zircon, and possibly tourmaline. In most cases, these minerals do not interfere significantly in subsequent characterization of the kerogen. Occasionally, small quantities of quartz remain, but these can usually be removed by repeated grinding and treatment with HCl—HF.

With some fine-grained, pyrite-rich samples, part of the FeS_2 remains, even after many treatments with $LiAlH_4$, a fact attributable to skins or membranes of organic matter enclosing and protecting framboidal pyrite from attack [52,53]. This problem of complete FeS_2 removal is more pronounced with milder reagents such as $NaBH_4$ and Zn—HCl, but is almost non-existent with HNO_3. These observations suggest that partial chemical attack of organic films is necessary to expose fine FeS_2 crystals to the reagent. Extensive fine grinding may also achieve such "exposure" but the ever-present possibility of surface oxidation of kerogen is increased, unless an inert atmosphere is used. Practical experience confirms that patience is required during numerous retreatments with $LiAlH_4$ (and HCl—HF) to remove the final traces of FeS_2 (and quartz).

Characterization of kerogen

Chemical separation is the first step towards the study of kerogen by methods inapplicable in the presence of various inorganic minerals. In other cases, techniques can profitably be applied both to the original sediment and isolated kerogen to determine how clays, carbonates, sulphides, etc. affect the chemical and physical properties of kerogen. As well as relating to the formation and exploitation of oil shales, such studies are aimed at showing how kerogen is altered by oxidation, reduction, polymerization, and cracking reactions under natural conditions. Initially, such reactions can lead to natural gases, petroleum, and more mature kerogens, whereas ultimately rocks either free of carbonaceous matter or containing graphite may be produced. Some of these methods of characterization will now be briefly considered. More details, particularly of early studies, have been given by Forsman [6] and Robinson [54].

Elemental composition

When an ash-free kerogen is available, direct analysis of carbon, hydrogen, nitrogen, sulphur, and oxygen is possible by macro- or microanalytical methods. When mineral matter is present, however, oxygen must usually be determined by difference, and calculation of ash-free analyses requires an accurate knowledge of the minerals present and their reactions under ashing conditions. It is usually desirable to determine the chlorine and fluorine contents in kerogens in order to estimate possible intercalation or addition reactions during acid treatment or the presence of insoluble chlorides and/or fluorides. Clearly, the reliability of kerogen analysis decreases rapidly with increasing mineral (and particularly pyrite) content.

Analytical data on kerogen can be used to calculate an empirical formula (e.g., $C_{215}H_{330}O_{12}N_5S$ for Green River Formation kerogen) or compared directly with data on other carbonaceous substances in various types of compositional diagrams [5,51,54]. The Ralston diagram [51] and triangular diagram of Forsman [6] use normalized C, H and O values, and separate bands are obtained on the latter for coals, coaly oil shales and non-coaly oil shales. The modified triangular diagram used by McIver [22] emphasizes differences in hydrogen content and enables diagenetic changes to be shown as the resultant of vectors representing loss of water, carbon dioxide, methane, or liquid hydrocarbons. A plot of H/C versus O/C ratios similar to that developed by Van Krevelen [55] for coals is a sensitive way of comparing kerogens and source materials. In Fig. 6-1, data from Table 6-III are plotted together with analytical data on some other oil shales [34,51]. For simplicity and because of uncertainties in oxygen determination, hydrogen contents or H/C ratios are often used as general indicators of terrestrial (low H/C) or marine (high H/C) source material [56].

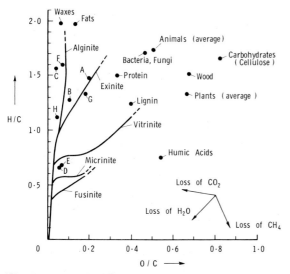

Fig. 6-1. Atomic H/C ratio versus O/C ratio diagram showing selected kerogens and average development lines of coal macerals. A = Coorong sediment; B = Julia Creek oil shale; C = Sydney Basin oil shale; D = Sydney Basin carbonaceous shale; E = Sydney Basin bituminous coal; F = Colorado oil shale (USA); G = Kohat oil shale (India); H = St Hilaire oil shale (France).

In general, a carbonate-poor oil shale contains kerogen with a low N/C ratio. Algal kerogens also exhibit low N/C ratios. As modern blue-green algal material is rich in nitrogen (60% protein, 9.6% N on a dry basis), a large proportion of the proteinaceous nitrogen must have been lost during shale formation [57]. Because of analytical difficulties, the organic sulphur content of kerogen has not often been systematically studied, although recent work indicates significant decreases in the S/C ratio on diagenesis [58].

Functional groups

The content of oxygen functional groups in kerogen varies widely, with ranges for carboxyl, ester, and hydroxyl oxygen being 1 to 64, 1 to 109, and 4 to 42 mg/g organic carbon, respectively [57]. In the case of Green River kerogen, 15% of the oxygen is present as carboxyl, 25% as ester, and 6.5% as hydroxyl, carbonyl and amide, whereas 52.5% is probably present in ether linkages [54]. Brower and Graham [59] found by reaction with chloro-sulphonic acid that Colorado oil-shale kerogen contains one double bond for each 22 carbon atoms. Using a modified iodine number method on Aleksinac oil shale, Pfendt and Vitorovic [60] observed complex reactions involving olefinic bonds and ketonic, aromatic, alcoholic, and ether structures, and concluded that ∼32% of olefinic bonds are terminal or conjugated.

Oxidation, reduction and hydrolysis

Controlled oxidation of kerogen has been widely used to yield small molecules which can be separated and identified by chromatography (and mass spectrometry) and which ideally can be "rebuilt" into the polymeric kerogen structure. Reagents which have been used include alkaline potassium permanganate [6,13,54], ozone [61], nitric acid [62,63], hydrogen peroxide [41], chromic acid [17,64], and air or oxygen [54]. Two effects are readily observed during alkaline permanganate oxidation: (a) a good yield of benzene carboxylic acids from highly-condensed aromatic structures, and (b) the resistance of fatty materials to attack. From this type of evidence, Green River kerogen, which yields mainly oxalic acid, volatile acids and carbon dioxide, has been assigned an essentially non-benzenoid, non-fatty structure [54]. In general, with non-aromatic groups and alkaline permanganate, oxidative attack is more likely to occur at branching points of aliphatic and isoprenoid chains [65].

Degradation with alkaline permanganate of kerogen from Australian torbanite, Dorset Kimmeridge Shale, and Yugoslavian Aleksinac Shale gave acidic products in yields of ∼20%, 40% and 60%, respectively. Considerable variations in the nature of the products from each kerogen were observed [13]. High resolution mass spectrometry and computer techniques have been used to detect oxycarboxylic and dicarboxylic acids from C_4 to C_{12}

produced in oxidation experiments on Green River kerogen [66]. Studies on kerogen from Tasmanian tasmanite including chromic acid oxidation indicate the presence of a random, saturated hydrocarbon polymer devoid of iso-prenoid groups [17]. Oxidation of kukersite kerogen with HNO_3 and $KMnO_4$ gave 1.54 and 2.04 wt.%, respectively, of C_2 to C_{10} monocarboxylic acids and traces of C_{11} to C_{15} acids, as well as dicarboxylic acids [63]. When nitric acid is used to degrade kerogen into carboxylic acids, etc., 60% HNO_3 (or $HNO_3-H_2SO_4$ mixtures) is commonly used for several hours at tempera-tures approaching 100°C [59] (i.e., much more vigorous conditions than those discussed earlier for pyrite removal during kerogen isolation).

As reducing agents ($LiAlH_4$, etc.) are used to remove pyrite during de-mineralization without greatly affecting the kerogen, exceedingly strong reducing conditions are needed to break up most kerogen structures. Reduction with hydrogen requires high temperatures and pressures. Hubbard and Fester [67] used 4,200 psig (hot pressure) at 355°C for 4 h with stannous chloride as catalyst to hydrogenate Colorado oil-shale kerogen. High temperatures are also necessary for the cleavage of ethers and other oxygen functional groups with hydriodic acid [68]. The possibility of thermal pyrolysis and molecular rearrangements under such drastic conditions limits the value of these techniques.

As mentioned earlier, some organic functional groups will be hydrolyzed during chemical isolation, whereas more resistant or inaccessible esters can subsequently be degraded by increasingly severe alkaline hydrolysis. The significance of the fatty and isoprenoid acids so released depends both on the distribution of products and the overall proportion of kerogen so hydro-lyzed (5—10% in the case of Green River kerogen). In all types of chemical degradation of kerogen (hydrolysis, oxidation, etc.) at least part of the product may result from "loosening" of the kerogen matrix and removal of entrapped compounds, which might subsequently react further [18].

Thermal decomposition

On heating kerogen at low temperatures, the first observable change is the loss of adsorbed water at ~100°C. Although moisture content has been used as an indicator of diagenesis in low-rank coals [55], the same methods have not been generally applied to kerogens. The generation at higher temperatures of water together with ammonia and hydrogen sulphide is another interesting area for research.

During both low-temperature pyrolysis (~300°C), which gives data on the potential of a kerogen to produce oil or gas, and high-temperature pyrolysis (~500°C), which relates more to the chemical nature of the kerogen polymer, the exact conditions of heating are crucial to an understanding of the results. Three points are of particular importance:

(1) Kerogen decomposition may be carried out in a vacuum or in an

atmosphere which is inert, oxidizing or reducing. This factor, together with the presence or absence of a solvent such as tetralin [54], will clearly affect the mechanism of pyrolysis.

(2) Primary reaction products will be subject to secondary cracking, polymerization, and oxidation or reduction, if not removed from the heated zone after formation. Solvent extraction during initial kerogen isolation will remove volatile components, which would otherwise distil from the sample during pyrolysis, but traces of the solvent may change the distribution of products.

(3) The method and rate of heating are significant variables and the catalytic effects of mineral matter in the kerogen and of surfaces, to which the reactants are exposed, may not always be negligible.

Gas chromatography and, to a lesser extent, mass spectrometry are commonly used to identify compounds formed during pyrolysis. The distribution of products up to undecane resulting from pyrolysis at 280°C has been suggested as a "fingerprint" for characterizing kerogen in sedimentary rocks [24,69]. Data from the degradation of Green River kerogen at 350°C in the presence of tetralin suggest an original structure containing 10—25% straight chain alkanes (C_{25} to C_{30}), 20—25% cycloalkanes, 10—15% aromatic structures (average of four rings per molecule), and 45—60% heterocyclic material [54]. Shul'man and Proskuryakov [70] have found that in the temperature range of 350—390°C, aliphatic C—C and ether C—O bonds are broken in kerogen from Baltic Sea kukersite. At 500°C, Green River kerogen yields 66% oil, 9% gas, 5% water, and 20% carbon residues [54].

For direct comparison with the volatile matter in coals (and particularly in vitrinite), which shows predictable variations with other chemical and physical characteristics [55], pyrolysis in an inert atmosphere at the conventional temperature (875—1050°C) is desirable. Using this approach, Gransch and Eisma [71] have determined the C_R/C_T ratio for a number of kerogens and related it to H/C ratios (C_R = residual organic carbon after pyrolysis at 900°C for 90 min under nitrogen, C_T = total organic carbon). In more recent studies, pyrolysis of oil shales using pulsed lasers has been described by Biscar [72], and flash pyrolysis of thin kerogen films in the high vacuum of a mass spectrometer has been advocated to minimize secondary reactions [73]. Similarly, the distribution of products from the gasification of kerogen in a microwave discharge may prove to be related to the original stucture in a significant way [74].

The kinetics of kerogen degradation, particularly at low temperatures, is of interest both from the viewpoint of oil-shale utilization and comparison of kerogens. The formation of total volatile products, as well as individual components such as methane, approximates to a first order reaction and follows the Arrhenius equation:

$$k = A\, e^{-E/RT} \tag{6-2}$$

where k is the rate constant, A is the frequency factor and E is the activation energy [75—77]. Abelson [75] has found that E is 40,250 cal/mole for Green River kerogen, while the uncatalyzed breaking of C—C bonds requires an activation energy of 57,000 cal/mole. There appears to be considerable scope for kinetic studies on the formation of individual alkanes, alkenes, etc. during pyrolysis of kerogens before and after chemical separation. Such data not only help to characterize oil-shale kerogen, but also to relate it directly to the formation of natural gas and petroleum by "natural", low-temperature pyrolysis in sedimentary basins [78—80].

Electron spin resonance

Molecular species containing free radicals are to be found in most carbonaceous solids and the unpaired electron spins are usually stabilized by delocalization over aromatic systems. ESR has been used to determine free spin concentrations and line widths for various organic sediments (particularly coals) and the results were related to analytical and maceral data [81,82]. The use of ESR as a geothermal indicator is of considerable interest, because the signal from an organic solid usually does not change until it is heated to a temperature higher than that to which it has previously been exposed. Marchand et al. [83] and Pusey [84] have shown that for certain kerogens the concentration of free electrons, the magnetic field location of the resonance point, and the width of the resonance signal all vary systematically with paleotemperature. A systematic, fundamental study of oil-shale kerogens using ESR could be of considerable interest.

Isotopic studies

Carbon-isotope studies of most kerogens reveal $\delta^{13}C$ values close to —26‰ [85]. Recent marine samples are often more positive, whereas Precambrian kerogens may be more negative. Degens [85] has discussed these values and similar restricted ranges for coals and petroleum. Thus, the carbon-isotope studies of oil-shale kerogen involve the interpretation of relatively small changes in $\delta^{13}C$, resulting from variable organic source material or more likely from differing maturation reactions (i.e., loss of heavy carbon dioxide or light methane, etc.).

Degens [85] and Baker and Claypool [86] have discussed the value of isotopic studies during thermal degradation of kerogen and the possibility of using differences in $\delta^{13}C$ between starting organic material and liberated methane as an index of diagenetic maturity. Sackett and Menendez [87] have measured $\delta^{13}C$ for a number of kerogens and compared values obtained for natural methane and methane evolved from kerogen during thermal cracking. Similar studies on coals illustrate some of the complexities to be expected [88]. Although carbon isotopes are clearly of most relevance to kerogen characterization, $^{32}S/^{34}S$, $^{14}N/^{15}N$, $^{16}O/^{18}O$ and $H/^{2}H$ ratios for carbonaceous matter may also be significant [89].

Infrared analysis

Infrared and, more recently, Raman spectra have been used to supply evidence on the structure of kerogen but, even when bands can be assigned unequivocally, the results are usually only qualitative. The following assignments have been made with varying degrees of certainty [6,54,90—93]:

3310—3390 cm^{-1}	OH and NH bonds
3000—3080 cm^{-1}	aromatic C—H bonds
2900 cm^{-1}	aliphatic C—H bonds
1680—1745 cm^{-1}	C=O bonds
1580—1650 cm^{-1}	C=C bonds, H$_2$O deformation, aromatic and graphitic structures, carboxyl salts, conjugated C=O bonds
1500—1520 cm^{-1}	aromatic rings
1400—1460 cm^{-1}	aliphatic CH$_2$ and CH$_3$ groups
1370—1380 cm^{-1}	CH$_3$ and cyclic CH$_2$ groups
1090—1250 cm^{-1}	C—O bonds
890— 980 cm^{-1}	C=C bonds
740— 850 cm^{-1}	condensed aromatic rings
720— 725 cm^{-1}	aliphatic chains greater than C$_4$

Infrared spectra are useful in detecting chemical changes in kerogen during demineralization, but allowance must be made for absorptions and other effects caused by unremoved inorganic minerals.

Microscopic techniques

The analytical techniques so far discussed lead, on the whole, to average data for a sample of isolated kerogen particles. Kerogen from most sediments, however, is not uniform, either chemically or physically, and differences in particles are revealed at the micron level by optical microscopy and scanning electron microscopy and at the macro-molecular level by electron microscopy. Examination by electron microscopy of organic matter from Toarcian sediments in the Paris Basin revealed differences before and after chloroform extraction [94] and selected area electron diffraction revealed the extent of molecular ordering [58].

Pollen grains and spores in kerogen are useful, not only in determining the age and environment of deposition of a sediment, but also in following the diagenetic and metamorphic history of the sediment. The degree of coalification of a particular pollen grain or spore and, hence, its thermal history are revealed in color changes from yellow to light brown to dark brown—black. Such changes in color or translucency may be determined under the microscope either visually or photoelectrically [95]. Giraud [69] has correlated spore carbonization data with degradation factors derived from kerogen pyrolysis. Diagenesis of Green River kerogens is revealed in color changes as well as in other chemical and spectral properties [26].

Petrologists have classified coal into the microscopic maceral groups vitrinite, exinite and inertinite, which may be associated in different ways to comprise a number of microlithotypes [96,97]. Although oil shales and kerogens dispersed in clayey and silty sediments may differ somewhat from coals in their paths of chemical alteration, similar classifications can at least tentatively be made. It is crucial that none of the kerogen is lost during isolation and that the presence of unremoved minerals (particularly pyrite) does not prevent accurate microscopic observation. Even kerogens from oil shale may vary considerably when accurate data are compared on the individual macerals of exinite, as well as on the presence or absence of vitrinite and inertinite. It is often assumed that the extremely fine "unidentifiable" organic remains in oil shales originate from algae and, to a lesser extent, other single-celled plants and animals such as diatoms and radiolaria [1,98].

As discussed earlier, chemical isolation of kerogen may result in chemical changes on a molecular level and, because of differing compositions, macerals will not all be affected similarly. Exinite, which is most resistant to attack, has been concentrated for particular study by treating kerogen with nitric acid or hydrogen peroxide, but an altered product must always be expected [99]. The term "sporopollenin" has been given to the exine material derived from spore and pollen grains after treatment with hot aqueous sodium hydroxide, hydrochloric acid, and 72% sulphuric acid or 85% phosphoric acid. An understanding of sporopollenin will clearly contribute to the knowledge on kerogen, particularly for older sediments [100,101]. As well as conventional microscopic techniques, ultraviolet fluorescence microscopy, cathodoluminescence, scanning electron microscopy and electron probe microanalysis have been applied to sporopollenin and other finely dispersed organic materials [102—105].

The reflectance of vitrinite in polished sections is a microscopic surface property often used as a measure of rank in bituminous coals [106]. A similar technique is applicable to kerogens, although special precautions are necessary for small ($\sim$10 μ) particles [107]. Bostick [108] has examined the reflectance of fragments in kerogens separated by a combination of chemical and physical methods and found that vitrinite-like material is the most useful measure of thermal alteration, although exinite reflectance may be relevant in low temperature situations. A correlation between reflectance and pyrolysis data for kerogens has also been investigated [109].

All these types of microscopic study are closely related to petroleum source rock research and theories of hydrocarbon generation from kerogen [90,110—115]. As far as oil shales are concerned, at least two questions need to be considered. Are oil shales petroleum source rocks which have yet to be subjected to the temperatures required for gas and petroleum generation? If so, can an oil shale that has produced all or most of its hydrocarbons be recognized from the type of organic matter (if any) that remains? Bell and Hunt [116] have suggested that in the extreme case, after considerable metamorphism, the former oil shales appear as graphitic shales, slates and schists. One of the challenges of kerogen research is to build up a unified picture of carbonaceous material in sediments by relating microscopic observations to chemical and physical data.

Miscellaneous techniques

Several physical properties of kerogen can readily be measured and usefully compared with those of coals [6]. These include refractive index, specific gravity, and swelling, softening, and plasticity parameters. A detailed study of the X-ray diffraction of kerogen is complex, but the broad peak observed in many cases is consistent with the interlayer spacings expected for predominantly alicyclic structures [117]. Diffraction-contrast techniques have also been applied to kerogen [118]. Broad-line nuclear magnetic resonance spectroscopy has been used to estimate oil yields from oil shale, and correlations with kerogen structure may prove possible in the future [119]. Solid-state ultraviolet spectra can indicate the presence or absence of aromatic structures [54], whereas visible fluorescent spectra of kerogens often resemble those emitted from long-chain polyene fatty acid polymers [120].

Thermal analysis methods have been applied to oil shales [93,121—123]. Results from differential thermal analysis, thermogravimetry, and evolved-gas analysis are greatly simplified if isolated kerogen is used but, even on the original shale, peaks due to the organic reactions can be distinguished from effects due to clays and other minerals [124,125]. Evidence from gel permeation chromatography suggests the presence of porphyrinic structures probably bonded to vanadium or nickel in the crosslinked kerogen molecules [126]. The trace element content of kerogens has not often been investigated, but is potentially of considerable interest [127,128].

Conclusion

It needs to be stressed that kerogen is not a single compound nor a homogeneous entity but a complex mixture of polymeric organic residues. Burlingame et al. [18] have shown diagrammatically accessible substituents on a possible kerogen "molecule" (Fig. 6-2). By definition, kerogen is insoluble in simple solvents and hence presents an exceedingly difficult characterization problem, particularly to organic chemists [129]. Cane [120] has even questioned the value of "attempting to unscramble the kerogen egg".

In this type of situation it is important not to detach kerogen studies (or more particularly oil-shale-kerogen studies) from the overall question of

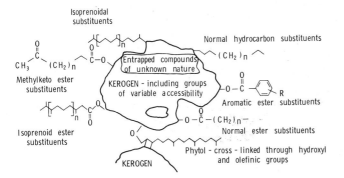

Fig. 6-2. Substituent structure suggested for kerogen. (Adapted from Burlingame et al. [18]).

organic matter in sediments. Many disciplines and techniques can contribute to such research on solid, liquid, and gaseous organic components in rocks at all levels of concentration. The particular value of chemistry in this multi-disciplinary approach is that usually quantitative data at the molecular level are obtained.

The essence of kerogen isolation by chemical methods is to carry out repeated treatments under the mildest conditions possible. Even solvent extraction, which requires penetration by solvent molecules to all soluble molecules, may rarely be complete in a single operation. Similarly, the failure of certain minerals to react during treatment can be attributed to the protecting effect of other material present, particularly in fine-grained sediments. The same principle no doubt accounts for the continued presence during demineralization of organic functional groups, which at first sight should have been oxidized, reduced, hydrolyzed, etc. Difficulty in removing pyrite by reduction is probably often due to skins or membranes of organic matter around and within pyrite framboids. Dilute nitric acid, which exposes and removes pyrite without difficulty, simultaneously oxidizes (and nitrates) most types of kerogen. There is merit in removing pyrite under both reducing ($LiAlH_4$) and oxidizing (HNO_3) conditions in the knowledge that the original kerogen has properties between the two resulting products, but more closely approaching the $LiAlH_4$ product. Overall, it is probably true that in recent years there have been few significant advances in the range of reagents and methods used in kerogen isolation. There is still a need for quantitative data on possible reactions of existing reagents with functional groups in kerogen, as well as the development of new separation methods, particularly for pyrite removal.

The characterization of isolated kerogen has benefited from recent advances in many techniques. Data from chemical, physical and microscopic methods are together leading to an understanding of kerogen-rich shales, comparable to that already established for coals. The complete picture will only emerge by combining results on bulk kerogen (e.g., by elemental analysis and spectral methods), on labile components (e.g., by oxidation and pyrolysis), and on microscopically observable particles. In particular, much remains to be documented on organic matter sparsely distributed in many essentially inorganic sediments. Although such material is of little economic importance at present, it is of scientific interest that the ultimate world "reserves" of finely disseminated kerogen are estimated to be $\sim 4 \cdot 10^{15}$ metric tons, a figure ~ 500 times that for coal, $\sim 10,000$ times that for oil shale, $\sim 20,000$ times that for petroleum, and $\sim 40,000$ times that for natural gas.

References

1. D.C. Duncan, "Geologic Setting of Oil Shale Deposits and World Prospects", *Proc. 7th World Pet. Congr.*, 3, 659—667 (1967).
2. E.T. Degens, *Geochemistry of Sediments*, Prentice-Hall, Englewood Cliffs (1965).
3. K.H. Wedepohl, *Handbook of Geochemistry*, Springer, Berlin (1969).
4. J.W. Smith and W.A. Robb, "Aragonite and the Genesis of Carbonates in Mahogany Zone Oil Shales of Colorado's Green River Formation", *U.S. Bur. Mines, Rep. Invest.*, 7727 (1973).
5. I.A. Breger, "Origin and Classification of Naturally Occurring Carbonaceous Substances", in: I.A. Breger (Editor), *Organic Geochemistry*, Pergamon, Oxford, Ch. 3, pp. 50—86 (1963).
6. J.P. Forsman, "Geochemistry of Kerogen", in: I.A. Breger (Editor), *Organic Geochemistry*, Pergamon, Oxford, Ch. 5, pp. 148—182 (1963).
7. W.E. Robinson, "Isolation Procedures for Kerogens and Associated Soluble Organic Materials", in: G. Eglinton and M.T.J. Murphy (Editors), *Organic Geochemistry*, Springer, Berlin, Ch. 6, pp. 181—195 (1969).
8. J.D. Saxby, "Isolation of Kerogen in Sediments by Chemical Methods", *Chem. Geol.*, 6, 173—184 (1970).
9. D. Leythaeuser, "Effects of Weathering on Organic Matter in Shales", *Geochim. Cosmochim. Acta*, 37, 113—120 (1973).
10. R.D. McIver, "Ultrasonics — a Rapid Method for Removing Soluble Organic Matter from Sediments", *Geochim. Cosmochim. Acta*, 26, 343—345 (1962).
11. D.E. Anders, F.G. Doolittle and W.E. Robinson, "Analysis of Some Aromatic Hydrocarbons in a Benzene-soluble Bitumen from Green River Shale", *Geochim. Cosmochim. Acta*, 37, 1213—1228 (1973).
12. J.R. Maxwell, C.T. Pillinger and G. Eglinton, "Organic Geochemistry", *Quart. Rev.*, 25, 571—628 (1971).
13. M.V. Djuricic, D. Vitorovic, B.D. Andresen, H.S. Hertz, R.C. Murphy, G. Preti and K. Biemann, "Acids Obtained by Oxidation of Kerogens of Ancient Sediments of Different Geographic Origin", *Adv. Org. Geochem., 1971, Proc. Int. Congr., 5th*, Pergamon, Oxford, pp. 305—321 (1972).
14. P.C. Wszolek, E. Gelpi and A.L. Burlingame, "A New Approach to the Isolation of Milligram Amounts of Significant Geochemical Compounds", *Adv. Org. Geochem., 1971, Proc. Int. Congr., 5th*, Pergamon, Oxford, pp. 229—247 (1972).
15. A.G. Douglas, K. Douraghi-Zadeh, G. Eglinton, J.R. Maxwell and J.N. Ramsay, "Fatty Acids in Sediments Including the Green River Shale (Eocene) and Scottish Torbanite (Carboniferous)", *Adv. Org. Geochem., 1966, Proc. Int. Congr., 3rd*, Pergamon, Oxford, pp. 315—334 (1970).
16. G. Steel and W. Henderson, "Isolation and Characterization of Stanols from the Green River Shale", *Nature*, 238, 148—149 (1972).

17. B.R. Simoneit and A.L. Burlingame, "Carboxylic Acids Derived from Tasmanian Tasmanite by Extractions and Kerogen Oxidations", *Geochim. Cosmochim. Acta, 37*, 595—610 (1973).
18. A.L. Burlingame, P.A. Haug, H.K. Schnoes and B.R. Simoneit, "Fatty Acids Derived from the Green River Formation Oil Shale by Extractions and Oxidations — A Review", *Adv. Org. Geochem., 1968, Proc. Int. Congr., 4th*, Pergamon, Oxford, pp. 85—129 (1969).
19. R.M. Mitterer and T.C. Hoering, "Production of Hydrocarbons from the Organic Matter in a Recent Sediment", *Carnegie Inst., Geophys. Lab., Ann. Rep.*, pp. 510—514 (1966—1967).
20. P.V. Smith, "The Origin of Petroleum: Occurrence of Hydrocarbons in Recent Sediments", *Bull. Am. Assoc. Pet. Geol., 38*, 377—404 (1954).
21. J.M. Hunt and G.W. Jamieson, "Oil and Organic Matter in Source Rocks of Petroleum", *Bull. Am. Assoc. Pet. Geol., 40*, 477—488 (1956).
22. R.D. McIver, "Composition of Kerogen — Clue to Its Role in the Origin of Petroleum", *Proc. 7th World Pet. Congr., 2*, 25—36 (1967).
23. G. Long, S. Neglia and L. Favretto, "The Metamorphism of the Kerogen from Triassic Black Shales, Southeast Sicily", *Geochim. Cosmochim. Acta, 32*, 647—656 (1968).
24. A. Combaz, "Thermal Degradation of Sporopollenin and Genesis of Hydrocarbons", in: J. Brooks, P.R. Grant, M. Muir, P. van Gijzel and G. Shaw (Editors), *Sporopollenin*, Academic Press, London, pp. 621—653 (1971).
25. N.L. Dilaktorskii, S.S. Baukov and M.M. Dilaktorskaya, "Application of Sedimento-metric Analysis for the Investigation of the Conditions of Accumulation of Shale Sediments", *Izv. Akad. Nauk Eston. S.S.R., Ser. Fiz.-Mat. i Tekh. Nauk, 10*, 130—142 (1961).
26. W.E. Robinson and G.L. Cook, "Compositional Variations of the Organic Material of Green River Oil Shale — Colorado No. 1 Core", *U.S. Bur. Mines, Rep. Invest., 7492* (1971).
27. D.E. Anders and W.E. Robinson, "Geochemical Aspects of the Saturated Hydrocarbon Constituents of Green River Oil Shale — Colorado No. 1 Core", *U.S. Bur. Mines, Rep. Invest., 7737* (1973).
28. D.K. Vitorovic and P.A. Pfendt, "Investigation of the Kerogen of a Yugoslav (Aleksinac) Oil-Shale", *Proc. 7th World Pet. Congr., 3*, 691—694 (1967).
29. W.R. Thompson and C.H. Prien, "Thermal Extraction and Solution of Oil-Shale Kerogen", *Ind. Eng. Chem., 50*, 359—364 (1958).
30. D. Vitorovic and L. Jovanovic, "Solubility of Aleksinac Oil-Shale Kerogen. III Solubility of Preheated Kerogen", *Glas. Hem. Drus., Beograd, 33*, 581—588 (1968).
31. P. Arpino and G. Ourisson, "Interactions Between Rock and Organic Matter. Esterification and Transesterification Induced in Sediments by Methanol and Ethanol", *Anal. Chem., 43*, 1656—1657 (1971).
32. R.D. Thomas and P.B. Lorenz, "Use of Centrifugal Separation to Investigate How Kerogen is Bound to the Minerals in Oil Shale", *U.S. Bur. Mines, Rep. Invest., 7378* (1970).
33. J.P. Forsman and J.M. Hunt, "Insoluble Organic Matter (Kerogen) in Sedimentary Rocks of Marine Origin", in: *Habitat of Oil*, Am. Assoc. Pet. Geol., Tulsa, pp. 747—778 (1958).
34. D.L. Lawlor, J.I. Fester and W.E. Robinson, "Pyrite Removal from Oil Shale Concentrates Using Lithium Aluminium Hydride", *Fuel, 42*, 239—244 (1963).
35. L. Reggel, R. Raymond, I. Wender and B. D. Blaustein, "Preparation of Ash-free, Pyrite-free Coal by Mild Chemical Treatment", *Abstr., 164th Nat. Meet., Am. Chem. Soc., Fuel, 10* (1972).

36. J.W. Hamersma, M.L. Kraft, E.P. Koutsoukos and R.A. Meyers, "Chemical Removal of Pyritic Sulphur from Coal", *Abstr., 164th Nat. Meet., Am. Chem. Soc., Fuel, 16* (1972).

37. F.J. Langmyhr, "Recent Development in the Use of Hydrofluoric Acid as Decomposing Agent for Inorganic Materials", *Acta Geol. Geogr. Univ. Comenianae, Geol., 15,* 23—33 (1968).

38. L.R. Moore, "Geomicrobiology and Geomicrobiological Attack on Sedimented Organic Matter", in: G. Eglinton and M.T.J. Murphy (Editors), *Organic Geochemistry,* Springer, Berlin, Ch. 11, pp. 265—303 (1969).

39. R.F. Cane, "Coorongite and the Genesis of Oil Shale", *Geochim. Cosmochim. Acta, 33,* 257—265 (1969).

40. I.P. Fedina and A.I. Danyushevskaya, "Extraction of Pyrite from Residual Organic Matter (Kerogen) in Sedimentary Rocks", *Nov. Metody Issled. Osad. Porod Tsel'yu Poiskov Blagopriyatnykh Nefte-Gazoobrazovaniu Usloviy,* 37—43 (1971).

41. T.E. Dancy and V. Giedroyc, "Further Researches on the Determination of the Chemical Composition of Oil Shales", *J. Inst. Pet., 36,* 593—603 (1950).

42. J.W. Smith, "Ultimate Composition of Organic Material in Green River Oil Shale", *U.S. Bur. Mines, Rep. Invest., 5725* (1961).

43. A.S. Fomina and L.A. Nappa, "Carbohydrates and Amino Acids in Kerogens of Ancient Bituminous Shales", *Khim. Tverd. Topl.,* (1) 8—16 (1967).

44. A.L. Burlingame and B.R. Simoneit, "Analysis of the Mineral Entrapped Fatty Acids Isolated from the Green River Formation", *Nature, 218,* 252—256 (1968).

45. W. Bergmann, "Geochemistry of Lipids", in: I.A. Breger (Editor), *Organic Chemistry,* Pergamon, Oxford, Ch. 12, pp. 503—542 (1963).

46. D.Vitorovic and M. Saban, "Solubility of Organic Components of Aleksinac Oil Shale. II. Solvents Boiling Between 100° and 207°", *Glas. Hem. Drus., Beograd, 33,* 569—580 (1968).

47. R.D. Thomas, "Use of Carbonic Acid to Concentrate Kerogen in Oil Shale", *Fuel, 48,* 75—80 (1969).

48. E.T. Degens and J.H. Reuter, "Analytical Techniques in the Field of Organic Geochemistry", *Adv. Org. Geochem., 1962, Proc. Int. Congr., 1st,* Pergamon, Oxford, pp. 377—402 (1962).

49. D.G. Jones and J.J. Dickert, "Composition and Reactions of Oil Shale of the Green River Formation", *Chem. Eng. Progr. Symp. Ser., 61,* 33—41 (1965).

50. J.W. Smith and N.B. Young, "Organic Composition of Kentucky's New Albany Shale: Determination and Uses", *Chem. Geol., 2,* 157—170 (1967).

51. G.W. Himus, "Observations on the Composition of Kerogen Rocks and the Chemical Constitution of Kerogen", in: G. Sell (Editor), *Oil Shale and Cannel Coal,* Institute of Petroleum, London, 2, 112—133 (1951).

52. L.G. Love and G.C. Amstutz, "Review of Microscopic Pyrite from the Devonian Chattanooga Shale and Rammelsberg Banded Ore", *Fortschr. Mineral., 43,* 273—309 (1966).

53. R.E. Sweeney, *Pyritization During Diagenesis of Marine Sediments,* Ph.D. Thesis, Univ. California, Los Angeles (1972).

54. W.E. Robinson, "Kerogen of the Green River Formation", in: G. Eglinton and M.T.J. Murphy (Editors), *Organic Geochemistry,* Springer, Berlin, Ch. 26, pp. 619—637 (1969).

55. D.W. van Krevelen, *Coal,* Elsevier, Amsterdam, 514 pp. (1961).

56. I.A. Breger and A. Brown, "Kerogen in the Chattanooga Shale", *Science, 137,* 221—224 (1962).

57. W.E. Robinson and G.U. Dinneen, "Constitutional Aspects of Oil-Shale Kerogen", *Proc. 7th World Pet. Congr., 3,* 669—680 (1967).

58. B. Durand, J. Espitalié, A. Combaz and G. Nicaise, "Etude de la Matière Organique Insoluble (Kérogène) des Argiles du Toarcien du Bassin de Paris. 1ère Partie: Etude par des Procédés Optiques. Analyse Elémentaire. Etude en Microscopie et Diffraction Electronique", *Rev. Inst. Fr. Pét., 27*, 865—884 (1972).

59. F.M. Brower and E.L. Graham, "Some Chemical Reactions of Colorado Oil Shale Kerogen", *Ind. Eng. Chem., 50*, 1059—1060 (1958).

60. P. Pfendt and D. Vitorovic, "Untersuchung der Struktur des Aleksinacer Olschiefer-kerogens mittels modifizierter Jodzahlmethoden. II. Der Einfluss des Bromwasser-stoffes", *Erdöl Kohle, 26*, 143—148 (1973).

61. M.C. Bitz and B. Nagy, "Ozonolysis of Polymer-type Material in Coal, Kerogen, and in the Orgueil Meteorite: A Preliminary Report", *Proc. Nat. Acad. Sci. U.S., 56*, 1383—1390 (1966).

62. E. Mannik, A.S. Fomina, T. Pehk and A. Mannik, "Component Composition of Dimethyl Esters of Dicarboxylic Acids Prepared by the Oxidation of Kukersite Kerogen", *Khim. Tverd. Topl., 3*, 142—144 (1972).

63. E. Bondar, R.E. Veski and A.S. Fomina, "Composition of Monocarboxylic Acids Formed in the Production of Dicarboxylic Acids from Kukersite Kerogen", *Esti NSV Tead. Akad. Toim., Keem., Geol., 21*, 129—132 (1972).

64. A.L. Burlingame and B.R. Simoneit, "High Resolution Mass Spectrometry of Green River Formation Kerogen Oxidations", *Nature, 222*, 741—747 (1969).

65. M. Djuricic, R.C. Murphy, D. Vitorovic and K. Biemann, "Organic Acids Obtained by Alkaline Permanganate Oxidation of Kerogen from the Green River (Colorado) Shale", *Geochim. Cosmochim. Acta, 35*, 1201—1207 (1971).

66. W.J. Richter, B.R. Simoneit, D.H. Smith and A.L. Burlingame, "Detection and Identification of Oxocarboxylic and Dicarboxylic Acids in Complex Mixtures by Reductive Silylation and Computer-aided Analysis of High Resolution Mass Spectral Data", *Anal. Chem., 41*, 1392—1396 (1969).

67. A.B. Hubbard and J.I. Fester, "A Hydrogenolysis Study of the Kerogen in Colorado Oil Shale", *U.S. Bur. Mines, Rep. Invest., 5458* (1958).

68. M.M. Petrunin and S.S. Semenov, "Effect of Hydriodic Acid on Baltic Shale Kerogen at High Temperatures", *Termokataliticheskie Metody Pererab. Uglevodorodnogo Syr'ya*, 206—212 (1969).

69. A. Giraud, "Application of Pyrolysis and Gas Chromatography to Geochemical Characterization of Kerogen in Sedimentary Rocks", *Bull. Am. Assoc. Pet. Geol., 54*, 439—455 (1970).

70. A.I. Shul'man and V.A. Proskuryakov, "Mechanism of the Decomposition of Kerogen from Baltic Sea Kukersite in the Bitumenization Stage", *Khim. Tverd. Topl.* (6), 73—81 (1971).

71. J.A. Gransch and E. Eisma, "Characterization of the Insoluble Organic Matter of Sediments by Pyrolysis", *Adv. Org. Geochem., 1966, Proc. Int. Congr., 3rd*, Pergamon, Oxford, pp. 407—426 (1970).

72. J.P. Biscar, "On-line Laser Pyrolysis Cell for Chromatography", *Anal. Chem., 43*, 982—983 (1971).

73. M. Blumer, "Chemical Fossils: Trends in Organic Geochemistry", *Pure Appl. Chem., 34*, 591—609 (1973).

74. Y.C. Fu, "Gasification of Fossil Fuels in a Microwave Discharge in Argon", *Chem. Ind. (Lond.)*, pp. 876—877 (1971).

75. P.H. Abelson, "Conversion of Biochemicals to Kerogen and n-Paraffins", in: P.H. Abelson (Editor), *Researches in Geochemistry*, Wiley, New York, 2, 63—86 (1967).

76. A.W. Weitkamp and L.C. Gutberlet, "Application of a Microretort to Problems in Shale Pyrolysis", *Ind. Eng. Chem. Process Design Develop., 9*, 386—395 (1970).

77. J.J. Cummins and W.E. Robinson, "Thermal Degradation of Green River Kerogen at 150° to 350°C", *U.S. Bur. Mines, Rep. Invest., 7620* (1972).

78. P.H. Abelson, "Organic Geochemistry and the Formation of Petroleum", *Proc. 6th World Pet. Congr.*, *1*, 397—407 (1963).

79. B. Tissot and R. Pelet, "Nouvelles Données sur les Mécanismes de Genèse et de Migration du Pétrole. Simulation Mathématique et Application à la Prospection", *Proc. 8th World Pet. Congr.*, *2*, 35—46 (1971).

80. D.H. Welte, "Petroleum Exploration and Organic Geochemistry", *J. Geochem. Explor.*, *1*, 117—136 (1972).

81. P.H. Given and C.R. Binder, "The Use of Electron Spin Resonance for Studying the History of Certain Organic Sediments", *Adv. Org. Geochem. 1964, Proc. Int. Congr.*, *2nd*, Pergamon, Oxford, pp. 147—164 (1966).

82. D.E.G. Austen, D.J.E. Ingram, P.H. Given, C.R. Binder and L.W. Hill, "Electron Spin Resonance Study of Pure Macerals", in: *Coal Science, Advan. Chem. Ser., Am. Chem. Soc.*, *55*, 344—362 (1966).

83. A. Marchand, P.A. Libert and A. Combaz, "Physicochemical Characterization of the Diagenesis of Several Biologically Homogeneous Organic Rocks", *Rev. Inst. Fr. Pét. Ann. Combust. Liquides*, *24*, 3—20 (1969).

84. W.C. Pusey, "The ESR-kerogen Method, a New Technique of Estimating the Organic Maturity of Sedimentary Rocks", *Pet. Times*, 21—26 (1973); *World Oil*, *176*, 71—75 (1973).

85. E.T. Degens, "Biogeochemistry of Stable Carbon Isotopes", in: G. Eglinton and M.T.J. Murphy (Editors), *Organic Geochemistry*, Springer, Berlin, Ch. 12, pp. 304—329 (1969).

86. D.R. Baker and G.E. Claypool, "Effects of Incipient Metamorphism on Organic Matter in Mudrock", *Bull. Am. Assoc. Pet. Geol.*, *54*, 456—468 (1970).

87. W.M. Sackett and R. Menendez, "Carbon Isotope Study and the Hydrocarbons and Kerogen in the Aquitaine Basin, Southwest France", *Adv. Org. Geochem. 1971, Proc. Int. Congr.*, *5th*, Pergamon, Oxford, pp. 523—533 (1972).

88. H.-U. Friedrich and H. Jüntgen, "Some Measurements of the $^{12}C/^{13}C$-ratio in Methane or Ethane Desorbed from Hard Coal or Released by Pyrolysis", *Adv. Org. Geochem. 1971, Proc. Int. Congr.*, *5th*, Pergamon, Oxford, pp. 639—646 (1972).

89. I.V. Grinberg, "Isotopic and Other Physicochemical Methods for Determining the Structure of a Kerogen-Coal Substance", *Khim. Tverd. Topl.*, (4), 110—119 (1969).

90. B. Tissot, Y. Califet-Bebyser, G. Deroo and J.L. Oudin, "Origin and Evolution of Hydrocarbons in Early Toarcian Shales, Paris Basin, France", *Bull. Am. Assoc. Pet. Geol.*, *55*, 2177—2193 (1971).

91. R.F. Cane and P.R. Albion, "The Phytochemical History of Torbanites", *J. Proc. R. Soc. N.S.W.*, *104*, 31—37 (1971); "The Organic Geochemistry of Torbanite Precursors", *Geochim. Cosmochim. Acta*, *37*, 1543—1549 (1973).

92. R.A. Friedel, J.A. Queiser and G.L. Carlson, "Infrared and Raman Spectra of Intractable Carbonaceous Substances — Reassignments in Coal Spectra", *Am. Chem. Soc., Div. Fuel Chem., Prepr. Pap.*, *15* (1), 123—136 (1971).

93. J. Espitalié, B. Durand, J.-C. Roussel and C. Souron, "Etude de la Matière Organique Insoluble (Kérogène) des Argiles du Toarcien du Bassin de Paris. 2ème Partie: Etudes en Spectroscopie Infrarouge et en Analyse Thermique Différentielle", *Rev. Inst. Fr. Pét.*, *28*, 37—66 (1973).

94 A. Oberlin, G. Terrière, B. Durand and C. Clinard, "Contribution de la Microscopie et de la Microdiffraction Electroniques à l'Etude de la Matière Organique Insoluble des Sédiments", *Adv. Org. Geochem. 1971, Proc. Int. Congr.*, *5th*, Pergamon, Oxford, pp. 577—589 (1972).

95. C.C.M. Gutjahr, "Carbonization Measurements of Pollen-grains and Spores and Their Application", *Leidse Geol. Mededel.*, *38*, 1—29 (1966).

96. H. Tschamler and E. de Ruiter, "A Comparative Study of Exinite, Vitrinite, and Micrinite", in: *Coal Science, Advan. Chem. Ser., Am. Chem. Soc.*, *55*, 332—343 (1966).

97. M. Teichmüller and R. Teichmüller, "Diagenesis of Coal (Coalification)", in: G. Larsen and G.V. Chilingar (Editors), *Diagenesis in Sediments*, Elsevier, New York, Ch. 8, pp. 391—415 (1967).

98. A.I. Ginzburg and G.V. Yavkhuta, "Characteristics of Oil Shales of the Volga River Basin", *Khim. Tverd. Topl.*, (6) 49—59 (1969).

99. B.S. Cooper and D.G. Murchison, "The Petrology and Geochemistry of Sporinite", in: J. Brooks, P.R. Grant, M. Muir, P. van Gijzel and G. Shaw (Editors), *Sporopollenin*, Academic Press, London, pp. 545—568 (1971).

100. J. Brooks and G. Shaw, "Identity of Sporopollenin with Older Kerogen and New Evidence for the Possible Biological Source of Chemicals in Sedimentary Rocks", *Nature, 220,* 678—679 (1968).

101. J. Brooks, P.R. Grant, M. Muir, P. van Gijzel and G. Shaw (Editors), *Sporopollenin*, Academic Press, London (1971).

102. M.D. Muir and P.R. Grant, "Application of Scanning Electron Microscope Techniques and Optical Microscopy to the Study of Sporopollenin", in: J. Brooks, P.R. Grant, M. Muir, P. Van Gijzel and G. Shaw (Editors), *Sporopollenin*, Academic Press, London, pp. 422—439 (1971).

103. M. Correia, "Diagenesis of Sporopollenin and Other Comparable Organic Substances: Application to Hydrocarbon Research", in: J. Brooks, P.R. Grant, M. Muir, P. van Gijzel and G. Shaw (Editors), *Sporopollenin*, Academic Press, London, pp. 569—620 (1971).

104. E. A. Baker and E. Parsons, "Scanning Electron Microscopy of Plant Cuticles", *J. Microscopy, 94,* 39—49 (1971).

105. B. Alpern, B. Durand, J. Espitalié and B. Tissot, "Localisation, Caractérisation et Classification Pétrographiques des Substances Organiques Sédimentaires Fossiles", *Adv. Org. Geochem. 1971, Proc. Int. Congr., 5th,* Pergamon, Oxford, pp. 1—28 (1972).

106. J. T. McCartney and M. Teichmüller, "Classification of Coals According to Degree of Coalification by Reflectance of the Vitrinite Component", *Fuel, 51,* 64—68 (1972).

107. R. Caye and J.P. Ragot, "Progrès Récents dans la Mesure de la Réflectance des Particules Carbonées Solides Disséminées dans les Roches", *Adv. Org. Geochem. 1971, Proc. Int. Congr., 5th,* Pergamon, Oxford, pp. 591—600 (1972).

108. N.H. Bostick, "Thermal Alteration of Classic Organic Particles as an Indicator of Contact and Burial Metamorphism in Sedimentary Rocks", *Geosci. Man., 3,* 83—92 (1971).

109. P. Leplat and R. Noel, "Etude par Pyrochromatographie en Phase Gazeuse et par Réflectance de l'Evolution de Quelques Kérogènes", *Adv. Org. Geochem. 1971, Proc. Int. Congr., 5th,* Pergamon, Oxford, pp. 567—576 (1972).

110. F.L. Staplin, "Sedimentary Organic Matter, Organic Metamorphism, and Oil and Gas Occurrence", *Bull. Can. Pet. Geol., 17,* 47—66 (1969).

111. B. Alpern, "Classification Pétrographique des Constituants Organiques Fossiles des Roches Sédimentaires", *Rev. Inst. Fr. Pét., 25,* 1233—1267 (1970).

112. A.A. Kartsev, N.B. Vassoevich, A.A. Geodekian, S.G. Neruchev and V.A. Sokolov, "The Principal Stage in the Formation of Petroleum", *Proc. 8th World Pet. Congr., 2,* 3—11 (1971).

113. R.J. Cordell, "Depths of Oil Origin and Primary Migration: A Review and Critique", *Bull. Am. Assoc. Pet. Geol., 56,* 2029—2067 (1972).

114. P. Besème, "Bitumes Figurés et Déplacés en Association dans Cinq Séries à Kérogène d'Anatolie (Turquie): Description et Origine de ces Kérabitumes", *Rev. Inst. Fr. Pét., 27,* 885—912 (1972).

115. H.D. Klemme, "Heat Influences Size of Oil Giants (Parts 1 and 2)", *Oil Gas J., 70* (29), 136—144 (1972); *70* (30), 76—78 (1972).

116. K.G. Bell and J.M. Hunt, "Native Bitumens Associated with Oil Shales", in: I.A. Breger (Editor), *Organic Geochemistry*, Pergamon, Oxford, Ch. 8, pp. 333—366 (1963).
117. S. Ergun, "X-ray Studies of Coals and Carbonaceous Materials", *U.S. Bur. Mines, Bull., 648* (1968).
118. A. Oberlin and G. Terrière, "Use of Diffraction Contrast Techniques to Study a Mixture of Highly Disorganized Carbonaceous Phases", *J. Microsc. (Paris), 14*, 1—6 (1972).
119. A.W. Decora, J.P. Flaherty, F.R. McDonald and G.L. Cook, "A Rapid Method for Estimating Oil Yields of Oil Shales by Broadline NMR Spectroscopy", *Am. Chem. Soc., Div. Fuel Chem., Prepr. Pap., 15* (1), 38—46 (1971).
120. R.F. Cane, "The Constitution and Synthesis of Oil Shale", *Proc. 7th World Pet. Congr., 3*, 681—689 (1967).
121. Y. Shahar and V. Wurzburger, "A New Oil Shale Deposit in the Northern Negev, Israel", *Proc. 7th World Pet. Congr., 3*, 719—728 (1967).
122. E.W. Cook, "Thermal Analysis of Oil Shales", *Q. Colo. Sch. Mines, 65*, 133—140 (1970).
123. A.I. Danyushevskaya, "Residual Organic Matter (Kerogen) in Mesozoic Formations of Northern-Central Siberia Studied by Thermal Methods", *Nov. Metody Issled. Osad. Porod Tsel'yu Poiskov Blagopriyatnykh Nefte-Gazoobrazovaniu Usloviy*, 44—50 (1971).
124. H.-R. v. Gaertner and H.-H. Schmitz, "Organic Matter in Posidonia Shales as an Indication of Residual Oil Deposit", *Proc. 6th World Pet. Congr., 1*, 355—363 (1963).
125. J.W. Smith and D.R. Johnson, "Multiple Thermal Analysis of Natural Materials", *Am. Lab., 3*, 8—14 (1971).
126. M. Blumer and W.D. Snyder, "Porphyrins of High Molecular Weight in a Triassic Oil Shale: Evidence from Gel Permeation Chromatography", *Chem. Geol., 2*, 35—45 (1967).
127. A.S. Houghton and W.W. Howe, "Organic Metal Complexes in the Uinta Basin", *Proc. 7th World Pet. Congr., 3*, 703—705 (1967).
128. J.D. Saxby, "Metal-organic Chemistry of the Geochemical Cycle", *Rev. Pure Appl. Chem. (Aust.), 19*, 131—150 (1969).
129. G. Eglinton, "Organic Geochemistry. The Organic Chemists' Approach", in: G. Eglinton and M.T.J. Murphy (Editors), *Organic Geochemistry*, Springer, Berlin, Ch. 2, pp. 20—73 (1969).

Chapter 7

STRUCTURAL ASPECTS OF ORGANIC COMPONENTS IN OIL SHALES

T.F. YEN

Introduction

Kerogen is the most abundant organic molecule on earth [1]. It has been estimated by McIver [2] that, whereas all the intercellular carbon in the biosphere amounts to $3 \cdot 10^{17}$ g, kerogen is at least ten thousand times as abundant. Kerogen, here, signifies the portion of organic sediments which exists in the dispersed form and is nonextractable by solvents [3]. In contrast, the extractable nonhydrocarbon portion is usually termed bitumen. Classification of organic matter in sediments is presented in Fig. 7-1. The organic material remaining in source rock after oil migration is usually referred to as kerogen. This kerogen can generate oil and gas as well as form graphite in sedimentary rocks.

Kerogen is present in all types of sediments as suggested by Hunt [4] and its properties may depend on diagenetic processes, chemical environments of deposition, and the particular kinds of biological sources. For example, Marchand et al. [5] characterized torbanite, coorongite, tasmanite, marahunite and a number of boghead deposits and found that there is a great variation in H/C ratio as shown by infrared spectrographic studies. Yen and Sprang

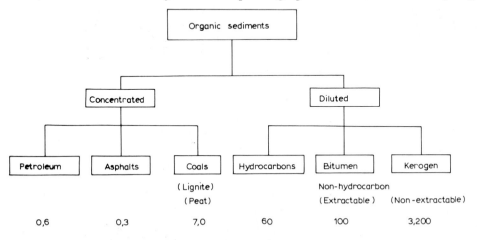

Fig. 7-1. Classification of organic sediments. The abundance of various organic sediments in the ecosphere is presented in trillion tons.

TABLE 7-I

Composition, age and precursors of some typical kerogens

Name and location of kerogen	Age	Precursor	Bitumen content (%)*	C (%)	H (%)	N (%)	S (%)	O (%)	Ng · 10[-18]**
Torbanite, Scotland[1]	Permian	*Pilaminima P. scotica (Botryococcus)*	1.6	79.1	9.8	0.80	—	9.2	1.4
Green River oil shale kerogen, Colo., USA	Eocene	—	2.0	56.1	7.2	2.5	2.6	13	—
Albertite, Utah, USA[2]	Eocene	—	1	83.4	8.4	1.8	1.0	5.4	8.5
Wurtzilite, Utah, USA[2]	Eocene	—	trace	83.5	11.5	1.6	3.7	0.5	0.53
Marahunite, Brazil[1]	Tertiary	*Botryococcus braunii*	1.7	58.9	5.5	1.0	2.3	26.4	0.66
Pseudocoal, So. Africa[2]	Permian	—	trace	81.3	8.6	2.5	0.5	6.8	15
Autun Boghead, France[1]	Permian	*Pila bibractensis (Botryococcus)*	0.53	76.9	10.4	1.5	0.9	7.6	0.35
Ingramite, Utah, USA[2]	Eocene	—	1	83.5	10.5	1.6	1.8	2.9	1.8
Kukersite, Estonia[1]	Ordovician	*Glecocapsomorpha prisca*	0.97	66.4	7.1	0.69	1.1	18	0.42
Alginite, Australia[1]	Permian	*Pila reinschia (Botryococcus)*	1.2	79.6	8.5	0.95	1.3	6.0	3.9
Tasmanite, Tasmania	Permian	—	5.6	72.5	9.1	1.1	3.0	10.5	0.42

Gilsonite, Utah, USA	Eocene	—	62	84.1	9.9	0.3	0.3	6.5	5.3
Anthroxolite, Quebec, Canada[2]	Ordovician	—	trace	87.1	4.8	0.6	0.3	8.6	28
Grahamite, Oklahoma, USA[2]	—	—	23	88.9	7.5	0.5	2.6	1.1	7.6
Coorongite, So. Australia[1]	Recent	*Elasophyton coorongina* (*Botryococcus*)	46	76.1	11.2	0.4	0.2	11.9	—
Fossil resin, France[1]	Cretaceous	—	63	70.3	8.5	0.2	0.3	14.1	0.28
Cutinite, Belgium[1]	Carboniferous	Cuticle	0.12	75.4	4.6	0.9	1.6	11.0	24
Cannel coal, Belgium[1]	Carboniferous	Spores	1.2	74.6	4.5	1.0	1.2	13.2	14

[1] Data of Marchand et al., [5].
[2] Data of Yen et al, [6].
*Referred to as benzene solubles normalized to percentages of benzene insolubles (kerogen).
**Spin density (per gram) from electron-spin-resonance data, see [8] for detail.

[6] have studied a number of asphaltoids and asphaltites, such as albertite, ingramite, wurtzilite, grahamite, etc., by electron spin resonance and differentiate them into coal-like series and asphaltene-like series based on Lande g-value differences. Structurally, these g-value differences can be correlated with the heterocyclic contributions of the given sample. It also should be pointed out that the aromaticity values differ greatly among different types of kerogen [6]. Usually, the more mature the kerogen, the higher its aromaticity value.

Kerogens can originate from different source materials, e.g., blue-green algae, red algae and green algae in a variety of environments, i.e., lacustrine, marine, inland sea, etc. The composition of kerogen also can vary with geological age. Compositions of some representative kerogens are presented in Table 7-I. The differences in composition reflect the diverse structures of organic compounds in kerogens.

Kerogen of Green River Formation

Oil shale of the Green River Formation is unique because of its exceedingly high content of carbonate minerals. A typical analysis of Green River oil shale from Colorado (see Fig. 1-3, p. 3) shows that the dolomite plus calcite content may reach 43%. During the Eocene period, large shallow lakes may have formed as a result of the water accumulation from the Rocky Mountain ranges. The fine-grained mineral debris may be the products of erosion and leaching from the older sediments. The saline minerals as well as carbonates may have been contemporaneously deposited with the organic degradation products.

The total organics content of the oil shale of Green River Formation usually ranges from 13 to 16% [7]. As shown in Table 7-I, the soluble bitumen content of Green River oil-shale sample is about 20%, whereas the kerogen content is about 80%. For the majority of the typical kerogens, the content of associated bitumens is commonly below 10%. These typical kerogens are conventionally classified under asphaltoids or asphaltic pyrobitumens. On the other hand, if the bitumens content is over 50%, kerogens usually fall in the class of asphaltites. Among these, gilsonite and grahamite are good examples. The kerogen of the Green River Formation belongs to the intermediate class, transitional between the asphaltoids and asphaltites.

The kerogen of the Green River Formation is one of the few which has a high oil yield per unit weight of organic carbon. Table 7-II presents compositions and oil yields of some of the world's common oil shales. The oil yield per unit weight of organic carbon of Piceance Creek oil shale of Colorado is of the same order of magnitude as those of organic carbon-rich oil shales (greater than 50% organic carbon content), with the exception of Alaskan and Australian oil shales. The high oil/gas ratio of some oil shales obtained

TABLE 7-II

Composition and oil yield of some oil shales

Location of sample	Org. C (%)	S (%)	N (%)	Ash (%)	Oil yield (gal/ton)
Kiligwa River, Alaska[1]	53.9	1.5	0.30	34.1	139
Piceance Creek, Colo.[1]	12.4	0.63	0.41	65.7	28
Elko, Nev.[2]	8.6	1.1	0.48	81.6	8.4
Dunnet, Scotland[1]	12.3	0.73	0.46	77.8	22
Ione, Ca.[2]	62.9	2.1	0.42	23	52
São Paulo, Brazil[1]	12.8	0.84	0.41	75.0	18
Puertollano, Spain[1]	26.0	1.7	0.55	62.8	47
Shale City, Oregon[1]	25.8	2.2	0.51	48.3	48
Coolaway Mt., Australia[1]	81.4	0.49	0.83	4.4	200
Soldiers Summit, Utah[2]	13.5	0.28	0.39	66.1	17
Ermelo, So. Africa[1]	52.2	0.74	0.84	33.6	100
New Glasgow, Canada[1]	7.92	0.70	0.54	84.0	9.4

[1] Data from Robinson and Dinneen [9].
[2] Data from McKee [10].

during retorting is an important feature, which can be correlated with aromaticity, maturity, and type of source material.

Structural models of complex organic molecules

Organic molecules can be represented by structural models ranging from simple to complex. Any structure is a shorthand representation of the molecular shape and contour showing an arrangement of atoms in groups. Different categories of organic components ranging from very simple to very complex are presented below.

(a) *Simple compound*. Simple compound has a low molecular weight and usually consists of specific skeleton and substituents. The specific location of atoms can be fully characterized by X-ray chromatography, e.g., β-methylnaphthalene.

(b) *Regular polymers*. Regular polymers are oligomers of high molecular weight and consist of regularly-spaced groups. They have a definite pattern of repeating sequences, e.g., polystyrene or polyimidazopyrrolone.

(c) *Random polymers*. Random polymers are similar to class (b), except that the building blocks occur in random fashion. Examples are biopolymers, such as lignin (Fig. 7-2) or melanin.

(d) *Intrinsic mixture*. Intrinsic mixture consists of a homogeneous collection of structurally similar compounds. In many cases, the strong association of π-electron in aromatic molecules greatly influences the physical properties.

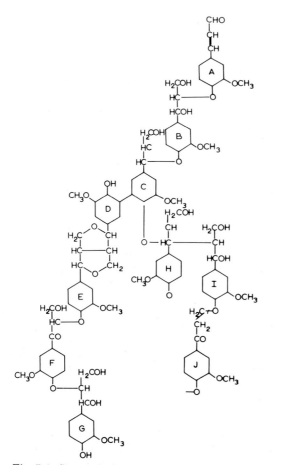

Fig. 7-2. Structure for a typical lignin slightly modified after Freudenberg [16].

An average structure can represent the entire array of similar molecules; examples are coal tar pitches (Fig. 7-3), petroleums, and cokes.

(e) *Multipolymers*. Multipolymers can be viewed as a combination of classes (c) and (d). These polymers have a large number of different building blocks. For example, copolymer (2 building blocks), terpolymer (3 building blocks), etc., to multipolymers (*n*-building blocks).

Coal, asphaltene, carbon, and kerogen belong to the multipolymer class.

In many cases, the structure of large molecules presents further problems, e.g., the presence of inter- or intra-crosslinking and inter- or intra-association. Actually, the development of technology of the fossil fuels depends heavily on the hypothetical models proposed. A good example is in the field of hydrodesulfurization of heavy fraction of petroleum. The structural model of asphaltene proposed by Yen et al. [11] enabled a successful catalytical

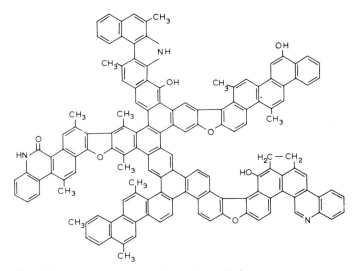

Fig. 7-3. Average molecule of a coal tar pitch.

conversion of petroleum stocks. Reference was made to this achievement by Beuther [12], Drushel [13], Ebel [14], and Mills [15].

The model is only an image representing the actual structure and reflects the properties of the actual substance. Although none of the proposed

Monomeric   Medium   Polymeric

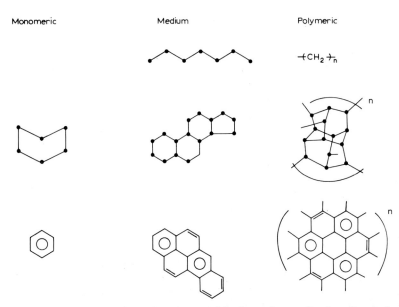

Fig. 7-4. Structure of various types of hydrocarbons; the top line is for paraffinic, the central line is for naphthenic, and the bottom line is for the aromatic. Only carbon skeleton is indicated. The polymeric forms include polyethylene, diamond, and graphite.

structures is final, it will approximate the actual substance through continuous modification.

Thus, the structural model is an abbreviation (shorthand version) of the complex structure of large molecules. Simple molecules can be precisely measured by the existing physical methods. Often, the structure of large molecules have to be deduced from those of the simple to medium molecules. Figure 7-4 is a representation of this approach. The large molecules of three types of hydrocarbons, i.e., paraffinic, naphthenic, and aromatic, are correlated with their simpler counterparts. Structures of large molecules such as polyethylene, diamond and graphite are thus derived.

Burlingame-Haug-Schnoes-Simoneit structural model

The proposed structures for kerogen of the Green River Formation are presented here chronologically. Burlingame et al. [17,18] oxidized a kerogen concentrate with 3 M chromic acid in sulfuric acid at reflux temperature for periods of 3—48 hours. The extracts isolated from the oxidation medium were analyzed by gas liquid chromatography (GLC) and by mass spectrometry (MS). Although the residue contained essentially no organic carbon (0.21% compared with 65.9% in the initial kerogen concentrate), yet the combined total extracts only represented about 8.8% of the carbon content of kerogen concentrate. The structural model proposed by these investigators, therefore, is of limited use because of the low values of carbon obtained by them (the remaining carbon is expected to be oxidized into CO_2).

The total yield of acids generated by this method increases with the duration of oxidation. Results indicate that there is a pronounced increase in yields of the more polar or more functionalized acids (ether-extractable acids) with the duration of oxidation. The isoprenoid acids decrease drastically in concentration compared with the normal, dicarboxylic and keto acids as oxidation progresses. Initial oxidation releases isoprenoid acids as well as predominant C_{16}-branched acid. In order to account for this concept, a structural model is proposed in Fig. 7-5. The essential feature of this model is an indication of the nature of substituents in the periphery of the kerogen nuclei.

The acids obtained by oxidation could arise by the following processes:

(a) Oxidative cleavage of carbon—carbon bonds.

(b) Hydrolysis of ester linkages to give acids and alcohols, the latter being subsequently oxidized to acids.

(c) "Loosening" of the kerogen matrix, thus liberating entrapped compounds.

Probably all of these processes can occur. Especially in the case of process (a), the chromic-acid oxidation usually cleaves the side chains from the nuclei of a large molecule. The presence of all these types of substituents shown in Fig. 7-5 have been supported by spectral evidence of the homologs of the oxidized products. The predominance of 4,8,12-trimethyl-tridecanoic

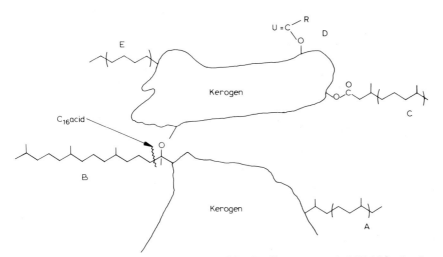

Fig. 7-5. Substituent structure suggested by Burlingame et al. [17,18]. A = isoprenoidal substituents; B = cross-linked phytol; the zig-zag line represents suggested site of chromic oxidation cleavage; C = isoprenoidal ester substituents; D = other ester substituents; R can be aromatic, normal alkano or methoxyalkano group; E = n-alkane.

acid in some oxidized fractions indicates crosslinking of the allyl rearrangement center in phytol during the formation of the large molecule.

Djuricic-Murphy-Vitorovic-Biemann kerogen structure

Djuricic et al. [19] used aqueous alkaline permanganate to oxidize the kerogen concentrate and consequently obtained 70% conversion of resultant carboxylic acids. The acids were converted to methyl esters and analyzed with GLC–MS computer system. The main products isolated were unbranched aliphatic acids (C_8–C_{29}), saturated dibasic acids (C_4–C_{17}), and isoprenoid acids (C_9,C_{12},C_{14}–C_{17},C_{19}–C_{22}) (see Table 7-III). In contrast to the findings of Burlingame et al. [18], keto and aromatic acids were found only in small quantities.

Permanganate oxidation is known to attack primarily at, or next to, a carbon atom bearing a functional group. It has been verified experimentally [20] that sites susceptible to the attack are those where quaternary carbons are present. Inasmuch as 70% of the carbon skeleton of kerogen has been degraded into acids, certain statements can be made concerning the structure of the kerogen nucleus. Djuricic et al. [19] concluded that the nucleus probably consists of long polymethylene bridges as shown in Fig. 7-6. The points of branching (indicated by tertiary or quaternary centers) are subjected to permanganate oxidation or to alkaline hydrolysis. Cleavage at a point of attachment of a saturated side chain would produce a monocarboxylic acid,

TABLE 7-III

Isoprenoid acids identified from permanganate oxidation [19]

Symbol[1]	Acid
C_9^α	2,6-dimethylheptanoic
C_{12}^δ	5,9-dimethyldecanoic
C_{14}^α	2,6,10-trimethylundecanoic
C_{15}^β	3,7,11-trimethyldodecanoic
C_{16}^γ	4,8,12-trimethyltridecanoic
C_{17}^δ	5,9,13-trimethyltetradecanoic
C_{19}^α	2,6,10,14-tetramethylpentadecanoic
C_{20}^β	3,7,11,15-tetramethylhexadecanoic
C_{21}^γ	4,8,12,16-tetramethylheptadecanoic
C_{22}^δ	5,9,13,17-tetramethyloctadecanoic

[1] $C_x^{\alpha-\delta}$ denotes isoprenoid acid containing a total of x carbon atoms with the first methyl branch at the position indicated by superscript Greek letter.

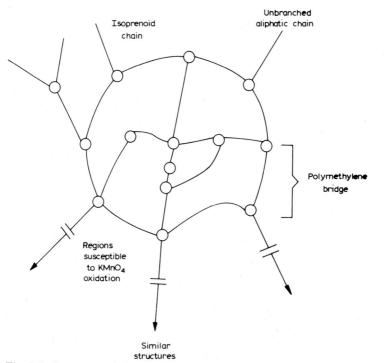

Fig. 7-6. Structure of the subunit of kerogen network modified after Djuricic et al. [19]. Lines between circles represent polymethylene chains. The circles represent junction of branching. Both n-paraffinic and isoprenoid chains are present.

whereas cleavage at a site of two carbon atoms connected by a polymethylene bridge would produce a dicarboxylic acid or even a tricarboxylic acid.

Contrary to the findings of Burlingame et al. [17], aromatic carboxylic acid was not isolated as a result of the permanganate oxidation. It is known that coals can be easily oxidized into families of aromatic acids under similar conditions [21]. Thus one can conclude that Green River kerogen contains only a few (or practically none) aromatic sites. Ketoacids are also not present. It is possible that chromic acid can cause β-oxidation of a paraffin.

Schmidt-Collerus and Prien kerogen structure

Schmidt-Collerus and Prien [22] used a combination of micropyrolysis and mass spectrometry to investigate the structure of Green River kerogen.

TABLE 7-IV

Principal fragmentation products of kerogen concentrated by micropyrolysis (According to Schmidt-Collerus and Prien [22])

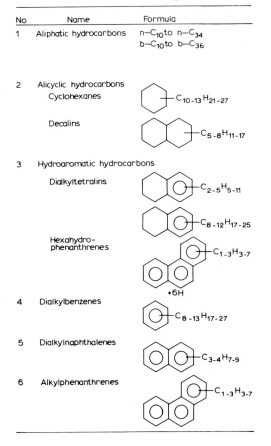

No	Name	Formula
1	Aliphatic hydrocarbons	$n-C_{10}$ to $n-C_{34}$ $b-C_{10}$ to $b-C_{36}$
2	Alicyclic hydrocarbons	
	Cyclohexanes	$C_{10-13}H_{21-27}$
	Decalins	$C_{5-8}H_{11-17}$
3	Hydroaromatic hydrocarbons	
	Dialkyltetralins	$C_{2-5}H_{5-11}$
		$C_{8-12}H_{17-25}$
	Hexahydro-phenanthrenes	$C_{1-3}H_{3-7}$ +6H
4	Dialkylbenzenes	$C_{8-13}H_{17-27}$
5	Dialkylnaphthalenes	$C_{3-4}H_{7-9}$
6	Alkylphenanthrenes	$C_{1-3}H_{3-7}$

Fig. 7-8.

Fig. 7-7.

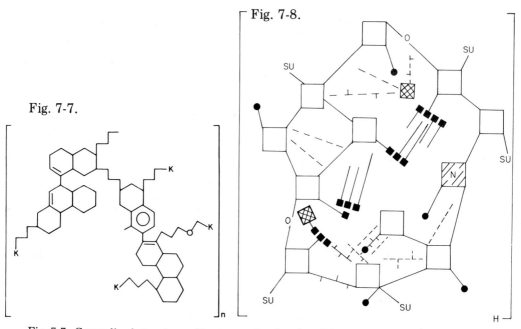

Fig. 7-7. Generalized structure of kerogen subunits after Schmidt-Collerus and Prien [22]. K indicates other kerogen units.

Fig. 7-8. Schematic structure of kerogen matrix modified after Schmidt-Collerus and Prien [22]. The squares represent subunits (SU). Small solid squares represent acidic functions; solid spheres represent methyl terminations. The dashed lines represent untrapped species. Hatched lines in subunits represent heterocyclic components. Lines represent alkanes.

Their results indicate that both α-kerogen and β-kerogen are present, with the latter representing only 5% of the total kerogen present. Microscopically, the α-kerogen behaves as alginite with low aromatic content, whereas β-kerogen contains high-aromatic (probably polycondensed) material. Under the controlled micropyrolysis, certain components were identified: (a) Normal and branched alkanes; (b) alkyl derivatives of decalins and tetralins (mostly orthosubstituted); (c) alkyl-substituted tricyclic terpenoid or phenanthroid-type derivatives. The structures of these compounds are summarized in Table 7-IV. Based on these subunits, a generalized kerogen structure was proposed as shown in Fig. 7-7. The major part of the subunits consists of alkyl-substituted decalins or tetralins, interlinked by normal or branched alkane bridges. In a kerogen matrix, many of these subunits are connected by alkane or ether linkages as shown in Fig. 7-8. There are also trapped subunits within this matrix.

The model proposed by Schmidt-Collerus and Prien [22] is useful, but is based on pyrolysis, which presents a considerable drawback. It is obvious that kerogen will be converted into pyrobitumens at elevated temperatures. Many of these observed compounds may have been changed due to pyrolysis, e.g., isoprenoids will form naphthenics by ring closure or even aromatics due to dehydrogenation. Recently, Scrima et al. [23] have demonstrated through thermal chromatography that the composition of pyrobitumen is entirely different from that of native bitumen.

Yen-Young-Shih kerogen structure

In structural studies, both physical and chemical methods are used concurrently and supplement each other. The chemical method involves stepwise permanganate oxidation of kerogen concentrate [24] as well as leached oil shale [25]. The efficiency of this mild oxidation is over 90%, i.e., the acids formed from the original organic carbon content of the kerogen constitute over 90% by weight. Ten different successive fractions are taken [24] ; each fraction is studied using a number of analytical methods, such as GLC, nuclear magnetic resonance (NMR), MS, and infrared spectroscopy (IR). On the other hand, the kerogen concentrate, as well as certain oil-shale samples from which certain minerals have been selectively removed (e.g., carbonate-free oil shale, pyrite-free oil shale, etc.) have been investigated using a number of physical methods. The X-ray diffraction technique, which has been previously developed by Yen et al. [26] for determination of asphaltenes, continues to be a powerful tool for studying kerogens (27). Electron spectroscopy for chemical analysis (ESCA), ESR and IR remain also as non-destructive tools for elucidation of the complex structure of this large multipolymer. Provisionally, the following conclusions can be reached from the experimental results obtained by several investigators [26,27,28]:

(a) Aromatic carbon systems are either absent or present in minute quantities in kerogen. Aromaticity approaches zero; however, this does not rule out the possibility of the presence of isolated double bonds such as those present in hydroaromatic or heterocyclic systems.

(b) The bulk of the carbon skeleton is naphthenic and contains 3—4 rings. It is possible that the carbon skeleton consists of these naphthenic clusters which are linked by heterocyclic or randomly-substituted branched hydrocarbon chains.

(c) Free-end and flexible long-chain linear polymethylene structures are absent. This does not rule out the crosslink structure of elaterite [3], which could be quaternary bonded by polymethylene chains or cycloparaffins.

(d) The polar groups, as well as heterocyclic atoms (such as N, S, O) are located at the outermost shell region.

(e) The degree of crosslinking for the central core and the outermost shell is different — the outermost shell contains more crosslinkings than the core region.

(f) The quantities of long-chain alkane substituents (ranging from C_{17} to

C_{31}) become more abundant toward the center of the core. The free end is probably entangled randomly.

(g) Loosely held "monomers" such as the major species identified in bitumen, e.g., stearanes, triterpanes, isoprenoids, and cyclic C_{40} carotenoids, may be entrapped in kerogen matrix. These molecules can be recovered by either heat or solvent.

(h) There is no regularity of crosslinking or branching in kerogen. There appears to be inter- and intra-molecular hydrogen bonding, as well as charge-transfer bonding.

(i) There is a possibility of the existence of diamond-like structures such as adamantane-type or caged macrocyclics.

In the light of the above-mentioned findings, a conceptual model is proposed, largely to accommodate the accumulated physical and chemical evidence. In doing so, the following guidelines are followed:

(1) Kerogen matrix is a multipolymer. Its insolubility qualifies kerogen to be considered as a non-uniform, 3-dimensional network of gel. The inhomogeneity is due to biogenesis and subsequent diagenesis.

(2) The "monomer" of this multipolymer consists of two types, i.e., (a) those containing difunctional bridges and (b) those consisting of multifunctional components. Both bridges and components can become terminators.

(3) Major components are isoprenoids, steroids, terpenoids, carotenoids, etc., as indicated in Fig. 7-9. The location of multifunctional link sites

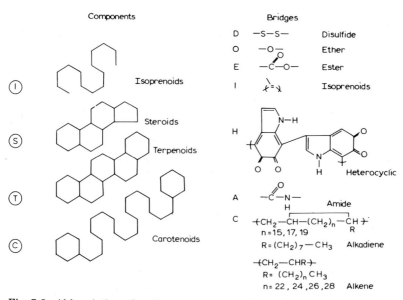

Fig. 7-9. Abbreviations for the common components and bridges in the organic portions of shales (see text for explanation).

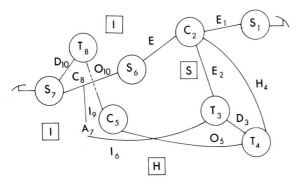

Fig. 7-10. Hypothetical structural model proposed by Yen [28] of a multipolymer representing the organic component of Green River oil shale. The nomenclature of the components is presented in Fig. 7-9. The circles represent essential components of kerogen. The crosslinks are indicated by bridges linked among components. The squares represent molecules trapped in the kerogen network which are bitumens. The subscript numerals indicate the sequence of monomers which have been exemplified in Fig. 7-11.

can remain as a variable. Due to diagenesis, the functional groups such as hydroxyl and double bond (unsaturation) are labile to the skeleton during isomerization. In the present chapter only skeletons are shown.

(4) Common bridges consist of disulfides, ethers, esters, isoprenics, heterocyclics, alkenes, and alkadienes (see Fig. 7-9). Incorporation of nitrogen-containing systems in kerogen during biostratinomy is known, e.g., the pyrrole system remains important due to the porphyrin pigment. The majority of algal hydrocarbons are long-chain α-olefins and alkadienes.

(5) The components are linked by bridges to form a kerogen matrix. Presence of loosely-held components and bridges in the matrix is also possible. This is hypothetically depicted in Fig. 7-10 [28].

In order to visualize such a structure, an example is constructed using the framework model (Fig. 7-11). This hypothetical model indicates a formula $C_{235}H_{397}O_{13}N_3S_5$ and measures $39 \times 27 \times 25$ Å^3. Robinson's formula for kerogen is $C_{215}H_{330}O_{12}N_5S$ (see Chapter 4) with H/C = 1.53. The H/C ratio of kerogen concentrate may range from 1.3 to 1.6.

Conclusions

A model is a working tool and should constantly undergo modification. It should be emphasized that at present the difficult task of elucidation of the structure of kerogen has not been accomplished. It is impractical to obtain a detailed structure with all the locations of atoms and the stereo-configuration of carbons. In complex molecules such as multipolymers, knowledge of an average structure is of great value, e.g., the hypothetical structure of asphaltics

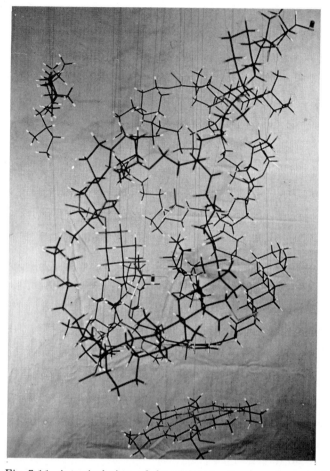

Fig. 7-11. A typical view of the molecular framework model for Green River kerogen and bitumen, which is based on the structure in Fig. 7-3. The following components are used for the model (numerals here refer to subscripts in Fig. 7-10): $1 = C_{17}H_{26}$; $2 = C_{32}H_{58}$; $3 = C_{27}H_{42}$; $4 = C_{22}H_{33}$; $5 = C_{29}H_{54}$; $6 = C_{20}H_{30}$; $7 = C_{17}H_{25}$; $8 = C_{25}H_{40}$. The following bridges are also used: $1 = CO_2$; $2 = CO_2$; $3 = S_2$; $4 = C_{16}H_6O_4N_2$; $5 = O$; $6 = C_{17}H_{34}$; $7 = CONH$; $8 = C_{17}H_{31}$; $9 = C_9H_{17}$; $10 = S_2$; $11 = O$; $12 = CO_2$.

[29] has helped to interpret a great number of basic as well as technological problems [30].

Another approach to the elucidation of the kerogen structure is the study of diagenesis of the hydrocarbons and lipids of microorganisms, which are known to be the precursors of the organics in shale. It is known that, by far, the most prominent producers of branched alkanes are the blue-green algae. In *Nostoc muscorum*, *Anacystis cyanea*, *Chroococcus turgidus*, *Phormidium luridum*, etc. the major components are 7- and 8-methylheptadecane (see

TABLE 7-V

Long-chain hydrocarbons produced by microorganisms

Hydrocarbons	Range and predominant carbon no.	Type of microorganisms	Ref.
n-Alkanes	$C_{16}-C_{33}, C_{17}$	*Anacystis cyanea, Chroococcus turgidus, Lyngbya aestuarii* (A)*	[32]
	$C_{13}-C_{19}$ $C_{25}-C_{29}, C_{29}$	*Sclerotinia sclerotiorum* (F)**	[36]
i-Alkanes	$C_{25}, C_{27}, C_{29}, C_{31}$	*Sphacelothica reiliana*	[35]
	C_{27}, C_{29}, C_{31}	*Ustilago maydis* *Urocystis agropyii*	[35] [33]
	$4-M_e\ C_{17}$	*Chlorogloea fritschii* (A)	[34]
	$7-M_e\ C_{17}$ $8-M_e\ C_{17}$	*Nostoc muscorum* *Anacystis cyanea* (A)	[32]
Alkenes	$n-C_{17}-\alpha$	*Chlorella pyrenoidosa* *Anacystis nidulans*	
	$n-C_{23}-\alpha, n-C_{25}-\alpha$	*Scendesmus quadricauda* (A)	[32]
	$n-C_{26}-\alpha, -C_{29}-\alpha$	*Anacystis montana* (A)	[32]
	$n-C_{25}-\alpha, n-C_{27}-\alpha$	*Chorella vulgaris* (A)	[32]
Alkadiene	$n-C_{27}-\Delta\ 1,18$ $n-C_{29}-\Delta\ 1,20$ $n-C_{31}-\Delta\ 1,22$	*Botryococcus braunii*	[37]
	botryococcene isobotryococcene (tetra-M_e acyclic triterpene)	(A)	
Isoprenoids	squalene	*Methylococcus capsulatus*	[38]
	hopene-22 [29]	*Methylococcus capsulatus*	[39]
	hopene-17 [21]	*Bacillus acidocaldarius*	[40]

*Algae (A).
**Fungi (F).

Table 7-V). Alkenes with terminal vinyl groups are frequently encountered in algal hydrocarbons, e.g., n-heptadecane-1 in *Chlorella pyrenoidosa*. Recently, sterols have been observed in prokaryotic organism, and squalene per se has been detected [31]. It is possible that quite a number of penta-cyclic triterpenes, such as hopene and maybe gammacerane, which have been identified in Green River oil shale, are derived from the biomass. In this manner, the higher homologs of carbon ($>C_{21}$) can be derived without con-

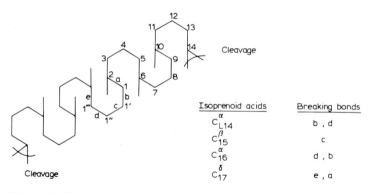

Fig. 7-12. Example of an acyclic tetraterpene, employed as a bridge for kerogen molecules. Upon permanganate oxidation, the two connecting ends are cleaved to form carboxylic acid. A series of different isoprenoid (branched) acids which could form are presented.

tribution from the specialized terrestrial plants. Some of the long-chain hydrocarbons derived from microorganisms are listed in Table 7-V.

The hypothetical model of Yen et al. [28] is compatible with the structures suggested by other investigators [17,19,22], and explains the observed results of many investigators. As an example, the isoparaffins obtained by Djuricic et al. [19] in Table 7-III can be further classified. In the Yen et al. [28] model, isoprenoid or terpenoid hydrocarbons can serve as either bridges or components. It is possible to assume that the acyclic terpene skeleton exists in the following simple monomers:

C_5 isoprene (I)
C_{10} myrcene (I)
C_{15} faresane (T) (sesquiterpene)
C_{20} phytane (T) (diterpene)
C_{30} squalene (T) (triterpene)
C_{40} lycopene (T) (tetraterpene)

The existence of isolated C_{14} to C_{17} branched paraffins can be explained by assuming a lycopene-type bridge. As shown in Fig. 7-12, cleavage at junctures will result in a carboxylic acid. Breaking bonds as indicated in Fig. 7-12 will yield C_{14}^{α}, C_{15}^{β}, C_{16}^{γ} and C_{17}^{δ} acids; otherwise it is difficult to form the patterns of the trimethyl sequences. Presence of other series such as C_{19}^{α} to C_{22}^{γ} can be explained similarly. The series of C_9^{α} to C_{12}^{δ} can be explained by postulating squalene as being the precursor.

Acknowledgement

This work was supported by NSF research grants GI-35683 and AER-74-23797 and A.G.A. BR-48-12. The help by Professor George V. Chilingar is greatly appreciated.

References

1. T.F. Yen, "Terrestrial and Extraterrestrial Stable Organic Molecules", in: R.F. Landel and A. Rembaum (Editors), *Chemistry in Space Research*, Am. Elsevier, New York, pp. 105—152 (1972).
2. R.D. McIver, "Composition of Kerogen — Clue to its Role in the Origin of Petroleum", *Proc. 7th World Pet. Congr., Vol. II*, Elsevier, Amsterdam, pp. 25—36 (1967).
3. T.F. Yen, "Chemical Aspects of Interfuel Conversion", *Energy Sources, 1* (1), 117—136 (1973).
4. J.M. Hunt, "Distribution of Hydrocarbons in Sedimentary Rocks", *Geochim. Cosmochim. Acta, 22,* 37—49 (1961).
5. A. Marchand, P. Libert and A. Combaz, "Essai de characterisation physico-chimique de la diagénèse de quelques roches organiques 'Biologiquement homogènes' ", *Rev. Inst. Fr. Pét., 24* (1), 3—20 (1969).
6. T.F. Yen and S.R. Sprang, "ESR g-values of Bituminous Materials", *ACS Div. Pet. Chem. Preprints, 15* (3), A65—A76 (1970).
7. J.W. Smith, "Ultimate Composition of Organic Material in Green River Oil Shale", *U.S. Bur. Mines, Rep. Invest. 5725,* 1—16 (1961).
8. T.F. Yen, J.G. Erdman and A.J. Saraceno, "Investigation of the Nature of Free Radicals in Petroleum Asphaltenes", *Anal. Chem., 34,* 694—700 (1962).
9. W.E. Robinson and G.U. Dinneen, "Constitutional Aspects of Oil Shale Kerogen", *Proc. 7th World Pet. Congr., Vol. III*, Elsevier, Amsterdam, 669—680 (1967).
10. R.H. McKee, *Shale Oil*, Chemical Catalog Co. (1925).
11. T.F. Yen, J.G. Erdman and S.S. Pollack, "Investigation of the Structure of Petroleum Asphaltenes by X-ray Diffraction", *Anal. Chem., 33,* 1587—1594 (1961).
12. H. Beuther and B.K. Schmid, "Reaction Mechanisms and Rates in Residue Hydrosulfurization", *Proc. 6th World Pet. Congr., Sect. III*, 297—310 (1963).
13. H.V. Drushel, "Analytical Characterization of Residua and Hydrotreated Products", *ACS Div. Pet. Chem. Preprints, 17* (4), F92—F101 (1972).
14. R.H. Ebel, "Recent Advances in Fuel Desulfurization Technology", *ACS Div. Pet. Chem. Preprints, 17* (3), C46—C55 (1972).
15. G.A. Mills, "Advances in Fuel Chemistry 1961—74", *ACS Div. Fuel Chem., 19* (3), 178—199 (1974).
16. F.E. Brauns and D.A. Brauns, *The Chemistry of Lignin*, Academic Press, pp. 616—629 (1960).
17. A.L. Burlingame and B.R. Simoneit, "High Resolution Mass Spectrometry of Green River Formation Kerogen Oxidations", *Nature, 222,* 741—747 (1969).
18. A.L. Burlingame, P.A. Haug, H.K. Schnoes and B.R. Simoneit, "Fatty Acids Derived from the Green River Formation Oil Shale by Extraction and Oxidation — A Review", *Adv. Org. Geochem. Proc. 4th Int. Congr. 1968*, (P.A. Schenck and I. Havenaar, Editors), Pergamon Press, pp. 68—71 (1969).
19. M. Djuricic, R.C. Murphy, D. Vitorovic and K. Biemann, "Organic Acids Obtained by Alkaline Permanganate Oxidation of Kerogen from the Green River (Colorado) Shale", *Geochim. Cosmochim. Acta, 35,* 1201—1207 (1971).
20. W.F. Sager and A. Bradley, "Oxidation of Trimethylmethane and Other Hydrocarbons by Acidified Dichromate", *J. Am. Chem. Soc., 78,* 1187—1190 (1956).
21. D.K. Young and T.F. Yen, "Oil Shale Kerogen Oxidation. I. Comparison to Lignite Oxidation", *Fuel*, in press (1975).
22. J.J. Schmidt-Collerus and C.H. Prien, "Investigation of the Hydrocarbon Structure of Kerogen from Oil Shale of the Green River Formation", *ACS Div. Fuel Chem., 19* (2), 100—108 (1974).

23. D.A. Scrima, T.F. Yen and P.L. Warren, "Thermal Chromatography of Green River Oil Shale. I. Bitumen and Kerogen", *Energy Sources, 1* (3), 321—336 (1974).

24. D.K. Young and T.F. Yen, "Fractional Oxidation of Green River Kerogen Concentrate by Alkaline Permanganate", unpublished results (1974).

25. D.K. Young, S. Shih and T.F. Yen, "Stepwise Oxidation of Bioleached Oil Shale", *ACS Div. Fuel Chem. Preprints, 19* (2), 169—174 (1974).

26. T.F. Yen and J.G. Erdman, "Asphaltenes (Petroleum) and Related Substances: X-ray Diffraction", in: C.L. Clark (Editor), *Encyclopedia of X-ray and Gamma-rays*, Reinhold, pp. 65—68 (1963).

27. J. Kwan and T.F. Yen, "X-ray Diffraction Studies of Kerogen Concentrates", unpublished results (1975).

28. T.F. Yen, "A New Structural Model of Oil Shale Kerogen", *ACS Div. Fuel Chem., 19* (2), 109—114 (1974).

29. J.P. Dickie and T.F. Yen, "Macrostructure of the Asphaltic Fractions by Various Instrumental Methods", *Anal. Chem., 39*, 1847—1852 (1967).

30. T.F. Yen, "Present Status of the Structure of Petroleum Heavy Ends and its Significance to Various Technical Applications", *ACS Div. Pet. Chem. Preprints, 17*, F102—F114 (1972).

31. E.W. Bird and J.M. Lynch, "Formation of Hydrocarbons by Microorganisms", *Chem. Soc. Rev., 3* (3), 309—328 (1974).

32. E. Gelpi, H. Schneider, J. Mann and J. Oro, "Hydrocarbons of Geochemical Significance in Microscopic Algae", *Phytochem., 9*, 603—612 (1970).

33. J. Han, E.D. McCarthy, W. van Hoeven, M. Calvin and W.H. Bradley, "Organic Geochemical Studies. II. A Preliminary Report on the Distribution of Aliphatic Hydrocarbons in Algae, in Bacteria, and in a Recent Lake Sediment", *Proc. Nat. Acad. Sci., 59*, 29—33 (1968).

34. J. Han and M. Calvin, "Hydrocarbon Distribution of Algae and Bacteria, and Microbiological Activity in Sediments", *Proc. Nat. Acad. Sci., 64*, 436—443 (1969).

35. J.D. Weete, J.L. Laseter, D.J. Weber, W.M. Hess and D.L. Stocks, "Hydrocarbons, Fatty Acids, and Ultrastructure of Smut Spores", *Phytopath., 59*, 545—548 (1969).

36. J.D. Weete, D.J. Weber and D. Le Tourneau, "Hydrocarbons, Free Fatty Acids, and Amino Acids of Sclerotia of *Sclerotinia sclerotiorum*", *Arch. Mikrobiol., 75*, 59—66 (1970).

37. A.C. Brown, B.A. Knights and E. Conway, "Hydrocarbon Content and its Relationship to Physiological State in the Green Algae *Botryococcus braunii*", *Phytochem., 8*, 543—547 (1969).

38. C.W. Bird, J.M. Lynch, S.J. Pirt, W.W. Reid, C.J.W. Brooks and B.S. Middleditch, "Steroids and Squalene in *Methylococcus capsulatus* Grown on Methane", *Nature, 230*, 473—474 (1971).

39. C.W. Bird, J.M. Lynch, S.J. Pirt and W.W. Reid, "The Identification of Hop-22 (29)-ene in Procaryotic Organisms", *Tetrahedron Lett., 34*, 3189—3190 (1971).

40. M. de Rosa, A. Gambarcorta, L. Minale and J.D. Bu'Lock, "Isoprenoids of *Bacillus acidocaldarius*", *Phytochem., 12*, 1117—1123 (1973).

Chapter 8

BIOLOGICAL FOSSIL HYDROCARBONS IN SHALES

E.J. GALLEGOS

Introduction

The importance of organic matter in petroleum reservoirs, coal fields, and shale deposits is probably self-evident in this age of energy crisis, pollution, and balance of payments problem.

Petroleum is at present an important source of fuel for energy. Products derived from oil through the efforts of the petrochemical industry, however, are becoming essential to a modern society.

"Every other source of energy should be found to replace wherever and as much as possible this precious oil which should in my opinion, in the future — not too distant, I hope — be used for the noble purpose of the petrochemical industry."[1]

A separate but related, and probably neglected, aspect of these organic compound-rich deposits is a study of the origin of individual organic components. Philosophically, this provides man with a look back towards chemical evolution and the origin of life. Practically, it can and does provide a powerful tool which can be used for improving methods for exploration and production of organic-compound-rich deposits. The practical and philosophical significance of the study of molecular fossils has been discussed recently by Blumer [1].

This chapter deals with one aspect of molecular paleontology, i.e., "biological marker" hydrocarbons in shales and other deposits.

The theory that organic materials in sediments are perhaps of biological origin owes its beginnings in part to the discovery of porphyrins in petroleum by Treibs [2]. This theory is a generally accepted concept supported by the presence of a variety of compounds in sediments that appear to be related to similar ones occurring in living organisms, i.e., amino acids, fatty acids, carbohydrates, sterols, terpanes, steranes, steroid-carboxylic acids, etc. [3—8].

Evidence continues to be uncovered showing that petroleum and organic compounds in shale and coal are, at least for the most part, derived from the organic remains of plants and animals. The biological origin theory of organic material in sediments is supported by optical activity, $^{12}C/^{13}C$ enrichment, and by the presence of "biological marker" compounds.

---

[1] Shahanshah Arya Mehr Mohammed Reza Pahlavi of Iran, as quoted in *Chemical and Engineering News*, p. 5, January 7, 1975.

Optical activity is generally associated with molecules of biological origin [9,10]. The ^{12}C enrichment in living matter through biological activity is also observed in organic material in sediments. Probably the most pressing argument for a biological origin of organic material in sediments is the presence of organic compounds, which have good chemical stability and skeletal features, related to compounds known to be produced by living systems. These are the "biological marker" compounds [2,11].

The "biological marker" hydrocarbons, i.e., paraffins, terpanes, steranes, carotanes, polyprenoids, and partially aromatized isoprenoids are amongst the most stable organic compounds found in sediments.

Once formed, these hydrocarbons not only resist modification over geological time, but they also resist change during isolation and analysis. Further, they are the easiest to isolate. They, therefore, have been subjected in recent years to intensive investigation by an increasingly large number of workers.

There are probably no sediments, regardless of depth, age, or presumed prehistory, known today which do not reveal at least one or the other type of stereo or structure of specific "biological marker" hydrocarbons.

This chapter attempts to summarize the state of the knowledge of these types of hydrocarbon "biological marker" compounds, which have been uncovered to date, and discuss their importance from the viewpoint of molecular origin.

These geochemically important compounds are reviewed in the following order: (1) normal and branched alkanes, (2) cyclic isoprenoids (1-5 ring), (3) the partially aromatized isoprenoids, (4) the polyprenoids, and (5) isoprenoids released from kerogen.

Branched and normal alkanes

Normal and branched paraffins, C_nH_{2n+2}, were the first hydrocarbons to be recognized and utilized in studies involving molecular geochemistry of organic deposits.

The structures presented in Figs. 8-1—8-13 summarize for the most part those C_nH_{2n+2} alkane types which have been uncovered thus far in extractable oil from sedimentary deposits.

A brief resumé of the principal workers responsible for these identifications are followed by a discussion and analysis of possible biological precursor molecules.

Bendoraitis [12] characterized a C_{21} isoprenoid in a petroleum as 2,6,10, 14-tetramethylheptadecane (Fig. 8-2). Johns et al. [13] also identified a C_{21} isoprenoid paraffin in a Soudan shale from Minnesota, $2.7 \cdot 10^9$ years old, and in an Antrim Shale from Michigan, $\sim 3 \cdot 10^6$ years old. Bendoraitis et al. [12] and Dean et al. [14] isolated and identified phytane, 2,6,10,14-tetramethylhexadecane (Fig. 8-3) in petroleum. Cummins and Robinson

Fig. 8-1. 2,6,10,15,19,23-Hexamethyltriacontane (squalane).

[15] reported in 1964 the identification of C_{13} to C_{32} n-paraffins and of a series of five isoprenoid compounds in Green River shale. These are the isoprenoid alkane series presented in Figs. 8-3—8-8.

The C_{17} isoprenoid (Fig. 8-6) has been identified recently in an Israeli shale [16] and earlier in a Devonian shale [17].

Recent work indicates that regular isoprenoids, i.e., head-to-tail attachment, from C_5 to at least C_{25}, are present in petroleum [12,18,19]. Only C_{14} through C_{21} regular, i.e., head-to-tail linked, isoprenoids have been found in shales or petroleum thus far. Squalane (Fig. 8-1) has been tentatively identified in Libyan [20] and Nigerian [21] crude oils. Squalane also occurs in nature [22]. Iso-(2-methyl)- (Fig. 8-10) and anteiso-(3-methyl)- (Fig. 8-11) alkanes have been isolated from rocks [23,13].

A homologous series of 2,6-dimethyl alkanes (Fig. 8-12) was identified in a marine shale of Cretaceous age from Italy [18].

Fig. 8-2. 2,6,10,14-Tetra-methylheptadecane

Fig. 8-3. 2,6,10,14-Tetra-methylhexadecane (Phytane)

Fig. 8-4. 2,6,10,14-Tetra-methylpentadecane (Pristane)

Fig. 8-5. 2,6,10-Trimethyl-pentadecane

Fig. 8-6. 2,6,10-Trimethyl-tetradecane

Fig. 8-7. 2,6,10-Trimethyl-tridecane

Fig. 8-8. 2,6,10-Trimethyl-dodecane (Farnesane)

Fig. 8-9. 2,6,10-Trimethyl-undecane

Fig. 8-10. Isoalkane

Fig. 8-11. Anteisoalkane

Fig. 8-12. 2,6-Dimethyl-alkanes

Fig. 8-13. n-Alkanes

Naturally occurring isoprenoids which have been cited as possible precursors to the isoprenoid alkanes uncovered in sediments include squalane, the polyprenoids, carotenoids [24], the phytol side chain of chlorophyll [12], the isoprenoid acids, alcohols, and other biolipids.

Current understanding suggests that, early during sedimentation, the proposed precursor isoprenoids are cleaved at one or another single or double bond biochemically or thermocatalytically. Following decarboxylation and/or dehydration, if oxygen is present on the molecule, one or more pieces characteristic of the original structure remain. These molecular artifacts are subsequently reduced to the hydrocarbon in the sediment. Molecular artifacts derived from alkylation or condensation products of biological precursors, which also have been reduced to the hydrocarbon, represent alternative biomarkers.

The diagenetic pathways are many from the isoprenoid precursors to the various isoprenoid alkanes uncovered in sediments. Any pathway or pathways should explain a principal presence in sediments of both phytane, C_{20}, and pristane, C_{19}, and an absence of the C_{17} isoprenoid in most sediments. C_{20} and C_{19} isoprenoids are generally the most widely distributed isoprenoid alkanes found and have been identified in crude oils and sediments of all ages, including the Precambrian [25]. The C_{17} isoprenoid is generally found in low concentrations, if at all [17,23].

The following discussion provides a look at the present views concerning possible precursors and pathways to the various isoprenoid alkanes found in sediments.

Squalane, C_{30}

Squalane (Fig. 8-14), because of a tail-to-tail linkage of two regular C_{15} isoprenoids, will on a single-bond cleavage pathway to a C_{20} or higher alkane give the irregular or 2, 6, 10, 15, etc., isoprenoid. So far, only the regular 2, 6, 10, 14, etc., types have been found in sediments. Squalane, however, could produce the regular C_{17} and lower molecular weight isoprenoids. From this analysis squalane is probably a minor contributor to the C_{18} and greater isoprenoid alkanes found in sediments.

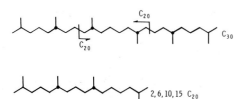

Fig. 8-14. Squalane C_{30} simple C—C cleavage to give the 2,6,10,15 C_{20} irregular isoprenoid.

Carotenoids, C_{40}

The carotenoid (Fig. 8-15) represents a tail-to-tail linkage of only two C_{20} regular isoprenoids. In this case, a break between C_{20} and C_{21} will give two pieces of the regular 2, 6, 10, 14, C_{20} isoprenoid alkane. The C_{24} and higher isoprenoids would have an irregular linkage; C_{22} and lower would be regularly linked. C_{17} and C_{23} presumably would be minor diagenetic products of carotenoids because of the need to break two C—C bonds.

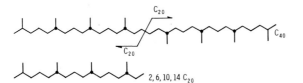

Fig. 8-15. Carotenoid C_{40} simple C—C cleavage to give the 2,6,10,14 C_{20} regular isoprenoid.

Polyprenoid, C_{30}—C_{100} (e.g., solanesol)

The polyprenoids (Fig. 8-16) are regularly linked, i.e., head to tail throughout. As a result, any part of polyprenoids on single C—C cleavage would give regularly linked isoprenoid alkanes, including C_{23}. Assuming no rearrangement and only single-bond cleavage, squalane can give the C_{17} regular and C_{22} irregular isoprenoid, carotenoids only the C_{22} regular isoprenoid, and the polyprenoids only the C_{23} regular isoprenoid. This ignores any higher or lower molecular weight possibilities.

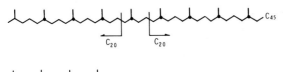

Fig. 8-16. Polyprenoid, e.g., solanesol C_{45} — simple C—C cleavage to give the 2,6,10,14 C_{20} regular isoprenoid.

Chlorophyll-a

The phytol side chain degraded from chlorophyll (Fig. 8-17) is the most commonly proposed progenitor to the chain isoprenoids found in sediments. The abundance of chlorophyll in nature and the discovery of phyloporphyrins, which could also be derived from chlorophyll, tend to support this proposal.

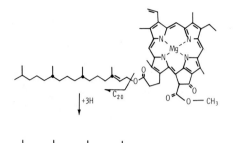

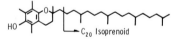

Fig. 8-17. Chlorophyll-a as a precursor to the 2,6,10,14 C_{20} regular isoprenoid.

The known presence of C_{21} and higher-molecular-weight isoprenoid alkanes in sediments must suggest the possibility of biological or non-biological alkylation if indeed the isoprenoid alkanes owe their origin mainly to degradation of chlorophyll. Recently, Cox et al. [26] have shown that phytanic acid and lower homologs in Green River shale have the same absolute stereochemistry as the phytol side chain of chlorophyll. If indeed the phytol side chain of chlorophyll is an important precursor to the regular iso-prenoid alkanes found in other deposits, then they too will show the same absolute stereochemistry.

Though apparently not abundant natural products, there are still other biolipids, which could act as precursors to the chain isoprenoids. These are:

(a) *Tocopherols* α, β, λ, and σ (Vitamin E)

β, λ, and σ tocopherols differ from α (Fig. 8-18) only in the number and location of methyl groups on the aromatic ring.

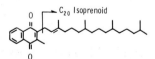

Fig. 8-18. α Tocopherol — possible precursor to the regular chain isoprenoids, up to C_{20}.

(b) *Vitamin K_1* (Fig. 8-19)

Fig. 8-19. Vitamin K_1 — possible precursor to the regular chain isoprenoids, up to C_{20}.

The phytyl side chain of the tocopherols and Vitamin K_1 have the same stereochemistries as the phytyl side chain of chlorophyll. Both were originally synthesized using phytol derived from chlorophyll [27].

(c) *Vitamin K_2* (Fig. 8-20)

(d) *Diphytanyl-phosphatidyl glycerophosphate* (Fig. 8-21)

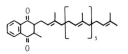

Fig. 8-20. Vitamin K_2 — possible precursor to the regular chain isoprenoids, up to C_{35}.

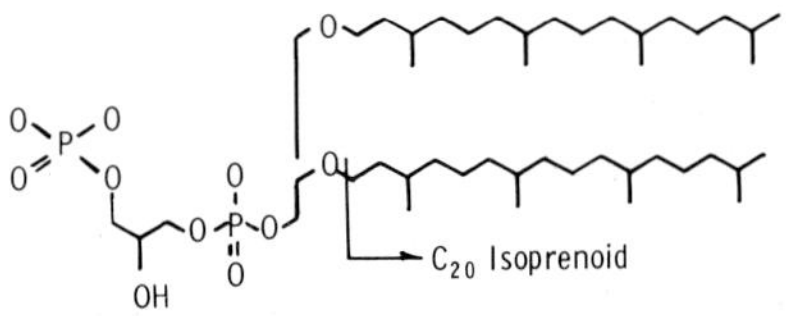

Fig. 8-21. Diphytanyl-phosphatidyl glycerophosphate — possible precursor to the regular chain isoprenoids, up to C_{20}.

This compound has been found in bacteria [28] and algae [29].

(e) *The ubiquinones* (Fig. 8-22)

(f) *Plastoquinone* (Fig. 8-23)

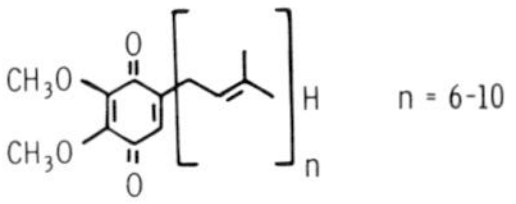

Fig. 8-22. The ubiquinones — possible precursor to the regular chain isoprenoids, up to C_{50}.

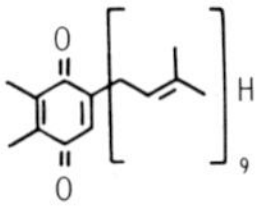

Fig. 8-23. Plastoquinone — possible precursor to the regular chain isoprenoids, up to C_{45}.

Tocopherol, Vitamins K_1 and K_2, the ubiquinone, and plastoquinones [27] are very likely minor contributors to isoprenoids found in sediments because of the relatively lower proportions of these compounds found in the biosphere in comparison to chlorophyll.

Acyclic sesquiterpenoids and diterpenoids found in nature are also likely contributors to the chain isoprenoid alkanes, such as:

(g) *Farnesol* (Fig. 8-24)

(h) *Phytol* (Fig. 8-25)

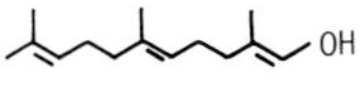

Fig. 8-24. Farnesol — possible precursor to the regular chain isoprenoids, up to C_{15}.

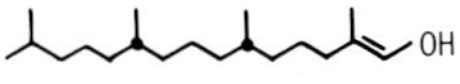

Fig. 8-25. Phytol — possible precursor to the regular chain isoprenoids, up to C_{20}.

(i) *Phytanic acid*

Phytanic acid (Fig. 8-26) is an unlikely precursor to phytane because this would require a complete reduction of a carboxylic group. A more likely saturated remnant of phytanic acid is pristane formed by decarboxylation and then followed by reduction. Very recently, Maxwell et al. [30] have determined the absolute stereochemistry of pristane in Green River shale. They show that the major portion, 80%, of 2,6,10,14-tetramethyl pentadecane from this shale has the 6(R), 10(s) configuration; whereas the remaining 20% are either 6(R), 10(R), or 6(s), 10(S) isomers or both. The 6(R), 10(S) configuration is characteristic of natural phytol. To produce C_{20}, C_{21}, and higher isoprenoid alkanes from phytanic acid also requires some sort of alkylation mechanism.

The low abundance of the C_{17} isoprenoid alkane (Fig. 8-27) in the geosphere is tentatively explained as follows [23]: Two carbon-carbon bonds must be broken to get a C_{17} from a regularly-linked chain isoprenoid; whereas C_{14}, C_{15}, C_{16}, C_{18}, and C_{19} require only one carbon-carbon bond rupture resulting in an expenditure of less time and energy.

These simplistic schemes ignore the absolute stereochemistry because of the lack of data. The generalized carbon skeleton schemes do serve as a guide in postulating the possible diagenetic pathways consistent with the presently available experimental data.

If the absolute stereochemistries of the isoprenoid alkanes found in the geosphere are consistent with the phytol side chain of chlorophyll, as has been implied, the question will arise as to whether or not potential precursors such as the carotenoids or polyprenoids were biogenetically reduced.

In contemporary higher plants, the odd-numbered n-alkanes predominate over even-numbered n-alkanes in the C_{27}–C_{33} molecular weight range. Young sediments also show this odd carbon number n-alkane dominance. Older sediments and crude oils, on the other hand, generally show a smoother distribution, i.e., the odd/even ratio is essentially equal to one, with a maximum at lower molecular weights [25].

The suggestion has been made that through diagenesis and maturation of precursors, such as straight-chain alcohols, fatty acids, and alkanes, there

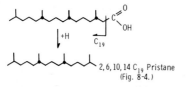

Fig. 8-26. Phytanic acid — possible simple C—C cleavage to give pristane.

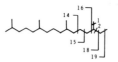

Fig. 8-27. A C_{17} regular isoprenoid from a C_{20} or greater regular isoprenoid requires two C—C bond cleavages, i.e., 1 and 2 above.

results a decrease in odd over even dominance of n-alkane distributions for some sediments. This suggests that decarboxylation of the acids during diagenesis and maturation provides the corresponding alkane [31]. This relationship does not always hold [25]; so there are other mechanisms of producing n-alkanes.

Cyclic isoprenoids

Monocyclics (C_nH_{2n})

The monocyclic terpanes are considered next. Johns et al. [13] reported the presence of n-alkylcyclohexanes C_{18} and C_{19} in an Antrim Shale from Michigan. These were identified by their highly characteristic mass spectra, i.e., a very intense m/e 83 ion.

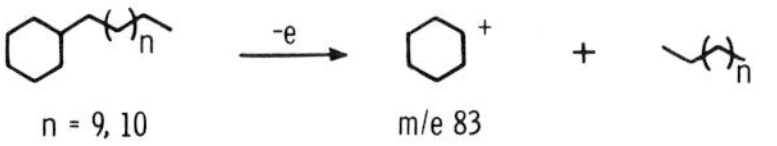

n = 9, 10   m/e 83

Fig. 8-28. n-Alkylcyclohexanes found in an Antrim Shale from Michigan. Electron impact route to m/e 83.

Recently, Anders and Robinson [32] reported the presence of at least 20 monocyclic alkanes from C_{13} to C_{24}, excluding the C_{17} compounds. The absence of the monocyclic C_{17} is consistent with the argument given for the virtual absence of the C_{17} isoprenoid alkane in sediments.

These cyclic compounds were isolated from Green River shale, distilled, and chromatographed to produce over 100 fractions which were subsequently analyzed by mass spectrometry. Of the 20 alkanes, 18 appeared to give the same fragmentation pattern as a tetraalkyl-substituted cyclohexane. One of the important fragments suggests the following structure (Fig. 8-29):

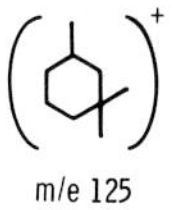

m/e 125

Fig. 8-29. Probable m/e 125 fragment ion structure from tetraalkyl-substituted cyclohexanes.

n = 4, 5, 6, 9-30

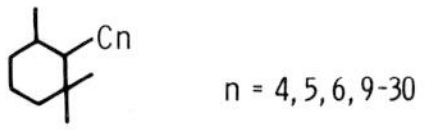

Fig. 8-30. Probable ring configuration of the tetraalkyl-substituted cyclohexanes isolated from Green River shale.

If so, these monocyclics are possibly of the types shown in Fig. 8-30.

The mass spectrum of the C_{40} monocyclic reported is consistent with the structure shown in Fig. 8-31a.

This C_{40} compound was the most abundant monocyclic hydrocarbon found in Green River shale. The concept of the carotenoids being precursors to monocyclics found in the geosphere is not new. Mair [33] refers to a

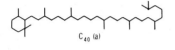

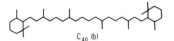

Fig. 8-31. Probable structure of a C_{40} monocyclic hydrocarbon (a) and perhydro-β-carotene (b) found in Green River shale.

number of low-molecular-weight monocyclics, which have skeletal features resembling fragments of the carotenoid molecule. This again stresses the apparent importance of carotenoids in the formation of acyclic and monocyclic debris in sediments.

Dicyclics (C_nH_{2n-2})

The first tetraterpane isolated from a geological sample was the dicyclic isoprenoid perhydro-β-carotene (Fig. 8-31b). Murphy et al. [34] isolated perhydro-β-carotene from the extractable fraction of the Green River shale. They prepared an authentic sample of perhydro-β-carotene by hydrogenation of β-carotene. Subsequent coinjection and comparison of spectra were used to confirm the structure of this important tetracyclic isoprenoid. Perhydro-β-carotene was found to constitute about 16% of the branched and cyclic alkane fraction of the Green River shale.

Any of the carotenoid types found in nature could be precursors to the perhydro-β-carotene. The requirement for conversion is possibly removal of oxygen, if present on a particular carotenoid, during a strongly reducing early diagenetic stage. Inasmuch as the carotenoids found in nature are quite reactive, hydrogenation must have occurred early after sedimentation. More than one perhydro-carotene has been reported in this fraction at very low levels, i.e., <0.1% content [35].

Additional dicyclic compounds other than carotenoids have recently been uncovered by Anders and Robinson [32] from Green River shale. They are $C_{14}H_{26}$ and $C_{20}H_{38}$—$C_{24}H_{46}$ dicyclics. The latter appear from their mass spectra to be of the dialkyl-substituted hexahydroindan variety.

Suggested potential source materials for these dicyclics are (1) the C and D rings of degraded steroids, (2) D and E rings of some degraded pentacyclic triterpenoids, or (3) the hexahydroindan portion of degraded Vitamin D.

Excluding perhydro-β-carotene, these additional dicyclics make up about 2% of the extractable saturates from the Green River shale. Recently, in an analysis of Eocene crude oils from the Jackson Sands Formation of South

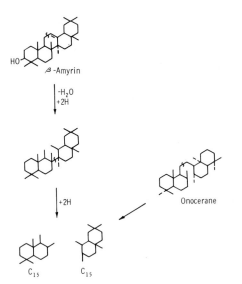

HO— β-Amyrin

-H₂O
+2H

+2H   Onocerane

C_{15} C_{15}

Fig. 8-32. Possible maturation route to the C_{15} dicyclics found in Jackson Sands Formation of South Texas.

Texas, Bendoraitis [36] identified a number of C_{15} and some C_{14} dicyclic compounds.

The two most intense peaks in the gas chromatograms of Loma Novia crude and saturate fraction from the Jackson Sands Formation were shown by NMR and mass spectra to be due very likely to the presence of penta-methyl decahydronaphthalenes. The C_{14} dicyclics showed similar mass spectra and by analogy were felt to be due to tetramethyl decahydro-naphthalenes. Bendoraitis [36] offered a maturation scheme, which embodies the conversion of a triterpane β-amyrin into methyl-substituted decahydro-naphthalenes, through a sequence of cracking reactions, as presented in Fig. 8-32. Simple bond cleavage of one of the onoceranes could also give two components with carbon skeleton and substituent arrangement similar to C_{15} isomers (Fig. 8-32).

Tricyclic terpenoids (C_nH_{2n-4})

A total of 12 tricyclic terpanes had been tentatively identified in Green River shale [32, 35]. The common feature of all the mass spectra of these tricyclics is a relatively intense parent ion, an important parent minus a methyl fragment, and a base peak of m/e 191. Budzikiewicz et al. [37] have shown that m/e 191, also produced from pentacyclic triterpanes, is due to a fragment which probably looks like the one shown in Fig. 8-33. This fixes the structure of the A/B rings of the tricyclics. The C-ring could be either 5-

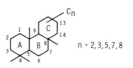

Fig. 8-33. Probable structure of the m/e 191 fragment ion produced by electron impact of many tri- and pentacyclic terpanes.

Fig. 8-34. Probable ring configuration of tricyclic terpanes identified in Green River shale.

membered or 6-membered. The 6-membered ring was assumed by Anders and Robinson [32] and Gallegos [35] because of the preponderance of 6-membered rings in terpenoid systems. Further, electron impact of a fused 5-membered C-ring attached to the structure (Fig. 8-33) may well not produce an important m/e 191 fragment ion. The most likely A/B/C ring configuration and substitution of the tricyclics is presented in Fig. 8-34.

Gallegos [35] found two isomers each of the C_{20}, C_{21}, C_{23}, C_{25}, and C_{26} tricyclic terpanes, all with very similar mass spectra. Further, the two C_{20} and the two C_{21} tricyclic terpanes constitute more than 80% of all tricyclics in the saturate fraction of the extractables in Green River shale. The m/e 191 mass chromatogram is shown in Fig. 8-35.

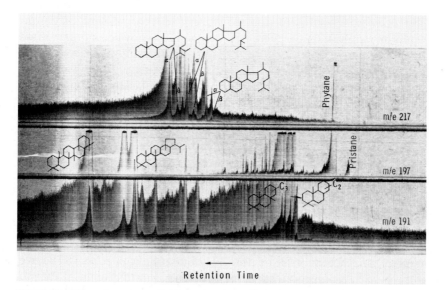

Fig. 8-35. Mass chromatic display of m/e 217 steranes, 191 terpanes and 197 paraffins in Green River shale bitumen saturate fraction.

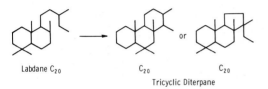

Labdane C_{20} C_{20} C_{20}
                   Tricyclic Diterpane

Fig. 8-36. Possible maturation route of a C_{20} labdane to give tricyclic diterpanes.

It appears that not one of the naturally-occurring tricyclic diterpanes has the same A/B/C ring carbon skeleton and substitution arrangement that would be required to produce those found in Green River shale. The naturally occurring tricyclic terpanes do not have a C-8 bridge-head methyl; whereas all those found in Green River shale do have it. The C-8 bridge-head methyl is presumed necessary to produce a large m/e 191 fragment in the mass spectra of terpanes.

Some diterpanes found in nature, however, with either ring closure or with ring opening could produce a tricyclic diterpane with the proper methyl substitution on Ring A and Carbons 8 and 10 (Fig. 8-36). The labdanes, for example, could give rise to Ring C on cyclization (Fig. 8-36).

The stachanes, kauranes, and trachylobanes might through ring opening produce similar tricyclic diterpanes as presented in Fig. 8-37.

If these are the only reasonable precursors to the tricyclic diterpanes found in Green River shale, then a question arises as to why there are only

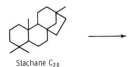

Stachane C_{20} C_{20}
                          Tricyclic Diterpane

Kaurane C_{20} C_{20}
                          Tricyclic Diterpane

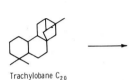

Trachylobane C_{20} C_{20}
                          Tricyclic Diterpane

Fig. 8-37. Possible maturation routes of C_{20} stachane, kaurane and trachylobane to give tricyclic diterpanes.

two isomers. The five-membered Ring C diterpane shown in Fig. 8-36 and tricyclic diterpane (C_{20}) structure resulting from maturation of kaurane in Fig. 8-37 can be eliminated because they would be expected to show an (M-29)+ fragment which was not found. In addition, both must show a base peak at m/e 191. Tentatively, the trachylobanes (Fig. 8-37) can be eliminated because, to produce the tricyclic terpane, two carbon-carbon bonds must be broken. This leaves only the two isomers, i.e., one resulting from the maturation of labdane, and the other from the maturation of stachane.

These two postulated structures explain the presence of two important C_{20} tricyclic diterpane isomers found in Green River shale. To account for the two important C_{21} diterpanes, however, some additional mechanism must come into play like microbiological methylation during sedimentation if they are to result in structures such as those resulting from the maturation of labdane (Fig. 8-36) and of stachane (Fig. 8-37). This type of mechanism has been postulated to account for the presence of homohopane, a C_{31} terpane, in Messel shale [38].

The higher homolog (C_{23} through C_{26} diterpane) pairs are present in a much lower concentration than the C_{20} or C_{21} diterpanes in the Colorado Green River shale. Their mechanism of formation, however, does offer a challenge to speculation. Perhaps some nonbiological transalkylation process occurred, such as the one suggested for the presence of a homologous series of alkyl porphyrins in petroleum [39,40]. The alternative explanation is nonbiological degradation during maturation of the pentacyclic terpanes through Ring D and Ring E opening. The problem with the latter explanation, however, is that nonbiological degradation of pentacyclic triterpanes should produce a multiplicity of tricyclic diterpane isomers. This is not what was found. The C_{20}, C_{21}, and C_{23} through C_{26} tricyclic terpanes showed only two isomers each in Green River shale. This implies stereospecific alteration, i.e., microbiological alkylation during sedimentation of terpanes such as stachane or kaurane or biological degradation of the cyclic triterpanes.

Tetracyclics (C_nH_{2n-6})

The first report of the presence of steranes in a geological source was made by Burlingame et al. [41]. They reported the identification of the C_{27}-, C_{28}-, and C_{29}-steranes in the branched-cyclic alkane fraction of the Green River shale, using gas chromatography, mass spectrometry, and combined GC—MS. They also indicated the very likely presence of more than one isomer of each type of sterane. Hills et al. [42] and Henderson et al. [43] provided further confirming identifications of these steranes.

By using GLC and GC—MS data, Henderson et al. [43] tentatively identified 5α- and 5β-cholestane and indicated the presence of ergostane and stigmastane (Figs. 8-41, 8-42, and 8-43).

In 1971, Gallegos [35] confirmed the presence of 5α- and 5β-cholestane

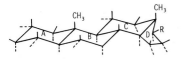

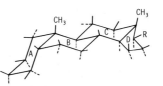

Fig. 8-38. Stereo representation of a 5α A/B trans-sterane.

Fig. 8-39. Stereo representation of a 5β A/B cis-sterane.

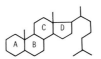

Fig. 8-40. 5α pregnane $C_{21}H_{36}$.

Fig. 8-41. 5α and 5β cholestane $C_{27}H_{48}$.

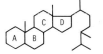

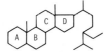

Fig. 8-42. 5α and 5β ergostane $C_{28}H_{50}$.

Fig. 8-43. 5α and 5β stigmastane $C_{29}H_{52}$.

(Fig. 8-41) and identified the 5α- and 5β-C_{28} and 5α- and 5β-C_{29} sterane isomers, ergostane (Fig. 8-42), and stigmastane (Fig. 8-43). The stereoconfigurations of the 5α and 5β steranes are shown in Figs. 8-38 and 8-39. In addition, he indicated the presence of 5α-pregnane C_{21} (Fig. 8-40).

These steranes, which were isolated analytically using combined mass spectrometry and gas chromatography, were tentatively identified solely from their mass spectra. The mass spectra of the isomeric steranes are practically identical, except for the relative intensities of the fragment ions m/e 151 and m/e 149. Tökes et al. [44,45] had shown previously that 5α- and 5β-pregnane showed these same m/e 149 and m/e 151 intensity differences. That is, the 5β isomer had an m/e 151 about equal in intensity to the 149 due to the cis arrangement, whereas the 5α isomer showed an m/e 149 fragment ion much larger than the m/e 151 fragment. Therefore, the ratio of intensities of 149/151 can be used to distinguish between the 5α and 5β isomers.

Seifert et al. [8] isolated and identified α- and β-bisnorcholanic C_{22} and cholanic C_{24} acids from a California crude. The hydrocarbons, 5α- and 5β-bisnorcholane C_{22} and cholane C_{24}, synthesized and used as proof of structure, showed the same m/e 149 to m/e 151 intensity difference distinguishing the 5α and 5β isomers. Since then, confirmation of the identification of the 5α- and 5β-steranes in Green River shale was made by both coinjection and

Fig. 8-44. Possible structure of a tetracyclic terpane, $C_{23}H_{40}$, found in Green River shale.

comparison of mass spectra of authentic C_{28} and C_{29} 5α- and 5β-steranes [46]. There are indications of a third C_{29} sterane, as shown in Fig. 8-35.

Sterane hydrocarbons have not been isolated from living systems thus far. The abundance of steroids found in nature, however, could, on dehydration and/or decarboxylation and hydrogenation provide the basic carbon skeleton needed to produce the steranes isolated from sediments.

The significance of the relative amounts of the 5α- versus the 5β-sterane isomers found in sediments is not clear. Presumably, both isomer precursors can be generated by either plants or animals.

Diagenetic alteration could also explain the relative concentrations of 5α- and 5β-steranes in the Green River shale. The ratio of 5α to 5β is roughly 3 : 1 for the C_{27}, C_{28}, and C_{29} steranes in the saturate fraction of the Green River shale.

Seifert [47] has recently discussed the possible animal contribution to petroleum on the basis of the observed ratio of the concentration of cis- to trans-A/B stereoisomers of the cholanic acid recently identified in petroleum from California. The *corresponding* hydrocarbons have not as yet been uncovered in shale or petroleum, though they very likely are present.

Additional tetracyclic terpenoids ($C_{23}H_{40}$ and isomers) were also identified by both Robinson et al. [32] and Gallegos [35]. The proposed structure (Fig. 8-44) is based on a dammarane- or lanostane-type tetracyclic triterpane, which best explains the observed mass spectra.

A biogenetic relationship between squalene and cholesterol via lanosterol has been proposed by Woodward and Block [48].

A lanosterol-like carbon skeleton provides a reasonable precursor source for the structure presented in Fig. 8-44 and isomers found in Green River shale.

Onocerane II and III (Fig. 8-45) have been tentatively identified in the alkane fraction of Green River shale [49].

Fig. 8-45. Onocerane $C_{30}H_{54}$.   Fig. 8-46. Gammacerane $C_{30}H_{52}$.

Pentacyclics (C_nH_{2n-8})

Gammacerane (Fig. 8-46) is the first pentacyclic triterpenoid hydrocarbon conclusively identified in a Nigerian crude [42]. The structure of gammacerane was elegantly and rigorously identified by Hills et al. [42], using high resolution gas chromatography, mass spectrometry, X-ray crystallography, and optical rotation measurements. Hills et al. [50] also reported the identification of an optically-active spirotriterpane from a Nigerian crude.

They felt that the spirotriterpane may be related to the 18-α oleonane system and, hence, might be formed from naturally-occurring triterpane of similar structure. Triterpanes containing a spiro A/B ring junction, such as oleonane presented in Fig. 8-47, have not been found in living systems. These workers also identified 18-αH oleonane (Fig. 8-48) in the Nigerian crude.

Fig. 8-47. 1(10-5α) abeo-3β-methyl-24β-nor-2α-18-αH oleonane $C_{30}H_{52}$.

Fig. 8-48. 18-αH oleonane $C_{30}H_{52}$.

Henderson et al. [43] tentatively identified hopane in Green River shale. Balough et al. [51] found that this C_{30} triterpane was (17 α,H) hopane identified by NMR analyses. (See Fig. 8-35.) Recently a homohopane C_{31} was identified in a Messel shale [38].

The presence in sedimentary rocks and petroleum of triterpanes with more than 30 carbon atoms in their skeleton has been noted previously [32,35,51].

In 1973, Ensminger et al. [52] reported the identification of a series of pentacyclic terpanes of the hopane type (Figs. 8-49 and 8-50), ranging from C_{27} to C_{35}. They also established that these hopanes were major components of crude oils and of organic matter in various sediments, oil shales, and coals. These workers used capillary columns GC—MS and capillary column coinjection of synthesized standards to identify the hopane series of triterpanes. The C_{28} hopane is apparently missing.

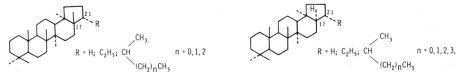

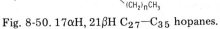

Fig. 8-49. 17βH, 21βH C_{27}—C_{32} hopanes.   Fig. 8-50. 17αH, 21βH C_{27}—C_{35} hopanes.

Ensminger et al. [52] suggested that these compounds might arise from alkylation reactions during early diagenesis, followed by reduction of some C_{30} precursors or degradation of a possible C_{35} precursor. They also pointed out that, whereas the (17βH, 21β) hopane skeleton (Fig. 8-49) has been found in living organisms, the (17αH, 21βH) hopane (Fig. 8-50) has not. This suggested to them that very probably the more stable hopane (Fig. 8-50) epimers are formed from the hopane (Fig. 8-49) series during diagenesis.

This assumption was strengthened by showing that cis-decalin can be isomerized to trans-decalin in the presence of montmorillonite at 100°C in two hours. Another type of terpane Ensminger et al. [52] found is the moretanes (17βH, 21αH) hopane presumably derived from acid isomerization of diploptene to hop-II-21-ene with subsequent hydrogenation.

Cyclization of the chair, chair, chair, chair, chair conformation of squalene produces the proper carbon skeleton stereo configuration for the hopanes and gammacerane [53]. Cyclization of the same squalene from both ends gives rise to the proper basic skeletal configuration for onocerane [53].

The first pentacyclic triterpenoid from an animal source, the protozoan tetrohymanol (gammacerane-3β-01), is structurally related to gammacerane.

In 1971, Bird et al. [54] identified hop-22(29)-ene in prokaryotic organisms, which is structurally related to the hopanes. Ensminger et al. [52] from their work concluded that, in general, a significant proportion of triterpane present in sediments and crude oils probably originates from lower organisms such as prokaryots.

Partially aromatized isoprenoids

Presumably during the course of hydrocarbon formation from biogenetic debris over geological time, first there is an aerobic modification of components during sedimentation, followed by anaerobic alteration and, finally, hydrogenation. Evidence is being uncovered to suggest that further maturation activity includes disproportionation reactions leading to aromatization, partial alkylation, and polymerization of resultant components.

The first part of this section deals with partially aromatized components, the skeletal types of which have been tentatively identified in sediments. Very little has been reported in the literature on the aromatics isolated from sediments. In 1973, Gallegos [55] and Anders et al. [56] have looked at the aromatics, principally the monoaromatics, in Green River shale.

Three general types of mono- or diaromatics were identified. These are the substituted phenylcyclohexyl alkanes (Fig. 8-51), alkylbenzenes (Fig. 8-54), and what appear to be monoaromatized terpanes or steranes (Fig. 8-52, 8-53, 8-55, and 8-56).

The monoaromatics in Green River shale show a dominance of compounds having a very intense fragment ion at m/e 119. Based on a combination of infrared mass spectra and analysis of dehydrogenation products of

Fig. 8-51. Proposed structure of some phenylcyclohexylalkanes found in Green River shale.

Fig. 8-52. Proposed structure of some benzodicycloalkanes found in Green River shale.

Fig. 8-53. Proposed structure of some benzotricycloalkanes found in Green River shale.

Fig. 8.54. Proposed structure of some alkylbenzenes found in Green River shale.

Fig. 8.55. Proposed structure of some tetralin cyclohexylalkanes found in Green River shale.

Fig. 8-56. Proposed structure of some alkyl tetralins found in Green River shale.

GC-trapped fractions, Anders et al. [56] concluded that 31% of the monoaromatics in Green River shale are due to substituted tetralins. The intense fragment ion at m/e 119 in the mass spectra of the isolated "tetralins", is, however, more compatible with alkylbenzenes or phenylcyclohexyl alkanes. Gallegos [55] from a thorough GC—MS analysis concluded that these C_nH_{2n-8} compounds with a base mass spectra peak at m/e 119 are in fact phenylcyclohexyl alkanes. Further, the m/e 119 fragment ion is shown to be consistent with an isoprenoid precursor via the relationship shown in Fig. 8-57.

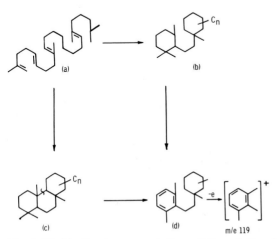

Fig. 8-57. Idealized representation of the relationship of the phenylcyclohexylalkanes to an isoprenoid precursor with possible intermediates.

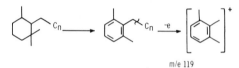

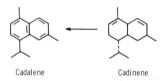

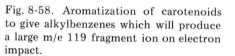

m/e 119   Cadalene   Cadinene

Fig. 8-58. Aromatization of carotenoids to give alkylbenzenes which will produce a large m/e 119 fragment ion on electron impact.

Fig. 8-59. Cadalene formation from the diagenetic dehydrogenation of naturally occurring cadinene.

Either route will produce a phenylcyclohexyl alkane, which would on electron impact give a large m/e 119 fragment. The aromatized carotanes during diagenesis could easily produce alkylbenzenes which will also give a large m/e 119 fragment by electron impact (Fig. 8-58).

All can be explained in terms of aromatization of a ring, ring opening, and/or bond cleavage.

Day and Erdman [57] heated a 1% solution of β-carotene in benzene at 188°C for 72 hours and produced significant amounts of toluene, m-xylene, ionene, and other aromatics. They also noted that a solution of β-carotene at 119°C in time also disrupts to the monoaromatics.

Bendoraitis [36] reported the identification of cadalene in three crudes from the Jackson Sands Formation in Texas. Bendoraitis [36] recognized cadinene (Fig. 8-59) as a possible precursor to cadalene.

According to Pliva et al. [58], among the many types of sesquiterpenic compounds, substances possessing the carbon skeleton 2,8-dimethyl-5-isopropylbicyclo(0.4.4)decane (Fig. 8-60) occur most frequently in nature.

Dehydrogenation of these naturally-occurring compounds possibly may form cadalene. Cadalene [59] has been considered as a possible hydrocarbon which could occur in petroleum as a result of the cyclization of farnesol (Fig. 8-24).

Bendoraitis [36] also isolated a $C_{28}H_{44}$ monoaromatic from Loma Novia crude, Jackson Sands Formation. The mass spectrum shows an exceptionally large parent less a methyl fragment ion at m/e 365. This mass spectrum and the isolation of C_{15} dicyclics (Fig. 8-32) from the same formation led Bendoraitis [36] to propose the structures presented in Fig. 8-61 to account for the $C_{28}H_{44}$ compound.

The β-amyrin (Fig. 8-32), as in the case of the two C_{15} saturates (Fig. 8-32), was used as an example of a possible precursor. Ring opening required here

Fig. 8-60. 2,8-Dimethyl-5-isopropylbicyclo (0.4.4) decane.

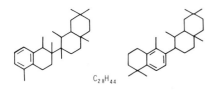

Fig. 8-61. Proposed tetracyclic structures favored to explain the mass spectrum of a monoaromatic fraction isolated from a Loma Novia crude.

Fig. 8-62. 3-Methyl-1,2-cyclopentanophenanthrene isolated from Ponca City crude.

to go from β-amyrin to the structures shown in Fig. 8-61 and Fig. 8-32 was also used to explain the presence of phenylcyclohexyl alkanes in Green River shale.

3-methyl-1,2-cyclopentanophenanthrene (Fig. 8-62) isolated from Ponca City crude by Rossini et al. [60] shows a large part of the skeletal structure of the steroids or tetracyclic triterpenoids. A series of methyl-substituted phenanthrenes was also isolated from the same crude by these workers. None showed substitution on the 4 or 5 position of the phenanthrene nucleus. The polycyclic terpenoids or steroids do not have methyl groups in position 5, which corresponds to the C-4 or C-5 position in phenanthrene. The absence of 4,5-substituted phenanthrene is consistent with terpenoid precursors.

Jarolim et al. [61] isolated structures presented in Fig. 8-63 from a Czechoslovakian lignite from Pilar near Karlovy Vary.

Progressive dehydrogenation of a pentacyclic triterpene, e.g., gamma-cerane, provides reasonable precursors to this series of compounds.

Albrecht and Ourisson [62] identified small amounts of dehydrogenated triterpenoids (Fig. 8-64) in a Messel oil shale located near Darmstadt, Germany.

Blumer [63] studied a Jurassic crinoid (fossil sea lillies) from northwestern Switzerland. The intensely colored fossil contained a number of crystallized pigments (fringelite) (Fig. 8-65) which, by reduction, particularly of the functional group, resemble aromatic hydrocarbons (Fig. 8-66) found in the same fossil.

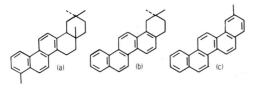

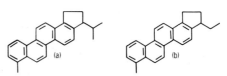

Fig. 8-63. Aromatics isolated from a Czechoslovakian lignite from Pila near Karlovy Vary.

Fig. 8-64. Dehydrogenated triterpenoids identified in Messel oil shale located near Darmstadt, Germany.

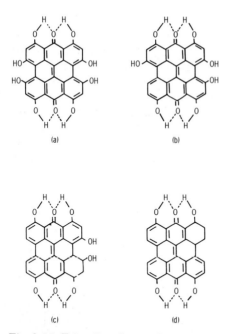

Fig. 8-65. Fringelites from a Jurassic crinoid from northwestern Switzerland.

Blumer [63] offered the following reasonable conclusions: The closely adjacent OH groups of fringelite (Fig. 8-65a) exert a strain on the normally planer aromatic ring. Reduction in the sediments has lessened this strain on fringelites (presented in Figs. 8-65b and 65c) and eliminated it, as shown in Fig. 8-65d. Hydrocarbons (presented in Fig. 8-66) are derived from the fossil pigments. Further, their concentration is influenced by the reversible redox equilibria.

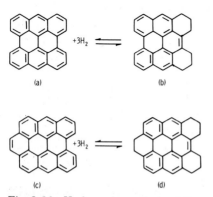

Fig. 8-66. Hydrocarbons derived from fossil pigments showing concentration effect of reversible redox equilibria.

Polycyclic isoprenoids

Recently Oelert et al. [64] in a field-ionization-mass spectrometric study of naphthenes in a Tia Juana crude residue, Maracaibo, Venezuela, suggested that a reasonably large number of compounds contained four to nine cata-condensed rings. Statistical analyses of the distribution curves of the high-molecular-weight naphthene types resulted in the development of reasonable models (Fig. 8-67), which best explain the maxima and shapes of these curves. These hypothetical structures are reasonable because they contain only well-known sterane or terpane skeletons and isoprenoids.

Further, they suggested that, based on reaction mechanisms of natural compounds, it is reasonable to assume that during petroleum genesis a carbon-carbon linkage might result in a stepwise growth of catacondensed ring cluster. If so, a nine-ring cluster, a combination of a sterane and triterpane, is also reasonable.

These data are consistent with a recent direct insertion probe mass spectrometric analysis of the high-molecular-weight extractable saturates (15%) from Green River shale [65]. The presence of polycyclic isoprenoids up to C_{80} was revealed. A low resolution mass spectrum at a probe temperature of 180°C of these polycyclics is shown in Fig. 8-68. The most intense ion in this range occurs at m/e 792, corresponding by high resolution measurement to $C_{58}H_{96}$, an 11-ring compound. There also appears a homologous series of compounds (A) starting at m/e 920 ($C_{67}H_{116}$) to m/e 1032 ($C_{75}H_{132}$),

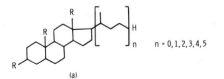

n = 0, 1, 2, 3, 4, 5

(a)

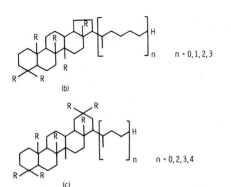

(b)   n = 0, 1, 2, 3

(c)   n = 0, 2, 3, 4

Fig. 8-67. Proposed structure of polyterpanes isolated from a Tia Juana residue.

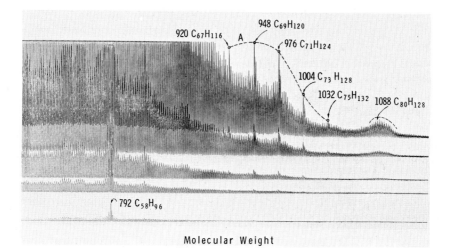

Fig. 8-68. Low resolution mass spectrum of the branched-cyclic hydrocarbon fraction of bitumen from Green River shale at 180°C probe temperature.

each separated by C_2H_4. These are 10-ring compounds. Also visible is an envelope of peaks centered at m/e 1088 ($C_{80}H_{128}$), i.e., $8 \times C_{10}H_{16}$, *or* an octaterpenoid which could contain 17 rings.

At a probe temperature of ~200°C, two additional homologous series of peaks appear, which are also separated by C_2H_4: (B) — an 8-ring series, starting at m/e 812 ($C_{59}H_{104}$), and (C) — a 13-ring series, starting at m/e 914 ($C_{67}H_{110}$), as shown in Fig. 8-69. All empirical formulas were determined from exact mass measurements.

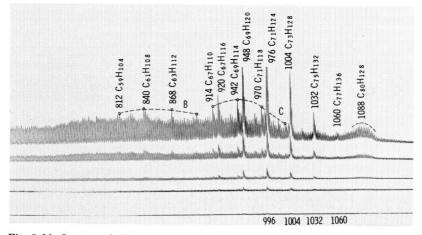

Fig. 8-69. Low resolution mass spectrum of the branched-cyclic hydrocarbon fraction of bitumen from Green River shale at 200°C probe temperature.

In view of the work of Oelert et al. [64], it is tempting to suggest that the observed profiles are due to compounds formed by condensing series (A) two pentacyclic triterpanes, series (B) two steranes, and, finally, (C) two steranes and a pentacyclic triterpane.

The next section on kerogen lends further support to these tentative concepts on high-molecular-weight polycyclics.

Kerogen

Kerogen is a term used here to describe the insoluble, non-volatile organic material found in sediments. Pyrolysis [66], oxidation [67], or catalytic reduction [68] have been reported as means of converting kerogen into a substance which can be analyzed by conventional means.

Recently [69], two related pyrolysis experiments were made on kerogen from the bitumen-free (solvent-extracted) shale of the Green River: (1) a

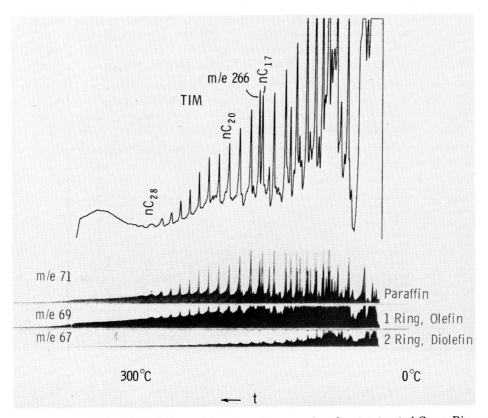

Fig. 8-70. Pyrolysis GC—MS chromatography of kerogen in solvent-extracted Green River shale.

pyrolysis GC—MS analysis of kerogen and (2) a GC—MS analysis of the saturate fraction of the pyrolysis oil from kerogen.

The kerogen sample was prepared by extracting the bitumen with a 50 : 50 benzene—methanol solvent for 222 hours prior to the pyrolysis experiments. Preliminary results are summarized graphically in Figs. 8-70, 8-8-71, and 8-72. Figure 8-71 shows the total ion monitor trace, TIM, and the m/e 71, 69, and 67 mass chromatograms generated by pyrolysis GC—MS of kerogen. The m/e 71 mass chromatogram monitors the alkane-like compounds, whereas the m/e 69 and 67 mass chromatograms monitor unsaturated or cyclic compounds. The saturated alkanes, mainly n-alkanes, appear to have the highest concentration.

Inasmuch as the py—GC—MS analysis was made on the total pyrolysis extractable material from kerogen, interpretation of the results is complicated by the presence of polyaromatics and hetero-atom-containing compounds.

This being the case, the pyrolysis oil from the Green River shale kerogen was separated over fully active alumina. Using cyclohexane as an eluant, a clear viscous saturate fraction was obtained for analysis by GC—MS. Surprisingly, infrared and Raman analysis of this fraction showed an absence of olefinic compounds. Fig. 8-71 shows the GC—MS mass chromatographic analysis of this saturate fraction of the pyrolysis oil from kerogen. Again, the n-alkanes identified by mass spectra are present in the highest concentration.

Figure 8-72 summarizes a terpane—sterane GC—MS analysis of the pyrolysis oil saturate fraction from Green River shale. Clearly most of the same terpanes and steranes found in the bitumen (solvent-extractable material) are also found in the saturate fraction of the pyrolysis oil from kerogen. Reten-

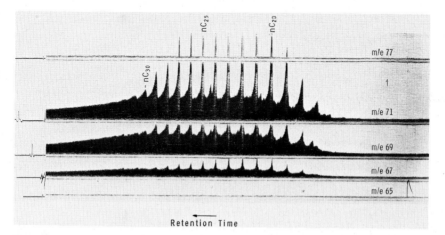

Fig. 8-71. Mass chromatography of the saturate fraction of vacuum pyrolysis oil from solvent-extracted Green River shale.

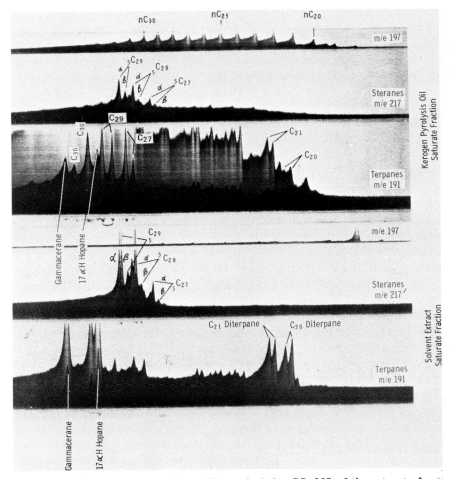

Fig. 8-72. Sterane, terpane, and paraffin analysis by GS—MS of the saturate fract: solvent-extractable oil (bitumen) and kerogen pyrolysis oil from Green River ......

tion times and complete mass spectra obtained by GC—MS confirms the terpane and sterane identifications. The terpanes and steranes are not bitumen residues. Thermal gravimetric analysis showed an absence of volatiles.

The conclusion from these experiments is that pyrolysis was able to release identifiable, fully saturated n-alkanes, terpanes, and steranes from kerogen in the Green River shale. Totally identified terpanes and steranes from C_{20} to C_{30} are present in concentrations of about 10% in the saturate fraction of the kerogen pyrolysis oil. This compares to a terpane—sterane C_{20} to C_{30} concentration of about 40% in the bitumen or extractable oil from the Green River shale.

These results suggest that known biological precursors are linked in some manner to form in part the complex network called kerogen. Kerogen presumably forms early during diagenesis, locking biological debris into its matrix. These biological components are very likely chemically bonded, making kerogen a good source of contamination-free "biological markers".

Conclusions

"Biological marker" hydrocarbons are priceless tools in the study of the geochemistry of organic matter in sediments. They carry detailed molecular information about their biological origin, mechanism of transformation, and diagenetic—epigenetic environment. In most cases, however, there are large data gaps between the presumed biological precursors and the "identified" hydrocarbons.

Studies of the organic components in young sediments, such as those being made by Ensminger et al. [38], are needed to close part of this gap. Further, the absolute stereochemistry of many of the "identified" hydrocarbons is not known. Determination of the biological precursors and diagenetic processing is highly dependent on this information.

Combined utilization of gas chromatography and mass spectroscopy presents a powerful analytical tool which is responsible for the provisional carbon skeleton identification of many of the reported "biological marker" hydrocarbons. This alone, however, will not necessarily fix the exact stereochemistry of molecules. Even synthesis and GC—MS coinjection sometimes will not give an unequivocal identification. Some isomers are expected to have practically identical mass spectra and retention times. Only isolation of individual components, followed by standard structure analysis techniques, similar to those used by Hills et al. [42] and Cox et al. [26], will give the final needed information.

Kerogen, which forms the greater part of organic material in sediments, represents a potential source of contamination-free "biological marker" compounds. Techniques should be developed so that "biological markers" can be quantitatively released from kerogen.

Acknowledgements

The author would like to thank Drs. A.L. McClellan, R.M. Teeter, and W.K. Seifert for helpful comments and suggestions. The thorough editing by Drs. T.F. Yen and G.V. Chilingar resulted in a much improved chapter.

References

1. M. Blumer, "Chemical Fossils: Trends in Organic Geochemistry", *Pure Appl. Chem.*, *34*, 591 (1973).
2. A. Treibs, "Chlorophyl und Hämin Derivate in Organischen Mineralstoffen," *Z. Angew. Chem.*, *49*, 682 (1936).
3. J.G. Palacas, *Geochemistry of Carbohydrates*, Thesis University of Minnesota (1959).
4. K.A. Kvenvolden, E. Peterson and G.A. Pollock, "Optical Configuration of Amino Acids in Precambrian Fig Tree Cherts", *Nature*, *221*, 141 (1969).
5. D.L. Lawlor and W.E. Robinson, "Fatty Acids in Green River Formation Oil Shale", *Am. Chem. Soc., Div. Pet. Chem., Rep. Meet., Detroit, April 4—9* (1965).
6. G. Mattern, P. Albrecht and G. Ourisson, "4-Methyl-Sterols and Sterols in Messel Shale (Eocene)", *Chem. Commun.*, 1570 (1970).
7. W. Henderson, W.E. Reed, G. Steel and M. Calvin, "Isolation and Identification of Sterols from a Pleistocene Sediment", *Nature*, *231*, 308 (1971).
8. W.K. Seifert, E.J. Gallegos and R.M. Teeter, "Proof of Structure of Steroid Carboxylic Acids in a California Petroleum by Labeling, Synthesis, and Mass Spectrometry", *J. Am. Chem. Soc.*, *94*, 5880 (1972).
9. T.S. Oakwood, D.S. Shriver, H.H. Fall, W.J. McAleer and P.R. Wunz, "Optical Activity of Petroleum", *Ind. Eng. Chem.*, *44*, 2568 (1952).
10. B.J. Mair, "Terpenoids, Fatty Acids, and Alcohols as Source Materials for Petroleum Hydrocarbons", *Geochim. Cosmochim. Acta*, *28*, 1303 (1964).
11. G. Eglinton, P.M. Scott and T. Belsky, *Hydrocarbons of Biological Origin from a One Billion Year-Old Sediment*, The National Academy of Sciences (1959).
12. J.G. Bendoraitis, B.L. Brown and L.S. Hepner, "Isoprenoid Hydrocarbons in Petroleum", *Anal. Chem.*, *34*, 49 (1962).
13. R.B. Johns, T. Belsky, E.D. McCarthy, A.L. Burlingame, P. Haug, H.K. Schnoes, W. Richter and M. Calvin, "The Organic Geochemistry of Ancient Sediments", *Geochim. Cosmochim. Acta*, *30*, 1191 (1966).
14. R.A. Dean and E.V. Whitehead, "The Occurrence of Phytane in Petroleum", *Tetrahedron Lett.*, *21*, 768 (1961).
15. J.J. Cummins and W.E. Robinson, "Normal and Isoprenoid Hydrocarbons Isolated from Oil-Shale Bitumen", *J. Chem. Eng. Data*, *9*, 304 (1964).
16. R. Ikan and A. Bortinger, "Normal and Isoprenoid Alkanes from an Israeli Shale", *Geochim. Cosmochim. Acta*, *35*, 1059 (1971).
17. E.D. McCarthy and M. Calvin, "The Isolation and Identification of the C_{17} Saturated Isoprenoid Hydrocarbon 2,6,10-Trimethyl Tetrodecane from a Devonian Shale", *Tetrahedron Lett.*, *23*, 2609 (1967).
18. K.E.H. Göhring, P.A. Schenck and E. Engelhardt, "A new Series of Isoprenoid Isoalkanes in Crude Oils and Cretaceous Bituminous Shales", *Nature*, *215*, 503 (1967).
19. J. Han and M. Calvin, "Occurrence of C_{22}—C_{25} Isoprenoids in Bell Creek Crude Oil", *Geochim. Cosmochim. Acta*, *33*, 733 (1969).
20. I.R. Hills, G.W. Smith and E.V. Whitehead, "Hydrocarbons from Fossil Fuels and Their Relationship With Living Organisms", *J. Inst. Pet. (Lond.)*, *56*, 127 (1970).
21. P.M. Gardner and E.V. Whitehead, "The Isolation of Squalane From a Nigerian Petroleum", *Geochim. Cosmochim. Acta*, *36*, 259 (1972).
22. E. Gelpi, H. Schneider, J. Mann and J. Oro, "Hydrocarbons of Geochemical Significance in Microscopic Algae", *Phytochemistry*, *9*, 603 (1970).
23. W. Van Hoeven, P. Haug, A.L. Burlingame and M. Calvin, "Hydrocarbons from Australian Oil, Two Hundred Million Years Old", *Nature*, *211*, 1361 (1966).
24. E.D. McCarthy, W. Van Hoeven and M. Calvin, "The Synthesis of Standards in the Characterization of a C_{21} Isoprenoid Alkane Isolated from Precambrian Sediments", *Tetrahedron Lett.*, *45*, 4437 (1967).

25. J.R. Maxwell, C.T. Pillinger and G. Eglinton, "Organic Geochemistry", *Quart. Rev.*, 25, 571 (1971).
26. R.E. Cox, J.R. Maxwell, G. Eglinton, C.T. Pillinger, R.G. Ackman and J.N. Hooper, "The Geological Fate of Chlorophyll: The Absolute Stereochemistries of a Series of Acyclic Isoprenoid Acids in a 50 Million Year-Old Lacustrine Sediment", *Chem. Commun.*, 1639 (1970).
27. L.F. Fieser and M. Fieser, *Advanced Organic Chemistry*, Reinhold, New York, 1011—1012 (1961).
28. M. Kates, L.S. Yengoyan and P.S. Sastry, "A Diether Analog of Phosphatidylglycerophosphate in *Halobacterium Cutirubrum*", *Biochim. Biophys. Acta*, 98, 252 (1965).
29. G.R. Whistance and D.R. Threlfall, "Isolation of Phytylplastoquinone and Phytylplastohydroquinone Monomethylether from *Euglena Gracilis*", *Phytochemistry*, 9, 213 (1970).
30. J.R. Maxwell, R.E. Cox, R.G. Ackman and J.N. Hooper, "The Diagenesis and Maturation of Phytol: The Stereochemistry of 2,6,10,14-Tetramethylpentadecane from an Ancient Sediment", in: H.R. v. Goetner and H. Wehner (Editors), *Advances in Organic Geochemistry*, Pergamon, Oxford, 277 (1971).
31. K.A. Kvenvolden, "Evidence for Transformations of Normal Fatty Acids in Sediments", in: G.O. Hobson and G.C. Speers (Editors), *Advances in Organic Geochemistry*, Pergamon, Oxford, 335 (1966).
32. D.E. Anders and W.E. Robinson, "Cycloalkane Constituents of the Bitumen from Green River Shale", *Geochim. Cosmochim. Acta*, 35, 661 (1971).
33. B.J. Mair, N.C. Kroukop and T.J. Mayer, "Composition of the Branched Paraffin—Cycloparaffin Portion of the Light Gas Oil Fraction", *J. Chem. Eng. Data*, 7, 420 (1962).
34. T.J. Murphy, A. McCormick and G. Eglinton, "Perhydro-β-Carotene in the Green River Shale", *Science*, 157, 1040 (1967).
35. E.J. Gallegos, "Identification of New Steranes, Terpanes, and Branched Paraffins in Green River Shale by Combined Capillary Gas Chromatography and Mass Spectrometry", *Anal. Chem.*, 43, 1151 (1971).
36. J.G. Bendoraitis, "Hydrocarbons of Biogenic Origin in Petroleum — Aromatic Triterpenes and Bicyclic Sesquiterpenes", Presented at *Sixth International Meeting on Organic Geochemistry, Rueil-Malmaison, France, September 18—21* (1973).
37. H. Budzikiewicz, J.M. Wilson and C. Djerassi, "Mass Spectrometry in Structural and Stereochemical Problems, XXXII Pentacyclic Triterpenes", *J. Am. Chem. Soc.*, 85, 3688 (1963).
38. A. Ensminger, P. Albrecht, G. Ourisson, B.J. Kimble, J.R. Maxwell and G. Eglinton, "Homohopane in Messel Oil Shale: First Identification of a C_{31} Pentacyclic Triterpane in Nature", *Tetrahedron Lett.*, 36, 3861 (1972).
39. E.W. Baker, "Mass Spectrometric Characterization of Petroporphyrins", *J. Am. Chem. Soc.*, 88, 2311 (1966).
40. T.F. Yen, L.J. Boucher, J.P. Dickie, E.C. Tynan and G.B. Vaughan, "Vanadium Complexes and Porphyrins in Asphaltenes", *J. Inst. Pet.*, 55, 87 (1969).
41. A.L. Burlingame, P. Haug, T. Belsky and M. Calvin, "Occurrence of Biogenic Steranes and Pentacyclic Triterpanes in an Eocene Shale (52 Million Years) and in an Early Precambrian Shale (2.7 Billion Years): A Preliminary Report", *Proc. Nat. Acad. Sci.*, 54, 1406 (1965).
42. I.R. Hills, E.V. Whitehead, D.E. Anders, J.J. Cummins and W.E. Robinson, "An Optically Active Triterpane, Gammacerane in Green River, Colorado, Oil Shale Bitumen", *Chem. Commun.*, 752 (1966).
43. W. Henderson, V. Wollrab and G. Eglinton, "Identification of Steroids and Triterpenes from a Geological Source by Capillary Gas-Liquid Chromatography and Mass Spectrometry", *Chem. Commun.*, 710 (1968).

44. L. Tökes, G. Jones and C. Djerassi, "Mass Spectrometry on Structural and Stereo-chemical Problems, CLXI, Elucidation of the Course of the Characteristic Ring D Fragmentation of Steroids", *J. Am. Chem. Soc.*, *90*, 5465 (1968).
45. L. Tökes and C. Djerassi, "Mass Spectrometry in Structural and Stereochemical Problems, CLXXVI, The Course of the Electron Impact Induced Fragmentation of Androstane", *J. Am. Chem. Soc.*, *91*, 5017 (1969).
46. E.J. Gallegos, unpublished results.
47. W.K. Seifert, "Steroid Acids in Petroleum — Animal Contribution to the Origin of Petroleum", *Pure Appl. Chem.*, *34*, 633 (1973).
48. R.B. Woodward and K. Block, "The Cyclization of Squalene in Cholesterol Synthesis", *J. Am. Chem. Soc.*, *75*, 2023 (1953).
49. W. Henderson, W. Wollrab and G. Eglinton, "Identification of Steranes and Triter-panes from a Geological Source by Capillary Gas—Liquid Chromatography and Mass Spectrometry", in: *Advances in Organic Geochemistry*, Pergamon, 181 (1968).
50. I.R. Hills, G.W. Smith and E.V. Whitehead, "Optically Active Spirotriterpane in Petroleum Distillates", *Nature*, *219*, 243 (1968).
51. B. Balough, D.M. Wilson, P. Christiansen and A.L. Burlingame, "Carbon-13 NMR Study of the Stereochemistry of Steranes From Oil Shale of the Green River Forma-tion (Eocene)", *Nature*, *242*, 603 (1973).
52. A. Ensminger, A. Van Dorsselaer, C.H. Spyckerelle, P. Albrecht and G. Ourisson, "Pentacyclic Triterpanes of the Hopane Type as Ubiquitous Geochemical Markers: Origin and Significance", Presented at *Sixth International Meeting on Organic Geo-chemistry, Rueil-Malmaison, France, September 18—21* (1973).
53. A.A. Newman, *Chemistry of Terpanes and Terpenoids*, Academic Press, London and New York (1972).
54. C.W. Bird, J.M. Lynch, S.J. Pirt and W.W. Reid, "The Identification of Hop-22(29)-ene in Prokaryotic Organisms", *Tetrahedron Lett.*, *34*, 3189 (1971).
55. E.J. Gallegos, "Identification of Phenylcycloparaffin Alkanes and Other Mono-aromatics in Green River Shale by Gas Chromatography-Mass Spectrometry", *Anal. Chem.*, *45*, 1399 (1973).
56. D.E. Anders, F.G. Doolittle and W.E. Robinson, "Analysis of Some Aromatic Hydro-carbons in a Benzene Soluble Bitumen From Green River Shale", *Geochim. Cosmo-chim. Acta*, *37*, 1213 (1973).
57. W.C. Day and J.G. Erdman, "Ionene: A Thermal Degradation Product of β-Carotene", *Science*, *141*, 808 (1963).
58. J. Pliva, V. Herout, B. Schneider and F. Sôrm, "On Terpenes, XLIII. Infrared Investi-gations of Terpenes IV", *Coll. Czech, Chim. Commun.*, *18*, 500 (1953).
59. L.F. Fieser and M. Fieser, *Topics in Organic Chemistry*, Reinhold, New York, pp. 184—185 (1963).
60. F.D. Rossini, B.J. Mair and A.J. Streiff, *Hydrocarbons from Petroleum*, Reinhold, New York, p. 402 (1953).
61. V. Jarolim, K. Hejno, F. Hemmert and F. Sôrm, "Über die Zusammensetzung der Braunkohle IX. Über einige Aromatische Kohlenwasserstoffe des Harzanteils des Montanwachses", *Coll. Czech. Chem. Commun.*, *30*, 873 (1965).
62. P. Albrecht and G. Ourisson, "Biogenic Substances in Sediments and Fossils", *Z. An-gew. Chem., Int. Ed.*, *10*, 209 (1971).
63. M. Blumer, "Organic Pigments: Their Long-Term Fate", *Science*, *149*, 722 (1965).
64. H.H. Oelert, D. Severin and H.J. Windhager, "Saturated Hydrocarbon Types From a Tia Juana Residue", *Erdöl and Kohle-Erdgas-Petrochemie vereinigt mit Brennstoff-Chemie*, *26*, 397 (1973).
65. E.J. Gallegos, unpublished results.
66. A.B. Hubbard and W.E. Robinson, "A Thermal Decomposition Study of Colorado Oil Shale", *U.S. Bur. Mines, Rep. Invest.*, *4744*, 24 (1958).

67. A.L. Burlingame, P.A. Haug, H.K. Schnoes and B.R. Simoneit, in: *Advances in Organic Geochemistry*, Pergamon, 88 (1969).
68. J.E. Flinn and G.F. Sachsel, "Exploratory Studies of a Process for Converting Oil Shale and Coal to Stable Hydrocarbons", *Ind. Eng. Chem. Process Design*, *1*, 143 (1968).
69. E.J. Gallegos, "Terpane and Sterane Release from Kerogen by Pyrolysis GC-MS", *Am. Soc. Mass Spectrom.*, *22nd Ann. Conf., May 9—24, Philadelphia, Penn.* (1974).

Chapter 9

RETORTING TECHNOLOGY OF OIL SHALE[1]

GERALD U. DINNEEN

Introduction

An efficient retorting process, either above- or underground, is a prerequisite for the utilization of oil shale. Many retorting systems have been suggested and quite a number tried over the last 100 years or so. Developments in recent years, however, have been mainly in the U.S.A., Brazil, and the U.S.S.R. on a limited number of systems. The present state of retorting technology in these countries is discussed in this chapter.

A major requirement for successfully utilizing oil shale as a source of liquid and gaseous fuels is a technically and economically feasible retorting process to thermally degrade the solid organic material (kerogen) in the shale. In such a process, which may be conducted either above- or belowground, the shale is heated to 425—475°C to decompose the kerogen to oil, gas, and a carbonaceous residue. Oil shale is normally retorted without beneficiation, but in some special circumstances concentration has been proposed [1].

The retorting process has an effect on the relative quantities and properties of the products obtained. Shale oil resembles petroleum but may differ from it in important respects, such as the nitrogen content of oil produced from Green River oil shale. The products normally produced from petroleum, however, can be obtained from shale oil if appropriate refining procedures are used.

Many aboveground retorting processes have been patented [2,3], and quite a number of these have been used at one time or another in commercial plants or have had some developmental work done on them [4]. Only a few retorting systems, however, have been applied or studied in the context of modern requirements for the efficient handling of large quantities of material. In recent years commercial operations have been conducted only in the U.S.S.R. and the People's Republic of China. Unfortunately, not enough information is available about the Chinese operations to permit a discussion of them. Hence, this paper will cover the status of retorting technology in the U.S.A., Brazil, and the U.S.S.R., which are the countries presently devoting considerable effort to utilize oil shale.

---

[1] The work upon which this chapter is based was done under a cooperative agreement between the Bureau of Mines, U.S. Department of the Interior, and the University of Wyoming.

Until rather recently, in-situ retorting processes had not generally received much attention. A notable exception was a full-scale application of the Ljungström process, begun in Sweden in 1944 [5]. In this process the oil shale was heated to 400° C by electric heaters in a hexagonal pattern of closely-spaced, shallow wells to produce a distillate oil containing about 50% gasoline. Utilization of this process, as well as other oil-shale activity in Sweden, however, was terminated a number of years ago. In the U.S.A. there has been heightened interest in underground processes in recent years, particularly as concern for the potential environmental effects of aboveground processing has increased. Hence, a discussion of present U.S.A. technology is included in this chapter.

Developments in the United States

Most attempts to utilize oil shales for the commercial production of fuels in the United States have been concerned with oil shales of the Green River Formation. The original interest in this formation, which occurs in the tri-state area (see Fig. 1-1 in the Introduction Chapter) of Colorado, Utah, and Wyoming, may have developed because a portion of it is readily accessible where it outcrops along an escarpment north of the Colorado River. More recent interest is due to the fact that the Green River oil shales contain a very large potential supply of energy — at least the equivalent of a hundred billion tons of petroleum — in relatively rich and thick deposits [6]. The traditional approach to utilizing the oil shale in the Green River Formation has involved mining and aboveground retorting of shale from the Mahogany zone along the south side of the Piceance Creek Basin. This shale, as indicated by the data in Fig. 9-1, is a heterogeneous material having a potential oil yield ranging from about 2 to nearly 30% by weight. Hence, selective mining can produce retort feeds of different average grades and a retorting process must be capable of handling a heterogeneous feed. The mining and aboveground retorting approach is still actively pursued because it will probably be the method used for the first commercial production of shale oil. An alternate approach involving in-situ retorting of the shale, however, has received considerable attention in recent years. This approach is attractive because it may be applicable to deposits of different thicknesses, grades, and depths of burial and because it avoids the problem of disposing of large quantities of spent shale.

Aboveground retorting

Although many aboveground retorting systems have been tried in an effort to develop a method for processing Green River shale in the last 60 years or so, only three have been tested on a large enough scale and with modern enough equipment so that some indication as to their advantages and dis-

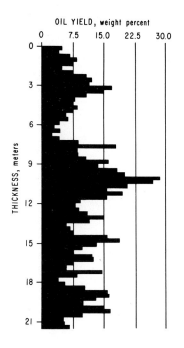

OIL YIELD, weight percent

Fig. 9-1. An oil-yield histogram for Mahogany zone of Green River Formation.

advantages is available. These are the gas combustion, Union Oil Company, and TOSCO II retorting systems which have been tested in pilot plants having capacities up to about 1,000 tons per day. They are considerably smaller than commercial-sized units which, as generally thought, will have to handle 5,000—10,000 tons per day each. A commercial plant might have about 10 of these units.

Gas combustion retort. From 1944 to 1956, pilot plant investigations of oil-shale retorting were conducted by the U.S. Bureau of Mines at facilities several miles west of the town of Rifle, Colorado. In the investigations, numerous types of retorts were evaluated. Of these, a process known as gas combustion retorting, which is shown schematically in Fig. 9-2, gave the most promising results and was studied the most extensively [7]. This retort is a vertical, refractory-lined vessel through which crushed shale moves downward by gravity, countercurrent to the retorting gases. Recycled gases enter the bottom of the retort and are heated by the hot retorted shale as they pass upward through the vessel. Air and some additional recycle gas, designated in Fig. 9-2 as dilution gas, are injected into the retort through a distributor system at a point approximately one-third of the way up from the bottom and are mixed with rising hot recycled gases. Combustion of the gases and of some residual carbon heats the shale immediately above the combustion

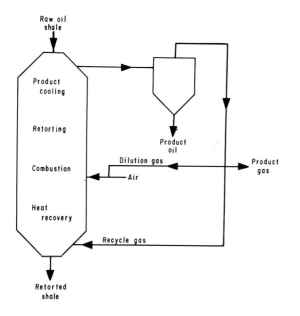

Fig. 9-2. Gas combustion retort.

zone to retorting temperature. Oil vapors and gases are cooled by the incoming shale, and the oil leaves the top of the retort as a mist.

Initial investigations of the process feasibility were made in a cylindrical retort 50 cm in diameter, which had a nominal capacity of 6 tons per day, and a rectangular retort rated at 25 tons per day. Operating variables were studied over a wide range of values during the investigations. The data for one test in the 25-ton retort are given in Table 9-I as an example of the conditions used. To develop the process further, a rectangular retort, 1.8 by 3.0 m, rated at 150 tons per day was constructed. Investigations were terminated in 1956, however, after only a small amount of work had been done on this retort and before operability of the process on this scale had been established.

Further developmental efforts on the gas combustion retort were conducted between 1964 and 1968 [8,9]. During this period, the Bureau of Mines facilities were leased by the Colorado School of Mines Research Foundation and were operated by it under a research contract with six oil companies: Mobil, which acted as a Project Manager, Humble, Phillips, Sinclair, Pan American, and Continental. This research utilized the same three retorts that the Bureau had built earlier and was concerned with such variables as shale flow in the retort and design of systems for injecting air into the retort. Results showed that the process could be operated at throughput rates about twice those achieved in the Bureau's operations without seriously decreasing the yield. All problems in operating the equipment were not solved, however,

TABLE 9-I

Data from a test in 25-ton-per-day pilot plant

Rates		
Raw shale	kg/h $\times$ m^2 bed area	1,480
Recycle gas	m^3/ton raw shale	470
Dilution gas	m^3/ton raw shale	35
Air	m^3/ton raw shale	153
Temperatures		
Product outlet	°C	58
Retorted shale outlet	°C	145
Yields		
Oil collected	vol. % of Fischer Assay	94
Gas vented	m^3/ton raw shale	240
Retorted shale	kg/ton raw shale	800
Water condensed	kg/ton raw shale	20
Material recovery	wt. %	101

particularly insofar as the largest of the three units was concerned.

The novel manner, in which retorting, combustion, heat exchange, and product recovery are accomplished in the gas combustion retort, gives high retorting and thermal efficiencies. The process does not require cooling water, which is an important advantage because the regions in which the oil-shale deposits occur are semi-arid. The retort uses lump shale (size distribution of minus 75 mm to plus 6 mm has given satisfactory results) and operates best on material having an oil yield of less than about 15% by weight. Because the process cannot use fine material, the latter would have to be briqueted or retorted in a different type of process. The gas combustion retort presents some operability problems, particularly in larger-sized equipment, in obtaining uniform shale flow, good air distribution, and adequate temperature control. These problems require additional developmental effort.

Union Oil Company retort. During the 1940's and 1950's, the Union Oil Company of California developed a process (Fig. 9-3) which was tested on a pilot-plant scale in 1957 and 1958 [10]. This system employs a counter-current flow of oil shale and air in a vertical refractory-lined vessel. It operates on a down-draft principle and the shale is moved upward through the retort by a charging mechanism referred to as a rock pump. Heat is supplied by combustion of the organic matter remaining in the retorted shale, and shale feed rates are adjusted to maintain the combustion zone a short distance below the surface of the bed. Some of the product (oil) is condensed by the cool, incoming shale and is recovered as a liquid, while the remainder exits

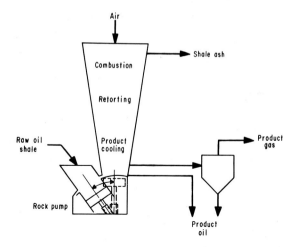

Fig. 9-3. Union Oil Company process.

with the gas. The retort uses lump shale of about the same size range as the gas combustion retort, requires removal of fine material, and does not need cooling water which, as mentioned previously, is an important feature.

Pilot-scale testing of the process was conducted in a plant near the headwaters of Parachute Creek in Western Colorado, where shale could be mined readily from an outcrop of the Mahogany zone. The pilot plant had a capacity of about 1,000 tons per day. It was announced after completion of the tests that operation of the process had been successful and it could be commercialized in the proper economic climate.

TOSCO II process. The TOSCO II process (Fig. 9-4) has been under development for a number of years by The Oil Shale Corporation. The retort is a rotary kiln type in which retorting is accomplished by mixing externally heated balls 15 mm in diameter with preheated shale crushed to a size of minus 12 mm [11,12]. The balls are separated from the hot spent shale on a trommel and recirculated through a ball heater. Products are drawn off to a collection system for removal of dust and recovery of liquids and gases. The process utilizes all the shale that is mined, has good heat transfer in the solid-to-solid system, and gives high yields. It is rather complex, however, and does require appreciable quantities of water to condense the liquid products and prevent dusting of the finely-divided spent shale.

A pilot plant designed for about 1,000 tons per day was operated at various times over a period of several years ending early in 1972. This plant was also located on Parachute Creek, not far from the operations by Union Oil Company. In the most recent investigations, it was operated by the Colony Development group with Atlantic Richfield Oil Company acting as a manager for the group, which also included Standard Oil Company of Ohio, The Oil

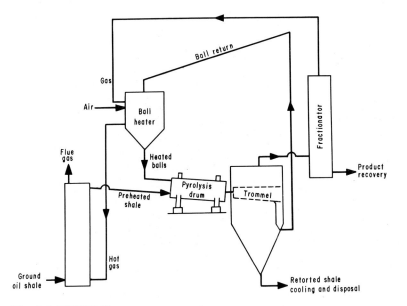

Fig. 9-4. TOSCO II process.

Shale Corporation, and Cleveland Cliffs Iron Company. When the testing program was terminated in April 1972, it was announced that evaluation of the data obtained would require some time before a decision would be made on constructing a commercial plant, which would presumably process in the order of 70,000 tons of shale per day. More recently, engineering design of a commercial plant has been started, though a decision on building it will not be reached until the design is completed, presumably sometime in 1976.

In-situ retorting

Because mining, crushing, and aboveground retorting make up a substantial portion (perhaps 60%) of the cost of producing shale oil, retorting oil shale in place has received some attention in the last 20 years as a possible means of reducing the cost of shale-oil production. This approach is attractive for several other reasons. It may be applicable to deposits of various thicknesses, grades, and amounts of overburden that are not readily amenable to mining. In addition, it eliminates the necessity of disposing of large quantities of spent shale. It may introduce other environmental problems, however, such as the possibility of groundwater leaching the soluble retorting products left underground. In spite of the potential advantages, only a relatively small amount of research has been done on the technique, and the technology is in the very early stages of development.

There are a number of ways in which underground processing might be accomplished. One of the simpler techniques, which is illustrated schematically

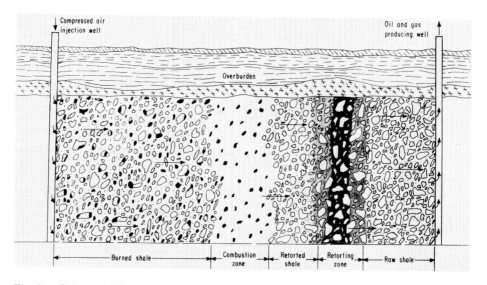

Fig. 9-5. Schematic diagram of in-situ oil-shale retorting process.

in Fig. 9-5, consists of drilling of wells having a predetermined pattern into the oil-shale formation, creating permeability among the wells if naturally-occurring permeability is low, igniting the shale in one or more of the wells, pumping compressed air down the ignition well to support combustion of some of the oil shale, forcing the hot combustion gases through the oil shale to convert the solid organic matter in it to oil, and recovering the oil thus generated from other wells in the pattern.

Although the preceding concept is simple, its actual development and application involve complex and difficult engineering problems. One of these that has received considerable attention is how to achieve the fracturing that may be required to give the necessary permeability. For the concept illustrated in Fig. 9-5, hydraulic pressure and/or chemical explosives have been tried, but there is difficulty in getting the required surface area, especially with deeper-lying shales. A method that has been suggested for the deeper shales is to use a nuclear explosive to create a large cylindrical cavity filled with several million tons of broken shale. In this case the retorting would probably be conducted from top to bottom of the cavity rather than horizontally as shown in Fig. 9-5. Although considerable study [13] has been devoted to this method, no field experiment has been conducted or is presently scheduled.

Past developments. In 1953, Sinclair Oil and Gas Company performed one of the early experiments aimed at in-situ retorting of oil shale [14]. In general, it used a concept similar to that presented in Fig. 9-5. From these tests and subsequent ones made during the following year, it was concluded that communication between wells could be established through induced or natural fracture systems, that wells could be ignited successfully, although high pressures were required to maintain injection rates during the heating period, and that combustion could be established and maintained in the shale bed. These were tests made near the outcrop in the southern part of the Piceance Creek Basin. Additional tests were made some years later at a depth of about 365 m in the north-central part of the Piceance Creek Basin. These latter tests were only partially successful, at least in part, because of an inability to obtain the required surface area for the heat transfer [15].

A different in-situ method was studied by Equity Oil Company of Salt Lake City [16]. The method consisted of injecting hot natural gas into the shale bed to retort the shale. One injection well and four producing wells were drilled into the shale formation. Gas was compressed to about 85 kg/cm^2, heated to 480°C, and delivered through insulated tubing to the retorting zone. The field experiment was conducted in an area of the Piceance Creek Basin having a naturally-occurring permeability and porosity due to the leaching of soluble salts. Based on results of the experiment and a mathematical model developed from them, it was concluded that this technique was feasible and potentially an economic method for recovering shale oil. The economics, however, are strongly influenced by the cost of natural gas and the amount required for make-up.

A more recent in-situ field testing program was conducted by Shell Oil Company from 1970 to 1972. Although not much information is available on this test, it apparently depends on the extraction of kerogen by hot miscible fluids containing solubilizing agents such as hydrogen sulfide.

Present programs. The major programs presently in progress, which are aimed at the development of in-situ retorting technology, are being conducted by the U.S. Bureau of Mines and Garrett Research and Development Company.

The Bureau's program involves laboratory studies, pilot scale simulation of underground operations, and field experiments. Many of the variables in retorting broken shale, such as the rate of combustion front travel, gas flows through broken shale, grade of shale, and particle-size distribution, can be advantageously studied in aboveground equipment simulating underground conditions. Other variables, however, such as the methods to obtain required permeability and control of underground reactions, can be studied effectively only in actual field experiments.

The Bureau's aboveground equipment for studying in-situ techniques consists of two retorts, one with a nominal capacity of 10 tons and the other with a nominal capacity of 150 tons. The two sizes of retorts are used because data may be obtained more quickly and inexpensively with the small one, but the larger one is required for obtaining meaningful data on some parameters. Because the fundamental difference between the two retorts is one of size, a description of only the 150-ton unit is presented here.

The 150-ton retort [17] shown in Fig. 9-6 is a refractory-lined, carbon-

Fig. 9-6. 150-ton batch oil shale retort.

steel cylindrical retort that is 4 m in diameter and 13.7 m high. It has an opening at the top for loading, using a hoist and bucket, and a hinged grate at the bottom for supporting the shale bed and discharging the retort. The refractory lining consists of 15 cm of firebrick backed by 10 cm of insulating castable refractory.

To charge the retort, a layer of crushed, sized granite is placed on the grate to prevent oil-shale fines from falling through and to protect the grate from excessive temperatures during retorting of the bottom portion of the oil-shale bed. After the crushed rock layer is placed, oil shale, which has generally been mine-run shale shown in the foreground of Fig. 9-6, is loaded into the retort, taking care to limit size degradation or segregation. During loading, sets of thermocouples, usually eight in number, are distributed over the cross-section of the retort at 1- or 2-m vertical intervals to measure bed tempera-tures during retorting.

After the retort is filled, it is closed and retorting is started by igniting the shale at the top with a natural gas burner. After the burner is turned off, combustion is maintained by injecting air and recycle gas, if used, into the top of the retort. The combustion zone travels down through the bed, retorting the oil shale ahead of it. A tank, mounted on load cells, is used to collect the liquid products so that a continuous record of retort output can be maintained. Gaseous products from the retort, which contain some oil and water, are passed through packed towers to remove most of the entrained materials. After passing through a blower, some of the gas stream may be recycled back into the retort, while the remainder vents through a stack equipped with a natural gas burner to oxidize combustible components.

So far, a series of nine runs has been made on the retort to determine the effects of the amount of oxygen in the retort gas and the gas velocity. Each one of these retorting variables was investigated at three levels: 7, 14, and 21% oxygen and 0.38, 0.61, and 0.84 m^3/m^2 bed cross section/min. Yields ranged from 40 to 65% of Fischer assay, with the higher results being obtained at the intermediate space velocity. Yields were not affected much by the oxygen content of the retorting gas.

The 10-ton retort has been used most recently to study the effects of shale grade. Successful operation of the retort has been achieved with shales having a potential oil yield as low as 4% by weight. With these lean shales the maximum yield obtained has been in the order of 50% of Fischer assay. The results indicate that zones of very lean shale should not interfere with the operability of an in situ recovery process.

Some of the parameters involved in underground processing of oil shale, such as obtaining required permeability for the passage of gases and liquids, ignition of a fractured oil-shale interval, achieving and maintaining combustion over a substantial thickness of the fractured interval, controlling direction of movement of the combustion front, and recovering the products of retorting, can be studied effectively only under field conditions. Hence, the Bureau of Mines has for several years been conducting field experiments in southwestern Wyoming between the towns of Rock Springs and Green River. In this area, an oil-shale interval about 6-m thick that yields about 8% by weight of oil per ton is relatively shallow. Experiments have been conducted at two sites, one where the shale is approximately 25 m deep and the other where it is approximately 120 m deep. So far eight experiments concerned with various fracturing and recovery methods have been conducted at the shallower site, and two fracturing experiments have been performed at the deeper site [18].

The most elaborate experiment [19] was one in which a set of test wells

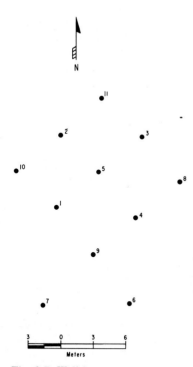

Fig. 9-7. Well locations for an in-situ experiment on recovery of oil from oil shale.

in the pattern shown in Fig. 9-7 was drilled through the 6-m interval of oil shale at 21—27 m below the surface of the ground. In order to achieve major fracturing of the shale in the central part of the well pattern, a series of electric, hydraulic, and explosive fracturing techniques was applied. The shale was ignited with a propane burner in the central well (No. 5) of the pattern, and shale combustion was then sustained in the formation by injection of air. The injection was continued for 5 weeks until the combustion front had reached several of the production wells; the injection of air was then discontinued. During this period about 31,000 l of oil were recovered aboveground.

To evaluate what had been achieved, a series of cores was taken after the combustion had been terminated [20]. Examination of these cores indicated that only a rather narrow shale interval of about 1.5 m had been heated and that some of the oil produced was apparently trapped in the unheated intervals, as cores from these intervals contained more oil than before the experiment started. A material balance based on core data before and after the experiment indicated that most of the potential oil originally present in the interval could be accounted for, though only a rather small part was obtained aboveground.

Garrett Research and Development Company is conducting in-situ experiments on the southwestern edge of the Piceance Creek Basin which utilize the combined mining and in situ processing technique patented by Garrett [21]. In this technique sufficient shale is mined from the lower part of a room to provide the desired porosity when the shale above the mined portion is collapsed. The broken shale in the room is then retorted from the top down in a manner similar to operation of the Bureau of Mines 150-ton retort. This field experiment, which presumably is on the scale of several thousand tons, has been in progress only since mid 1972. When the results of this experiment become available, they should answer many questions about the feasibility of underground retorting of large quantities of broken shale.

Developments in Brazil

In Brazil, the government corporation, Petrobrás, has had an oil-shale development program in progress for some years [22]. This program resulted in the development of the Petrosix process (Fig. 9-8) in which oil-shale fragments ranging in size up to 15 cm enter the top of a vertical retort and move by gravity through the zones of heating, retorting, and cooling. The retorted shale fragments discharge into a sump where they are mixed with waste water and transported to the disposal area. Process heat is furnished by a stream of preheated recycle gas that enters the retort at the middle level and combines with a second recycle gas stream which is injected into the bottom of the vessel. The second gas stream flowing upward recovers heat from the downward-moving retorted shale fragments. In this manner, the

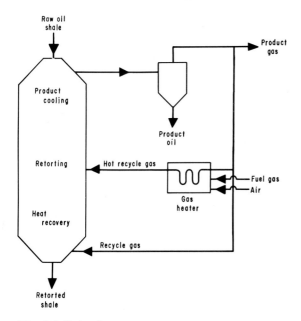

Fig. 9-8. Petrosix process.

retorted shale fragments are cooled and the recycled gas recovers heat. Because the process uses external combustion to heat the retorting gas, it should eliminate by more precise temperature control the clinker of agglomerate problems that have occurred in other gravity-flow retorts, such as the gas-combustion type. It is the use of this externally-heated gas stream that primarily distinguishes the Petrosix from the gas-combustion retort.

The Brazilian developments have culminated in the construction of a large pilot plant at São Mateus do Sul, State of Paraná, which started operation in the summer of 1972. The plant utilizes shale from the Iratí Formation obtained by open-pit mining of two intervals that have thicknesses of 3.2 and 6.5 m and an average oil yield of 7.4% by weight. The Petrosix retort in the plant is designed to process 2,500 tons of shale daily with yields of approximately 1,000 barrels of oil, 1 million cubic ft of gas, and 20 tons of sulfur. The operation of this large-scale plant should give valuable information as to the operability and economics of the Petrosix process.

Developments in U.S.S.R.

Oil-shale processing in the U.S.S.R. utilizes the kukersite found in the Baltic Basin, which is situated in the northwestern part of the country, primarily around the city of Kohtla-Järva in the eastern part of the Estonian S.S.R. The industry has operated continuously for about 50 years and presently utilizes about 25 million tons of oil shale annually [23]. This oil shale is obtained from both underground and surface mines. Roughly half of the mined oil shale, which averages about 35% by weight of organic material and has a maximum fragment size of 25 mm, is utilized directly as a power plant fuel. The other half, the fragment size of which ranges from 25 to 125 mm, is used to produce town gas, liquid fuels, and chemicals. Although the major thrust of the oil-shale industry in the Soviet Union was for many years the production of town gas, the future for gas production is not promising owing to increasing competition from natural gas. Hence, it has become expedient to readjust the oil-shale industry toward the production of petrochemicals, and at the present time more than 35 different products are being made. This change in emphasis on the output of products desired has had an effect on retort development. At present, two retorting systems — gas generator and chamber oven — are in use, and a third — solid heat carrier — is under development. An older method — low-temperature coking in tunnel ovens — has not undergone fundamental improvements in recent years and has largely been phased out of operations.

Gas generator retorting system

The gas generator retorting system is used for low-temperature coking of kukersite [24]. Although only half of the shale that is processed is retorted

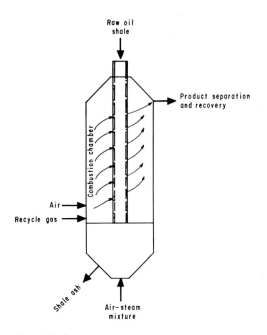

Fig. 9-9. Gas generator.

in these units, they produce about 60% of the shale oil, because the chamber ovens are operated primarily for the production of town gas. Fig. 9-9 shows a simplified diagram of one modern version of the gas generator system. This version consists of a vertical cylindrical shaft with a built-in gas-combustion chamber near the center of the shaft, where air is injected together with recycle gas. A steam—air mixture is also injected into the lower part of the generator to gasify residual carbonaceous material in the retorted shale. Retorting is achieved by a cross-flow stream of hot gas passing horizontally through a thin bed of shale moving downward through the gas generator. The products from the retort are liquid hydrocarbons and a low-heating-value gas.

The present gas generator retort has evolved after numerous design changes that were made in an effort to overcome the deficiencies of earlier types, i.e., low throughput (35 tons/day) and unstable operation that required frequent rodding and cleaning of bituminous deposits. Empirical design changes did not produce notable improvement, and it was only after a study of the specific retorting characteristics of Baltic shale, that progress was made. A major improvement was achieved in the 1950's by arranging for central distribution of the heat-carrier gas. Subsequently, the design illustrated in Fig. 9-9 was developed to achieve a throughput of 185 tons/day and to reduce the manpower requirements, because it is adaptable to automatic control. Even the improved present-day design, however, recovers only about

75% of Fischer assay. Further improvements seem possible by measures such as careful sizing of the charge, recovery of light oil carried out with the gas, and improved grate design.

Chamber ovens

Chamber—ovens (Fig. 9-10) are used primarily for high-temperature pyrolysis (about 800°C) of oil shale to produce town gas [25]. Each chamber measures 4 × 0.4 × 10 m and has a daily capacity of 20 tons of oil shale. Each chamber is separated from adjacent chambers by heating flues in which

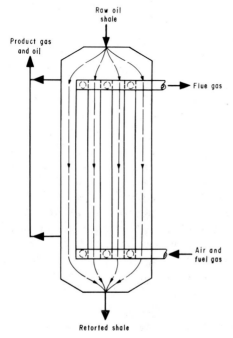

Fig. 9-10. Chamber oven.

the low-heating-value off-gas from the gas generators is utilized as fuel. The yield of gas from a chamber oven may be as high as 300 m³/ton and it may have a heating value of 4000 kcal/m³. The gas contains about 30% hydrogen, 25% hydrocarbons, and 10—13% carbon monoxide. In addition, the chamber ovens produce as byproducts some high-temperature tar and natural gasoline.

Solid heat-carrier retort

For several years development of a new highly efficient retort utilizing hot spent shale ash as the heat-carrying medium has received attention [26]. In this system, which is similar in principle to the TOSCO II process discussed in a previous section, shale fragments with a maximum size of 15—18 mm are fed to a rotating drum along with the heat carrier. The heat carrier is produced by burning spent shale in an auxiliary ebulliating bed with air injection. So far, a 500-ton-per-day unit has been constructed and operated successfully. The advantages of the process are high efficiency and production of a wide range of products the composition of which can be flexibly regulated. In one reported operation, the products consisted of 17% high-heating-value gas, 21% gasoline and light distillate, and 61% of a mixture of medium and heavy distillates. It is thought that the process can be scaled up so that eventually a unit can be designed that will handle 10,000 tons per day [1].

Conclusions

A very large number of different retorts have been suggested during the last 100 years for the aboveground processing of oil shale, and a substantial number of these have actually been tried at some time during that period. Within recent years, however, the only retorts that have received appreciable attention are the gas combustion, Union Oil Company, and TOSCO II retorts in the U.S.A.; the Petrosix retort in Brazil; and the gas generator, chamber oven, and solid heat-carrier retorts in the U.S.S.R. The retorts in the U.S.A. and Brazil are being tried on pilot-plant scales ranging from about 300 to 2,500 tons per day. Although the retorts show promise, their actual operability on a commercial scale has yet to be demonstrated. In U.S.S.R., the retorts are being used or developed in connection with an industry that processes about 10 million tons of oil shale a year. Each one of the retorts has advantages and disadvantages, so that the best retort for a given situation will depend on the particular conditions existing in that specific situation.

In addition to the aboveground retorting of oil shale, which is the traditional approach, the possibility of retorting the oil shale in situ has received attention in recent years. This technique may have economic and environmental advantages. It is in the early stages of development, however, and its technical feasibility has not yet been established.

References

1. M.I. Podkletnov, "Main Methods and New Trends in Oil Shale Processing in the U.S.S.R.", *Prepr., U. N. Symp. Develop. Utiliz. Oil Shale Resour., Tallinn, Eston. S.S.R., Sect. III, Pap. B1*, 23 pp. (1968).
2. S. Klosky, "An Index of Oil-Shale Patents", *U.S. Bur. Mines Bull., 468,* 650 pp. (1949).
3. S. Klosky, "Index of Oil Shale and Shale Oil Patents: 1946-1956", A supplement to Bull. *468, U.S. Bur. Mines Bull., 574,* I. U.S. Patents, 1958, 134 pp.; II. United Kingdom Patents, 1958, 75 pp.; III. European Patents, 1959, 45 pp.
4. G. Sell, (Editor), *Oil Shale and Cannel Coal*, Institute of Petroleum, London, England, 2 (1951).
5. G. Salomonsson, "The Ljungström In Situ Method for Shale-Oil Recovery", in: *Oil Shale and Cannel Coal*, Institute of Petroleum, London, England, 2, 260—280 (1951).

6. D.C. Duncan and V.E. Swanson, "Organic-rich Shale of the United States and World Land Areas", *U.S. Geol. Surv. Circ.*, *523*, 30 pp. (1966).

7. A. Matzick, R.O. Dannenburg, J.R. Ruark, J.E. Phillips, J.D. Lankford and B. Guthrie, "Development of the Bureau of Mines Gas-Combustion Oil-Shale Retorting Process", *U.S. Bur. Mines Bull.*, *635*, 99 pp. (1966).

8. J.R. Ruark, H.W. Sohns and H.C. Carpenter, "Gas Combustion Retorting of Oil Shale Under the Anvil Points Lease Agreement: Stage I", *U.S. Bur. Mines, Rep. Invest.*, *7303*, 109 pp. (1969).

9. J.R. Ruark, H.W. Sohns and H.C. Carpenter, "Gas Combustion Retorting of Oil Shale Under the Anvil Points Lease Agreement: Stage II", *U.S. Bur. Mines, Rep. Invest.*, *7540*, 74 pp. (1971).

10. C. Berg, "Retorting of Oil Shale", in: *Oil Shale and Cannel Coal*, Institute of Petroleum, London, England, *2*, 419—427 (1951).

11. R.J. Cameron, "Technology for Utilization of Green River Oil Shale", *Proc., 8th World Pet. Congr.*, Applied Science Publishers Ltd., Essex, England, *4*, 25—34 (1971).

12. A.F. Lenhart, "TOSCO Process Shale Oil Yields", *Prepr., U.N. Symp. Develop. Utiliz. Oil Shale Resour.*, Tallinn, Eston. S.S.R., Sect. III, Pap. F-2, 20 pp. (1968).

13. *Bronco Oil Shale Study*, prepared by U.S. Atomic Energy Commission, U.S. Department of the Interior, CER-Geonuclear Corp., and Lawrence Radiation Laboratory, PNE-1400, Clearinghouse for Federal Scientific and Technical Information, Springfield, Va., 64 pp. (1967).

14. B.F. Grant, "Retorting Oil Shale Underground — Problems and Possibilities", *Q. Colo. Sch. Mines*, *59* (3), 39—46 (1964).

15. A.L. Barnes and R.T. Ellington, "A Look at Oil Shale Retorting Methods Based on Limited Heat Transfer Contact Surfaces", *Q. Colo. Sch. Mines.*, *63* (4), 83—108 (1968).

16. P.M. Dougan, F.S. Reynolds and P.J. Root, "The Potential for In Situ Retorting of Oil Shale in the Piceance Creek Basin of Northwestern Colorado", *Q. Colo. Sch. Mines*, *65* (4), 57—72 (1970).

17. A.E.Harak, L. Dockter and H.C. Carpenter, "Some Results from the Operation of a 150-ton Oil-Shale Retort", *U.S. Bur. Mines, TPR 30*, 14 pp. (1971).

18. H.E. Thomas, H.C. Carpenter and T. E. Sterner, "Hydraulic Fracturing of Wyoming Green River Oil Shale: Field Experiments, Phase I", *U.S. Bur. Mines, Rep. Invest.*, *7596*, 18 pp. (1972).

19. E.L. Burwell, T.E. Sterner and H.C. Carpenter, "Shale Oil Recovery by In Situ Retorting — a Pilot Study", *J. Pet. Technol.*, *22*, 1520—1524 (1970).

20. H.C. Carpenter, E.L. Burwell and H.W. Sohns, "Evaluation of an In Situ Retorting Experiment in Green River Oil Shale", *J. Pet. Technol.*, *24*, 21—26 (1972).

21. D.E. Garrett, *In Situ Process for Recovery of Carbonaceous Materials from Subterranean Deposits*, U.S. Patent 3,661, 423 (1972).

22. C.E. Bruni, D. Vasconcelos and V.T. Padula, "Brazilian Oil Shale Development", *Proc., 8th World Pet. Congr.*, Applied Science Publishers Ltd., Essex, England, *4*, 13—24 (1971).

23. G.V. Ozerov, A.Y. Aarna, H.T. Raudsepp, M.Y. Gubergritz, S.I. Faingold, A.S. Fomina, A.M. Kotov, G.M. Mamedaliev, N.S. Nametkin, N.D. Serebryannikov, V.M. Yefimov and N.I. Zelenin, "Processing and Utilization of Oil Shale of the Baltic Basin of the U.S.S.R." *Proc. 8th World Pet. Congr.*, Applied Science Publishers Ltd., Essex, England, *4*, 3—12 (1971).

24. V.M. Yefimov and E.E. Piik, "Processing of Oil Shale in Gas Generators", *Prepr., U.N. Symp. Develop. Utiliz. Oil Shale Resour.*, Tallinn, Eston. S.S.R., Sect. III, Pap. C3, 28 pp. (1968).

25. N.D. Serebryannikov, "Production of Town Gas from Oil Shale", *Prepr., U.N. Symp. Develop. Utiliz. Oil Shale Resour.*, Tallinn, Eston. S.S.R., Sect. III, Pap. E2, 24 pp. (1968).

Chapter 10

EVALUATION OF OIL SHALES USING GEOPHYSICAL WELL-LOGGING TECHNIQUES

WALTER H. FERTL

Introduction to geophysical well-logging

Generally speaking, *well logging* denotes any operation wherein some characteristic data of the formation penetrated by a borehole are recorded in terms of depth. Such a record is called a *log*. The log of a well, for example, may simply be a chart on which abridged descriptions of cores are written opposite the depths from which cores were taken. A log may also be a graphic plot with respect to depth of various characteristics of these cores, including porosity, horizontal and vertical permeability, and water and hydrocarbon saturations.

In *geophysical well logging*, a probe is lowered in the well at the end of an insulated cable, and physical measurements are performed and recorded in graphical form as functions of depth. These records are called *geophysical well logs*, *well logs*, or simply *logs*. Often, when there is no ambiguity, *geophysical well-logging operations* are referred to shortly as *well logging* or *logging*.

Various types of measuring devices can be lowered on cables in the borehole for the sole purpose of measuring (logging) both borehole and in-situ formation properties. These logging tools, or logging sondes, contain sensors which measure the desired downhole properties, whether thermal, magnetic, electric, radioactive, or acoustic. Insulated conductive cables not only lower these sondes in the borehole but also pass power to the sondes and transmit recorded signals (data) to the surface, where the latter are recorded as a log. Hence, geophysical well-logging methods provide a detailed and economical evaluation of the entire length of drilled hole. Most of these logging operations are performed with the sonde moving uphole. Most well-logging methods available today have been initially designed and developed to assist in answering some major questions associated with exploration, evaluation, and production of oil and gas [9,11,20,21,23,24,41].

Today, however, many of these logging sondes and associated interpretation concepts are equally successful applied in exploring and evaluating metallic deposits [3,6,7,8,41] and nonmetallic minerals [5,36], and have also found application in mine design [17].

Well logging, as it is known today, was born on September 5, 1927, when the first resistivity log was run in well Diffenbach No. 2905, Pechelbronn Oil

Field, Alsace, France. It came out of experiments intended to achieve another purpose, a feature which is not uncommon in scientific research.

Well logs provide one of the main keys to realistic formation evaluation. The latter is as a blend of science and art used to determine the composition and physical or chemical rock properties in situ and the nature and amount of fluids contained in the pore space, thereby giving an indication of the economic worth of natural resources accumulated in the subsurface, such as oil, gas, coal, uranium, etc.

Despite major technical advances over the last several decades, it is practically impossible as yet to directly measure in-situ engineering and economically important properties of geologic formations penetrated by exploratory holes. Hence, the oil and mining industry has to resort to measurements of specific secondary rock properties (resistivity, radioactivity, etc.), which are then empirically related to the amount of oil and gas in-place, the quality and size of coal deposits, the "richness" of particular ore concentrations in host rocks, oil yield per ton in oil-shale deposits, etc.

Geophysical well logs for oil-shale evaluation

Several geophysical well logs can be used to evaluate oil-shale deposits, as far as lithology variations, thickness, and oil yield are concerned. Before starting a discussion of properly selected logging programs and associated interpretation methods, however, geophysical well logs applicable for oil shale evaluation will be reviewed briefly.

Caliper log

The caliper log basically measures and records the size (diameter) of the borehole. Basically, large flexible springs or arms, which ride against the wall of the borehole, are mounted on the body of a sonde. Owing to changes in hole size, the movement of these springs or arms generates voltages within the sonde which are then transmitted to the surface and recorded in terms of hole diameter. The caliper log works equally well in boreholes filled with fresh- or salt-water muds (drilling fluids), oil-base drilling fluids, or gas (e.g., air).

Non-focused electric logs

These types of logging sondes basically measure the resistivity of materials surrounding the logging sonde, and frequently several different electrode configurations are used in combination to measure various resistivity parameters [23,40]. Quality of measurements depends on the type of borehole fluid and, obviously, electric logs cannot be run in air-filled holes or in oil-base muds.

Focused conductivity—induction type logs

The induction log basically measures the electric conductivity of formations traversed by the borehole to obtain an estimate of the true formation resistivity [13,14,35]. Generally speaking, the formations are energized by electromagnetic induction. The resulting electromagnetic forces (eddy currents) are detected by receiver coils and transmitted to the surface where both formation conductivity and its reciprocal resistivity are recorded. Measured resistivities in excess of 100 ohm-m^2/m, however, generally are unsatisfactory. With the exception of very saline (salty) borehole fluids, the induction log works equally well in gas-filled holes and in oil-base or fresh-water muds.

Focused resistivity logs

Several types of focused resistivity logs are routinely used by the oil industry for the purpose of measuring the apparent resistivity of a thin segment of the formation perpendicular to the borehole. These logging sondes perform well in the salt-water muds and in detecting highly resistive and relatively thin zones, but are ineffective in gas-filled boreholes and in oil-base muds.

Generally speaking, the resistivity is measured by recording the voltage at a central electrode from which a constant current is so focused that it goes laterally a certain distance into the formation and then fans out vertically. This focusing is accomplished by a proper arrangement of electrodes, situated above and below the measuring electrode. These electrodes are maintained at the same potential as the measuring electrode [10,13].

Gamma-ray log

The gamma-ray log is used as a lithology log and to determine shaliness and/or radioactive heavy minerals in zones investigated. It basically measures the intensity of the natural gamma rays of the formations penetrated by the borehole. The natural radiation intensity is measured by proper downhole detectors, amplified, and then transmitted to the surface. The gamma-ray log can be run in cased or uncased holes and is independent of the type of fluid in the borehole [16,19].

Scattered gamma-ray density logs

Formation density logs basically measure the electron density (i.e., number of electrons per cubic centimeter) of downhole formations. This electron density is directly related to the true bulk density which, in turn, is a function of the composition of rock matrix material, the formation porosity, and the density of the fluids and/or gases filling the pore space.

A gamma-ray source emits medium energy gamma rays into the formation where collision takes place with electrons in the rock. This collision causes a backscattering and a decrease in gamma-ray energy (Compton effect). These scattered gamma rays reaching the detector (on the logging sonde), which is at a fixed distance from the radioactive source, are then recorded as a measure of formation density. These values can then be used to estimate formation porosity. Density logs can be run equally well in all types of borehole fluids [1,32,38].

Acoustic (sonic) logs

Sonic logs record the time required for a compressional sound wave to traverse one foot of formation. This *interval transit time* is the reciprocal of the velocity of the compressional sound wave and is a function of formation lithology, porosity, and types of fluids in the pore space [19,22,34,39]. Hence, the sonic log (1) is a good porosity tool, provided the lithology is known; (2) assists in interpreting seismic data; and (3) indicates the quality of cement bonds in cased holes [15].

A transducer creates elastic wave pulses which travel a given distance through the formation and are then picked up at receivers in logging sonde. Travel time, total acoustic wave trains, signal amplitudes, etc., can be recorded.

Acoustic logs can be run in any type of borehole fluids but not in air-filled or gas-filled holes.

Neutron logs

The basic purpose of neutron logs is to measure the abundance of hydrogen atoms in downhole formations or the relative abundance of epithermal neutrons arriving at the detector.

High-energy, fast neutrons are continuously emitted from a radioactive source which is mounted in the sonde. Owing to collision with nuclei of the rock, the neutrons will be slowed down until finally they are captured by the nuclei of atoms, such as chlorine, hydrogen, silicon, etc. Thereby, the capturing nucleus emits a high-energy gamma ray of capture.

Depending on the type of the neutron logging sonde, either these capture gamma rays or neutrons themselves are counted by a detector in the sonde [31,33]. Usually, the neutron logs can be run equally well in uncased and cased boreholes and are independent of the type of fluid present in the borehole.

Hot-film anemometry

A hot-film flow logging technique developed by U.S. Bureau of Mines has proved to be a valuable formation evaluation tool for in-situ oil shale and underground mining experiments. Detailed descriptions of two modes of sensor operation, i.e., constant current and constant temperature, have been given by Thomas and Sterner [30]. Fractures in oil shales can be located and characterized using this technique. In addition, flow characteristics can be determined before and after artificial stimulation and during and after retorting.

Concluding remarks on logging tools

For the purpose of logging shallow oil-shale deposits, both maximum pressure and temperature ratings of the appropriate logging sondes are of no interest, because most tools withstand approximately 20,000 psi pressure and 400°F temperature. In the above review of logging tools, however, attention has been given to the fact that some of these tools can be run in water-filled and/or empty (air- or gas-filled) boreholes, whereas others are limited only to fluid-filled holes.

Oil-yield determinations using geophysical well logs

Basic considerations

Coring provides the only *direct* measurement of oil yield in oil shales. This approach, however, is time-consuming and expensive, particularly if large and rather thick oil-shale deposits are to be sampled and evaluated by a multi-well program. *Geophysical well-logging techniques* provide *indirect* oil yield estimates which result in a faster, economical, and more attractive evaluation of oil-shale deposits. Nevertheless, core analysis data (such as Fischer assay values), in at least the first test hole, is always desirable to allow an *empirical* correlation between the measured oil yield and the response of geophysical well-logging sondes.

The oil-yield estimates from geophysical well logging measurements are based on several basic important assumptions. These include:

(1) Correlation between physical rock property and oil yield. A direct empirical relationship has to exist between a physical rock property, as measured from a well log, and the oil yield of an oil shale. The literature presents many attempts of correlating oil yield with density, resistivity, acoustic properties, etc., of oil-shale deposits [2,4,27,37].

Lean oil shales tend to be brittle and to fracture under stress, whereas rich oil shales tend to be tough and resilient, resist fracture by bonding, and yield plastically under stress. Smith and Trudell [26] stated that the organic matter content is the only significant compositional difference between the fractured and non-fractured layers.

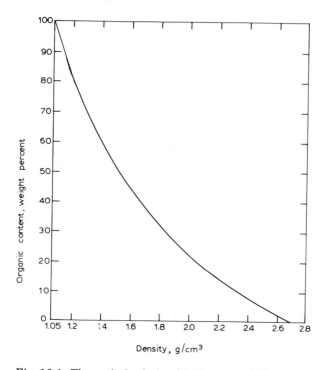

Fig. 10-1. Theoretical relationship between shale density (2.70 g/cm³) and organic matter content (density = 1.05 g/cm³) typical for Green River oil shale, Colorado. (After Smith et al. [27].)

Figure 10-1 illustrates the theoretical relationship between the shale density and the organic matter content, i.e., oil yield. Assuming a shale density of 2.70 g/cm³ and organic matter density of 1.05 g/cm³, a hyperbolic correlation is derived. These density data closely approach the actual values in the Green River oil shale [27].

Regression-type analysis of log-derived bulk densities (g/cm³) and oil yields (gal/ton) then resulted in linear and quadratic-type correlations such as:

Oil yield = 144.39 − 56.05 × (density)   (10-1)

with a standard error of estimate of 3.36 gal/ton.

Oil yield = −5.004 + 91.721 × (density) − 36.318 × (density)²   (10-2)

with a standard error of estimate of 3.19 gal/ton.

Several other empirical relationships between the oil shale yields and density have been proposed [4,28,37]. A comparison of these correlations is shown in Fig. 10-2. The closest agreement is observed over the range of main interest, i.e., an oil yield of 13 to 27 gal/ton.

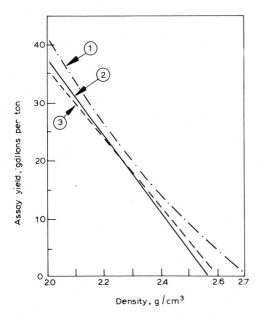

Fig. 10-2. Several empirical relationships between oil-shale assay yield and density:
(*1*) Yield = 31.563 × (density)^2 − 205.998 × (density) + 326.624 (after Stanfield et al. [28]);
(*2*) Yield = 167.92 − 65.15 × (density) (after Bardsley and Algermissen [4]);
(*3*) Yield = 154.81 − 59.43 × (density) (after Tixier and Curtis [37]).

(2) Mineral composition in oil shales. Uniformity of mineral composition in oil shales should exist. For example, mineral composition in the oil-yielding sections of the Green River Formation is quite uniform [27]. X-ray diffraction analysis studies showed a rather consistent distribution of quartz, dolomite, calcite, and illite in every sample. Soda and potash feldspars were present in 85 to 95% of the examined samples, and pyrite was found in more than one-half of the samples.

(3) Porosity development in oil shales. Oil shales should be uniformly non-porous in the zones examined. Laboratory investigations, however, have established the presence of relatively low porosity with water-filled pores in several oil-shale deposits. As well logging tools respond to the matrix composition of the oil shale (i.e., mineral components *plus* organics) and the amount and type of fluid in the pore space, any porosity development will introduce an error in quantitative oil-yield estimates. This error increases with increasing porosity. In nonporous oil shales, however, this problem is nonexistent. If a density log is used to evaluate an oil shale, porosity (ϕ) relates to the oil shale density as follows:

$$\phi = (\rho_{ma} - \rho_b)/(\rho_{ma} - \rho_w) \tag{10-3}$$

where ϕ = water-filled pore space (including vugs, fractures) in oil shale, percent of bulk volume; ρ_{ma} = matrix density of oil shale (nonporous), which is a function of mineral and organic components of the rock, g/cm^3; ρ_b = bulk density of oil shale measured by density log, g/cm^3; ρ_w = density of water in the pore space of oil shale, g/cm^3.

For quantitative oil-yield estimates using the density log, the apparent density error (E, %) due to the porosity effects can be expressed as follows:

$$E = 100[1 - (\rho_b/\rho_{ma})] \qquad (10\text{-}4)$$

Presence of even low porosity ($<5\%$), if not accounted for, will introduce substantial errors in oil-yield estimates, as much as 10 gal/ton or more. Hence, the above correction factor should be applied to the log-derived density values before estimating oil yield. Multiplying the density log reading (ρ_b) by the value $[100/(100 - E)]$ will then adjust the logging data to approximate the true density of the nonporous matrix (ρ_{ma}).

(4) Borehole enlargements, hole rugosity, leached mineral zones. A gauge hole and/or little if any rugosity of the borehole wall should be present. Major washouts and other hole enlargements affect the response and, thus, quality of any logging measurement. This is particularly true for pad-type logging sondes, such as the density log, which require smooth borehole walls for reliable pad-to-wall contact.

For example, poor wall contact results in density measurements that are too low, which, in turn, give too optimistic (i.e., too high) oil-yield estimates. This may be due to (1) improperly applied drilling techniques, (2) presence of water-filled vugs or fracture systems, or (3) presence of major amounts of dawsonite [$NaAl(OH)_2CO_3$], nahcolite [$NaHCO_3$], halite, and other sodium minerals in the oil shale facies [25]. These minerals may occur as single, discontinuous crystals or crystal masses. The latter sometimes represent more than 50% of the rock volume.

For example, *nahcolite* has a density of about 2.2 g/cm^3, which is equal to that of an oil shale yielding 25 gal/ton [27]. Unfortunately, it is not always possible from the density log alone to differentiate between a 25 gal/ton oil shale and a nahcolite streak. Three-arm *caliper* logs, however, can be used successfully to locate such mineral zones, which frequently wash out during drilling operation with water-base muds or have large vugs due to natural leaching in the past [29].

(5) Comparative sampling procedures. One has to select proper, representative sampling procedures when correlating core and logging data, in order to obtain meaningful relationships. Sample size for Fischer assays (i.e., one-foot cores or small selective plugs) should correspond with the response (i.e., vertical resolution) of the specific logging tool used. These considerations are of ut-

most importance in oil-shale deposits where lean and very rich laminated
zones drastically vary over distances of a few inches.

Discussion of field cases

Quantitative correlation of the density log response and assay oil yield in
gallons per ton has been first suggested by Bardsley and Algermissen [4].
Similar correlations have also been reported by Baldwin et al. [2] for slim-
hole logging, Tixier and Curtis [37], and Smith et al. [27].

Figure 10-3 illustrates the relationship of assay oil yield and log-derived
bulk density in a test hole drilled in the Piceance Basin, Rio Blanco County,

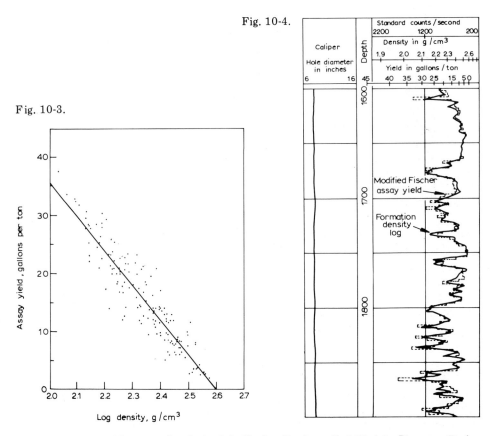

Fig. 10-3. Oil yield versus log-derived bulk density in well drilled in Piceance Basin,
Rio Blanco County, Colorado. Yield = 154.81 − 59.43 × (bulk density); standard de-
viation = 2.94 gal/ton. (After Tixier and Curtis [37].)

Fig. 10-4. Comparison of oil-shale assay yield and density log response in Piceance Basin
well, Colorado. (After Tixier and Curtis [37].) Depth is in ft.

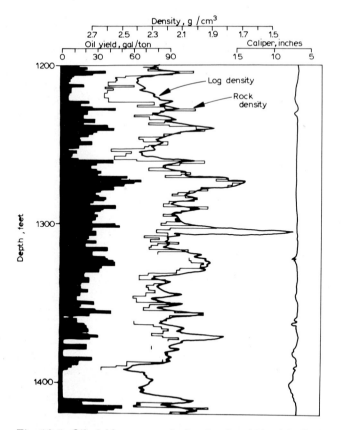

Fig. 10-5. Oil-yield assay, rock density, log-derived bulk density, and caliper log in Colorado corehole no. 2. (After Smith et al. [27].)

Colorado. Figure 10-4 shows the excellent agreement of core and well logging data in the subject well plotted on compatible scales. The caliper log shows a gauge hole, which is indicative of optimum borehole conditions for such empirical correlations.

Figure 10-5 shows oil-yield assay, oil-shale matrix density (i.e., density of mineral components plus organic matter), log-derived bulk-density values, and the caliper curve in a test hole drilled through the Green River Formation, Colorado. The interval shown in Fig. 10-5 includes the so-called Mahogany zone with a porous, tuffaceous zone from 1,206 ft to 1,223 ft in the top section. A large difference between the bulk and matrix densities reflects good porosity development in the tuff. A leached zone begins at about 1,300 ft, containing localized cavities, breccia, and earthy intervals. At a depth of 1,400 ft, there is a lean black shale marker at the base of the Mahogany zone.

Table 10-I lists the average values for assay oil yield, bulk and matrix

TABLE 10-I

Oil-shale assay yield, rock density, and log-derived bulk density in corehole no. 2, Colorado (after Smith et al. [27])

Interval (ft)	Oil yield (gal/ton)	Rock density (g/cm^3)	Bulk density from well log (g/cm^3)	Apparent porosity (%)
1200—1250	16.54	2.338	2.265	3
1250—1300	28.08	2.139	2.110	1
1300—1350	24.60	2.212	2.103	5
1350—1400	19.40	2.302	2.222	3
1400—1450	21.21	2.283	2.222	3
1450—1500	25.76	2.210	2.126	4
1500—1550	20.45	2.292	2.221	3
1550—1600	23.16	2.280	2.186	4
1600—1650	12.58	2.483	2.278	8
1650—1700	18.74	2.351	2.243	5
1700—1750	31.78	2.116	2.001	5
1750—1800	38.73	2.037	1.994	2
1800—1850	37.54	2.043	1.971	4
1850—1900	41.47	1.984	1.946	2
1900—1950	27.59	2.147	2.011	6
1950—2000	30.71	2.094	1.966	6
2000—2050	35.41	2.020	1.866	8
2050—2070.5	46.59	1.888	1.712	9

density values, and porosity development in this test hole. Smith et al. [27] have chosen 50-ft intervals to average out the highly localized porosity variations. The log-derived bulk-density values are consistently lower than the oil-shale matrix densities, with the difference being a function of the porosity development in the oil-shale section. These apparent porosity values are listed in the last column of Table 10-I.

Additional data are available in Table 10-II, which compares oil-yield

TABLE 10-II

Comparison of oil-yield estimates from geophysical well logs and core samples in slim holes (after Baldwin et al. [2])

Well	Interval (ft)	Average oil yield (gal/ton)		
		Fischer assay	sonic log	density log
A	692—748	34	31	37
B	794—872	27.5	25	23
C	744—810	32	29	27

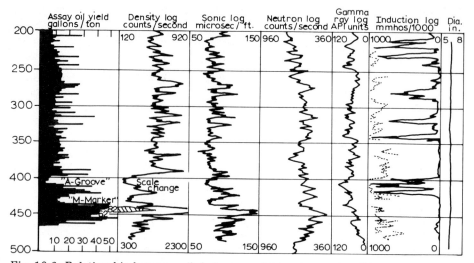

Fig. 10-6. Relationship between oil-shale assay yield and several well-log responses. (After Bardsley and Algermissen, [4].) Figures on left-hand side = depth in ft; A-Groove = lean oil shale marker; and Dia. in. = borehole diameter in inches from caliper log.

values and log-derived density values in several slim holes (i.e., 3-inch diameter holes) drilled in Colorado oil shales. Small diameter (1.75-inch OD) logging sondes, both gamma-gamma density tools and acoustic devices,

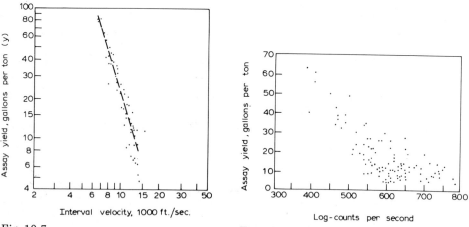

Fig. 10-7.   Fig. 10-8.

Fig. 10-7. Relationship between oil-shale assay yield, Y (gal/ton), and interval velocity, V (ft/sec); $\log_{10}(Y) = 15.25 - 3.48 \times \log_{10}(V)$. (After Bardsley and Algermissen, [4].)

Fig. 10-8. Relationship between oil-shale assay yield and neutron log response. (After Bardsley and Algermissen, [4].)

were successfully used to make quantitative in situ oil-yield estimates.

Figure 10-6 compares the oil-yield assay, determined on core samples, and the response of several types of well logging sondes in a test hole in the Green River oil shale. In this gauge hole (see caliper curve) both the density and sonic log responses indicate a quantitative relationship (Figs. 10-2 and 10-7). At the present time, however, a semilogarithmic (yield versus log Δt) rather than a log-log type correlation is used, as shown in Fig. 10-7.

The neutron log response, however, shows a large scatter of data points, indicative of a non-quantitative relationship between assay oil yield and the well-log response (Fig. 10-8).

The gamma-ray response in Fig. 10-6 shows a general decrease in shale content in the richer oil shale streaks and, as expected, increasing shaliness in the leaner zones, such as A-groove and M-marker. Due to the complex composition of oil shales, however, no simple, quantitative relationship between oil yield and gamma-ray response should be expected.

The induction log curve shows very low resistivity (i.e., high conductivity) over most of the zone of interest (Fig. 10-6). Only drastic variations in lithology (coupled with significant water-filled porosity development) in thick enough streaks, to overcome the vertical resolution limitations of the induction tool, are recorded. In laminated intervals consisting of rather thin streaks of lean, rich, and/or tuffaceous composition, resistivity logging tools with better, more detailed resolution would be preferable.

References and bibliography

1. R.P. Alger, L.L. Raymer, W.R. Hoyle and M.P. Tixier, "Formation Density Log Applications in Liquid-Filled Holes," *J. Pet. Technol.*, *15*, 321—333 (1963).
2. W.F. Baldwin, R.L. Caldwell and E.E. Glenn, "Slim Hole Logging in Colorado Oil Shale", *Trans. SPWLA*, Paper C, 1—17 (1966).
3. R.W. Baltosser and H.W. Lawrence, "Application of Well Logging Techniques in Metallic Mineral Mining", *Geophysics*, *35* (1), 143—152 (1970).
4. S.R. Bardsley and S.T. Algermissen, "Evaluating Oil Shale by Log Analysis", *J. Pet. Technol.*, *15*, 81—84 (1963), also *Quart. Colo. Sch. Mines*, *58* (4), 178—184 (1963) and *World Oil*, *161* (2), 94—96 (1965).
5. L.O. Bond, R.P. Alger and A.W. Schmidt, "Well Log Applications in Coal Mining and Rock Mechanics", *Trans. Soc. Min. Eng.*, *250* (12), 355—362 (1971).
6. R.A. Broding, C.W. Zimmerman, E.V. Somers, E.S. Wilhelm and A.A. Stripling, "Magnetic Well Logging", *Geophysics*, *17* (1), 1—26 (1952).
7. J.A. Czubec, "Recent Russian and European Developments in Nuclear Geophysics Applied to Mineral Exploration and Mining", *The Log Analyst*, 20—34, Nov.—Dec. (1971).
8. J.A. Czubec, "Pulsed Neutron Method for Uranium Well Logging", *Geophysics*, *37* (1), 160—173 (1972).
9. V.N. Dakhnov, *Geophysical Well Logging.* Moscow, Gostoptekhizdat (1959). In Russian; Translated into English by G.V. Keller, Colorado School of Mines, Golden, Colorado (1962).

10. C.J. Decker and M. Martin, "The Laterolog and Salt Mud Logging in Kansas", *Oil Gas J., 50* (41), 119—129 (1952).
11. R. Desbrandes, *Théorie et Interprétation des Diagraphies*, Editions Technip, Paris, 545 pp. (1968).
12. H.G. Doll, "Introduction to Induction Logging", *J. Pet. Technol., 1* (6), 148—162 (1949).
13. H.G. Doll, "The Laterolog — A New Resistivity Logging Method with Electrodes Using an Automatic Focusing System", *Trans. AIME, 192*, 305—316 (1951).
14. J.L. Dumanoir, M.P. Tixier and M. Martin, "Interpretation of the Induction-Electrical Log in Fresh Mud", *J. Pet. Technol., 9* (7), 202—218 (1957).
15. W.H. Fertl, P.E. Pilkington and J.B. Scott, "A Look at Cement Bond Logs", *J. Pet. Technol., 26*, 607—617 (1974).
16. W.G. Green and R.E. Fearon, "Well Logging by Radioactivity", *Geophysics, 5* (3), 272—283 (1940).
17. J.C. Jenkings, "Practical Application of Well Logging to Mine Design", *SME — Preprint 69-F-73*, AIME Ann. Meet., Washington, D.C., Feb. (1969).
18. F.P. Kokesh, "Gamma Ray Logging", *Oil Gas J., 50* (12), 284—298 (1951).
19. F.P. Kokesh, R.J. Schwartz, W.B. Wall and R.L. Morris, "A New Approach to Sonic Logging and Other Acoustic Measurements", *J. Pet. Technol., 17* (3), 282—287 (1965).
20. E.J. Lynch, *Formation Evaluation*, Harper and Row, New York, Evanston, and London, 422 pp. (1962).
21. R. Meinhold, *Geophysikalische Messverfahren in Bohrungen*, Akademische Verlagsgesellschaft Geest und Portig K.G., Leipzig, 237 pp. (1965).
22. G.R. Pickett, "Acoustic Character Logs and Their Applications in Formation Evaluations", *J. Pet. Technol., 15*, 659—668 (1963).
23. S.J. Pirson, *Handbook of Well Log Analysis for Oil and Gas Formation Evaluation*, Prentice-Hall Inc., Englewood Cliffs, 326 pp. (1963).
24. S.J. Pirson, *Geologic Well Logging Analysis*, Gulf Publishing Co., Houston, Texas, 370 pp. (1970).
25. J.J. Schmidt-Collerus and R.D. Hollingshead, "Investigations into the Nature of Dawsonite in the Green River Formation", in: *5th Symposium on Oil Shale, Quar t. Colo. Sch. Mines, 63* (4), 143—167 (1968).
26. J.W. Smith and L.G. Trudell, "Wyoming Corehole No. 1 — A Potential Site for Production of Shale Oil in Place", in: *5th Symposium on Oil Shale, Quart. Colo. Sch. Mines, 63* (4), 55—69 (1968).
27. J.W. Smith, H.E. Thomas and L.G. Trudell, "Geologic Factors Affecting Density Logs in Oil Shale", *Trans. SPWLA*, Paper P, 1—17 (1968).
28. K.E. Stanfield, J.W. Smith, H.N. Smith and W.A. Robb, "Oil Yields of Sections of Green River Oil Shale in Colorado, 1954—57", *U.S. Dep. Interior, Bur. Mines*, Washington, D.C., *Rep. 5614*, 186 pp. (1960).
29. H.E. Thomas and J.W. Smith, "Caliper Location of Leached Zones in Colorado Oil Shale", *Log Analyst, 11* (4), 12—16 (1970).
30. H.E. Thomas and T.E. Sterner, "Hot-Film Flow Logging As Applied to In Situ Oil Shale and Mining Experiments", *Trans. SPWLA*, Paper L, 1—14 (1972).
31. C.W. Tittle, H. Faul and C. Goodman, "Neutron Logging of Drill Holes: The Neutron—Neutron Method", *Geophysics, 16* (4), 626—658 (1951).
32. J. Tittman and J.S. Wahl, "The Physical Foundations of Formation Density Logging (Gamma—Gamma)", *Geophysics, 30* (2), 284—296 (1965).
33. J. Tittman, H. Sherman, W.A. Nagel and R.P. Alger, "The Sidewall Epithermal Neutron Porosity Log", *J. Pet. Technol., 18*, 1351—1363 (1966).
34. M.P. Tixier, R.P. Alger and C.A. Doh, "Sonic Logging", *J. Pet. Technol., 11*, 106—114 (1959).

35. M.P. Tixier, R.P. Alger and D.R. Tanguy, "New Developments in Induction and Sonic Logging", *J. Pet. Technol.*, *12* (5), 79—88 (1960).
36. M.P. Tixier and R.P. Alger, "Log Evaluation of Non-Metallic Mineral Deposits", *Trans. SPWLA*, Paper R, 1—22 (1967).
37. M.P. Tixier and M.R. Curtis, "Oil Shale Yield Predicted From Well Log", *Proc. 7th World Pet. Congr.*, Mexico City, Mexico, *3*, 713—715 (1967).
38. J.S. Wahl, J. Tittman and C.W. Johnstone, "The Dual Spacing Formation Density Log", *J. Pet. Technol.*, *16*, 1411—1417 (1964).
39. M.R.J. Wyllie, A.R. Gregory and G.H.F. Gardner, "An Experimental Investigation of Factors Affecting Elastic Wave Velocities in Porous Media", *Geophysics*, *23*, 459—494 (1958).
40. M.R.J. Wyllie, *The Fundamentals of Well Log Interpretation*, Academic Press, New York and London, 240 pp. (1963).
41. C.J. Zablocki, "Some Applications of Geophysical Well Logging Methods in Mineral Exploration Drill Holes", *Trans. SPWLA*, Paper U, 13 pp. (1966).

Chapter 11

ENVIRONMENTAL ANALYSIS OF AN OIL-SHALE INDUSTRY
IN THE UPPER COLORADO REGION

D.W. HENDRICKS and J.C. WARD

Introduction

The oil-shale deposits found in the Green River Formation in the states of Colorado, Utah, and Wyoming are by far the largest in the U.S.A., accounting for about 80% of the known world deposits. In these states oil-shale deposits occur beneath 25,000 sq miles (16 million acres) of lands, of which about 17,000 sq miles (11 million acres) are believed to contain oil shale of commercial potential. The oil contained in these deposits in the Green River Formation amounts to about 1,800 billion barrels of recoverable oil. Figure 1-1 in Chapter 1 shows the distribution of these deposits. The area shown comprises to a large extent the Upper Colorado Region, which is the upper half of the Colorado River Basin.

Industry development

Much of the land in the oil-shale regions is federally owned and administered by the U.S. Bureau of Land Management. The development of an oil-shale industry, therefore, is contingent upon the viability of a federal lease program. Such a program was initiated in 1973 with public bidding for six prototype leases — two each in Colorado, Wyoming, and Utah — of not more than 5,120 acres each. Figure 1-1 in Chapter 1 shows the approximate locations of the leasing sites. These sites were conceived as permitting a production level of 250,000 bbl/day by 1979. A one million barrel per day industry is anticipated by 1985 through further leasing. Table 11-I shows a possible time table for achieving the one million barrel per day production level.

The technology used in mining and processing of oil shale ore pertains strongly to questions of environmental effects. Three mining methods, i.e., surface, underground, and in-situ, are contemplated. Table 11-I also anticipates a possible technology mix for mining. Underground mining probably will predominate, because in most oil-shale areas the deposits are found at depths of 1,000 ft or greater. From Table 11-I, about 25% of the shale for a one million barrel per day industry would be mined by surface methods. According to most experts, perfection of the in-situ technology by 1985 seems questionable.

Processing technology involves crushing the ore and then retorting (see

TABLE 11-I

Projected possible development pattern for a 1,000,000-bbl/day industry by 1985 (After U.S. Department of Interior: Final Environmental Impact Statement, 1973 [4])

Year	Colorado		Utah	Wyoming	Technology assumed[1]	Total oil production[2]
	Public land	Private land	Public land	Public land		
1973	—	—	—	—	—	—
1974	—	—	—	—	—	—
1975	—	—	—	—	—	—
1976	—	50	—	—	1-U	50
1977	—	—	—	—	—	50
1978	50	50	—	—	2-U	150
1979	100	—	—	—	1-S	250
1980	—	—	50	—	1-U	300
1981	—	50	—	50	1-U, 1-I	400
1982					2-U, 1-I	550
1983					3-U	700
1984					1-S_1	850
1985					1-U, 2-I	1,000
					17 total plants	

[1] Legend:
1-U = one 50,000-bbl/day underground mine
1-S = one 100,000-bbl/day surface mine
1-I = one 50,000-bbl/day in-situ mine
1-S_1 = one 150,000-bbl/day surface mine
2-U = two 50,000-bbl/day underground mines
2-I = two 50,000-bbl/day in-situ mines
3-U = three 50,000-bbl/day underground mines
[2]Numerical data in table refers to plant capacities in thousands of barrels per day.

Chapter 9 for details). Retorting involves heating the crushed oil shale, to about 900° F, such that the *kerogen* (the solid organic matter) is converted to gases and oil vapors. The three major retorting technologies are: (1) the Union Oil retort, (2) the TOSCO II retort, and (3) the Gas-combustion retort. These are merely different approaches to achieve the necessary heat transfer. Although the residues are different in particle size and to some extent in chemical composition, they all represent substantial disposal problems.

Characteristics of the region

General description

The Upper Colorado Region is traditionally "western rural" in character; this is true in both image and fact. The landscapes are vast open spaces in all

TABLE 11-II

Land characteristics and land uses of the Upper Colorado region (From Upper Colorado Region Comprehensive Framework Study, 1971 [3])

Land Resource Groups	Area	Cropland Irrig.	Dry	Grazing	Timber Production	Urban and Industrial	Developed Recreation & Classified Watershed	Primitive Areas (Wilderness)	Developed Mineral Production	Trans. and Utilities	Developed Fish and Wildlife
					Area (Thousands of Acres)						
UPPER COLORADO REGION-1930											
Alpine	1,329	-	-	257	-	3	22	417	-	6	-
Forest	27,152	-	-	19,926	9,351	10	155	777	-	108	-
Range	37,050	-	-	33,944	-	11	69	156	-	151	-
Cropland	1,571	1,056	515	-	-	-	-	-	-	-	-
Pasture	1,395	738	57	600	-	-	-	-	-	-	-
Urban (Priv)	392	-	-	-	-	185	-	-	-	198	-
Water & misc.	3,268	-	-	1,231	-	147	156	64	71	169	393
Total Land	72,157	1,794	572	55,958	9,351	356	402	1,414	71	632	393
Water (areas 40 ac.)	482	-	-	-	-	-	351	-	-	-	-
TOTAL	72,639	1,794	572	55,958	9,351	356	753	1,414	71	632	393

three states consisting of extensive sparsely vegetated plains with low escarpments, some forests, and several imposing mountain ranges. Elevations range from 5,000 to 10,000 ft above sea level. Precipitation varies from about 7 inches in the Wyoming plains to 14 inches in the high plateau areas of Colorado. Table 11-II gives a general statistical picture of the basic land categories and the various activities common to the region as related to land use. The "western rural" character is also evident from the numerical data given.

Population

Population density is also consistent with the "western rural" designation. Density of population is about three persons per sq mile. Table 11-III shows

TABLE 11-III

The 1970 population distribution in oil-shale areas (From 1970 Census of Population, General Social and Economic Characteristics, U.S. Department of Commerce, Washington, D.C., 1972)

State	County	Population
Colorado	Garfield	14,800
	Mesa	54,300
	Rio Blanco	4,800
Utah	Duchesne	7,300
	Uintah	12,700
Wyoming	Sweetwater	18,400
	Uintah	7,100
		119,400

the 1970 population distribution by county for the three-state region.

Towns in the region include: Grand Junction (20,000), Rifle (2,500), Meeker (1,597), Craig (4,205), and Rangley (1,591), in Colorado; Vernal (4,000) in Utah; and Rock Springs (11,700) in Wyoming. Denver and Salt Lake City are the two nearest major metropolitan areas.

Water

The rate-limiting factor in further development of the region is probably the availability of water. Water is also a major factor in the development of oil-shale resources. The average annual flow in the Colorado River at Lee's Ferry, the accepted division point between the upper and lower basins, is 12,710,000 acre-ft. Of this, 5.8 million acre-ft is available for upper basin depletion. The environmental impact statement estimates 341,000 acre-ft of this water could be made available for depletion by oil shale. During the period 1949—1968, water-rights applications by oil companies in the Colorado oil shale area totaled 1,103,348 acre-ft of water claimed. These applications have the status of filings and conditional decrees, which does not assure the availability of water. In some cases, irrigated land has been purchased in order to obtain water rights, but this does not assure that the water can be made available for the oil-shale development, especially if the point of diversion must be changed.

Another important factor which must be taken into consideration in any water-use plan, is the potential salt loading of the Colorado River. The average annual salinity concentration of the Colorado River at Imperial Dam during the period 1941—1970 was 757 mg/l. It is anticipated that this concentration level will increase well beyond 1,000 mg/l by 1980. The economic damages associated with these higher salinity levels are significant and have been the subject of extensive economic studies.

Mineral resources

Energy resources in addition to oil shale are extensive over the three-state oil-shale area. Recoverable natural gas is estimated at 85 trillion cu ft, whereas crude oil reserves are estimated at 680 million barrels. Coal deposits are estimated at 6—8 billion tons; two-thirds of these deposits are in Wyoming and one-third is in Colorado.

In connection with the oil-shale development, surveys have shown that about 27 billion tons of alumina are present in the central Piceance Creek Basin, along with about 30 billion tons of nahcolite. These minerals could be mined in conjunction with oil shale. This means that a single plant that produces 35,000 bbl/day of upgraded shale oil could also yield about 3% of the 1980 anticipated need for aluminum and 15% of the nation's 1980 need for soda ash (sodium carbonate). These figures are based upon assays showing 11% by weight of dawsonite and 15% by weight of nahcolite.

Ecology

Ecologically, the Upper Colorado River Region is highly valued. Due to the limited human population and extensive areas of public lands, the region has retained its essentially natural character. Big game animals include mule deer, antelope, bighorn sheep, black bear, elk, moose, and mountain lion. Mule-deer population in the Piceance Basin numbers 30,000—60,000 animals. The herd is one of the largest in the United States of America and is considered especially valuable. Herds are also large in the Uintah Basin and in Wyoming. Elk herds are also substantial. In addition, there are a number of species of small game, 27 species of migratory waterfowl and shore birds, six species of upland game birds, five species of fur bearers, 21 species of nongame animals, 200 species of nongame birds, and 24 species of raptors. Several wild-horse herds are also found in the region.

Fishery habitat in the Upper Colorado Region includes 36,000 acres in natural lakes, 275,000 acres in impoundments, and 9,000 miles of fishing streams. There is little fishery habitat in the oil-shale areas.

Plant communities depend upon the life zone represented. These are listed as follows for the oil-shale areas: sagebrush — 6,240,000 acres; salt brush—greasewood — 2,720,000 acres; juniper pinyon woodland — 2,640,000 acres; mountain mahogany—oak scrub — 1,280,000 acres; Douglas fir forest — 1,280,000 acres; pine—Douglas fir forest — 960,000 acres; great basin sagebrush — 320,000 acres; and foothills prairie — 80,000 acres.

Much of this information is summarized in Table 11-IV, which shows the general ecological character of the overall region.

Recreation

Outdoor recreation in the region is considered of high quality due to the vastness of the essentially pristine natural environments and to the scenic and ecological richness of the area.

Hunting in October and November is one of the major recreational activities. In the Piceance Basin, mule deer hunter-days number in the order of 40,000 per year with an annual harvest of over 5,000 mule deer.

Some of the scenic areas in the region include Dinosaur, Arches, Canyonlands, and Black Canyon National Monuments, and numerous less well-known areas in the White River and Uncompahgre National Forests. Some notable areas in Rio Blanco County, Colorado, for example, include: Flat Tops Wilderness area, Douglas Creek, Moon Canyon, Cathedral Bluffs, Raven Ridge, and Piceance Creek. Ski areas in the region are numerous and include Snowmass, Aspen, and Vail.

TABLE 11-IV

Representation of the life zones along the southern continental divide (From: Final Environmental Statement, 1973 [4])

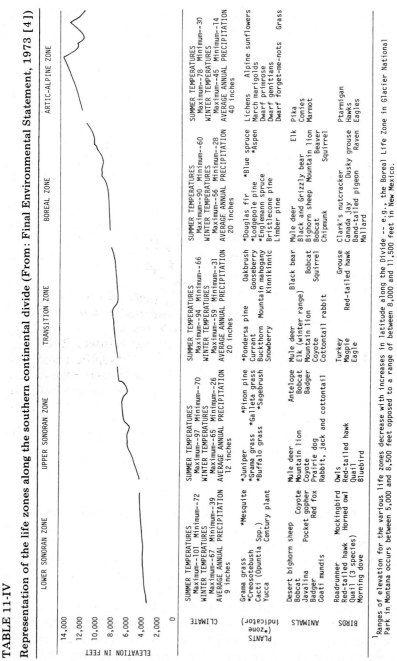

ELEVATION IN FEET: 14,000 / 12,000 / 10,000 / 8,000 / 6,000 / 4,000 / 2,000 / 0

	LOWER SONORAN ZONE	UPPER SONORAN ZONE	TRANSITION ZONE	BOREAL ZONE	ARTIC-ALPINE ZONE
CLIMATE	SUMMER TEMPERATURES Maximum--101 Minimum--72 WINTER TEMPERATURES Maximum--67 Minimum--39 AVERAGE ANNUAL PRECIPITATION 9 inches	SUMMER TEMPERATURES Maximum--97 Minimum--70 WINTER TEMPERATURES Maximum--65 Minimum--26 AVERAGE ANNUAL PRECIPITATION 12 inches	SUMMER TEMPERATURES Maximum--94 Minimum--66 WINTER TEMPERATURES Maximum--59 Minimum--31 AVERAGE ANNUAL PRECIPITATION 20 inches	SUMMER TEMPERATURES Maximum--90 Minimum--60 WINTER TEMPERATURES Maximum--56 Minimum--28 AVERAGE ANNUAL PRECIPITATION 20 inches	SUMMER TEMPERATURES Maximum--78 Minimum--30 WINTER TEMPERATURES Maximum--45 Minimum--14 AVERAGE ANNUAL PRECIPITATION 40 inches
PLANTS (*Zone Indicator)	Grama grass *Mesquite *Creosotebush Cacti (Opuntia Spp.) Yucca Century plant	*Juniper *Pinon pine *Grama grass *Galleta grass *Buffalo grass *Sagebrush	*Ponderosa pine Oakbrush Currant Gooseberry Buckthorn Mountain mahogany Snowberry Kinnikinnic	*Douglas fir *Blue spruce *Lodgepole pine *Aspen *Engelmann spruce Bristlecone pine Limber pine	Lichens Alpine sunflowers March marigolds Dwarf primrose Dwarf gentians Dwarf forget-me-nots Grass
ANIMALS	Desert bighorn sheep Bobcat Coyote Javalina Pocket gopher Badger Red fox Coati mundis	Mule deer Antelope Mountain lion Bobcat Coyote Badger Prairie dog Rabbit, jack and cottontail	Mule deer Black bear Elk (winter range) Bobcat Mountain lion Squirrel Coyote Cottontail rabbit	Mule deer Elk Black and Grizzly bear Bighorn sheep Mountain lion Bobcat Beaver Chipmunk Squirrel	Pika Conies Marmot
BIRDS	Roadrunner Mockingbird Red-tailed hawk Horned owl Quail (3 species) Morning dove	Owls Red-tailed hawk Quail Bluebird	Turkey Grouse Magpie Red-tailed hawk Eagle	Clark's nutcracker Canada jay Dusky grouse Band-tailed pigeon Raven Mallard	Ptarmigan Hawks Eagles

¹Ranges of elevation for the various life zones decrease with increases in latitude along the Divide -- e.g., the Boreal Life Zone in Glacier National Park in Montana occurs between 5,000 and 8,500 feet opposed to a range of between 8,000 and 11,500 feet in New Mexico.

Source: Reference Amberger, 1954.

Private ranches

Some 25 private ranches in the Piceance Creek oil-shale region cater to hunting and fishing clientele. Many others catering to hunting clientele exist outside the shale areas. In Colorado, these ranches number about 78.

Incremental changes

Evaluating change

It is generally accepted that the development of an oil-shale industry will cause fundamental changes to the western rural character of the Upper Colorado Region. The effects of the industry will be both direct and indirect on the region. The *direct effects* are those resulting from the activity of producing shale oil. The visual disharmony (smoke stacks, landfills of spent ore, buildings, roads, pipelines, etc.) is an esthetic intrusion imposed on vast natural landscapes having great scenic qualities and an otherwise tranquil character. Pollution from the mining and processing of the shale is another direct effect. So is the loss of habitat for various animals due to spatial competition from oil-shale development activities.

Indirect effects, on the other hand, would be the *induced* effects, which are not immediately caused by an oil-shale development activity. Whereas the emergence of various support services and populations would be direct effects, the consequent additional *activity pressures* on ecological systems would be indirect. These, however, should not be considered precise definitions, but merely functional ones. The definitions may change depending upon the situation and interpretation. At any rate, the analysis should not suffer if the definitions are somewhat elastic, or even if there is some misinterpretation from what is intended.

In assessing the environmental effects caused by an activity, it is important to evaluate the *changes*. Once identified, changes may be assessed in terms of *importance* and *magnitude* [2]. The *importance* term is a subjective one. The pristine natural character of the land would be important to some persons but not to others. For example, the fact that the bald eagle or the mountain lion is thriving in the region, constitutes an ecological value highly important to certain segments of the population, but it is unimportant to others who have different interests.

The idea of *value* is central to the question. Health, education, ecology, etc. are types of value. All have different weights depending upon the individual who must make the choices, in the event there is competition. In the case of non-public goods, such as food, housing, automobiles, etc., the goods have *exchange value*. Thus, individuals can allocate their personal wealth for these goods through the *market* mechanism. In the case of public goods — scenery, ecological systems, public lands, etc. — the values must be weighed and allocations made through the political process. In the case of oil-shale development or any other decisions regarding public lands or public resources, such as air and water, it is the political-legal system, consisting of legislation, regulations, and court decisions, which must allocate these resources. Such resources represent essentially a *capital stock*. Thus, the value weighting, and hence the importance, must be assigned commensurately. Those animals on the rare and endangered species list would certainly figure prominently in any value weighting, because this list represents a collective judgement, through the political process, of what is important. The commitment of land for a particular use then involves a "tradeoff", which essentially uses or depletes various categories of capital stock resources (i.e., ecological habitats, open space, water quality, etc.).

The other term of change is *magnitude*, i.e., *how much* change will take place, especially in relation to the total resource. For example, how many mule deer will be affected in relation to the size of herd? How much land will be needed for the oil-shale development versus the total land in the basin? How many similar areas of pristine natural character would remain in the nation if the upper Colorado region is industrialized?

Formulating the questions to succinctly articulate the most significant issues, requires both value sensitivity, issue perception, and professional knowledge. Developing the factual data in the context of the significant questions will then permit a systematic evaluation and good understanding of what will happen as a result of a proposed activity.

Overall changes

Table 11-V presents a summary of some of the changes which will occur or are anticipated as a result of the development of an oil-shale industry. The list is not inclusive nor is it highly selective in categories included. It is intended, however, to provide a general understanding of what will happen to the region as a result of imposing a 1,000,000-bbl/day oil-shale industry on the region.

In examining Table 11-V, it is seen that large quantities of ore and residue must be moved, i.e., about 10 billion cu ft of ore each year or 37 million cubic yards. By comparison, Fort Peck Dam on the Missouri River, the largest earth-fill dam in the world, required 125.6 million cubic yards of material. Consequently, the earth-moving task is monumental. Some of this material will be returned to the underground cavities, but it is contemplated that, in addition, some 17 canyons will be filled to depths of some 200 ft.

Land and water

Land required for oil-shale development totals about 80,000 acres. This factor is not decisive when compared with the 16 million acres of lands in

TABLE 11-V

Baseline conditions and changes anticipated for various system categories in the Upper Colorado River region due to development of a 1,000,000-bbl/day oil-shale industry

System	System Indicator	Dimension	Pre-oil shale industry (1973 or earlier)	Post-oil shale industry[1] (1985 or later)
Industry	Oil production			
	ore mined	tons/yr	-0-	550 million
		ft^3/yr	-0-	8-9 billion
	ore residue	tons/yr	-0-	
		ft^3/yr	-0-	9-10 billion
	Land requirements			
	production processes	acres	-0-	50,000 by 1985
		acres/yr	-0-	1,200 after 1985
	urban development	acres	-0-	20,000
	utility rights of way	acres	-0-	10,000
	Water requirements			
	diversion	acre-ft	-0-	145,000
	consumption	acre-ft	-0-	90,000
	Energy requirements			
		KWH/yr	-0-	66.7 million
	Labor force			
	temporary	persons employed	-0-	29,000
	permanent	persons employed	-0-	42,400
	Taxes			
	Industry paid	dollars/yr	-0-	218 million in 1981
	taxes	dollars/yr		165 million
Community	population	persons	119,000 in 1970	234,000
	housing	dwellings	37,400	+13,000 for 42,000 new permanent employes
	water	acre-ft	35,700	17,000 additional
	energy	KWH/yr	N.A.	2,000 additional
	total employment	persons employed in 1970	44,000	86,400
	Taxes-oil shale produced			
	Federal	dollars/yr	4.9 million	541 million
	State	dollars/yr	3.5 million	86 million
	local	dollars/yr	-0-	132 million
Esthetics	None	none	natural landforms	symmetric forms i.e., buildings, stacks, roads, pipelines, power lines, etc.
Recreation	Hunting			
	Piceance Basin	deer/yr	5,000	reduced
Colorado River at Lee's Ferry	Annual flow	acre-ft/yr	12,710,000	diminished by Upper Basin depletions
	Salt flow	tons/yr	8,642,000	Unknown
	Leachable salts from annual production of oil shale residue	tons	-0-	4,920,000
	Salt concentration average	mg/L	499	
Air	Dust	tons/day	-0-	20-100 (for 17 plants)
	Stack gases			
	SO$_2$ emission	tons/day	-0-	70-200
	SO$_2$ ambient from 900' stack @10 mi.	μg/m^2	-0-	4
	SO$_2$ Colorado Stack emission standard	μg/L	10	500
	NO$_x$	tons/day	-0-	80-150
	ambient standard	μg/m^3	none	100
Ecological	Mule deer			
	Wyoming	individuals	39,650	no estimate
	Piceance Basin	individuals	20,000-60,000	10% or more reduction
	Elk-Wyoming		3,950	
	Mountain Lions	individuals	15-20 in Colo.	fewer

[1] Numerical data taken from: Environmental Impact Statement, 1973.

the oil-shale area. The water requirement of 145,000 acre-ft does not appear excessive either, especially when compared with the 12,710,000 acre-ft average annual flow in the Colorado River at Lee's Ferry. Small increments of water, however, are significant in the Colorado River system, and incrementally this amount of water is decisive in that other water uses (i.e., agricultural) must be eliminated if oil shale is to be developed. If water could be traded on the free market, oil-shale industry probably would outbid agriculture. Water transfers, however, are not permitted to take place quite so freely and water availability will be a critical limiting factor. Whether the water will be made available or not will be determined by the non-market decision processes.

Salt loading

Small increments of salt loading on the Colorado system are also highly significant; the system is very much economically sensitive to salts. This has been ascertained in several years of economic studies (about 1966—1970) sponsored by the Federal Water Quality Administration (now EPA).

The potential salt loading from oil-shale residues could be appreciable. Calculations in the Final Environmental Impact Statement (U.S. Department of the Interior, 1973 [4]), based upon experiments at Colorado State University by Ward et al. [6], indicate that a 6-hr storm having an intensity of 0.3—0.5 inch/hr, if assumed to completely leach a 700-acre area of spent shale residue to a depth of 12 inches, would result in 16,740 tons of salts. If there are 17 such sites and each site had one such storm each year, the additional annual salt load would be 284,580 tons. As shown in Table 11-V, this compares with a present-day figure of 8,642,000 tons/yr at Lee's Ferry on the Colorado River. This mode of leaching is merely a speculation in order to give some order of magnitude idea of what might conceivably happen.

In estimating additional salt loading it is difficult (1) to determine how much water will come into contact with the spent shale each year and (2) to predict the amount of salt which will be leached by the moisture that does make contact. The former question can be dealt with as a stochastic phenomena using records of precipitation. Ward et al. [6] have an empirical equation which can give an estimate for the latter question. Their equation was developed through snowfall and rainfall—runoff testing on field plots. It relates concentrations of salinity in the surface water runoff from rainfall as a function of spent oil-shale residue bulk density, permeability of the spent oil-shale residue, moisture content deficit of the spent oil-shale residue, slope of the spent oil-shale residue surface, length of overland flow, rainfall intensity, storm duration, and water temperature. In further work on snowfall, Ward and Reinecke [7] developed a similar empirical equation, which includes the same parameters as above but in which snowmelt runoff intensity and cumulative volume of snowmelt runoff per unit area are sub-

TABLE 11-VI

Hypothetical rain and snow storm

Parameter	Assumed		dimensions
	rain	snow	
volume runoff/unit width	8.3	8.3	ft^3/ft
Porosity	0.345	0.345	dimensionless
$\frac{w}{w_s}$ where, w = soil moisture content, cm^3/g w_s = saturation soil moisture content, cm^3/g	0.362	0.362	dimensionless
length of overland flow	226	226	feet
precipitation salinity	0	0	mg/l
rainfall intensity or rate at which snow melts to water	0.0123*	0.0235	ft/hr
surface runoff intensity	0.0123	0.00240	ft/hr
	Calculated		
	rain	snow	
mass of salt leached per unit area of horizontal surface	45,100	171	mg/ft^2
average salinity in runoff	43,500	165	mg/l
initial value of salinity in runoff	289,000	1,100	mg/l

*Based on a 1 year frequency, 3 hour rain at Grand Junction, Colorado.

stituted for the rainfall parameters. Ward and Reinecke [7] also developed from the empirical studies a rational overland flow water quality model, which was successfully applied to their experimental results from both rainfall and snowfall experiments. This model predicts the concentration of dissolved solids in the runoff from rainfall or melting snow as a function of (1) the cumulative volume of runoff per unit width, (2) the porosity of the oil-shale retorting residue, (3) the moisture content of the spent oil-shale residue, (4) the rainfall or snowmelt rate, and (5) the fraction of the rainfall or snowmelt water that appears as runoff.

Table 11-VI outlines the necessary data and the information that can be predicted for a given rain or snow storm by the overland flow water quality model. As shown in Table 11-VI, a three-hour rain storm having an intensity of 0.0123 ft/hr will result in a runoff with an average TDS (total dissolved solids) concentration of 43,500 mg/l. A storm of the intensity and duration assumed will result in 25.83 acre-ft of runoff if the site area is 700 acres. For example, for 17 such sites and 20 such storms per year (2.95 inches rain/yr), the total runoff volume of water having surface contact with oil shale is 8,782 acre-ft. Assuming the length of run is 226 ft (to conform with the test plot and to have some order of magnitude idea of salt loading), the average salt concentration of the surface runoff water is 43,500 mg/l, giving a total salt loading of 518 tons/yr. This figure is, of course, a rough lower limit calculation of what might be expected in salt loading from rainfall. The assumption that the simulated rainfall on the test plots did not penetrate the oil-shale residue, accounts for the identical figures in Table 11-VI between rainfall intensity and surface runoff intensity. The water-pollution potential of snow is much less than that of rain. Melting snow, however, does alter the physical characteristics of the residue and will percolate into the residue at least 1 or 2 ft.

Until more time is spent on this problem, the 284,580 tons/year of salts probably is not an unreasonable figure to assume. To give some idea of an upper limit of salt leaching from spent shale residues, Ward et al. [6] also conducted leaching experiments. Their tests showed that up to 1,120 mg of salts can be leached from 100 g of spent shale from the TOSCO process. Based upon the amount of material mined and retorted annually for a 1,000,000-bbl/day industry, about 4,920,000 tons of leachable salts are contained in the spent oil shale mined over a one-year period. These salts are accessible to the Colorado River through the hydrologic processes. Whereas it is unlikely that this amount of salt will be leached annually, the salt will leave the spent shale eventually through leaching over the years, decades, or centuries. Another problem relating to salt is the fact that some of the oil-shale formations must be reached by mining through ground-water aquifers which are highly saline. Thus, ground-water salinity, combined with the leaching of the shale residue, implies that the additional salinity which could be imposed on the Colorado River system is a potential problem of major proportions.

Urbanizing trends

Whereas an additional 115,000 population by 1985 is not significant by urban metropolitan standards, it will cause a large *incremental* effect on community systems in the region and on the natural environment. Measured against the 1970 population of 119,000, the new populations will require a doubling of existing capacity for community services. Pressures on the natural environments will also increase. But of equal concern is an overall regional *trend* toward urbanization, which the oil-shale industry could likely precipitate. In addition to the new support services, always associated with new basic industries, additional independent industries are often stimulated to move into new developing areas. Water may not be rate limiting for such new expansions, because transfers of water rights are not uncommon.

Ecology

Ecologically the region is rich, as stressed previously; Table 11-V gives some indication of this. In this sense, the region should be compared to what is available nationally. In other words, how much poorer will the nation be in pristine natural regions if the Upper Colorado Region is destined to become one of primarily industrial-urban character. To assess and even articulate this concern is a much more difficult task than comparing measurable changes against some total measurable quantity, such as salt loadings in the Colorado River. But it should be done so that the decision to commit the region to potential industrialization can be accomplished with deliberate and full knowledge of the significant tradeoffs.

Regional system

Macroscale system

Whereas many of the specific changes, which will occur in the region, are enumerated in Table 11-V, it does not provide a sufficient grasp of the *system* nature of the changes. Any changes on any part of any of the sub-systems will be felt through the entire system. Thus, not only are individual elements of the system affected, but also because of this the system must find a new equilibrium and, in doing so, becomes a different system. This is really the key concern in an environmental assessment, i.e., to describe the changes in individual elements of a system, which can be anticipated as a result of a proposed activity and then to grasp the fact that a new system may well emerge from these changes in aggregate. Whether this new system is wanted or not, is a value question to be settled politically.

The Upper Colorado Region contains both human systems and natural systems. These systems will be affected by three key characteristics of an oil-shale industry: (1) the process of creation (i.e., construction activities), (2) the existence of an industry infrastructure, and (3) the metabolism of the industry.

Figure 11-1 illustrates some of the system interactions which will be induced by introduction of an oil-shale industry. The emphasis in Fig. 11-1 is on the changes induced. As noted, some effects are direct and some are indirect. The essential message, however, is that it is a *system* that will be

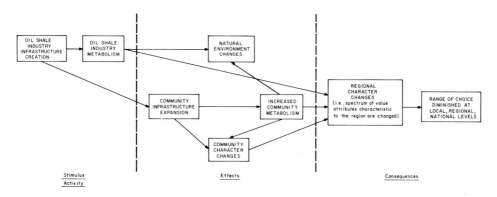

Fig. 11-1. Interactions of regional subsystems as affected by introduction of an oil-shale industry.

changed and will be modified in many of its basic character attributes as compared to the same system prior to the oil-shale development. New *equilibrium conditions* will be the result and the system will have different *state conditions*, ecologically, socially, economically, etc.

System disaggregation

It is difficult to find a single scheme which can permit a comprehensive analysis of system interactions without going to a fairly detailed degree of resolution. When this is done, the depiction of the system becomes unwieldy and the larger picture is lost, being obscured by too much detail. Keeping in mind that the purpose of the analysis of the interactions for the system is to keep the focus on the *whole*, the disaggregation process must be sensitive to the question of aggregation. In other words, should one examine salt loading of the Colorado River in terms of average concentration over a long time period, by extremes, or by monthly averages? Whether dealing with questions of salt loading, population, economic production, *ad infinitum*, aggregation is of critical concern. The aggregation is accomplished by selecting appropriate indicators. If appropriate indicators can be chosen, a reasonable quantitative picture of the regional system might be gleaned for both before and after the introduction of an oil-shale industry. Figure 11-2 shows some of the systems which will be affected by an oil-shale industry, whereas Fig. 11-3 is a disaggregation of Fig. 11-2. In Fig. 11-2, the goal was to select appropriate aggregating indicators such that a reasonable "picture" of the before and after systems could be gleaned.

In constructing Fig. 11-3 some themes were borrowed from the physical and biological sciences. The ·analysis of the regional system can be better

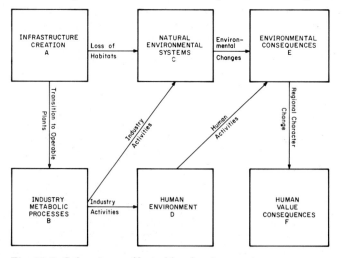

Fig. 11-2. Subsystems affected by development.

structured using these concepts, which are defined as follows:

(1) *Infrastructure*: the array of physical structures (power plants, transmission lines, dams, canals, pipelines, buildings, etc.) and management structures and institutions (private enterprise, laws and regulations, the judicial system, volunteer organizations, etc.), which facilitate the functioning of an organized society. The physical infrastructure both permits and directs the functioning of the management infrastructure.

(2) *Metabolism*: the relations between inputs and outputs together with internal movements, activities, and functions defines a system metabolism.

(3) *State*: the condition of a system as determined by the aggregate of indicators. For a community, this could include employment level, population, per capita income, age distribution, etc. For a terrestrial ecosystem, it might include counts of various species and trophic level distribution.

(4) *Process*: the transition relationship between states. States are changed by a process which may be the result of the creation of new infrastructures or expansion of existing ones, or by new inputs to a system. In each case, the system equilibrium is disturbed and a new equilibrium level must emerge.

(5) *Equilibrium*: a system at rest is in equilibrium with its surroundings. Human and natural systems are in *dynamic* equilibrium, that is, if the inputs, outputs, and processes are steady state, the system is in equilibrium. If a disturbing factor is imposed, the system must emerge to a new state.

System interactions

Whereas Table 11-V develops a general picture of some of the important elements of the Upper Colorado region and some of the possible changes which could result from a 1,000,000-bbl/day oil-shale industry, it is not a sufficient analysis to permit an *understanding* of the human and natural systems, and their interactions. The above definitions in the context of Figs. 11-2 and 11-3, can help to provide this grasp of the overall system.

As evident in Figs. 11-2 and 11-3, the system is complex and in order to understand the environmental effects of an oil-shale industry, this complexity must be at least partially understood. Through this delineation of some of the system interactions, it becomes evident that no one single problem exists which is isolated from any of the others, and that all of these interactions, in aggregate, combine to result in a different system. Thus, it is not individually the pollution effects of sulfur dioxide on a deer herd, or the visual disharmony of a large smoke stack, or the increased community services demanded by the industry labor force, ad infinitum (as perhaps implied in Table 11-V), which is the essential issue, however important each individual effect may be, but rather it is the fact that all of these changes in aggregate will change the essential character of the overall system. In terms of value consequences to people in the region and in the nation as well, this is of great significance.

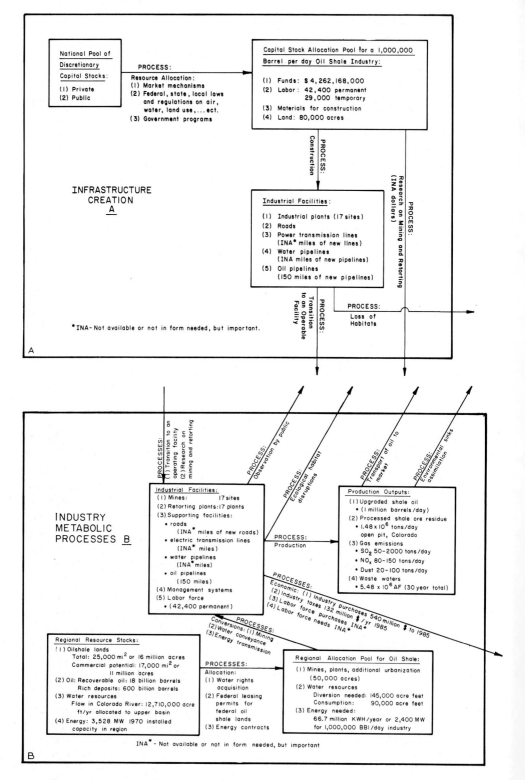

Fig. 11-3. Expansion of individual subsystems.

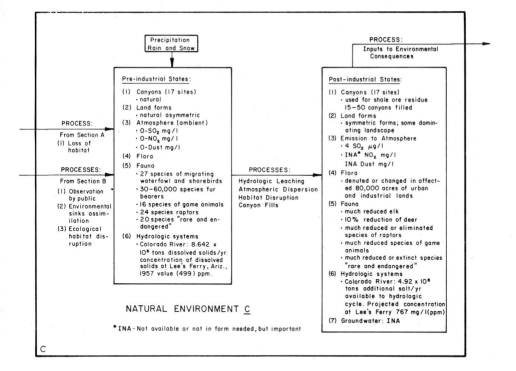

Precipitation
Rain and Snow

PROCESS:
Inputs to Environmental
Consequences

PROCESS:
From Section A
(1) Loss of
habitat

PROCESSES:
From Section B
(1) Observation
by public
(2) Environmental
sinks assim-
ilation
(3) Ecological
habitat dis-
ruption

Pre-industrial States:

(1) Canyons (17 sites)
· natural
(2) Land forms
· natural asymmetric
(3) Atmosphere (ambient)
· O-SO$_2$ mg/l
· O-NO$_x$ mg/l
· O- Dust mg/l
(4) Flora
(5) Fauna
· 27 species of migrating
waterfowl and shorebirds
· 30–60,000 species fur
bearers
· 16 species of game animals
· 24 species raptors
· 20 species "rare and endangered"
(6) Hydrologic systems
· Colorado River: 8.642 x
10^6 tons dissolved solids/yr.
concentration of dissolved
solids at Lee's Ferry, Ariz.,
1957 value (499) ppm.

PROCESSES:
Hydrologic Leaching
Atmospheric Dispersion
Habitat Disruption
Canyon Fills

Post-industrial States:

(1) Canyons (17 sites)
· used for shale ore residue
15–50 canyons filled
(2) Land forms
· symmetric forms; some domin-
ating landscape
(3) Emission to Atmosphere
· 4 SO$_2$ μg/l
· INA* NO$_x$ mg/l
INA Dust mg/l
(4) Flora
· denuted or changed in affected 80,000 acres of urban
and industrial lands
(5) Fauna
· much reduced elk
· 10% reduction of deer
· much reduced or eliminated
species of raptors
· much reduced species of game
animals
· much reduced or extinct species
"rare and endangered"
(6) Hydrologic systems
· Colorado River: 4.92 x 10^6
tons additional salt/yr
available to hydrologic
cycle. Projected concentration
at Lee's Ferry 767 mg/l(ppm)
(7) Groundwater: INA

NATURAL ENVIRONMENT C

*INA-Not available or not in form needed, but important

C

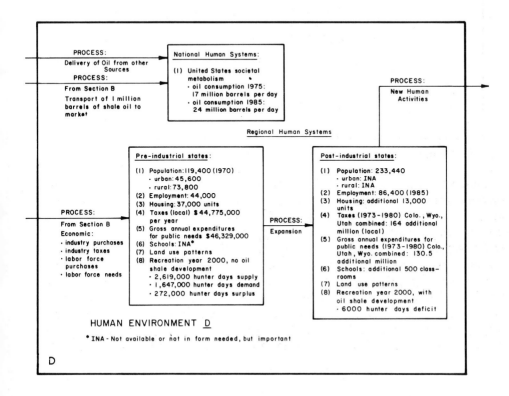

PROCESS:
Delivery of Oil from other
Sources

PROCESS:
From Section B
Transport of 1 million
barrels of shale oil to
market

National Human Systems:

(1) United States societal
metabolism
· oil consumption 1975:
17 million barrels per day
· oil consumption 1985:
24 million barrels per day

PROCESS:
New Human
Activities

Regional Human Systems

PROCESS:
From Section B
Economic:
· industry purchases
· industry taxes
· labor force
purchases
· labor force needs

Pre-industrial states:

(1) Population:119,400 (1970)
· urban: 45,600
· rural: 73,800
(2) Employment: 44,000
(3) Housing: 37,000 units
(4) Taxes (local) $44,775,000
per year
(5) Gross annual expenditures
for public needs $46,329,000
(6) Schools: INA*
(7) Land use patterns
(8) Recreation year 2000, no oil
shale development
· 2,619,000 hunter days supply
· 1,647,000 hunter days demand
· 272,000 hunter days surplus

PROCESS:
Expansion

Post-industrial states:

(1) Population: 233,440
· urban: INA
· rural: INA
(2) Employment: 86,400 (1985)
(3) Housing: additional 13,000
units
(4) Taxes (1973-1980) Colo., Wyo.,
Utah combined: 164 additional
million (local)
(5) Gross annual expenditures for
public needs (1973-1980) Colo.,
Utah, Wyo. combined: 130.5
additional million
(6) Schools: additional 500 class-
rooms
(7) Land use patterns
(8) Recreation year 2000, with
oil shale development
· 6000 hunter days deficit

HUMAN ENVIRONMENT D

*INA-Not available or not in form needed, but important

D

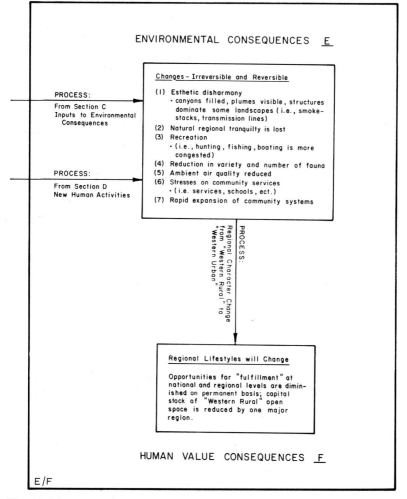

ENVIRONMENTAL CONSEQUENCES <u>E</u>

Changes – Irreversible and Reversible

PROCESS:

From Section C
Inputs to Environmental
Consequences

(1) Esthetic disharmony
      · canyons filled, plumes visible, structures
        dominate some landscapes (i.e., smoke-
        stacks, transmission lines)
(2) Natural regional tranquilty is lost
(3) Recreation
      · (i.e., hunting, fishing, boating is more
        congested)
(4) Reduction in variety and number of fauna
(5) Ambient air quality reduced
(6) Stresses on community services
      · (i.e. services, schools, ect.)
(7) Rapid expansion of community systems

PROCESS:

From Section D
New Human Activities

PROCESS:
Regional Character Change
from "Western Rural" to
"Western Urban"

Regional Lifestyles will Change

Opportunities for "fulfillment" at
national and regional levels are diminished on permanent basis; capital
stock of "Western Rural" open
space is reduced by one major
region.

HUMAN VALUE CONSEQUENCES <u>F</u>

E/F

Fig. 11-3 (continued).

The 1973 Upper Colorado system existed in an *equilibrium*, that is, the sub-systems were not changing with time. The *state* of the system (the aggregate of all conditions in the system, i.e., animal populations, annual rainfall, human populations, employment levels, salt loadings in the Colorado River, etc.) was designated previously as "western rural". The imposition of a 1,000,000-bbl/day oil-shale industry on this system would require a new equilibrium, that is, new *states* must emerge. Whether these new states would be appreciably different from the previous ones, may be difficult to determine. To determine the effect of SO_2 emissions on ambient air quality, for example, a dispersion *model* must be used. Whereas this particular effect can be evaluated by such a determinate model, other interactions are sometimes indeterminate.

Block	Block or Process Category	Item	
A. Infrastructure Creation	Capital Stock Allocation pool	(1)	$426,216,800 is estimated cost for a 100,000 barrel plant; figure given is multiplied by ten for a 1,000,000 barrel per day plant
	Industrial facilities	(5)	Final Environmental Statement, Vol. I, Chapter I, p. 89
B. Industry Metabolic Processes	Industrial facilities	(3)	Ibid, I, II, 89
	Production outputs	(2) (3) (4)	Ibid, I, III, 14 Ibid, I, III, 134 Ibid I, III, 60; 30 year total for surface mining
	Economic processes	indust. purch.	Ibid, I, III, 216
	Regional resource stocks	(3) (4)	Ibid, I, II, 23 (upper basin allocation) Ibid I, III, 38
	Regional allocation pool for oil shale	(3)	Ibid, I, II, 38
C. Natural Environment	Pre-industrial states	(5) (6)	Ibid, I, II, 63; I, III, 185 Ibid, I, II, 99
	Post-industrial states	(1) (3) (5) (6)	Ibid, I, III, 194 Ibid, I, III, 145 Ibid, deer-I, III, 179 rare and endangered, I, III, 171 4.92×10^6 tons/yr dissolved solids are leachable from shale oil residue calculated from laboratory data by Ward, et al (1971) Ibid, I, II, 34
D. Human Environment	United States Societal metabolism		1985 oil production: American Petroleum Institute, CPA, Oilman's fact finder 1973 oil production, Energy Resources Report, Business Publishers Report, Silver Springs, Md., Oct. 19, 1973, p. 316
	Pre-industrial states	(1) (2) (4) (5) (8)	Ibid, I, II, 97 Ibid, I, III, 206 Ibid, I, II, 209, 253, 307 Ibid, I, II, 209, 253, 307 Ibid, I, III, 190
	Post-industrial states	(1) (2) (3) (4) (5) (8)	Ibid, I, III, 206 Ibid, I, III, 206 Ibid, I, III, 222 Ibid, I, III, 215, 220 Ibid, I, III, 215, 216 Ibid, I, III, 191

Fig. 11-3 (continued). Documentation for portion of numerical data.

In such cases, it may be sufficient to assert merely that *new states* are *accessible* and could possibly emerge. Identifying these new accessible states then becomes the task. Decisions can then be based upon knowledge on whether or not the new states are likely to emerge as a result of the change influence, but it is not known whether they *will* emerge. This type of systematic evaluation can aid in bringing planning and management into the domain of deliberate choice vis a vis random guess or avoidance of choice by lack of knowledge.

The analysis in Figs. 11-2 and 11-3 is intended to illustrate the interactions of the overall system and so it does not contain sufficient resolution for highly-detailed interpretation. Neither is the analysis comprehensive, in that some of the important elements (e.g., the overall employment sector) for the region are not included. The emphasis is on change and on understanding the system nature of the problem.

The overall aggregate changes imposed on the system will result in a new equilibrium for the regional system, which will likely result in a new character of the Upper Colorado Region. It is possible, then, to better understand the changes which will be imposed on the Upper Colorado Region and through this understanding to make more deliberate choices. In the long term, as stressed previously, this happens through the political system, because the choices are essentially non-market in nature. But an understanding of the effects which may be induced will aid in making informed decisions and help in determining measures which may mitigate some of the adverse effects.

Acknowledgements

Most data for this analysis were obtained from the Final Environmental Statement for the Oil Shale Leasing Program. The analysis schemes were based upon Chapter 1 in *Environmental Design for Public Projects.*

References

1. D.W. Hendricks, E. Vlachos, L.S. Tucker and J.C. Kellogg (Editors), *Environmental Design for Public Projects*, Water Resources Press, Fort Collins, Colo. (1974).
2. L.B. Leopold, F.E. Clarke, B.B. Hanshaw and J.R. Balsley, "A Procedure for Evaluating Environmental Impact", *U.S. Geol. Surv. Circ. 645*, Washington, D.C. (1971).
3. Upper Colorado Region State-Federal Inter-Agency Group, Pacific Southwest Inter-Agency Committee and Water Resources Council, *Upper Colorado Comprehensive Framework Study* (1971).
4. U.S. Department of the Interior, Final Environmental Statement for the Prototype Oil Shale Leasing Program, Vol. I, *Regional Impacts of Oil Shale Development*, U.S. Government Printing Office, Washington, D.C. (1973).
5. J.C. Ward, G.A. Margheim and G.O.G. Löf, *Water Pollution Potential of Oil Shale Residues from Above-Ground Retorting*, Presented by J.C. Ward at the symposium on Shale Oil, Tar Sands, and Related Materials, Division of Fuel Chemistry and Petroleum Chemistry, Am. Chem. Soc., Los Angeles, March 29, 1971; *15* (1) 13—20, preprints of papers presented.
6. J.C. Ward, G.A. Margheim and G.O.G. Löf, *Water Pollution Potential of Rainfall on Spent Oil Shale Residues*, Environmental Protection Agency, Water Pollution Control Research Series 140 30 EDB, December, 1971, 124 pp. For sale by the Superintendent of Documents, U.S. Government Printing Office, Washington, D.C. 20402. (Catalogue No. EPI.16:14030EDB 12/71; Stock No. 5501 0197).
7. J.C. Ward and S.E. Reinecke, *Water Pollution Potential of Snowfall on Spent Oil Shale Residues*, June, 1971, 56 pp., National Technical Information Service, U.S. Department of Commerce, Springfield, Virginia 22151. Accession No. PB 210 930.
8. J.C. Ward, *Water Pollution Potential of Snowfall on Spent Oil Shale Residues*, paper presented at the *Western Snow Conference*, Grand Junction, Colorado (April, 1973).

Chapter 12

SURVEY OF OIL-SHALE RESEARCH IN THE LAST THREE DECADES

CHARLES H. PRIEN

Introduction

The past thirty years (1944—1974) have been a period of major activity in oil-shale research and development. New understandings of the chemical structure of oil-shale kerogen and its thermochemistry have been reported. Old technologies in oil-shale processing have disappeared, and new retorting processes have emerged. In a number of countries long existing oil-shale industries have been discontinued, whereas in several others, national oil-shale industries are about to begin.

Sufficient energy in all forms is a matter of increasing world concern, as are also the environmental problems associated with its production. In the past five years the latter have become of special importance for an oil-shale industry, with its inherently enormous problems of waste disposal.

In this concluding chapter, a survey of those major oil-shale developments during the past three decades, which are believed by the author to be of particular significance, is presented. It is an overall assessment of the subject from the viewpoint of an intimate, personal association with oil-shale research and development over these past thirty years.

Oil-shale industries have developed over the past one hundred years in France, Scotland, Sweden, Spain, South Africa, Australia, the Estonian S.S.R., and the People's Republic of China. Only industries in the U.S.S.R. and in mainland China are in existence today. Although most of the remainder attained maximum throughputs as high as one million to three million tons of shale annually during their life-span, it is perhaps significant that they all discontinued operations during the last twenty years of the period under examination. A brief historical review of the individual principal world-shale industries, past and present, is presented first [1].

Major world shale industries

A little more than 100 years ago, James Young completed his first plant for low temperature distillation of cannel coal in Scotland, and shortly thereafter, in 1862, changed to the processing of the local oil shales. This was the beginning of the Scottish oil-shale industry, which flourished continuously for over a century. In its peak year (1913), it reached a throughput of 3.3 million tons of shale annually. In 1962, however, this shale industry was discontinued for economic reasons and does not exist any longer.

The Swedish Shale Oil Company was formed in 1940, primarily to create an alternate domestic fuel source in the event of World War II. The industry reached a level of processing of over 2 million tons of shale per year before its discontinuation in 1966, when its economic future was no longer considered promising in the future fuel economy of the nation. Today, the oil-shale industry in Sweden no longer exists.

The Australian torbanites of New South Wales are among the richest oil-shale deposits in the world, with yields averaging over 120 gallons of shale oil per ton (500 liters/metric ton). The most significant attempt to develop these shales was started in 1940. At maximum production in 1947, a throughput of some 350,000 tons of torbanite shales per year was attained. The plant was closed, however, for economic reasons in 1952.

Oil-shale operations in Spain, at Puertollano, reached a level of 1 million tons per year in the late 1950's, but ceased in 1966. South African shale production at Ermelo began in 1935 and reached a level of over one quarter million tons per year; however, depletion of the deposit forced the operation to close in 1962. The French oil-shale industry, among the oldest in the world to process shale on a substantial scale, attained a maximum throughput of one-half million tons per year in 1950. But, after years of intermittent output, all operations were closed down by 1957. Today, the oil-shale industries in Australia, in Spain, in South Africa, and in France no longer exist.

Significant production of the kukersite shales of Estonia began in the 1920's. At the present time (1973) some 20 million tons of shale are mined annually in the Estonian S.S.R., and an additional 6 million tons per year in the Leningrad area. There is also minor production in the Volga Basin. With its total 1973 annual throughput of more than 26 million tons/year, the U.S.S.R. has one of the only two present (1975) commercial-scale shale industries in the world.

The U.S.S.R. shale industry has been characterized in the past by the use of its oil shales primarily for power and town gas production. Competition from natural gas and petroleum is changing this picture, however, as is also the pressures of the New Economic Reform, with its goal that Soviet industries each individually become a self-contained "profitable" operation. As a result, the U.S.S.R. oil-shale industry is turning increasingly to the production of petrochemicals as a major orientation. Any future planned expansion in actual raw shale throughput capacity will probably continue to be primarily for increased power generation.

The largest present oil-shale processing country in the world is the People's Republic of China, which is estimated to be utilizing some 35—50 million tons of shale per year at Fushun, Manchuria, plus an unconfirmed additional 10—20 million tons/year at Mowming, Kwangtung Province. The future status of the Chinese shale industry is simply unknown at present, until more data are available, but all indications are that it is still expanding.

The annual throughput of each of the above-described major world shale industries has reached at least one-third to one-half million tons/year or more during their existence. Respectable oil-shale reserves exist in at least 15 other countries, but none of these countries have attained the above-mentioned levels of utilization.[1] This includes the two countries with the world's largest presently known oil-shale deposits, the United States and Brazil.

In the United States of America many small oil-shale pilot plants have been constructed during the past 50 years by both government and private industry. The U.S. Bureau of Mines has conducted a more or less continuous research effort on oil-shale processing during this entire period. But it was the Synthetic Fuels Act of 1944, which was the primary stimulus for initiation of a comprehensive, $23-million Bureau of Mines program of research and development on all aspects of oil-shale mining and retorting, and shale-oil refining, in the period 1944—1955. This included a demonstration size room and pillar mine and, finally, the design of the U.S.B.M. gas-combustion type retort. Research on this retorting process was continued at the government's Anvil Points, Colorado, facilities by a group of six petroleum companies. In 1967, throughputs of 360 tons/day were attained. Recently, a further modified gas combustion process, called the Paraho retort, is under study at Anvil Points, by a consortium of 17 sponsoring private companies.

Two retorting plants in the United States have attained sustained operation at levels of 1000—1200 tons per day during the past three decades. One of these was that of the Union Oil Company near Grand Valley, Colorado, in 1958. The other was the currently existing plant of the Colony Development Operation, in the same locale. Full-scale, 50,000-ton/day commercial versions of each of these processes are hopefully to be completed in the period 1979—1980.

In Brazil, a 2500-ton/day semi-works plant using the Petrosix retort (a modified gas combustion type) has recently been placed on stream at São Mateus do Sul, in the State of Paraná. The oil shales being used are those of the Irati Formation; they first occur in the State of São Paulo and extend southward continuously in a great "S" shape, for 1,700 km to the Uruguay border.

In summarizing, then, this brief historical review, it might be said that over the past 100 years six countries with attractive oil-shale reserves (i.e., Scotland, Sweden, France, Australia, Spain, and South Africa) have attempted to establish national oil-shale industries. Each industry has flourished for a period of time, but all have become economically unprofitable during the past twenty years for one reason or another and, now, none of the six any longer exists.

---

[1] At Dotterhausen, West Germany, a modest-size plant, completed in 1961, has used local shales to produce cement and electric power.

Two countries, the U.S.S.R. and the People's Republic of China, have suc-
ceeded in establishing and maintaining industries which are now in the range
of more than 26 and perhaps 50 million tons per year, respectively. But, the
U.S.S.R. oil-shale industry, although commendably large and, certainly, of
great industrial importance to the Soviet economy, faces increasing questions
as to its profitability and strong pressures from alternate fuel sources. In the
case of China, it would appear that its shale industry is still expanding, but
any conclusions here must be tempered by a lack of sufficient information
for an adequate economic appraisal.

Finally, the two countries with the world's largest oil-shale reserves, U.S.A.
and Brazil, have not as yet attained commercial levels of production. The
United States, however, is projecting a possible growth to a one million barrels per day shale-oil production by circa 1990. In Brazil, which has recently
initiated several thousand tons per day throughput in a semi-works plant,
after 15 years of operation of a series of small pilot plants, an industry of
perhaps 60,000—100,000 bbl/day capacity by the mid 1980's is predicted.

Reports continue to persist of new plants to exploit the oil-shale reserves
in the Democratic Republic of the Congo, Italy (Sicily), Thailand, Burma,
Israel, and Yugoslavia. It is obvious from recent developments, therefore, that
despite the discouraging history of industry terminations of the past two decades, certain of the world's oil-shale resources are still considered to be potentially significant factors in future world energy supplies. The extent to
which this is true and the reasons which prompt this conclusion are discussed
in later sections of this chapter.

Overall status of oil-shale research

Several important international conferences on oil shale, and a series of
seven annual U.S.A. symposia on the subject have been held during the past
three decades. Those have served to summarize progress in oil-shale research
and technology at appropriate intervals. In 1950, the Institute of Petroleum
(London) held its *Second* Oil Shale and Cannel Coal Conference in Glasgow.
A total of 49 papers were presented by various international authorities [2]
on geology, mineralogy, mining, and retorting of the world's oil shales and
cannel coals and shale-oil refining and uses of its by-products.

A successor "Third" Conference to the above, scheduled for the United
States in the mid-1960's, was never convened. Fortunately, however, international progress in oil-shale research was brought up to date in a timely
United Nation's Symposium on the Development and Utilization of Oil Shale
Resources, which met in Tallinn, Estonian S.S.R., in 1968. Some 90 papers
were presented [3] from over 10 countries, in four major categories; (1) geology, mineralogy, and mining; (2) geochemistry of kerogen; (3) retorting,
refining, combustion, and uses of by-products; and (4) economics of oil-shale
utilization.

In the United States, developments in oil-shale research and technology over the last ten years have been described in a series of seven national Oil Shale Symposia held at the Colorado School of Mines, Golden, Colorado. The collected papers [4—6] of these almost annual symposia constitute a detailed chronology of both fundamental and applied research on U.S.A. oil shales during the period 1964—1974. For the earlier part of the 30 years under survey, reference is made to the annual review of research on the Pyrolysis of Coal and Shale by the author, which appeared in each September issue of the American Chemical Society publication, *Industrial and Engineering Chemistry*, for 16 years, between 1948 and 1963 [7]. This was an annual annotated compilation of selected, significant international papers on basic shale-research, retorting processes, shale oil and its by-products, and analytical methods.

The above four references are suggested as useful overall source compendia of research and development in oil shale for the past three decades, which can be consulted for more detailed information.

Oil-shale characteristics, classification, and constitution

The geology, mineralogy, geochemistry, structural configuration of kerogens, and physical properties of oil shales are examined in considerable detail by other authors in this book. A few observations as to the characteristics, classification, and constitution of oil shales, however, might be in order.

Characteristics of oil shales

Schlatter [8] has pointed out that the term "oil shale", although a well-known misnomer, is short, convenient and so well-entrenched in the English language that it is probably impossible to replace it. The same is true of the term "bituminous shale" in the Latin languages. If a substitute were to be selected, Schlatter suggested "kerogenous rock" (and such translations thereof as "roche à kérogène" or "roca kerógena"). He believes that the best short definition of an oil shale appears to be "a sapropelite containing a variable amount of kerogen which, on destructive distillation, yields shale oil."

In the past three decades considerable progress in geological and geochemical research has enlarged the concept of the formation and preservation of kerogenous rocks. It is the modern view that both oil shales and oil-source rocks form in all three possible types of aquatic environment, i.e., marine, brackish, and fresh-water. There is probably no genetic difference between petroleum source rock and oil shale.[1] The two most important prerequisites

---

[1]See H.H. Rieke and G.V. Chilingarian, 1974, *Compaction of Argillaceous Sediments*, Elsevier, for possible reasons why oil shales did not act as source rocks. (Editorial comment.)

for the generation of kerogenous rocks are an abundance of lipid-rich organic matter, predominantly phytoplankton, and anaerobic conditions for the preservation of the dead organisms. Schlatter has indicated that the bulk of the known and richest shales were formed in fresh-water lacustrine environments, ranging from small lakes to extensive intracontinental or intramontane basins.

Classification of oil shales

Attempts at oil-shale classification have been made according to variations in organic matter, petrography of the mineral constituents, chemical composition or genetic considerations, environment of deposition, geologic age, or any various combinations of such criteria. All of these may have some academic value, but none have proved satisfactory for practical application. The only practical criterion is the yield of oil shale, which means that classification must be based upon a system of quantitative grading. Therefore, agreement is urgently needed on an international standard grading system, which would facilitate the evaluation and comparison of oil shales the world over. Recognizing this, an international committee for establishing a system of fundamental definitions, terminology, and classification of the oil-shale deposits of the world was established at the previously mentioned United Nations oil-shale symposium in Tallinn in 1968.

Ozerov and Polozov [9] have addressed themselves to the task of devising a commercial classification system for shales. They showed that the organic content of the world's shales varied from a few percent to well over 40%, with 15—35% as perhaps representative. From 18 to 66% of this organic matter is converted to shale oil upon pyrolysis, with the higher yields (plus 50%) obtainable from the sapropelic shales. Both the chemical composition and the boiling range of the resulting distillates vary considerably. Phenols content, for example, fluctuates from very low to over 20%. Sulfur in the oil ranges from 0.5% to over 8%, and nitrogen from 0 to nearly 2%. The "gasoline" boiling fraction yield ranges from as low as 5% to as high as 25%.

Such variations are not surprising in view of the diversification in paleogeographical conditions under which kerogen was formed world-wide and the changes in rate of sediment accumulation and subsequent lithification. According to Ozerov and Polozov [9], it would appear that there are two main shale genetic types: sapropelic and sapropelitic-humic. The organic matter of the sapropelic shales is more homogeneous, produces high yields of oil (over 50% conversion of organic matter to oil), and has high heating value. In sapropelitic-humic shales, organic matter is more heterogeneous, with resulting greater range in its percent conversion (15—50%) to oil.

Mineral composition of the world's oil shales also varies widely. It is suggested that three types of oil shales exist, based on the combined percentage of CaO and MgO present in the mineral matrix, as follows:

Type:	Percent CaO plus MgO:
Carbonate	More than 20%
Silica-alumina carbonate	10—20%
Silica-alumina	Less than 10%

As a result of their studies, Ozerov and Polozov have proposed an *industrial* classification of shales into four types, designated as shales for the production of (1) power, (2) gas and oil, (3) power and chemicals, and (4) oil only. Each class was characterized as to the ranges of heats of combustion, oil yield, sulfur content of oil, and genetic type. This first attempt at a commercial classification system, while admittedly imperfect, is most worthwhile as a starting point for future more elaborate efforts.

Constitution of oil shales

It is perhaps worthwhile to review briefly the status of our knowledge of the constitution of the oil shales of the world's three largest deposits, i.e., those in the United States of America, U.S.S.R., and Brazil.

The Green River Formation oil shales of the western United States have been well described in a U.S. Bureau of Mines paper [10] as follows: The oil shale is an organic-rich, dolomitic marlstone. Average content of minerals, in weight-percent, are: dolomite, 32; calcite, 16; quartz, 15; illite, 19; feldspars, 16; and other minerals, 2. Certain zones in the formation contain dawsonite, nahcolite, and halite. The oil shale is a highly-consolidated, inorganic—organic system with no significant micropore structure, pore volume, internal surface, or permeability. The inorganic portion consists of small, non-spherical particles. Estimates of the surface area of these particles suggest that only a small part of the organic matter is bonded to them. Thermal conductivity of the raw shale is low: only about 1 W/m°K.

Concentration of the organic material by removal of the mineral constituents is difficult without altering the composition of the organic material. The organic matter consists of about 10 wt % bitumen and 90 wt % kerogen. A number of compounds (*n*-alkanes, fatty acids, chain-isoprenoids, steranes, etc.) that have been identified in the bitumen, indicate the biological origin of the organic material. Data from several methods for degrading and characterizing the kerogen are consistent in showing that it is a macro-molecular material having predominantly a linearly-condensed, saturated cyclic structure, with heteroatoms of oxygen, nitrogen and sulfur.

Schmidt-Collerus and Prien [11] propose that two different forms of Green River kerogen exist. Predominating (95% of the total kerogen) type is an alpha-form, which is an alginite-like material of low aromatic content. The remaining 5% is a beta-form, with a much higher content of aromatic (probably polycondensed) structures. (See Chapters 7 and 8 on the structure of the organic material in oil shales.)

Fomina and co-workers have spent many years in examining the chemical nature of the Baltic kukersite and dictyonema (bituminous alum) shales of the U.S.S.R. [12]. On the basis of their investigations they postulate that Baltic kukersite kerogen consists of polymers of lipocarbohydrate type, in which trehalose or polysaccharides represent the alcoholic part, whereas C_{14} to C_{30} fatty acids represent the acidic part. This type of lipocarbohydrates has been isolated by the biologists from pathogenic bacteria. During diagenesis, physical and chemical changes occurred which resulted in the formation of kerogen, while retaining structural elements of carbohydrate nature. When oxidized, these elements decompose to form CO_2 and oxalic acid.

By contrast, results from hydrolysis and other studies indicate that dictyonema-shale kerogen contains considerable quantities of melanoide-type substances and from 10 to 20% of nitrogen-containing matter.

The Baltic kukersite shales have 20—60% organic matter, 25—40% calcium and magnesium carbonates, 20—45% clastic and clayey material, and 2—4% pyrites [13]. Many aggregates of oil shale and limestone occur, as well as strata which are either pure oil shale, or basically pure limestone.

Whereas deposits of oil shale have been found in many states of Brazil, it is the Tertiary shales of the Paraiba Valley northeast of São Paulo and the Permian oil shales of the Irati Formation, extending from São Paulo and Paraná states southward to the Uruguay border, which are of greatest commercial interest.

The Paraiba shales are the richest, with organic contents being equivalent to 21—33 gallons of oil/ton of rock. The run-of-the-mine water content of the shale is very high (approximately 80—90 gal/ton), however, and this complicates the processing. The organic matter is low in nitrogen and sulfur contents, and the mineral matter is very low in carbonates [14].

The black Permian Irati shales are the most extensive and commercially the most attractive. In southern Paraná State and Rio Grande do Sul State they exist as two distinct beds of oil shale, separated by shale and limestone strata [15]. The total organic matter content is 20—30%, with an average equivalent oil yield of approximately 20 gal/ton. The finely-grained, finely-laminated rock is composed mostly of micas and various clay minerals, with minor amounts of pyrite, calcite and/or dolomite, and quartz. A detailed examination of the composition of the Irati shale organic matter has recently been reported by Costa Neto [16] and his co-workers, at an international oil-shale symposium in Brazil.

Oil-shale technology

The remainder of this chapter is devoted to a discussion of the current status of world oil-shale technology, as it has evolved as a result of research and development during the past three decades. As the oil-shale industries of

Scotland, France, Sweden, Australia, and South Africa have all ceased production during this period, it has not been deemed pertinent to consider these discontinued technologies here. Adequate descriptions of all of these industries may be found in the technical literature.

Only the technology in three countries with significant, well-documented, current (1974) oil-shale activity, i.e., United States of America, U.S.S.R., and Brazil, is discussed here. It is recognized that there is a noticeable omission in not including the People's Republic of China, with perhaps the world's largest oil-shale industry. Sufficiently detailed and reliable information on developments of oil-shale technology in China, however, is just not available at the present time.

Oil-shale developments in the three selected countries are interesting case studies in contrasts, and provide an excellent opportunity to emphasize the importance of individual national energy economies in creating a favorable climate for the utilization of this fossil fuel resource. Collectively, these three nations have probably most of the world's oil-shale reserves. Two of these countries, the United States of America and Brazil, are believed to be on the verge of initiating national industries. The third country, i.e., the Soviet Union, is struggling to adapt a well-established industry to a changing national energy situation.

Attention is first directed to the evolvement of oil shale technology in the U.S.A., because it serves to illustrate the many elements which influence the industrial development of a new fuel resource.

United States oil-shale technology

Brief history of U.S.A. shale activity. The history to date of attempts to establish commercial shale oil production from western U.S.A. oil shales has been that of a series of boom and bust cycles. A number of small pilot plants, which were established prior to 1920, became the victims of newly discovered cheap Texas oil and, hence, discontinued production. From 1920 to 1944, industrial interest in oil-shale processing was essentially non-existent. The issuance of Federal oil-shale patents (fee-titles) to private industry and individuals, however, was most active in this period, resulting in transfer of over 300,000 acres of land (with 50 billion barrels of reserves) to private holdings.

Beginning with the thirty-year period under current review and continuing from 1944 to 1955, the U.S. Bureau of Mines, as a result of the new Synthetic Fuels Act, created and operated a demonstration oil-shale mine at Anvil Points, Colorado, and investigated a series of retorting methods, resulting in development of its Gas Combustion process. In the 1954—1958 period, Sinclair Oil Co. conducted field tests on the in-situ recovery of shale oil on its property on Haystack Mountain in Western Colorado, while Union Oil

Co. built and successfully operated a 1200-ton/day vertical retort on its property on upper Parachute Creek in Garfield County, Colorado, using its Rock-Pump process.

In 1956, Denver Research Institute began research (in Denver) on the Tosco process of oil-shale retorting, which resulted in a successful pilot plant of 24 tons/day that continued operation until 1966. The Oil Shale Corporation then continued these activities under its own direction. From 1961 to 1968 Mobil Oil and later Equity Oil (1967—1968) conducted experiments on in-situ retorting on their shale properties. From 1964 to 1967, a consortium of six petroleum companies (Mobil Oil, Pan American, Continental Oil Co., Phillips Petroleum, Humble Oil, Sinclair Oil) leased the Bureau of Mines Anvil Points facilities and increased the capacity of the U.S.B.M. gas combustion process to a throughput of 350 tons/day.

In the last six years (1967—1974), the Colony Development Operation (Cleveland Cliffs, Sohio, Oil Shale Corporation, Atlantic Richfield, and later Ashland Oil and Shell Oil) has successfully expanded the Tosco II process (previously mentioned) to 1,000 tons/day at its Parachute Creek western Colorado site, and is contemplating full-scale (50,000 barrels/day) commercial production by 1980. In 1972, Occidental Petroleum Corporation initiated tests on a new method of in-situ recovery, having a current, daily production rate of 30 barrels. Superior Oil Company has indicated interest in initiating a multi-mineral oil-shale process, including recovery of saline minerals, in the Piceance Basin, by drilling a 9° inclined shaft underground to deposits at a depth of 1,800 ft.

In early 1974, Paraho Development Corporation, a consortium of 17 companies, began the investigation of its vertical kiln, modified gas combustion process, at Anvil Points, Colorado. A 35-ton/day, 2.5 ft in diameter, experimental Paraho-DEI Type I kiln, which is currently in operation, was followed by the construction of an 8.5 ft in diameter, 700-ton/day semi-works retort. In mid-1974, Union Oil Corporation announced that its SGR (steam gas recirculation) oil-shale process would be tested in a 1,500-ton/day demonstration retort and a subsequent 5,000-ton/day prototype plant on its property in Western Colorado, in anticipation of a 50,000-bbl/day full-scale plant to be operational by the early 1980's.

In early 1974, the U.S. Secretary of Interior launched a Prototype Federal Oil Shale Leasing Program in the three western oil-shale states (Colorado, Utah, and Wyoming). Four government sites have presently been leased to various energy companies. This activity, in conjunction with that by private industry on its own lands, could result in a 300,000 barrels/day oil-shale industry by 1980, and a 1,000,000 barrels/day industry by 1985 (4% of a projected U.S.A. 1985 demand of 25 million barrels of petroleum per day). Whereas these are modest inputs to total U.S.A. energy demands, they are very substantial potential contributions to U.S.A. future energy deficits during the next decade.

Fig. 12-1. Western United States oil-shale deposits. (Denver Research Institute photo.)

Western U.S.A. oil-shale reserves. As a result of improved methods of geologic prospecting during the past thirty years, the total in-place reserves of equivalent shale oil in the 16,000 sq miles of the western oil shales of the Green River Formation of Colorado, Utah and Wyoming are now estimated to be over 2 trillion barrels. There are 730 billion barrels of oil in shales averaging 25 gal/ton and in strata 10 ft or more in thickness, which are considered to be commercially exploitable in the foreseeable future. The latter reserves, however, are nearly twice as large as the currently quoted Middle East petroleum reserves.

The presently most economically-attractive shale reserves, averaging 30 gal/ton or more, are in strata 30 ft or more in thickness and less than 1,500 ft below ground level (Fig. 12-1). The most favorably located of these premium-grade deposits alone contains 170 billion barrels of equivalent oil, or a 27-year supply for the U.S.A. at our 1974 rates of petroleum consumption. Some 83% of the "commercially exploitable" shale reserves are located in Colorado (Piceance Creek Basin), 9% in Utah (Uinta Basin), and 8% in Wyoming (Green River, Washakie, and Sand Wash basins).

It is necessary to point out that the above figures are "in-place" reserves, of which no more than 50% are *recoverable* by presently-known technology[1]. But even at only 40% recovery efficiency, the reserves available are enormous. For example, the 170 billion barrels of 30 gal/ton premium grade "reserves", previously mentioned, at a 40% recovery rate, would alone supply a one million barrel/day shale industry for 190 years. Some 22% of these premium reserves are located on private lands and 78% on federal lands. About 85% are located in Colorado and 12% in Utah.

In addition to the oil shale there are large reserves of saline minerals associated with the oil shale, particularly in Colorado's Piceance Creek Basin. These include halite (NaCl), nahcolite $(NaHCO_3)$, trona $(Na_2CO_3 \cdot NaHCO_3 \cdot 2H_2O)$, and dawsonite $[NaAl(OH)_2CO_3]$, which occur basically in zones extending intermittently from 1,800 to more than 2,600 ft below the surface.

It is obvious that the resource base for the development of a U.S.A. oil shale industry is more than adequate, at both present and projected future levels of technology.

Overview of current U.S.A. technology. As a result of research and development by government and industry in U.S.A. during the past three decades, a processing sequence of mining and above-ground "retorting" has evolved to produce shale oil, or by hydrogasification above-ground, a high-Btu pipeline gas. In later years improved technology may also permit the use of in-situ retorting or gasification, thus reducing the materials handling required. It is useful to first present a brief *overview* of the current state of U.S.A. oil-shale technology and then to examine certain of the processing steps in greater detail.

As now contemplated, an oil-shale industry will be the world's largest low-grade minerals processing industry, mining and handling solids at a magnitude not heretofore generally accomplished on an industrial scale. The following example, using 30 gal/ton shale, will illustrate the point:

For every 2,000 lb of shale mined and then retorted, one would obtain approximately only 230 lb (11.5% of original weight) of shale oil product, plus 40 lb of undiluted retort gases, 30 lb of water, and 80 lb of residual organic carbonaceous coating (a potential fuel) on the spent shale. The total weight of "useful" organic material is, therefore, about 350 lb, or only about 17.5% of the original weight of the mined shale. Thus, 82% of the shale mined (86% if the carbonaceous coating is not used as fuel) must be discarded as waste material.

---

[1] Future improvements in mining and retorting methods, or the successful development of in-situ technology in the next 5 to 10 years could make leaner shale strata economically attractive, at which point they would be added to the "recoverable reserves".

A 50,000-bbl/day plant will mine about 73,000 tons of shale per day (24 million tons/year) and discard approximately 59,000 tons/day (20 million tons/year) of waste spent shale. A projected one million barrels per day industry will require the mining of 480 million tons of shale annually, which is nearly equal to the approximate current annual level of U.S.A. coal production (600 million tons per year). Annually, 390 million tons of waste shale will be produced.

All of this processing must be done in a region in which water for processing and domestic use is very limited. Finally, the shale oil produced must be transported 700–1,200 miles to substantial markets.

The ultimate result of the above constraints is that enormous care must be taken to ensure (a) cheap, large-scale materials handling methods at all stages of oil-shale processing (mining, retorting, spent shale disposal); (b) maximum heat recovery in retorting and upgrading; and (c) minimum use of water and power. Only in this way can the resulting shale oil be produced in U.S.A. at a price competitive with conventional petroleum.

The majority of shale mining is expected to be by the underground room-and-pillar method (Fig. 12-2), using approximately 60 ft square rooms and pillars some 60–75 ft in height, at depths up to 1,500 ft, with a recovery of

Fig. 12-2. Underground room-and-pillar oil-shale mining. (U.S. Bureau of Mines photo.)

55—70% of a mined strata. Surface mining may be applicable to 15—20% of the mineable shale reserves, predominantly by open pit (rather than strip mining) techniques, in areas where the ratio of overburden plus interbedded waste to ore is between 0.5 and 2.5 to 1. In the case of oil shale, the usual advantages of surface mining an ore body, i.e., lower-cost, are considerably offset by the reduced costs made possible by large-scale underground operations. It is possible that a combination of surface and underground mining will be employed where unusually deep pits would otherwise be required.

Between 80—85% of all mined shale must be discarded as spent shale residue, of which at least 40% must be permanently stored above ground, compacted, and revegetated. With open pit mining, the overburden and residue must initially be stored off mine site, until pit disposal is feasible.

Above-ground retorting of shale is of three general types, involving the use of (a) recycled hot solids, (b) retorts with internal combustion zones, and (c) retorts with external furnaces. Included in these three classes are the Tosco II, Lurgi-Ruhrgas, Union, Gas Combustion, Paraho, and Petrosix retorting processes, which are the leading processes in the U.S. at the present time. Each one of these retorting processes has its own peculiar advantages and drawbacks. The resulting shale oil produced from most of these processes will probably be up-graded by hydrotreating.

In-situ processing of shale involves a combination of suitable fracturing (or rubblization) and in-place retorting and recovery techniques. The "state-of-the-art" is probably 5 years less advanced than mining plus surface retorting. Because of its potential to reduce environmental impacts, however, active research on the in-situ processing is continuing, with the Occidental Petroleum method being the latest entry in the field.

This, then, is a brief encapsulation of the present status of oil-shale technology in the United States of America. In the two sections immediately following, the mining, crushing, shale-residue disposal and retorting technologies currently available for U.S.A. shale-oil production are examined in more detail. The ultimate processing sequence ultimately employed may involve any combination of a mining method and retorting method from among those mentioned above, depending upon the nature of the deposit, its location, the yield of the oil shale, etc.

Mining, crushing, residue disposal.

Underground mining. It is expected that in U.S.A., commercial underground mining will primarily use the room and pillar method. It will initially be confined mainly to those portions of the Mahogany zone shales which are 1,500 ft or less below the surface and which average 30 gal/ton or more in beds 30—90 ft in thickness. These limitations are imposed as a result of the costs currently encountered in underground mining, and could be expected to be relaxed as improved "second-generation" technology becomes available in later years.

Large-scale room and pillar mining was demonstrated by the Bureau of Mines at Anvil Points, Colorado, in the late 1940's; by Union Oil Company in the mid-1950's at its Parachute Creek site; and between 1967—1972 by Colony Development Operation near Grand Valley, Colorado [17]. Several million tons of shale have been mined at these sites by this method, at rates of 1,200 tons/day and higher. A commercial mine will require a scale up to 73,000 tons/day, approximately 60 times greater than the present technology would allow; however, this can be accomplished by using a combination of smaller unit mines. In all of the above cases, mine access to the producing horizon was by (horizontal) adit from an escarpment. As the number of locations in the shale region where adit entry is possible are limited, it is likely that a vertical shaft or even an occasional incline entry will also often be used.

In room and pillar mining, a series of "rooms" are created underground, with 30—45% of the deposit left standing as pillars for support. (In the U.S.B.M. mine, room openings and pillars were each 60 ft square. The total mineable section (room height) was 73 ft, at two levels of 39 ft and 34 ft, respectively). Pillar size, room dimensions, and percent recovery of ore for a given site are obviously functions of the thickness of overburden present. (A 50,000-B/D plant, mining 73,000 tons of 30 gal/ton raw shale/day in a U.S.B.M.-type underground mine, would utilize an underground area of about 170—200 acres per year, including pillars).

At the scale of underground mining contemplated, large mechanized equipment can be used, including multiple rotary drill jumbos, 20-cu yd front-end loaders, 100-ton or larger trucks (or large capacity conveyors), etc. Explosives will probably be of the ammonium nitrate-fuel oil type.

In the latter stages of mine development some 60% of the spent shale residue could begin to be returned to the mine, by conveyor or perhaps as a slurry. Little or no surface subsidence is expected from room and pillar mining of the type described. It is possible that underground waters could pose a problem in a few mining locations, although more data are still needed in this regard.

Surface mining. For the western U.S.A. oil-shale deposits surface mining could involve either open pitting or stripping, but will probably be primarily of open pit type. The shale strata should average 25 gal/ton or more. The ratio of "overburden plus interbedded waste" to ore should be in the range of 0.5 : 1 to 2.5 : 1, depending upon richness of the ore and the amount of hauling of overburden that would be required. Open-pit mining of oil shale itself on a large scale has not yet been attempted, but this method has been used at very high production levels for low-grade copper ores, brown coals, and tar sands. Oil-shale open-pit mining should be at a level of over 100,000 tons/day for greatest efficiency. It will require some period of time to develop a pit to reach this production level.

It will generally be necessary to dispose of overburden off the minesite for the first 10 years of operation, prior to the time that it can then be continuously discarded in mined-out pit areas while further mining proceeds. (As an example, for a site with a 1 : 1 overburden-waste to ore ratio, a thickness of 500 ft of 30 gal/ton shale, and a production rate of 144,000 tons of raw shale/day, there would be required 1,000 acres of off-minesite area for overburden storage, at 250 ft average pile depth, over a 10-year period). This off-site overburden storage area would be permanent and would be revegetated. Spent shale would also be stored above ground during the initial years of open pit development, but could thereafter be returned to the pit (see discussion below).

In some areas of the western U.S.A. oil-shale region (e.g., Piceance Creek Basin), saline waters at depth could present a serious disposal problem in open-pit mining, if the water was not all utilized in subsequent processing. The extent of this problem is not known at the present time. Hauling of mined, interbedded *lean* shale layers to separate dump areas could pose a substantial economic burden on open-pit mining, in terms of excessive transportation costs.

Open-pit mining will require large rotary drills for drilling and blasting, and the use of big shovels, trucks and conveyors to move material. Large draglines might also sometimes be used. In the rare cases where strip mining might be feasible, such draglines would be employed to move blasted overburden into previously mined areas.

There is a recent proposal by the Department of Interior, now under study, to create a *very large* unitized open-pit operation in the Piceance Creek Basin, with a pit as much as 2,000 ft deep. The concept is that this would permit simultaneous economical recovery of both lower-grade shales (e.g., 20 gal/ton) and any associated saline minerals. The entire area involved would be made part of the "unitized system", which could eventually include a combination of both open-pit mining and underground mining. The pit would subsequently be filled and the ground revegetated, thus restoring the entire disturbed area.

Crushing and screening. Whereas oil shale can be readily drilled and blasted, it tends to be unusually resilient to crushing (probably because of its kerogen content) and abrasive (due to the silica present), with a tendency to slab. Any crushing system must allow for these characteristics, as well as to provide effective means for dust control.

The size of the crushed shale required depends on the retorting process employed. Some retorts use a minus 2-inch or minus 3-inch feed devoid of fines <1/8 inch in size, thus requiring open circuit primary and secondary crushing. Others need a minus 1/2-inch product, which requires additional, closed-circuit tertiary crushing, but the retort will accept the fines produced.

The crushing systems employed to date have included jaw crushers, gyratory crushers, roller crushers, and/or impact mills. It has not yet been precisely shown, however, which system is the most efficient, although this will be determined as pilot-plant operations continue.

Disposal of spent shale residue. The disposal of the solid spent shale residue from retorting (ca. 80—85% of the weight of the shale mined) would cause the most obvious environmental impact of oil-shale processing [17]. The residue may contain 2—5% of a carbonaceous coating (on spent shale), or may be nearly completely denuded of carbonaceous matter (shale ash), depending upon the retorting process used.

For surface disposal, this residue will be transported by truck or belt conveyor, preferably to adjacent canyons, gullies or similar land depressions, wetted with about 15% by weight of water and compacted to a specific weight of 80—100 lb/cu ft [18]. To prevent downstream pollution by leaching of soluble components, the disposal sites will be guarded by adequate culverts, dams, and diversion ditches. Slurry disposal systems might be used, but only if added water supplies exist, or if low-grade saline aquifer waters could be used.

Upon completion of a residue disposal site, it will be contoured, topsoil added (or the top several feet leached to create a salt-free upper layer), fertilizer applied, and the area revegetated. A number of years of continuous care, including watering and re-fertilizing, are expected to be required until the new vegetation is self-sustaining. It is not believed, however, that this will impose an excessive added economic burden on industry costs. Additional development work is still required in order to better define the best plant types and regimes for revegetation. Colony Development Operation continues to conduct active research in this area, as well as Colorado State University and other organizations.

If all of the shale residue from a 50,000-bbl/day plant mining 30 gal/ton shale were to be stored above ground in 250 deep spoil piles, up to 75 acres/year of storage area would be required, or 1,500 acres over 20 years of operation [17]. But, it may be possible to return as much as 60% of the shale residue to the mine by conveyor, or as a slurry if water availability and drainage would permit. Because of the larger void space and hence greater volume of shale residues resulting from crushing, all of the residue will not "fit" back in the mined-out rooms. For the remaining 40% to be stored above ground, 30 acres/year will be required, or 600 acres over 20 years of plant operation. Specific weight after compaction both above and below ground should be approximately 80—100 lb/cu ft.

In the case of open-pit mining, the shale residue, like the overburden, will initially be stored off-site for at least the first 5 years of operation (but probably longer), and then could be returned to the mine by truck or belt conveyor. The mined-out area required for disposal depends upon the depth of the pit, but would approximate 75 acres/year for each 250 ft of depth.

Retorting processes. The only commercially acceptable method for producing shale oil at present in U.S.A. is to crush the rock and then heat it to 900° F or higher. At this temperature, the organic matter decomposes (pyrolyzes) to yield oily vapors (which condense to a viscous liquid shale oil), gases, and a carbonaceous residue on the remaining rock. This process is called "retorting". The carbonaceous residue may or may not be burned for fuel.

As a result of the past thirty years of research, three basic "methods" for above-ground retorting have reached the stage of potential industrial scale-up in the United States at the present time. Their classification is based upon the way heat is supplied to the retorting process. These methods include the use of (a) recycled hot solids (Tosco II process and Lurgi-Ruhrgas process), (b) an internal combustion zone within the retort (Union Rock Pump retort — Type A, Bureau of Mines Gas Combustion retort, Paraho Type I kiln), and (c) retorts with an external, fuel-fired furnace or gasifier (Union Oil SGR process, Paraho Type II process, Petrosix process).

Only two of these processes, Tosco II and the Union Rock Pump retort (Type A), have reached capacities of 1,000—1,200 tons/day under sustained operation on U.S.A. oil shale and could, therefore, be considered ready for early scale-up to, for example, a 10,000 ton/day commercial unit. The Petrosix retort has recently been put into operation in Brazil, at a designed throughput rate of 2,500 tons/day. The improved Gas Combustion retort reached a capacity of 350 tons/day at the U.S.B.M., Anvil Points, Colorado, plant site in 1966. A 35 ton/day experimental Paraho-DEI Type I kiln 2.5 ft in diameter has been placed in operation at Anvil Points, Colorado, and an 8.5-ft diameter semi-works retort with a nominal capacity of 700 tons/day was completed and placed on-stream at this same U.S.B.M. site later in 1974. A small (16—25 ton/day) Lurgi-Ruhrgas plant has been used to retort Colorado oil shale in West Germany.

The union Oil SGR (steam gas recirculation) process has been investigated for several years in a 3 ton/day retort in California, and plans for the construction of a 1,500 ton/day demonstration retort and a 5,000 tons/day prototype reciprocating solids-pump unit in Colorado were announced in mid-1974. A Paraho Type II process retort was also constructed at Anvil Points, Colorado. These two processes both use external furnaces, or gasifiers. Mention should also be made of the extensive research program on direct surface hydrogasification of oil shale (IGT), conducted by the Illinois Institute of Technology since 1960, U.S. Bureau of Mines and other organizations. The IGT process, employing excess hydrogen at pressures up to 500 lb/sq inch and temperatures of 1,200—1,400°F, in a three-zone reactor, results in a pipeline quality gas [19]. A 12-inch, one-ton per day unit is now (1974) under construction in Chicago.

An excellent, detailed discussion of various oil-shale retorting processes is given in Chapter 9 by Dinneen (see also [20]). A short discussion on the comparison between various processes, however, might be useful here. The Tosco II process (rotating kiln) and Lurgi-Ruhrgas process (screw conveyor) are both horizontal retorts. All other processes employ vertical retorts.

The Tosco II and Lurgi retorts both utilize solid-to-solid heat transfer, which results in high heat transfer rates and leads to high throughput capacities. The rotating kiln Tosco retort will accept a wide range of raw shale feeds, without the necessity of removing fines. The retort off-gases are not diluted with combustion products and are, hence, a high-Btu fuel. The solid wastes from the Tosco or Lurgi processes are more finely divided and, therefore, require greater care for dust removal and for disposal.

Vertical retorts generally accept a larger raw shale feed and, hence, have lower crushing costs. Most of these retorts, however, require the screening out of fines, which partially offsets this advantage. Vertical retorts tend to "bridge" and hang-up when richer portions of shale occur in the feed. This is avoided by more elaborate solids feed and discharge mechanisms, or in the case of the Union retort, by using a reciprocating piston upflow feeder. These feed and discharge mechanisms are also included to minimize the channeling, which always presents a problem as vertical retorts (Union, Gas Combustion, Paraho, Petrosix) are scaled-up.

The combination of the combustion and the retorting zones and both pre-heat and cooling zones in the single vessel of a vertical retort improves heat economy, but does result in diluted, lower-Btu retort off-gases. The latter disadvantage is overcome, of course, when an external furnace or gasifier and recycle gases are used. The feed and spent shale residues in vertical retorts are of larger particle size, which tend to decrease dusting problems, and aids in creating stable dump sites through the use of traditional soil-compaction techniques.

It is important to note that a variety of retort designs will compete with one another as the oil-shale industry grows, each with its own peculiar advantages and disadvantages.

In-situ processing. Retorting of the oil shale in-place has always been an attractive alternative to mining and above-ground retorting, because it eliminates both of these materials-handling steps, as well as the necessity to dispose of the spent shale. The usual approach to in-situ processing is to drill a pattern of wells, consisting of a central well surrounded by 4 or 5 off-take wells, into the shale deposits. The shale is fractured between wells by using hydraulic pressure, electricity, chemical explosives, or, as has been proposed, even nuclear explosives. Compressed air is injected into the central well, the shale is ignited, and the hot combustion gases are forced through the shale to convert the organic matter to oil, which is pumped up from the peripheral off-take wells. In the place of underground ignition, the heat required might be furnished by hot gases (e.g., methane) or liquids.

In-situ retorting has not been economically or technically successful to date, although field tests have been conducted during the past 15 years by Sinclair, Mobil, Equity, Shell, and the Bureau of Mines, among others. In 1972, Occidental Petroleum Corporation began the most recent in-situ field tests in western Colorado, using a process involving a combination of some mining (15–20%) plus in-place retorting [21]. Because of its potential to reduce environmental impact on the surface of the shale lands, and assuming no adverse underground impacts, in-situ oil-shale processing is expected to be an active subject of continuing research in the decade ahead.

Upgrading, by-products, saline minerals. The high-pour point, viscous shale oil obtained from above-ground retorting of western U.S.A. shales must usually be subjected to either coking or visbreaking in order to produce a pipeline crude which is pumpable without heating. This must be done at the shale plant, prior to pipeline transportation to market.

In addition, as shale oil is high in nitrogen content (1.8%) and contains moderate quantities of sulfur (0.8%), it is necessary that these be removed prior to finished refining to end-products. This is usually accomplished by hydrotreating processes, which convert the nitrogen to ammonia, and the sulfur compounds first to hydrogen sulfide and then to sulfur. it is possible to carry out these partial refining steps at the shale plant, or wait to remove sulfur and nitrogen until the shale oil has been transported by pipeline to the refinery. In any case, one can expect that a 50,000-bbl/day shale-oil plant will yield, as by-products, approximately 150 tons/day of ammonia, 180 tons/day of sulfur, and up to 800 tons/day of petroleum coke.

If the deeper shales of the Piceance Creek Basin of Colorado are processed, nahcolite and dawsonite could be recovered in some cases. Based upon average concentrations of 11% dawsonite and 15% nahcolite, it has been estimated by the U.S. Dept. of Interior [17] that a 50,000-bbl/day shale plant also recovering saline minerals could supply approximately 4% of the anticipated U.S.A. need for aluminium in 1980 and 20% of the nation's projected needs for soda ash. This does not include nahcolite's proposed use for sulfur removal from stack gases.

In order to recover the saline minerals along with the deeper shales, Superior Oil Co. has indicated interest in drilling a 9° inclined shaft from an outcrop on the edge of the northern Piceance Creek Basin, to a depth of 1,800 ft. The concept is to remain always below the saline aquifer of the leached zone and, thus, avoid water infiltration problems [22].

Water and power requirements, air emissions, socio-economic impacts.

Water requirements. The water requirements for mining and above-ground retorting of oil shale and upgrading of the shale oil vary with the processes involved. For a typical 50,000-bbl/day plant, the process water consumed (exclusive of power generation) would be 20 acre-ft/day (6,900 acre-ft/year), which approximately constitutes 3 barrels of water per barrel of shale oil produced. Some 55% of this water is used for wetting, compaction, and revegetation of the discarded spent shale, 30% for shale oil upgrading by hydrotreating, and the remaining 15% for mining, crushing, and retorting. All water diverted for use, eventually will be consumed somewhere in the process. It is not comtemplated, therefore, that degradation of the water quality of existing western U.S.A. streams would occur.

It is very possible that, as the U.S.A. shale-oil industry grows toward a million barrels per day in the next 15 years, available surface waters in the three western states will not be sufficient. Continued industry expansion will, therefore, require either further technological reduction of present water requirements or access to other sources of water.

One such alternate water source is a saline aquifer 400 ft deep, the top of which is located 1,000—1,650 ft beneath the surface of the Piceance Creek Basin in Colorado. It contains up to 25 million acre-ft of water according to the recent United States Geological Survey (USGS) estimates. Salinity is estimated to vary from 2,000 to 63,000 ppm. Whereas the high salinity may restrict the application of this ground water in oil-shale processing, it is likely that it could be used at least for wetting and compaction of spent shale, which, as previously stated, consumes 55% of direct process water requirements.

Power requirements. Surface retorting plus underground mining requires a consumptive power capacity of approximately 1 kW for each one bbl/day of shale-oil production. A 50,000-bbl/day plant will, therefore, have a consumptive power requirement of 50,000 kW; and a 1,000,000-bbl/day industry will need a capacity of approximately 1,000 MW (installed capacity would be as much as 50% higher). The domestic power requirements of the associated communities would increase these figures by an additional 10%.

Air emissions. The principal sources of air emissions and, hence, potential air pollution from U.S.A. oil-shale development will be (1) dust and vehicular emissions during construction; (2) solid particulates resulting from blasting and mining, as well as from the overburden and spent shale disposal operations; (3) dust produced during crushing and retorting operations; and (4) gases from retorting and oil upgrading operations. Included in the retorting and refining gases will be the gases from the burning of various process fuels. Utilization of these gases is expected to be largely on-site, to serve process needs.

The five major types of emissions will be solid particulates, sulfur dioxide, nitrogen oxides, carbon monoxide, and trace hydrocarbons. Each one of these categories of potential pollutants will be controlled so as to meet U.S.A. national and state air quality standards, using conventional industrial control equipment.

The estimated residual amounts of the various contaminants varies with the mining, retorting, and upgrading processes used. The only detailed analysis of the pollution problem currently available is the 1974 data of the Colony Development Operation [23], which are based upon underground mining, TOSCO II retorting, and upgrading of product by partial hydrogenation. For a 50,000-bbl/day plant, Colony Development Operation estimates the following maximum rates of emissions: solid particulates, 1,040 lb/hr; sulfur dioxide, 1,700 lb/hr; nitrogen oxides, 6,200 lb/hr; carbon monoxide, 60 lb/hr; and trace hydrocarbons, 290 lb/hr.

In order to minimize the effect of inversions, it is expected that most shale plants in Colorado's Piceance Creek Basin will be located on top of the mesas, rather than in existing valleys.

Socio-economic impacts. Only a brief description of the socio-economic impacts of the U.S.A. oil-shale industry upon the western three-state shale region, which is at present rural in character with a relatively low population density (see [24]), is presented here. One 50,000-bbl/day plant will add approximately 11,000 new permanent residents to the region, 90,000 new people when the industry reaches 500,000 bbl/day, and 160,000 added population for a 1,000,000-bbl/day industry. (The growth is not quite linear). These estimates are exclusive of the transient population involved during the construction phase, which would probably increase these figures by 50%.

Among the social and economic changes to be encountered will be the need for new public services of all kinds (water, sewage, libraries, schools, hospitals, roads, etc.), most of which must be started and reach a high level of completion *before* the tax revenues exist for their financing (the lag is approximately six years). Government assistance will be required to alleviate this problem.

U.S.S.R. oil-shale industry

Attention is next directed to the oil-shale industry in the Soviet Union. In contrast to shale processing in both the United States of America and Brazil, which are still only on the verge of commercial development, the U.S.S.R. has long had a mature, operating shale industry, as is amply attested by the 60 excellent research papers so ably presented at the 1968 oil-shale conference in Tallinn, Estonian SSR [3]. A study of this industry, therefore, presents excellent means to examine the opportunities and the problems of large-scale utilization of oil shale as an energy source.

This section is an attempt to summarize the significant developments in U.S.S.R. oil-shale technology, particularly during the past three decades. Portions of the section are adapted, with grateful acknowledgement to the Brazilian Academy of Sciences, from an assessment of world oil-shale technology recently presented by the author to an oil-shale symposium in Brazil [1].

The Soviet shale industry is estimated to have mined some 400 million metric tons of oil shale over the past three decades. If all of this shale had been converted to shale oil, which was not the case, the equivalent output of oil over this period would have been approximately 600 million barrels[1], or a 30-year average of 55,000 bbl/day. At the 1973 mining rate of 26 million tons per year, the equivalent total oil output would be 110,000 bbl/day.

The major portion of U.S.S.R. shale is used for power generation and not to obtain oil. Nevertheless, these "equivalent" oil production rates are presented in order to confirm the Soviet industry's proper claim to being a full-scale industrial oil-shale operation; and also as means to equate its size with previously quoted projections for a future U.S.A. oil-shale industry. By comparison, the present estimated output of the shale industry of mainland China is believed to be between 40,000 and 60,000 bbl/day.

Reserves and mining in U.S.S.R. The Baltic Basin shale reserves of the U.S.S.R. are extensive, totalling 21 billion tons. The commercially attractive reserves are about 11.3 billion tons (8.4 billion tons in Estonia and 2.9 billion in the Leningrad area). In Estonia, these commercially attractive beds have an average thickness of 3 m, with 10—40 m of overburden, whereas the Leningrad deposits are 1—2 m in thickness. The shales are 2—3 times higher in kerogen content than those in either the U.S.A. or Brazil. Organic content varies from 20 to 60%, with an average of 35%, yielding an equivalent of 50—70 gallons of oil/ton. Oil-shale reserves totalling perhaps 3—4 times those in the Baltic Basin exist in the Volga Basin, the Ukranian S.S.R., and the Central Asian Republics, but are still largely unexplored.

Some 26 million tons of shale were mined in 1973 in Estonia. The major production (80%) in the past has been from 15 underground mines, with the balance from open-pit mines. But in the late 1960's, a new open-pit mine with a rated annual capacity of 4 million tons was placed in operation, and plans for another with a capacity of 9 million tons/year were approved. When fully completed, this latter complex will be the largest surface mine in the Soviet Union. As a result of these changes, in the near future open-pit mining will probably account for nearly 50% of total U.S.S.R. shale production.

Power generation in U.S.S.R. The emphasis on open-pit mining is due to the fact that two-thirds of all U.S.S.R. oil shale mined (i.e., 18 million tons/year) is burned for power generation. The average heating value of this fuel has been 4,000 Btu/lb (= 2,200 kcal/kg). But in 1965, the Soviet State Planning Committee (Gosplan) established a new price schedule for shale of 3.2 rubles per metric ton (= $3.20/short ton), based upon richer shale of 3,200 kcal/kg (5,800 Btu/lb) heating value, with a particle size ranging from a fraction of a mm to 25 mm. The price of all other grades of shale was to be determined from this price base. The understandable result has been that many mines

---

[1] Using an average kukersite organic content of 35% and estimating a 70% conversion of kerogen to shale oil.

often now tend to "high-grade" their deposits, which inevitably increases the percentage of material rejected [25].

The largest oil-shale power plants are the 1,625-MW units of the Baltic Thermal Power Station at Narva and the 1,600-MW plant of the Estonian Central Electric Station nearby, which together supply demand for power in the northwestern U.S.S.R. It is expected that increasing power demands will result in a corresponding increase in oil-shale mining output to 30—35 million tons per year in the next few years.

Over 10 million tons of waste ash are currently produced annually from power generation, of which as much as two-thirds may be stack-gas fly-ash. This will increase proportionately, as new power generating capacity increases. A portion of this ash is used for construction materials (kukersite cement, refractories, etc.), but the majority must be disposed of as waste. In addition, the inefficient operation of the older stack gas dust collectors has created an almost insurmountable air-pollution problem in the Estonian oil-shale area.

As the ash content of the shale used as fuel is so high (60—75%), fouling and corrosion of heat transfer surfaces in exchangers is a constant problem in power generation. The deposits are primarily calcium sulfate (from lime—sulfur oxides reactions) and alkali sulfates and chlorides, the latter forming because of the 0.6—1% chlorine content of the kukersite shales. In order to avoid these problems, Soviet scientists are considering the economic trade-offs involved in first retorting the oil shale and then burning the ash-free liquid and gaseous hydrocarbons. Alternate designs to the present pulverized-shale boilers are currently also being examined, as a possible way to avoid excessive fly-ash problems.

Retorting. Whereas 66% of all U.S.S.R. oil shale mined is used for power generation, the remaining 33% (i.e., 9 million tons per year) is the raw material for high- or low-temperature retorting in the production of fuel gas, liquid hydrocarbons, and chemicals. This 9 million tons/year of raw shale feed which is retorted, would yield approximately 38,000 bbl/day in equivalent shale oil, if Soviet retorting technology were primarily petroleum-crude oriented, which is the case in both the U.S.A. and Brazil.

At the present time, however, 50% of the 9 million tons of shale retorted annually is subjected to high-temperature pyrolysis (at 700—800°C) in the continuous chamber ovens. The remaining 60% is semi-coked in either low-temperature cross-flow gas generator (Pintsch-type) retorts (54%) or tunnel-ovens (6%).

The high-temperature chamber ovens are operated primarily on a 25—125 mm shale feed to produce a high gas yield; however, some liquid oils, including crude naphtha, are also obtained. The naphtha is cracked to obtain additional gas, whereas the liquids, including high-temperature tars, are processed further to oil products and petrochemicals.

The lower-temperature Pintsch retorts, also operating on 25—125 mm shale, produce liquid-hydrocarbon oils for further processing (including petrochemicals) and a 110 Btu/cu ft of retort off-gas. The off-gas is used primarily to heat the chamber ovens. The relatively small shale throughput of the out-moded low-temperature tunnel ovens, which are, however, well suited to process richer shales showing a plastic transition range, is used to produce (1) liquid oils for further processing and (2) a high calorific gas (900 Btu/cu ft) to further supplement the industry's total gas production.

The overall principal products of the chamber gas generators, the Pintsch gas retorts, and the tunnel ovens are thus: (1) fuel gas; (2) liquid products for further processing to fuel oils, impregnating oils, and petrochemicals; and (3) by-product electrode coke, phenols, and sulfur. Whereas motor gasoline, diesel oil, and other conventional petroleum fractions have been refined in the past, this is no longer done for economic reasons. Emphasis instead is being placed upon gas production and upon petrochemicals.

At present, a total of nearly one billion m^3 (350 billion std cu ft) of fuel gas, with an average heating value of 4,000 kcal/m^3 (450 Btu/std cu ft) is produced annually from the Baltic shales [26]. The future for gas production from oil shale, however, is not promising, due to increasing competition from natural gas. At least five natural gas pipelines have now been completed in the Baltic region between Leningrad and Riga, and additional lines are under study. It is doubtful, therefore, that any significant future expansion will occur in Soviet gas output from oil shale.

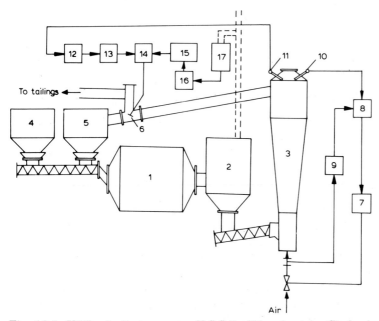

Fig. 12-3. UTT retorting process, U.S.S.R. (Flowsheet by Cleslewicz, 1971, [25].) *1* = retort, *2* = dust chamber, *3* = reheat furnace.

For the past ten years or more, a new retorting process employing solid heat carriers has been under development at the KIVIOLI works, Estonian S.S.R. and in Leningrad. The process, designated UTT (Fig. 12-3), is quite similar to that of the TOSCO II process of The Oil Shale Corporation in the U.S.A., previously described, and may have evolved from the same original, patented concepts. Finely divided oil shale, usually less than 25 mm in size, is fed to a rotating drum along with a heat carrier. The carrier is hot spent shale ash, produced by burning shale semi-coke (spent shale residue after retorting) in an auxiliary ebulliating bed, with air injection. A 500-ton/day unit (UTT-500) has been constructed and operated successfully [27].

This new retort, with its high throughput, high yields and flexibility to operate either at high temperature (650—780°C) for maximum gas production, or under semi-coking conditions (470—520°C) for maximum yield of liquid products, can process oil shale at an estimated one-half the cost of the present chamber ovens. Under maximum gas conditions a high calorific fuel gas of 1,100 Btu/cu ft (10,000 kcal/m^3) could be furnished for power generation, thus eliminating direct shale burning. At periods of reduced power demand, the UTT process could be switched to low-temperature retorting and liquid products can be produced as intermediates for petrochemicals.

It has been stated that the UTT process is capable of scale-up to throughputs of 2,000 tons of shale per day per retort. One would expect, therefore, that its commercialization would be one of the next steps in Soviet oil-shale technology.

Petrochemicals. It was stated earlier in this paper that increased production of petrochemicals is a major future goal of the U.S.S.R. oil-shale industry. The objective is to emphasize multi-purpose plants with combined power generation and chemicals production. The latter are competitive in the northwestern part of U.S.S.R. with petrochemicals produced from petroleum. Soviet scientists have made a herculean effort to date to isolate every possible chemical of commercial value from the kukersite shales and their by-products, and this research continues.

Particular attention has been paid to the isolation and utilization of phenol homologues, including both the water-soluble phenols in waste waters and the low- and high-boiling alkyl phenol fractions from retorting. Alkyl derivatives of resorcinol predominate in the aqueous fractions, whereas alkyl derivatives of phenol and naphthol abound in the higher-boiling oil fractions. These phenol derivatives are of interest as raw materials for the manufacture of detergents and other surfactants, and for the synthesis of polymers, varnishes, adhesives, and tanning agents.

The crude gasoline portion from low-temperature retorting in the chamber ovens contains up to 70% of aromatics and other unsaturated hydrocarbons. Fractionation and pyrolysis of this distillate results in high yields of C_6 to C_9 aromatic hydrocarbons (benzene, toluene and their methyl and ethyl homologues; styrene and its homologues, indene, etc.) suitable for synthesis of polymers. Wood preservatives are produced from blends of various shale oil fractions.

Research has shown [26] that the kukersite organic matter (kerogen) itself is a suitable raw material for chemical synthesis, without retorting. Accordingly, economical beneficiation methods have been developed to produce concentrates containing 70—90% kerogen, from raw oil shale. Controlled oxidation of these concentrates (with nitric acid and/or oxygen) results in the production of dibasic acid mixtures suitable for the synthesis of plasticizers, polyurethane foams, plant growth stimulators, and other organic chemicals.

The flexibility of the UTT solid heat carrier process for either gas generation or for obtaining liquid materials has prompted studies for multi-energy processing complexes capable of both power and chemicals production. Two interesting versions of such complexes, each with a throughput of 16 million tons of raw shale per year, have been proposed [28].

In the first version, 2,000-kcal/kg (3,600-Btu/lb) shales are used to generate power (rated capacity of 14 MW) and produce chemicals. The fuels for power generation are topped shale-oil fractions, residual gas after separation of olefins, and carbonaceous spent shale. The chemicals include water-soluble phenols, aromatic liquids, and electrode coke. The thermal fuels represent 66% of the raw shale's original heating value, whereas the chemical products constitute 25%.

In the second processing sequence, practically all of the liquid and gaseous retorting products are used for power generation (rated capacity of 2,200 MW). The exceptions are the aromatic hydrocarbons, obtained during gas oil pyrolysis, and the water soluble phenols, both of which are converted into chemical products. Some 91% of the original raw shale's heating value is utilized for power generation in this processing approach.

Neither of these industrial processing complexes has been approved for construction to date. They are mentioned here as examples of the highly sophisticated level of development of U.S.S.R. oil-shale technology and the potential of this technology to contribute to future Soviet energy and chemical markets.

Environmental problems. The U.S.S.R. shale industry is giving increasing attention to its environmental pollution problems. Projections indicate [25] that some 23,000 ha (57,000 U.S. acres) will eventually be occupied by open-pit mines in Estonia, if present plans for expanding shale production are carried out. As a result, land reclamation studies involving restoring land contours, creating lakes, and reforestation have been initiated, principally to reduce the volumes of wind-blown dusts and water pollution.

The spent shale dumps, some 200—300-ft high, pose a special "land pollution" problem, especially near the power plants. In addition, there is spontaneous combustion of stockpiles and waste dumps, which often continues for years, evolving H_2S, sulfur oxides, incomplete distillation products, resinous substances, and carbon monoxide. These often reach 3—9 times (or more) permissible levels, especially during the winter months. Sulfur oxides are one of the worst air pollutants, with concentrations as high as 2—4 mg/m^3 (i.e., 8 times "permissible" norm) near the power stations. Dust pollution is another serious problem, again especially during the winter.

Pollution of existing water resources is a continuing concern. A portion of the problem has been alleviated through the previously-described extraction of the water-soluble phenols from retort waters, for subsequent use as chemical raw materials. This has reduced total waste water phenol concentrations by 96—99%. But much more still remains to be done.

A great deal of effort has been spent to examine the toxic and, particularly, the carcinogenic effects of the intermediates and final products of shale processing. Whereas carcinogenic hydrocarbons (e.g., 3,4 benzopyrene) have been detected in Baltic shale products, suitably strict prophylactic measures have been taken to protect working personnel. As a result, the Ministry of Health has indicated [29] that, to date, no occupational cancer has even been recorded in the U.S.S.R. oil-shale industry.

One cannot avoid the conclusion that the Soviet shale industry is well aware that environmental pollution is still one of its major problems. The effort to solve it will be expensive and, undoubtedly, much more costly than if suitable measures of environmental protection had been undertaken at an early stage of the industry's growth. This latter fact is the important lesson which should be earnestly learned by the embryonic U.S.A. and Brazilian oil-shale industries.

Oil-shale developments in Brazil

Brief history. Oil-shale deposits have been identified in at least ten states in Brazil. Whereas the complete extent of these deposits is still undetermined, they probably total at least one trillion barrels of equivalent oil and, hence, constitute the world's second largest known oil-shale reserves. The two deposits of major commercial interest, however, have been the Tertiary shales of the Paraiba Valley and the black Permian shales of southern Brazil.

Initial pilot plant efforts during the past three decades were devoted to studies of the Paraiba Valley shales, beginning in the early 1940's and continuing, after the mid-1950's, under the direction of the national corporation, Petrobrás. A pilot plant was constructed by Foster Wheeler Co.; Cameron and Jones, Inc. was employed as consultant for over 15 years.

Because of the less favorable processing characteristics of the Paraiba shales, work was shifted in 1957 to Irati oil shales, which were shipped to the Tremembe pilot plant facilities. The encouraging results with these shales resulted in the development, by Petrobrás engineers, of the Petrosix process,

Fig. 12-4. Petrosix oil shale plant at São Mateus do Sul, Brazil. (Denver Research Institute photo.)

and initiation of plans for the construction of a semi-works plant of 2,200 metric tons/day nominal capacity at one site of the Irati shale deposits, São Mateus do Sul, State of Paraná. This latter plant is now complete and has recently been placed in full-scale operation (Fig. 12-4).

Petrosix retorting process. The Petrosix modified gas-combustion-type retorting process, with its use of an external furnace for heating, is an excellent example of the fact that shale processing technology must always be specifically tailored to the unique physical and chemical properties of each country's reserves and to the product mix of its energy market. It is very rare that a given country's shale technology can be *directly* transferred to another country, although such attempts have been all too common in the past history of world oil-shale development.

Petrosix engineers have incorporated desirable features of the U.S. Bureau of Mines gas combustion process, as modified by Cameron Engineers, into their own retort design, while at the same time improving the process so as to avoid both the clinker formation occasionally encountered with Irati shale and off-gas dilution problems [30]. As a result, the products of the Petrosix retort, in addition to shale oil, include a high-Btu fuel gas, LPG, and sulfur, all of which are in great demand in Brazil's economy. The 0.8—0.9% nitrogen content and 1% sulfur content of the shale oil obtained, together with its high content of olefins, require the use of subsequent hydrofining for up-grading, but these are well-known refining processes.

At the São Mateus do Sul plant, the black Irati shale is mined by the open-pit method, from both an upper and lower bed totalling 30 ft in thickness, with a combined average oil content of about 7.4% (18—20 gal/ton) [15]. There are approximately 100 ft of overburden. After crushing to minus 6 inches and removing some fines, the shale is fed to the top of the vertical Petrosix retort. It then flows downward by gravity, countercurrent to up-flowing hot gases and entrained oil vapors.

Retorting heat is furnished by heating a stream of retort off-gas in an ex-ternal furnace and then returning it to a mid-point (the retorting zone) in the retort. This avoids dilution with combustion gases in the retort itself. Fuel for the external furnace may be a shale-oil fraction, process fuel gas, or even residual carbon on spent shale. A second, cool stream of unheated recycle gas is returned to the lower section of the retort, to recover heat from the hot spent shale.

An oil vapors—retort gas mixture is withdrawn from the top of the retort, with the oil droplets in a mist suspension. This mixture flows to cyclones and electrostatic precipitators and a condenser for oil removal. The residual gas product is in part recycled, as mentioned above, and the balance sent to a sulfur-recovery plant, resulting in the LPG gas for final sale.

Two unusual features of the Petrosix retort design are its anti-segregation feeder and its annular, hydraulically-controlled discharge grate. These act to reduce channelling in the retort, thus avoiding a reduction in oil yield. In the semi-works plant the spent shale is conveyed to waste as a slurry, but this method will not be used in a full-scale commercial design.

It has been estimated [15,20] that the 2,000—2,200 ton/day semi-works plant at São Mateus do Sol, at steady state, will produce 1,000 barrels of oil, 14—17 tons of sulfur, and 1.2—1.3 million cu ft of fuel gas daily. A full-scale commercial plant with a throughput of 108,000 metric tons of shale per day from 16 retorts has been projected [15]. Gross production of shale oil would be 63,000 bbl/day (or 45,000 bbl/day net, if 18,000 bbl/day were used as in-plant fuel). The oil would contain 1% sulfur and 0.8% nitrogen, which would be removed by subsequent hydrofining. Fuel gas production would be 60 million cu ft/day and nearly 1,000 tons of elemental sulfur will be obtained daily. Both sulfur and LPG are in short supply in the growing Brazilian economy.

As Brazil imports over one-half of its petroleum requirements and demand is growing at a rate of about 8% per year, it is obviously in the national in-terest to develop the nation's indigenous oil-shale deposits as a supplemental fuel and sulfur source. This will improve the country's foreign exchange balance. The oil-shale reserves, which are located adjacent to the more in-dustrialized southern part of the country, are favorably situated with respect to major fuel markets.

Summary

In the past twenty years, six world oil-shale industries, i.e., those in Scotland, Sweden, Spain, France, Australia, and South Africa, have ceased to operate. Almost all of these industries, during their lifetime, attained throughputs of one to three million tons of shale annually.

Only the shale industry of the U.S.S.R., with an annual capacity of 26 million tons of shale, and that of the People's Republic of China, with a throughput of somewhere between 35 and 50 million tons of shale per year are still in operation. The Soviet industry is facing increasing competition from natural gas and is, therefore, turning increasingly to the production of chemical products and intermediates. Throughput continues to expand, however, with all new growth projected to be devoted almost entirely to power production. It is reasonable to expect, in the light of future energy requirements, that mainland China's shale industry capacity will also continue to rise.

Increasing world energy demand and the prospect of near term energy shortages in the U.S.A. during at least the coming decade are resulting in a re-assessment of all U.S.A. energy sources, including oil shale. This is lending impetus to the development of a U.S.A. oil-shale industry, on both private and federal lands. Recent improvements in technology [31] have reduced U.S.A. shale-oil costs to the point where they are already more than competitive with those of the new domestic petroleum. The future uncertainty of foreign import sources and the prospect of intolerably unfavorable future balance of payments is adding further incentive to developing shale oil. As a result, the early initiation of the U.S.A. oil-shale industry at long last appears to be economically feasible and desirable in the national interest.

The embryonic Brazilian oil-shale industry is now ready to proceed through the prototype, semi-commercial stages, which are the normal predecessors of full-scale production. Like its U.S.A. counterpart, Brazilian oil-shale development has, in part, awaited the time when the necessary combination of economic and technological factors were all favorable. This situation would certainly appear now to exist.

Environmental pollution problems associated with energy production for all sources has become a major concern throughout the world. The processing of oil shale is no exception. Indeed, with its high percentage of waste material, shale processing is particularly vulnerable to attack by environmentally-concerned citizens. The established Soviet industry is facing this problem in terms of costly modifications in currently existing plants. The embryonic U.S.A. and Brazilian industries both need to include proper air, water, and solid waste pollution controls as planned normal components of their projected full-scale operations, in order not to face delays due to an increasingly ecologically-oriented populace, and also costly plant revisions at later stages. The peoples of the world must collectively agree, whatever their political and ideological differences, not to contribute unnecessarily to the future pollution of the planet earth.

References

1. C.H. Prien, "Current Developments in World Oil Shale Technology", preprint, *Symposium on Science and Technology of Shale, Brazilian Academy of Sciences*, Curitiba, Parana, Brazil (1971).
2. G. Sell (Editor), *Oil Shale and Cannel Coal*, Vol. 2, Institute of Petroleum, London, 832 pp. (1941).
3. Ministry of Gas and Gas Chemicals Industry, U.S.S.R., Research Institute for Shale, *Exploitation and Use of Combustible Shale Resources*, Balgus Publishing House, Tallinn, 624 pp. (1970).
4. J.H. Gary and E.H. Crabtree (Editors), *Proceedings of the First Five Oil Shale Symposia, 1964—1968*, Colo. Sch. Mines Quart., Golden, Colo., 911 pp.
5. J.H. Gary (Editor), "Synthetic Liquid Fuels from Oil Shale, Tar Sands, and Coal, A Hydrocarbon Symposium", *Colo. Sch. Mines Quart.*, 65 (4) 1—241 (1970).
6. J.H. Gary (Editor), "Proceedings of the Seventh Oil Shale Symposium", *Colo. Sch. Mines Quart.*, 69, (2) 1—231 (1974).
7. C.H. Prien, "Pyrolysis of Coal and Shale", *Ind. Eng. Chem.*, Annual September Issue, 16 reviews, Vols. 40 (1948) through 55 (1963).
8. L.E. Schlatter, "Definition, Formation and Classification of Oil Shale", Preprint, *United Nations Symposium on the Development and Utilization of Oil Shale Resources, Tallinn* (1968).
9. I.M. Ozerov and V.F. Polozov, "Principles of Oil Shale Commercial Classification, Preprint, *United Nations Symposium on the Development and Utilization of Oil Shale Resources, Tallinn* (1968).
10. G.U. Dinneen, J.W. Smith, P.R. Tisot and W.E. Robinson, "Constitution of Green River Oil Shale", Preprint, *United Nations Symposium on the Development and Utilization of Oil Shale Resources, Tallinn* (1968).
11. J.J. Schmidt-Collerus and C.H. Prien, "Investigation of the Hydrocarbon Structure of Kerogen from Oil Shale of the Green River Formation", *167th Nat. Meet., Am. Chem. Soc., Div. Fuel Chem., Preprint*, 19 (2) 10—103 (April, 1974).
12. A.S. Fomina, Z.A. Degtereva, L.A. Nappa and L.Y. Pobul, "Chemical Composition of Baltic Oil Shale Kerogen", Preprint, *United Nations Symposium on the Development and Utilization of Oil Shale Resources, Tallinn* (1968).
13. V.A. Kotlukov, "Geology and Prospects of Studies of Oil Shales in the U.S.S.R.", Preprint, *United Nations Symposium on the Development and Utilization of Oil Shale Reserves, Tallinn* (1968).
14. United Nations Dept. of Economic and Social Affairs, *Utilization of Oil Shale — Progress and Prospects*, United Nations, New York (1967).
15. C.E. Bruni, D. Vasoncelos and V.T. Padula, "Brazilian Oil Shale Developments", *Proc. Eighth World Pet. Congr.*, Paper No. PD 10 (2), Moscow (1971).
16. C. Costa Neto, "Chemistry of the Shale from Irati", Preprint, *Symposium on Science and Technology of Shale, Brazilian Academy of Sciences, Curitiba, Parana, Brazil* (1971).
17. United States Dept. of Interior, *Final Environmental Statement for the Prototype Oil Shale Leasing Program*, Vols. I—VI (Supt. of Documents Stock No. 2400-00785; $6.15) (1973).

18. T.D. Nevens, W.C. Culbertson and R. Hollingshead, *Disposal and Uses of Oil Shale Ash*, Final Rep., U.S. Bur. Mines Project No. SWD-8, U.S. Dep. of Interior (April, 1970).
19. S.A. Weil, H.L. Feldkirchner and P.B. Tarman, "Hydrogasification of Oil Shale", *167th Nat. Meet., Am. Chem. Soc., Div. Fuel Chem. Preprint, 19* (2) 123—146 (April, 1974).
20. T.A. Hendrickson, "Oil Shale Processing Methods", *Proc. 7th Oil Shale Symposium, Colo. Sch. Mines Quart., 69* (2) 45—69 (1974).
21. D.E. Garrett (to Occidental Petroleum Corp.), *In-Situ Process for Recovery of Carbonaceous Materials from Subterranean Deposits*, U.S. Patent No. 3,661,423 (May 9, 1972).
22. B. Weichman, "The Superior Process for Development of Oil Shale and Associated Minerals", *Proc. 7th Oil Shale Symp., Colo. Sch. Mines Quart., 69* (2) 25—43 (1974).
23. *An Environmental Impact Analysis for a Shale Oil Complex at Parachute Creek, Colorado, Part I, Plant Complex and Service Corridor*, Colony Development Operation, Denver, Colo. (1974).
24. J.S. Gilmore and M.K. Duff, "Impact of Oil Shale — Boom or Bust", *Proc. 7th Oil Shale Symp., Colo. Sch. Mines Quart., 69* (2) 119—123 (1974).
25. W.J. Cleslewicz, "Selected Topics of Recent Estonian—Russian Oil Shale Research and Development", *Colo. Sch. Mines Quart., 66* (1) 154 pp. (1971).
26. I.M. Ozerov et al., "Processing and Utilization of Oil Shales of the Baltic Basin of the U.S.S.R.", *Proc. Eighth World Pet. Congr.*, Paper No. PD10(1), Moscow (1971).
27. Y.S. Ulanen, "Retorting Shale Fines in a Process with a Solid Heat Carrier", Preprint, *United Nations Symposium on the Development and Utilization of Oil Shale Resources, Tallinn* (1968).
28. B.I. Tyagunov et al., "Energo-Technological Utilization of Baltic Oil Shales", Preprint, *United Nations Symposium on the Development and Utilization of Oil Shale Resources, Tallinn* (1968).
29. G.M. Gortalum, "Shale Coking as a Method for the Investigation of Carcinogenic Compounds Present in Shale Oil", Preprint, *United Nations Symposium on the Development and Utilization of Oil Shale Resources, Tallinn* (1968).
30. A. Variso, "The Petrosix Process — Irati Prototype Plant" (in Portuguese), Preprint, *Symposium on Science and Technology of Shale, Brazilian Academy of Sciences, Curitiba, Parana, Brazil* (1971).
31. E.W. Cook, "Oil Shale Technology in the USA", *Fuel, 53,* 146—151 (1974).

REFERENCES INDEX*

Aarna, A.Y., 52, *59*, 194, *198*
Abelson, P.H., 32, *57*, 69, 70, *78*, *79*, 117, *125*, *126*
Ackman, R.G., 154, 156, 176, *178*
Albion, P.R., 36, 39, 45, 52, *58*, *59*, 118, *126*
Albrecht, P., 149, 162, 165, 166, 169, 176, *177*, *178*, *179*
Alger, R.P., 198, 201, 202, *211*, *212*, *213*
Algermissen, S.T., 203, 204, 205, 207, 210, *211*
Alpern, B., 119, *127*
Amstutz, G.C., 112, *124*
Anders, D.E., 65, 68, 69, 72, 77, *78*, 104, *122*, *123*, 157, 158, 159, 160, 162, 164, 165, 166, 167, 176, *178*, *179*
Andersen, B.D., 104, 114, *122*
Anderson, P.C., 66, 77
Appleman, M.D., 10, *11*
Arpino, P., 104, *123*
Auslen, D.E.G., 117, *126*
Axelrod, J.M., 89, 99, *101*

Baalen, C.V., 33, *57*
Baker, D.R., 117, *126*
Baker, E.A., 119, *127*
Baker, E.W., 162, *178*
Baldwin, W.F., 203, 207, 209, *211*
Balough, B., 74, *79*, 165, *179*
Balsley, J.R., 221, *234*
Baltosser, R.W., 199, *211*
Bardsley, S.R., 203, 204, 205, 207, 210, *211*
Barnes, A.L., 189, *198*
Bankov, S.S., 104, *123*
Belcher, J.H., 51, *59*
Bell, K.G., 120, *128*
Belser, C., 62, 77
Belsky, T., 36, *58*, 66, 77, 150, 151, 157, *177*, *178*

Bendoraitis, J.G., 150, 151, 152, 159, 168, *177*, *178*
Benther, H., 135, *147*
Berg, C., 185, *198*
Bergmann, W., 109, *124*
Bertrand, C.E., 49, *59*
Bertrand, P., 50, *59*
Besème, P., 119, *127*
Biemann, K., 70, 71, *79*, 104, 144, *122*, *125*, 137, 138, 146, *147*
Binder, C.R., 117, 126
Bird, C.W., 145, *148*, 166, *179*
Biscar, J.P., 116, *125*
Biscaye, P.E., 98, *102*
Bitz, M.C., 114, *125*
Blackburn, K.B., 51, *59*
Blaustein, B.D., 105, *123*
Block, K., 164, *179*
Blumer, M., 116, 120, *125*, *128*, 149, 169, 170, *177*, *179*
Bondar, E., 114, 115, *125*
Bond, L.O., 199, *211*
Bortinger, A., 151, *177*
Bostick, N.H., 119, *127*
Boucher, L.J., 162, *178*
Bradley, A., 29, 44, *57*, 62, 63, 72, 73, 74, 76, *77*, *79*, 85, 88, 89, 91, 97, 98, 99, *100*, *101*, *102*, 137, *147*
Brauns, D.A., 134, *147*
Brauns, F.E., 134, *147*
Bray, E.E., 31, 36, *58*
Breger, I.A., 30, 43, 54, 56, *57*, *58*, *60*, 104, 113, *122*, *124*
Bricker, O.P., 99, *102*
Brobst, D.A., 95, *102*
Broding, R.A., 199, *211*
Brooks, J., 36, *58*, 119, *127*
Broughton, A.C., 50, *59*
Brower, F.M., 114, 115, *125*
Brown, Andrew, 43, 54, *58*, 113, *124*
Brown, A.C., 52, *59*

---

*Prepared by Georgette Alexander and Safwat S. Farag.

SUBJECT INDEX*

---

*Prepared by S. Dougherty and H. Josephbeck.